Limitless

Rebecca Denae

Foreword by
Pastor Rocky McKinley

Foreword

The Merriam-Webster online dictionary defines the word *limitless* as "being or seeming to be without limits." Sounds a little vague. So, I looked up the word *limit* to better define the answer I was looking for. It said that a *limit* is something that bounds, restrains, or confines. Therefore, if something is *limitless*, it is not bound, restrained, or confined. I don't know if there is a better word to describe Rebecca Denae.

This book is the story of Rebecca's journey of tragedy and triumph. Diagnosed with cancer at the young age of 18, she refused to play the victim. Time and time again, she has willed her way to victory overcoming the most difficult of challenges. Don't get me wrong, within these pages are life-shattering prognoses that could have justified her giving up. However, once you get to know her, you will agree giving up is not an option for this brave soul.

I remember meeting Rebecca for the first time. It was after a Sunday morning worship service and my wife and I were standing in the foyer. She walked up and I couldn't help but notice the scar on her leg. She did not shy away from telling me her testimony and the obstacles she had already overcome. I could tell by the smile on her face and her outgoing personality she was different. Cancer would not define her. She was an overcomer. Little did we know her story was just beginning. We have had the privilege of watching it unfold from a front row seat. Even when she couldn't stand physically, she stood tall in her perseverance and fortitude.

Stories like this remind me that every victory starts with a fight. To experience the victor's crown, you must first engage in the battle. You can't sit on the sidelines and expect to receive your reward. You must put on your helmet, lace up your boots, pick up your sword and shield, and fight like your life depends on it. Rebecca didn't necessarily pick the fight, but she didn't back down from it. Her life literally depended on it. She didn't give up. She fought through every emotion, every pain, and every setback. She is *limitless*.

I pray the words on the following pages inspire you and challenge you. I pray whatever you are going through will not hold you bound, restrained, or confined. Weeping may endure for the night, but joy comes in the morning. Get ready to become *limitless*.

—Pastor Rocky McKinley

For Mom. Thank you for being my biggest cheerleader and supporting me in all my wildest dreams. I wouldn't be who I am today if not for your love.

"Life is a matter of the right chaos in the correct order."
-Trevor Turner

Author's Note

This is a work on nonfiction. To write this book, I relied on journals, pictures, accounts from others, and my own memory. Others may remember details or events differently. The dates used are approximated to aid the timeline of the story. Any misinterpretations or errors are my own.

Be advised: *Limitless* is a memoir of my journey through cancer and amputation. This story includes elements that might not be suitable for some readers. Some triggers include medical trauma and descriptions of medical procedures and settings (throughout), descriptions of scars (throughout), mentions of death (throughout), and mentions of events that could be triggering to those who have experienced sexual abuse, sexual misuse, or physical abuse (Chapter 26).

Prologue

"Ms. Rebecca, can you confirm your date of birth?"

"June 9, 2000"

I had given that answer so many times in the last few years that it didn't matter where my head was at that moment. I was distracted by the very beginnings of sensory overload. Enough doctors were crammed into the small pre-op room that it seemed to close in even more. I felt the IV in my right arm a little more than I preferred, and I was trying not to bend my arm with it placed. My attention couldn't be torn from the cold, rubbery scent of the oxygen I was receiving through the tube under my nose; the prongs pointed toward my nose just far enough apart that they rubbed against it every time I spoke.

"Rebecca is a 22-year-old female with a history of localized Ewing's Sarcoma to her proximal left tibia and surrounding soft tissue. Previous surgery was a proximal tibia resection with an allograft and plate. The allograft and plate are currently broken. Rebecca, can you confirm again what you're here for?"

I took a breath of the rubber-oxygen. I had answered this question at least five times already, but this time, I knew it was the last time I'd have to. And once those words crossed the line into existence, setting the team of anesthesiologists and surgeons into motion, there would be little time to reverse the decision I had already made.

It wasn't fear but a finality that what I was about to do was very permanent.

"I'm here to have my left lower leg amputated."

The events of the past few years that led to the sentence I just uttered all raced through my mind. Mere heartbeats and I was being turned to my side, the anesthesia team explaining what they were doing to prepare to place the nerve blocks. A few breaths, and I would be waking up to a new reality.

These were the last few moments, seconds really, that I would be spending as a person with both legs. I thought of the "Goodbye" written on my foot, a joke from a friend as we all said bye to my foot the previous night. I had made peace with the decision, but there was something very real about the fact that what would seem to be a few seconds later for me, I would wake up without part of my leg. I decided I would spend those last seconds in prayer.

It wasn't coherent, and to be honest I am not sure that it was even words. I just felt, and knew God was making meaning out of those feelings. I felt the trust I had put in Him to get me through what was ahead of me. I felt the finality of my choice. Most of all I felt His presence there with me, bringing me comfort.

I asked the nurse closest to me if she would hold my hand until I was out. She grabbed my hand and squeezed just before I watched the liquid disappear from the syringe in her hand. I felt ice shoot through the vein in my arm and then weight swirling through my skull. My brain was impossibly light and airy and heavy as molten steel at the same time. I knew I had milliseconds, so I sent up one last prayer.

"Be with me."

The room contorted, condensed, then faded.

Part One: Cancer

Chapter 1

January 3, 2019

Let's back up a few years. Long before the words "Ewing's Sarcoma," "resection," "allograft," and "amputation" became a part of my regular vocabulary, my struggles were much more typical for an 18-year-old fresh out of high school. My concerns had been with adapting to college life as a freshman at Florida Southern College, my dream school.

I had worked for years to get into FSC. From the first semester of my freshman year of high school, I was dual enrolling at one of the local colleges, hoping to graduate with my associate's degree when I graduated with my High School Diploma. It was quite the goal to strive for, considering academics were not the only thing on my mind. While my goal might have been to be at the top of my class with a college degree at my high school graduation, my passion found its place in a different part of my high school campus: the band room.

Yep, I was a band nerd. Ever since seventh grade, I had spent any time I wasn't studying playing drums. What started as in-class rehearsals in my school's concert band ended up with me becoming a member of the marching band's drumline. By the time I reached my

1

sophomore year of high school, I had even auditioned for an independent indoor drumline.

Between dual enrollment and drumming, I spent my four years of high school in a never-ending flurry of action. If it wasn't studying, writing papers, and passing handfuls of certifications for the Business Academy I was involved in, it was rehearsals, competitions, and performances. I thrived in the chaos, and by the time I crossed the stage for my high school graduation, I had a folder full of certifications and a 4.3 GPA. I had competed and placed Superior at state-level music competitions, and as for the AA I had been striving for, I had graduated with honors during the winter commencement ceremony a semester prior.

It only made sense for the chaos to continue, and I embraced it. I was accepted into Florida Southern's Marine Biology Program and made it through the audition process to become a member of their concert band. My days were full of classes, exams, rehearsals, and performances.

Just as I had in high school, I had big plans—and even backup plans. But what I didn't have plans—or backup plans—for was hearing the words, "I'm sorry, what you have is malignant."

That life-changing one-liner was the culmination of a year-long battle to get answers for the knee pain that had started my senior year of high school. When my left knee started to ache, I thought it was the years of marching drumline catching up to me. It made sense, considering I had spent too many days to count rehearsing for six to twelve hours at a time.

I thought things would ease up when I moved to college since they did not have a marching band. Instead, they only got worse, even to the point of nearly collapsing, when my knee went out from under me one morning. That pushed me to visit one of the Urgent Care Centers in Lakeland.

I was clueless. For most of my life, I had only gone to my family medicine doctor for things like allergies. I walked into the small clinic, totally unprepared for the process. I could still barely remember my social security number, and I had written academic

2

papers shorter than the stack of paperwork I had to fill out. I persisted, though.

Things went smoothly once I got through the paperwork and triage questions. Everyone was so kind as I was taken back for X-rays and then left in a private room to await the results. I was hopeful that, with everything going as well as it seemed to, I would be getting a solution to my problem. The doctor who entered my room was thorough, taking my leg through the typical range of motion tests.

Everything continued to go well until he brought out an ace bandage to wrap my knee in, told me to take Tylenol, and dismissed me. It didn't sit well with me, but he assured me it could only be inflammation.

I ignored the nagging feeling in my gut. I had been raised to trust doctors, so if he said it was inflammation, I would believe him. But months went on, and things only got worse. I could barely make it up the stairs to my second-story dorm room, and I dreaded the long walks I once enjoyed across campus to the science and music departments. When I got home for winter break, I tried to hide the constant limp that showed in my gait. Nothing makes it past a mom's watchful eye, though.

My Mom, Sherry, and I had been two peas in a pod my whole life. Despite the ups and downs my volatile teenage years brought us, she had always been my biggest supporter and closest friend. It was her guidance that shaped me into the person I had grown into during high school. Our relationship held firm during my first semester at Florida Southern, with me calling and texting her all day, every day. She knew me like the back of her hand, so it took her all of five minutes to see the limp I had been trying to hide.

Despite my insistence that I was fine and that the doctor told me it was just inflammation, her requests to seek another opinion won over. I found myself in a different, much less friendly Urgent Care Clinic. It seemed that from the moment I entered, I was inconveniencing the staff there. After I filled out the novella of paperwork, they begrudgingly took their own X-rays and continued to treat me with indifference. That is, of course, until they got the X-

3

ray results back. Then, I was the most exciting thing they had seen that day.

They showed me the X-ray, and I could see why their mood changed so quickly. Nearly half of my tibia was covered in wicked-looking white fibers. They thought I had Fibrous Dysplasia and referred me to an Orthopedic Clinic for further testing.

It was a relief to not be sent away again without answers. Though I had no idea what Fibrous Dysplasia was, they reassured me it was like a benign growth, something that could be treated easily to rid me of the pain. I felt lighter than I had in a few months by the time I arrived for my appointment at the Ortho Clinic. I had even started to get the hang of the paperwork I had to fill out. They reviewed the X-rays sent over by the Urgent Care Clinic, and I didn't even bat an eye when I was told I would be getting an MRI that day.

I had never had an MRI before, but I wasn't nervous in the slightest. I was just happy that someone was finally taking my concerns seriously. If it weren't for the banging and humming of the impossibly small tube I was in for the MRI, I probably would have fallen asleep. I was blissfully content.

While I waited for the call with the results of my MRI to come in, I enjoyed the reprieve from school. A lot of my time was spent catching up with my best friend, Anthony. He was two years my junior in high school, and we became close after I introduced him to the joys of drumline. Though we spent plenty of time on the phone during my time away at college, there was nothing better than being back in person. It was hard to play drums together from three hours away. He was even by my side when I got pulled over for the first time that winter break. Even though it was just a headlight that had gone out in my car, I was freaking out. His method of calming me was to hassle me about the whole situation, but that was our dynamic.

When the call finally came with the MRI results, I was excited. I felt so close to a potential solution, after all the time and energy I spent fighting for answers. What I did not expect was the vague explanation that what they found in the MRI was outside of their

4

specialty. Instead of continuing care with their orthopedic specialists, I would be referred to an Orthopedic Oncologist.

Oncologist, as in a cancer specialist.

To say I freaked out was an understatement. Mom had already left for work that morning, so I was home alone. I didn't want to hit her with that kind of news in the middle of her workday, and certainly not when I hadn't even processed the information, so I did the only thing I knew to do to calm my nerves. I went on a run.

To be clear, I was never a runner. I hated running. However, during my semester at Florida Southern, I learned that physical activity was an amazing cure for stress. I spent months handling my stress in Zumba classes and knew that the physical exertion would help clear my mind so I could process the idea of seeing an oncologist. Unfortunately, getting into a Zumba class in my small town would be impossible, so I went for the next best thing.

I threw on my workout clothes and took off without even warming up. I ran until the muscles in my legs felt as if they would give out at any moment, and the cold air burned my chest through my heavy breaths. I wasn't even aware of the flaring pain in my left knee until I was hobbling back to my front porch.

But, as I expected, my head had cleared. I sat in silence for long enough, thinking through the possibilities of what might happen next.

Up until that morning, whatever had been causing my pain had been deemed benign. As if a switch had flipped, I wasn't so sure anymore. If I was being sent to an oncologist, there must have been some questions. But on the flip side, they didn't know for sure. For all I knew from the vague phone conversation I had, it could be a precaution.

That was it. It had to be a precaution.

Limitless

Chapter 2

Mom offered to come with me for the appointment at Ortho, but I told her I wanted to handle it. I was set in my ways of being Little Miss Independent and wanted to continue to handle things on my own. I didn't know what to expect, but I assumed it would be similar to what I had already experienced.

I couldn't have been farther off the mark.

I was halted by the bustling crowds and vaulted ceilings on the first floor of the Ortho office. Signs were posted everywhere, directing patrons to the various services, and I was thankful I had been told to go straight to the fourth floor. I was directionally challenged enough.

I barely had to wait before a nurse escorted me to get all the imaging the oncologist needed. Apparently, they needed everything they could get. I was herded around from floor to floor, getting an X-ray, CT scan, and MRI. I was left by one nurse, only to be picked up by another when each scan was done.

No one bothered to tell me anything, and I was getting too overwhelmed to ask any questions. It took three hours of various scans before I was taken to a room, and the only information I was given was that I could expect to wait at least an hour while the results came through.

I nearly begged the nurse to let me escape long enough to get lunch. I hadn't eaten anything for breakfast that morning because I expected a much quicker process. I assumed my X-rays and MRI results would be sent over from the previous clinic, so I figured it would be a quick consultation. I planned on grabbing lunch on my way home, but with three hours already behind me and at least two more ahead of me, I knew I wouldn't make it that long.

The nurse told me to be back within an hour, so I picked a place nearby and drove myself over. Before I could even get out of the car, I realized I had an IV still in my arm from the IV contrast and a medical identification bracelet on. Not exactly the best look in a town with major hospitals.

I threw on a jacket, even though it was a fairly warm day. The jacket was so much better than the looks I could imagine I'd get for showing up to a Tijuana Flats with an IV hanging out of my arm.

For the first time in the past few hours, I could actually slow down and process what was happening. Even though my nachos were brought out quickly, I took as much time as I could eating them so I could have an excuse to sit and think.

The confidence I had leading up to the appointment that being sent to an oncologist was just a precaution was starting to crumble. I hadn't been able to get answers from anyone when I managed to speak up and ask what was happening. I was just told I would have to wait to talk to the oncologist. That didn't ease my mind.

I started to regret not letting Mom come with me. She would have been able to tell me what she thought was going on and could have helped keep me calm. But instead, I insisted on trying to be independent, and that left me pondering what was about to happen over a plate of nachos.

I spent what time I had convincing myself that everything was going to be fine. See, it wasn't that I thought I was invincible, as some believe 18-year-olds think. It's that I couldn't imagine cancer, of all things being relevant to me. I had knee pain, but I was a relatively healthy person. I didn't feel sick. So, it had to just be a precaution.

By the time I made it back to the exam room at the clinic, I had convinced myself that it wasn't anything to worry about. I didn't have a clue what that conversation might look like, but in my head, I hoped it would look like sending me on my way with plans to monitor whatever was in my leg and letting the longest day of my life come to an end.

When not one but two orthopedic surgeons who specialized in oncology came into my room, my heart sank. One surgeon was bad enough. Two couldn't mean anything good.

We traded short introductions; luckily, they didn't ask for the rundown of how I ended up in their clinic. I was already getting tired of retelling that story for every new doctor I saw. What really stumped me, though, was what they decided to focus on when examining my leg.

They were intent on this knot on my leg, just to the side of my knee. It had been there for nearly a decade, and no other doctor had even bothered to mention it. When it first popped up when I was nine, Mom pushed our family medicine doctor to check it out. After a few scans, we were told it was nothing. Unless it started hurting, it wasn't something to worry about.

Suddenly, it seemed that it became something to worry about, though I hadn't caught onto that as quickly as they had. The pain I was having was in my knee joint, and I had lived for so long with this knot that we called an abnormality that I almost forgot it existed. I almost started laughing when they began referring to the knot as a tumor. I had been told for years it was nothing to worry about, and I couldn't fathom that it was now a problem.

Even more to my shock, when the two surgeons finally looked up from my knee, one of them told me I would need a biopsy of the tumor and that he could do it the next day.

I was pretty convinced he was crazy, and I expressed as much. I was going to need a better explanation about how it was related to my knee pain before letting them cut me open. On top of it sounding insane, I had to move back to Florida Southern for my second semester the next day, and if anything was going to stop me, it would have to be important.

In explanation, the surgeon pulled up the results of the MRI on his computer to show me. I had expected the white fibers going down my tibia since I had already seen them on a previous X-ray, but I did not expect to see just how big the tumor was or that it connected to the fibers on my tibia.

To the eye, my tumor seemed to be about the size of a plum. According to the MRI, it was nearly the size of an orange. I had to question how they thought it could be related to my knee pain. Though they were careful not to mention anything like cancer, they said it was possible that the tumor on my leg could be causing some deeper issues, and they needed a biopsy to make sure they were treating it properly.

Finally, I relented. The sight of the MRI was jarring enough to convince me.

The second I agreed, I was rushed around again. Thankfully, they left the IV from the contrast MRI in, so I didn't have to get stabbed again for pre-op labs. After labs, I was brought back into a room with a nurse who explained what I could expect the next day. It was information overload. I hardly processed what she was saying before being handed the consent forms.

They were pretty straightforward, and by that point, I would have signed almost anything just to be able to leave and have some peace and quiet, so I signed.

By the time I made it back to my car, I sat in the driver's seat and let my head fall against the steering wheel. I was exhausted. I had spent over six hours in the clinic, had to face my fear of needles, and had surgery scheduled for the following day. I knew I needed to call Mom and let her know what was happening, but I just needed a minute to decompress.

I didn't know what to think anymore. I didn't want to believe that maybe what was wrong with me was cancer, and it wasn't something I wanted to worry about before having some kind of proof. I still couldn't reconcile that possibility, though. I had no other symptoms aside from pain and a tumor.

I couldn't even believe I had started referring to the knot on my leg as a tumor.

Whether it was denial or simply the inability to process the looming possibility, I held fast to the idea that maybe it was nothing. I called Mom and told her about the surgery I scheduled. She was so calm, as she always had been. She told me she would call off the next day at work so she could be there for me, and when we got off the phone, I turned my car radio up as loud as I could stand it and let whatever rock songs I had on my playlist keep my mind busy on the drive home.

January 8, 2019

I woke up in a private recovery room, not a recovery unit that separated me from every other post-op patient by a curtain. This room was fully closed in by glass doors, with curtains behind the glass doors for added privacy. Mom, my boyfriend's mom, and my dad were all in the room with me. That was normal, but what wasn't was the fact that my dad couldn't bring himself to make eye contact with me. I thought he was just stressed that I had to go through surgery. As soon as I felt up to talking, I kept an easy conversation going so that I wouldn't have to think about the fact that I was in a private room after having a tumor biopsied by an orthopedic oncologist.

When my surgeon came in, I didn't even see how Mom and my boyfriend's mom moved to the head of my bed in anticipation of the news they had already been told, holding handfuls of tissues just out of my sight.

Everyone expected the waterworks. Everyone braced themselves as the words left my surgeon's mouth, but instead of catatonic grief, they were met with curiosity. My only question to my surgeon was to ask, "So, you're telling me I can't go back to school this semester?"

It seemed to break the tension in the room as he giggled and told me I likely wouldn't be going back to school for longer than a semester. At that moment, that news was more devastating than a cancer diagnosis. I loved learning, and for once, I also loved the subjects I was learning. I thought it was audacious for cancer to take that away from me.

I had even signed up for private lessons on the drum set. My percussion instructor had spent an entire semester trying to help me learn keyboard instruments like the marimba until he realized my heart wasn't in the keyboards, but in the drums. When he agreed to teach me drum set, I was ecstatic. But now, I wouldn't be able to learn drum set, or anything else I had looked forward to, for that matter.

Processing that over the next few hours as I waited to be discharged was a very methodical process for me. I saw aspects of my life that would certainly be affected by cancer treatment, I allowed myself to understand that those things were no longer so easily within my grasp, and I let them go one by one. I didn't try to grieve for them, as there seemed too many to grieve. I just held them in the hands of my mind and opened those hands to let the thoughts fall where they may.

It was later, on the long ride home, when Mom decided to ask me if I really understood that I had cancer. It was a hard question. I wasn't in denial by any means. But I also wasn't distraught. Of all things, I was at peace. It was very early in my faith journey, and both my knowledge of God, as well as my relationship with Him, had not been deepened.

I had no idea what to expect, and thankfully, I could not peer into my future to see the things that I would endure in the following months and years. One thing I knew very clearly, though, was that as surprised as I was, God was not. I also knew so deeply I knew it must have come from my spirit and not my mind that God allows things to happen for a reason. I was sure He was not the author of tragedy, though He had allowed it to happen in my life. I let myself be at peace knowing that He had a reason and that even if I never got to understand that reason, He was worth trusting, and it would all work out for the good.

I opened my eyes the next morning, expecting something to be different. I had cancer, after all. Things had to change. But the sun still brightened up the space in my room, gently bringing me out of slumber. The woodpecker that pecked against the side of the house outside my window still returned for his morning routine. The deer still grazed in the backyard. The squirrels still tried, just like they did the day before, to find their way to the top of the bird feeder. I had cancer, but the world still went about its peaceful business as if nothing had happened.

I slowly realized that the only thing different was the immobilization brace wrapped around my leg from my biopsy the previous day and the fact that I had to get around on crutches. It would have been no different than if I had had a repair surgery for one of the many injuries I thought had been causing my pain. But instead of looking at a quick recovery, I was looking at the bleak unknown. I didn't even know what kind of cancer I had. Just that this clump of rogue cells in my body was turning my life upside down.

I tried to process that. To run the events of the last few months in my head over and over again, to try to make some kind of sense out of them. But what was there to process? I didn't have an official diagnosis. That was probably a good thing, as there was nothing to Google. Still, even without a diagnosis, some members of my family had managed to call Mom, convinced that I was going to die because they Googled it. Twice.

I thought the idea of dying of cancer was ridiculous. There was simply no way; it wouldn't be me. But I still contemplated what my life would look like, and for how long. I knew I would be getting a port - a small device placed under the skin of my chest that would be used to draw blood and deliver my chemo.

Chemo. I would be getting that. Would I lose my hair? How sick would I be? How long would my treatment be?

And that was the cycle of thoughts every day. It was like Katniss in *The Hunger Games*. "My name is Rebecca. I have cancer.

I don't know what kind it is. I also don't know anything else," and repeat, over and over.

Anyone I talked to seemed to treat me like glass, like I was going to shatter at any moment. Only Anthony seemed to take the news in stride. For everyone else, though, the news was devastating. I understood. Even looking at myself in a mirror seemed to have a cascade of thoughts of the unknown.

I tried to imagine myself bald. That was the main physical result of chemo that I could recall. No amount of mirror staring could make that happen, so I tried to imagine myself with that rail-thin, frail, pale look that I saw in so many portrayals of cancer patients. At 18, I was overweight, and trying to imagine myself as sickly and thin seemed impossible. I always took pride in my ability to keep a decent tan, so I couldn't imagine being pale, either. Most of all, I couldn't imagine myself being sick. The worst I could remember being sick was the once-a-year fight I had with pollen. But even my allergies hadn't kept me from school. I couldn't fathom sickness so bad it could change my whole body.

Truth be told, the more I thought about it, the more it started to scare me. I didn't even know how or in what way. Maybe it was just the idea that not only my life but my person, my body, and maybe even my personality could change. It wasn't a fear of death because there was simply no way I was going to be dying at such a young age from something like cancer. That had been ingrained in my thoughts since the moment cancer became a reality in my life. But since the only option between life and death for me was to live, what would living even look like? I couldn't even begin to see so far in the future as to imagine how this would change the lives of 25, 30, or 50-year-old Rebecca. Even trying to imagine the life of a 20-year-old Rebecca while 18-year-old Rebecca had cancer was too much.

At the point when trying to overthink the whole situation had proven to be a weird combo of horrifying and annoying, I decided to try to take it day by day. That seemed safer. No thoughts of baldness or paleness or sickness. It seemed easy enough. Until I got around almost any human being.

14

For some reason, people thought it would be comforting to tell me about how their friend's cousin's sister-in-law had breast cancer and how she was so sick and miserable all the time. Or how frail someone else's brother's best friend was after chemo and how he never seemed to recover. Or, my personal favorite, when my pastor at the time announced to our small church that I had been diagnosed with cancer, followed by the caution that I may not be in church much anymore, as I would likely not be leaving the vicinity of my bathroom because I would be puking my guts out for the next few months. As if I didn't have enough to worry about already.

How most of these people thought they were being helpful, I have no idea. We didn't even have a diagnosis, much less a prognosis. We didn't know what chemo I would be getting, much less the effect it would have on my body. We knew that different chemo regimens could have different side effects. Apparently, no one else did. Every time I had to listen to these "comforting" attempts, smiling and nodding along because it was polite, I felt my stomach turn. I was trying so hard to take it day by day, and everyone on the planet seemed to be bent on filling me with fear.

I would often end up stressed out, telling Mom about what another well-meaning person told me when she got home from work at night. She would have to reassure me that every person's journey with cancer and cancer treatment is different. Just about the time I had my fears back under control, we were back to square one of freaking out because someone I knew just had to tell me how terrible cancer treatment was. It was exhausting.

Limitless

Chapter 3

January 15, 2019

    Entering the hospital where I was to spend the duration of my treatment cycles was an assault on the senses. It was a sea of people - moving, rushing, meandering, going all different directions at all different speeds. The smell was a mix of bland cafeteria food, antiseptic, and hand sanitizer. The paint, in an effort to seem fun and friendly, was a mix of colors and grand designs, though all of the colors seemed just a few shades off as if the fluorescent lights corrupted their attempt at beauty. Compared to the sterile white of the adult cancer center where I had my biopsy, it felt like a circus gone horribly wrong.

    The room I found myself in after checking in for admission was worse. So little light came in from the tiny window that faced the side of another building that even though the glaringly bright fluorescent lights were on, the room felt dim. The colors seemed to turn an even more muted version of themselves. The air, heavily filtered, seemed sickly. I avoided the hospital bed, opting for a seat on the small couch under the window to ponder my new situation. When the heavy door thudded closed, it felt for a split second as if it would not open again at my will. I felt as if I were forbidden from roaming freely. The shackle of an identification bracelet solidified my feeling of being trapped, and I fought the urge to rip it off.

The realization had set in that I was being treated in a pediatric cancer unit. When I received a call from the doctor who would be my oncologist, she did not indicate that this would be the case. She hadn't even referred to the building where I would receive treatment as a children's treatment center. It was simply "The North Tower." The growing anxiety spilled over at this realization in the form of agitation. I was an adult, had been seen by many adult physicians, and was frustrated at the idea that I found myself in a unit where I had to see overly happy cartoon characters lining the walls on the path to my treatment room.

Mom had to explain to me that because of the type of cancer I had - a sarcoma - I was referred to a sarcoma specialist. Who just happened to be a pediatric specialist since sarcomas were usually diagnosed in children.

It didn't help my agitation that I had been kept mostly in the dark about the nature of my current admission. The phone call I had received telling me when to come in for my first treatment had yielded little insight outside of where to go, and I had been herded from the admissions floor to the fourth-floor cancer unit with less info still.

As I sat on the couch, trying to keep my anxiety at bay, I shifted my thoughts to the one piece of info I could squeeze out of that phone call: my hair. I ran my hands through the length of it, much shorter now than it was before. Less than a week prior, my hair had been halfway down my back and was thick and wavy. It had never been shorter than shoulder blade length until then, where one side was nearly shaved, and the other didn't even go past my ears. An asymmetrical pixie of sorts.

The one question I was able to ask on the phone call with my oncologist was if I would be losing my hair due to my treatment. I was put off by her tone despite her affirmation that I would. Slightly condescending, as if she thought it vain of me to worry about my hair in the face of a cancer diagnosis. What she didn't know was that I had read that hair could not be donated after a chemo treatment, and I was determined that if I couldn't have my hair, someone else should be able to have it as a wig to help them through their treatment. Before I came in for my first treatment, I had my hair cut to donate.

I had completely zoned out in my thoughts and was jarred back to reality when a nurse knocked and entered my room. She told me she needed me on the bed so she could start an IV. I approached the bed like it was booby-trapped. It even had a continence pad that I ripped off before sitting down. I knew it was standard housekeeping practice, but it felt so demeaning.

I knew my veins were difficult to find, but it seemed like they had agreed to disappear. Eventually, I had three nurses in my room with a vein light, trying desperately to get the IV placed. My arms were dotted with failed attempts, and I was on the verge of passing out. When one of the nurses finally did get the IV placed, somehow, blood started pouring from my arm. Before they could tell me not to look, I looked down to see my blood and passed out. It was an ordeal and a half, but they finally got the IV placed, and I was attached to the IV pole at the side of my bed. It felt like a leash, further enforcing the feeling of imprisonment.

The following hours were full of questions. Not questions from me, but from a flurry of different doctors. By the time I had retold my story of diagnosis, and medical history, and answered the same questions four times, my patience had run dangerously thin. I had been in that place for hours and still had no clue what was happening.

At one point, I had an ultrasound technologist trying to get scans of my heart by shoving the probe as deeply into my ribs as he could while an impatient doctor tried to pry answers out of me. Both were too impatient to allow the other to finish so I wouldn't be overwhelmed.

Finally, as I rested on the razor-thin edge of my patience, my oncologist entered my room, flanked by a team of doctors. She outlined the plan that I was being prepped for another surgery to take place the next day to place my port - a small device inserted under the skin of my chest with a direct line to a major blood vessel - and to have a bone marrow biopsy done to make sure my cancer had not spread there. After that, I would start my treatment.

The tone that had been so grating on the phone had followed her into the room. She spoke as if to a child, not to an adult who could comprehend her situation and make her own decisions. I tried to convince myself that, despite that, I liked her. I felt I had to since she was the specialist who held my future.

By the evening, I had blessedly been left in peace. Teams of doctors no longer interrogated me, and I was left alone to try to rest. Try being the keyword. If nurses weren't coming in to check on the IV fluids or draw labs, Patient Care Assistants - PCAs - were in my room taking my vitals. Every time I seemed to wind down and relax, someone else was in my room.

I tried to sleep, but I couldn't even get comfortable with the IV in my arm. I was still so terrified of the tube going into the vein that I tried to sleep with my arm completely straight. Even if I hadn't been afraid of bending my arm, I would soon learn that when I did, the machine connected to my IV would start beeping incessantly and that there was some blockage. I spent most of my night tossing and turning on the thin mattress.

By the time I managed to drift into a fitful sleep, morning rounds came as a very unpleasant surprise. All the lights were on in my room, and a full team of doctors were crowding around me. Before I could even think, I was being bombarded with questions I could barely answer.

How was I feeling?
Was I in any pain?
Had I eaten yet?
How did I sleep?

To add insult to injury, they all seemed so perky, and it was like they expected that from me as well. My glowering morning attitude must have been as unpleasant for them as the wake-up call was for me.

To my growing agitations, they told me I would not be allowed to eat anything since I was waiting for my surgery to place my port. That wouldn't have been so bad if they could have answered the question of when my surgery would be. Instead, I was told I would go in when an opening came up that day if nothing else more pressing came up.

I waited, getting hangrier with every passing moment. It didn't help that the only entertainment in the unit was the TV in each room. I had hardly ever been huge on watching TV, not that I ever had the time in high school and college, and I could only scroll through Facebook so many times before I started getting antsy.

The morning passed, as did the afternoon, and despite our questioning, Mom and I got no answers. It wasn't until after 4:00 p.m. that we were told no space had opened up to fit me into the surgeon's schedule. To their credit, they tried to assure us that I would be put on the morning schedule for the next day.

When dinner finally came, I devoured it within minutes. I was hardly concerned about the flavor. I needed sustenance. In solidarity, Mom had decided not to eat until I could as well, so she was quick to get something from the cafe downstairs.

After being busy almost constantly, both at college and at home, sitting in a hospital bed all day watching TV felt like a monumental waste of my day. Worse, since I didn't do anything to exert energy, I wasn't even tired when the time came to try to sleep.

I tried not to let my mind wander to all the questions that had been circulating in my mind since I got diagnosed. There wasn't any use worrying about it, but it's not like I had much else to think about. I tried to pray, but I didn't even know what to pray about.

After another fitful night of sleep, another early awakening, and another morning with no breakfast, I was headed to the OR for what was probably the easiest surgery I would endure. I could be mostly prepped in my room, and all that would need to be done in pre-op is administering anesthesia. Before I knew it, I was waking back up on my way to my room, being transferred onto my bed, and left alone to rest.

As my senses came back to me and the anesthesia wore off, I found myself terribly sore. The left side of my chest, just below my collarbone where my port was placed, ached deeply with every movement. My lower back, where two bandages covered the entry points from the bone marrow biopsy, was just as sore. I tried to roll onto my side to ease the pain in my back but quickly realized how terrible it was for my newly placed port. The Tylenol I was offered did little to dull the pain, so the rest of the day into the night was even less restful than the previous days.

I woke up utterly exhausted and even more sore than the day before. No rounds had invaded my precious little rest that morning, and I was not about to complain about it. But when a team of doctors even larger than the usual five or six entered my room that afternoon, the blood drained from my face. I could only imagine what could possibly be wrong if all of those doctors were there to witness it.

Of course, they asked questions, and my anxiety and temper worsened with each second that I had to answer questions while questions raced through my head. When I reached the point of nearly snapping at them to tell me what was going on, I was informed that I was being discharged and that my treatment was being postponed because they had not been able to diagnose me accurately.

At this point, I was barely concerned about the lack of a diagnosis and the lack of information that came with it, as I was excited to be going home. I wanted sunlight, and fresh air, and to be free to go where I wanted, when I wanted. The discharge papers could not get in my hands fast enough, and I wasted no time in rushing us out of the horribly colored halls to freedom.

Once I was home, I spent a decent bit of my time trying to find a way to rest that wouldn't agitate both my back and my chest. My chest hurt much worse as the muscles and skin adjusted to the new device implanted there, so I chose a backache over the pain in my chest.

Once I felt rested after a few days, I tried to go back to my usual. My usual was, unfortunately, much more difficult with the addition of my port. I couldn't fix the mess of curls that had become my hair, because I couldn't lift my left arm above my head. I did the best I could since I made plans to go out to brunch with Anthony and catch him up.

I found the next barrier the minute I got into my car. My seatbelt rested directly on top of my newly placed port. I had been driving long enough that putting on my seatbelt and letting it snap against me was a habit, but it only took a few times before the pain taught me to tuck my seatbelt down around my arm.

I filled Anthony in on what had transpired at the hospital over pancakes - pancakes that were way better than those I had tried at the hospital, by the way. It was such a relief to be around my best friend. In contrast to the way everyone usually treated me following my diagnosis, he was one of the few people I could stand to be around for long. The only difference in the way he treated me was that he ended up giving me a few more hugs than he normally would have. Other than that, instead of the usual pity and speculation, he just kept reminding me that I would be fine.

January 28, 2019

It was hard to try to go about my normal life with cancer hanging over my head. I constantly wondered if that would be the day my oncologist would call and summon me back. If my oncologist never called me back to the hospital, it would have been too soon. But she did call about a week and a half later with a diagnosis.

I had Stage III Ewing's Sarcoma.

As far as stages go, Stage III is far from ideal with sarcomas. Though it had not yet metastasized - spread anywhere else - it was in multiple places along the bone and surrounding soft tissue and was considered high-grade. I found out that it had taken my oncology team so long to diagnose it as Ewing's because the kind I had was somewhat of a mutation of Ewing's.

Staying with the habit of keeping me mostly in the dark until they were ready to share more, that was all the info I received outside of being told when to come back for my first treatment and that I should plan to be there at least five days. I had a few days until I was scheduled to come in, and knowing that I would be going back sent me into a kind of paralysis. I felt the urge to try to live it up, to do whatever I could before starting chemo, but figuring out what to do was nearly impossible. Anthony's winter break had ended, and he was back in the routine of school and rehearsals, so my options were limited.

All too soon, I was again surrounded by the awful colors of my fourth-floor unit. Luckily, I never had to face the madness of the hospital alone since Mom promised to be with me for every treatment.

At least this time, I had some idea of what to expect, so it wasn't a surprise when nurses came into my room to draw blood and set up fluids. This time, however, they accessed my port. I was pleasantly surprised that it was far simpler than an IV and much less stressful. They even had a spray to numb the area just before they inserted the needle into my chest, making sure I felt nothing. The needle connected to the small plastic device just under my skin, and since it was connected to a major blood vessel, it could be used like an IV.

This time, I had no time to get too far into my head before a nurse educator showed up to, quite frankly, bombard me with info about what felt like every single aspect of my treatment.

To start, I was told much of what I had already figured out about my cancer. Ewing's was a bone and soft tissue cancer, and mine was high-grade, so I would likely need chemo, radiation, and surgery. After that, it was a crash course on the kind of chemo I would receive.

My treatments would total fourteen cycles, each cycle lasting two weeks. The protocol was VDC/IE, which took me days to remember. It took me even longer to remember what it all stood for - vincristine, doxorubicin, cyclophosphamide, ifosfamide, and etoposide. I would be in for five days to receive doses of the first three, VDC. I would have nine days to recover before starting a two-day cycle with the latter two, IE, and ending with 12 days off. Seven cycles of VDC, seven cycles of IE, and I would be done. Only eight months of treatment, the nurse said. Only.

The more daunting thing I would learn was the side effects. But to understand the side effects, I was given a lesson on hematology, or how my blood would be affected. Knowing that, I could understand that because of how chemo affected my red blood cells, I would be very low on energy. If my platelets were low, as they likely would be, I could bruise very easily or, at worst, bleed out from something as simple as a nosebleed. My ability to fight infections would be low once chemo took out my white blood cells, so things as simple as a cold could also be detrimental.

On top of that, because chemo would attack all cells in my body that were fast replicating, as cancer was, it would also attack mucous membranes in my body, like the lining of my GI tract, nose, and mouth. Nicely put, I could get wicked mouth sores.

Cyclophosphamide and ifosfamide could cause severe bladder damage, so I would be given extra fluids to flush them out of my system quickly.

Vincristine could damage my nerves, leading to peripheral neuropathy - nerve damage - so I could lose sensation in my fingers and toes.

Doxorubicin could damage my heart, so I would be given steroids before each dose.

Etoposide would lower my blood pressure, so I would be lightheaded and might have spells of passing out.

Last but certainly not least, in an absolutely worst-case scenario, this combination of drugs could cause leukemia in the future.

Yep, the drugs used to treat my cancer could cause another kind of cancer. Just another fact of living as a cancer survivor, another fact so easily thrown into the education I was being given.

It was safe to say I was overwhelmed at that point, but we were not done. Over the next few hours, the next eight months of my life were explained to me. When I would come for treatments, blood tests, and blood transfusions. What actions I would take for each and every possible scenario. What would happen if, what we would do if, what would happen when, and how we would deal with anything that could possibly happen. I had words thrown at me that I couldn't possibly keep up with, concepts that I felt like I needed a degree to

25

understand. Yet I was reassured, not so reassuringly, that I would be an expert at these subjects before long.

Because every 18-year-old wants to be an expert in their newly diagnosed chronic illness.

I still felt horribly unprepared for the path that was ahead of me, but I processed what I could and vowed to ask questions about what I couldn't. By the time this nurse left, smiling as if she hadn't just told me how much hell I was about to walk through, all I wanted was a nap. But no rest for the weary. My team was coming through the door, telling me I would receive my first dose of chemo that night. I was eating dinner and was immediately terrified of finishing it if I was starting chemo.

My nurse came in to start the pre-med cocktail of steroids and nausea meds. I was still eating as she worked, not paying much attention to what she was doing. Just as I took a bite of green beans, a horrible sensation flooded my senses. Something between a taste and a smell of rubber overtook the flavor of the green beans, and I gagged. I had just learned the hard way that it was possible to "taste" saline and other things that were flushed quickly through my port. That was a lesson I would not soon forget and one that I still laugh at.

Before we started chemo, my oncologist came in to explain one more aspect of the treatment I was receiving. I was told that this chemo was likely to affect my reproductive system and that I would be put on a certain type of birth control that would shut that system down to minimize the effects of chemo on it. I was told that because my cancer was so aggressive, waiting for hormonal treatments to harvest my eggs for the future was not feasible and was incredibly expensive.

And that was that, plain and simple. The choice of my ability to have children was so easily taken from me. We didn't know at the time that we could have pushed back and made ourselves a part of the decision. We were so overwhelmed that we just placed our trust in these doctors, with the hope that they knew best. I was so overloaded that I was hardly able to process just how quickly that decision was made for me.

Then, the time finally came for my chemo to start, and I was nearly frozen to the bed in fear. In order to even connect the bags of chemo - a totally-not-daunting yellow bio-hazard warning label stamped to the side of the bag it came in - the nurses had to wear a mask, gloves, and special gowns. That made me feel so much better about the fact that this stuff was going to be pumped into my veins.

I had just been told exactly what to expect, but I had no idea what to expect. I knew what side effects I should be experiencing, but they forgot to mention exactly when they would happen. I assumed that they would happen as the drugs were being infused, so I tried to sleep during the infusion, hoping to avoid them. Unfortunately, I was too worried to get any rest. I just waited anxiously for the first wave of nausea to hit me as my body rejected the poison it was being given.

After a while, I realized that maybe, for the moment, I was safe from the nausea and started to relax as much as I could. By the time my infusion was over, I was ready to get some sleep for the night.

Only, there would be no sleep.

As I was warned, the extra fluids started the second I was disconnected from the chemo. Within half an hour, I was headed to the bathroom. I was still optimistic about the coming night of sleep. I climbed back in bed, got comfortable, and just started drifting into the sweet bliss of sleep when...*beep*

...*beep.*

...*beep.*

...*beep.*

Ten minutes later, after my nurse changed my empty bag of fluids, I was desperate. I was determined to get some rest. I had finally fallen asleep, and I could feel deeper sleep overtaking me when a knock sounded at my door. I thought that if I just acted like I had been asleep, maybe I'd be left alone. Wishful thinking. It was time for vitals.

All night, just as I had been on the verge of falling asleep or getting deeper sleep, I had to use the bathroom. Or the machine started beeping. Or it was time for meds. Or it was time for vitals.

By the time breakfast was being brought in, I decided that there was no point in trying to sleep. I woke up, steeled myself for another day of chemo, and hoped for a decent night of sleep the following night.

Each day, I waited for the side effects to hit me, but they never did. It was just five long, frustrating days of being attached to the IV pole. It took me about two days to really lose it over the IV pole. Every time I had to get up to use the bathroom, which was every 45 minutes, I had to unplug it from the wall and drag it around the foot of my bed to get to the bathroom. The bathroom was too small to get the IV pole inside with me, so I had to close the door around the line that was attached to my chest, hoping I wouldn't detach the needle accessing the port in my chest. When I was done, I'd have to drag it back to be plugged in.

That process got old the first five times I had to do it. By the tenth time, I had grumpily called my IV pole "stupid." In an attempt to help my mood, Mom suggested nicknaming the IV pole Stoopid. Within a few days, she had a t-shirt we could attach to the IV pole with the name Stoopid written in goofy letters, and I had a pin that said "I'm with Stoopid."

Within a few days of my stay, I got used to the constant knocks on my door and stopped flaring with anxiety every time someone new came into my room. To my surprise, someone had knocked, and they weren't in scrubs or a lab coat.

The girl who entered my room was around my age and was in jeans and a T-shirt. She told me she was from an organization called Streetlight. The people in Streetlight, the Streeples, were undergrad students who volunteered to be peer visitors to patients in the North Tower. I thought it was a cool idea, especially to have something interesting to look forward to during the endless hours of treatments I was looking at.

She spent the afternoon with us, even telling us that we could get a wheelchair to take me out of my room. We didn't know where to go, so she took us to what became one of my favorite spots in the following months. After crossing to the other side of the street to the

28

South Tower through an underground transport tunnel, she led us outside to the Fountain of Hope. Even with the chaos of the city around us, it was a little haven of fresh air and beautiful scenery.

February 1, 2019

By the end of my five days of chemo, I could feel the effects start to take hold of my body. When I finally got home, I could barely drag myself into the house from my car. Throughout the week, I did not feel sick and didn't even throw up, but it took its toll on my energy. That, combined with the fact that I couldn't get uninterrupted sleep for longer than 45 minutes at a time. The first thing I did at home was shower. The second was to get in my own bed and sleep. And I slept like I hadn't known sleep in years. I realized, at this point, why sleep deprivation is considered an advanced interrogation technique.

Over the next few days, things only got worse.

Where there was once a steady, confident hand, I reached out to find my hand trembling. Where there were once bright eyes looking back at me from the mirror, there were now tired, dull eyes. Where there was a sharp mind, it now felt like I was thinking in slow motion.

Either way, I was just happy I wasn't throwing up. If the worst of it was feeling like I had a horrible version of the flu, I wouldn't complain.

Throughout the process of getting diagnosed and enduring my first treatment, everyone kept wondering when the breakdown would come. Though I had seemed to handle things just fine, I still hadn't cried about it. I had dealt with the whole situation, relatively speaking, pretty well.

I continued to handle it well until I woke up one morning just a few days after coming home, ran my hand through my hair as I always did, and looked at my hand to see a handful of hair had come with it.

I had expected a gradual loss of my hair, maybe a few strands here or there for a few days, to ease me into the loss. Instead, it was instantaneous. One day, my hair was just as strong and thick as it had always been. The next, it was falling out by the handful, and I was devastated. I could handle the shaky, weak feeling. I could talk myself around it. But pulling my hair out in clumps was too drastic of a sign that I may now be on the path to becoming what I had feared: A Cancer Patient.

You know, the sickly, bald, weak, pale character on TV who could barely lift their head off their pillow. "Half dead," I had once described them. I could fake it past feeling fatigued. I could avoid letting people see my hand shaking. I couldn't avoid this irreversible, visible step into becoming what I had feared.

I climbed into the shower and lost it. In hindsight, the shower was the worst place to have this breakdown since I would end up watching my hair swirling down the drain. After nearly a month, I finally cried. Not because I cared so much about my hair that I thought I would never be able to show my face again out of embarrassment, but because that was my life. I wouldn't be able to hide, and people would see that I was a Cancer Patient. They would pity me because that's what people do when they see a young person with cancer. They don't tell them how strong they are or what a warrior they are. That seems to come only after they make it to survivorship.

After I broke down, I accepted my new fate and texted Mom to let her know. I also decided at that moment that I wouldn't wait until survivorship to be considered strong. I had been surviving cancer from the moment it became an active threat in my body, and I would not be called a cancer patient. Instead, I would be called a cancer survivor. Despite my impending baldness, paling skin, and dull eyes, I would not allow anyone else to define me based on what I could not control. I would be defined by how I handled those things.

After three days, I understood what it meant to have thick hair. I couldn't move without my hair being everywhere. In the drains, on my clothes, on my sheets, all over my floor, and when it came to the

30

point that I was leaving a trail of hair wherever I walked and I still had a head full of hair, I got fed up. I called Mom and told her that I would likely go insane if we didn't bite the bullet and shave my head. It was bound to happen eventually, and I certainly was not going to wait until I had less hair than Gollum to do it.

Mom set up an appointment with a local hairdresser after hours so we could take that step in private. After she got off work, I met her at the small salon and made it two steps through the door before I froze. My whole body started to tremble, and I couldn't force my legs to carry me forward. When I finally got to the salon chair, I started to cry again. Even though I had expected it and decided to do it, it had become more real than what I was prepared to feel.

Before the hairdresser started, I looked at Mom, who was on the verge of tears. Knowing I couldn't handle seeing her cry with me, I told her only one of us was allowed to cry. I was trying to joke and make light of the situation, but Mom took me seriously and became the strong one for both of us. In hindsight, telling a mother she was not allowed to cry watching her daughter have her head shaved was cruel. But I was sobbing, the hairdresser was sobbing, and for Heaven's sake, someone needed to hold it together for us. Mom had always been where I drew my strength, and I needed that strength in those moments.

I didn't look in the mirror when it was done. I just thanked the hairdresser, who had shared this heart-wrenching moment with me. I grabbed my beanie, covered my head, and let Mom lead me to my car. She told me she would order my favorite pizza and would meet me at home when I was ready. She knew I would need to take the long way home.

During the whole ordeal, Mom had offered to shave her head to support me. I had to think about that during my drive. The fact that she would offer such a drastic show of support warmed my heart, but I couldn't bear to see myself without hair, much less the image mirrored in Mom. I had no choice in my hair loss, but I wouldn't put her through the same. Instead, I decided I wanted her to cut her hair and donate it. It was a show of support enough and would go to a good cause. She agreed that it was a good compromise.

Limitless

By the time I got home, I was ready to be the strong cancer survivor I was so determined for people to see. I joked and laughed like I would any other night, even through tear-swollen eyes. I wasn't going to let cancer steal my spark.

Chapter 4

February 7, 2019

Being a cancer survivor was like a full-time job. It would be nice to think that after every treatment, I got to spend the rest of my time until the next one at home, in peace.

If only.

My body was already weakened to the point where I no longer felt the usual urge to get out, move, and exert energy. I was content to relax more. In that relaxation, I would find myself trying to visualize life after cancer. I tried to hold onto what it felt like to stand without my body trembling. Then, I tried to visualize what I might do when my body could handle the activity again. My love was still drumming, and I tried to visualize myself performing with an indoor drumline, strong and full of life again. It was hard to imagine, considering I hadn't even had the strength in my hands to pick up my beloved drumsticks.

Within a few days of being home from treatment, though, I was back at the hospital in the clinic, getting blood drawn for labs. At first, I wouldn't even let them touch me with a normal IV blood draw. I hated needles, and I had a port for a reason. Though the logic was that accessing my port too much could increase my risk of getting an infection, the port was much less stressful, so that's what I wanted to do. Despite my reservations, I did find one nurse I would trust to do an IV blood draw.

This nurse, Megan, was one of the sweetest people I had ever met. It made me trust her instantly, and when she was able to find a vein on the first try with almost no pain, she became my go-to. If she wasn't there, we accessed my port, and everyone knew that when she was there, she was my nurse.

After my lab results came back, I would get to see a member of my oncology team, and I was usually bombarded by questions.

How was I feeling?

What was my pain level?

Had I been eating?

Had I been using the bathroom?

Did I have any mouth sores?

Had I been bruising easily?

Did I have any numbness in my fingers?

Did I feel fatigued?

Had I been nauseous?

In general, I felt like I had the flu if the flu was about a thousand times worse than normal. My hands trembled constantly, as if I could barely hold the weight of my arms. In fact, I felt as if I could barely hold the weight of my own body up. My stomach constantly churned, though I had not thrown up yet. I had started sleeping longer but never felt as if I had slept long enough. My brain seemed to be swimming inside my skull.

After talking about side effects to make sure they weren't bad enough to warrant more medications to keep them under control, we talked about the results of my blood work.

Every time I took chemo, it would cause my red blood cell, white blood cell, and platelet counts to drop. To receive another treatment, those counts would have to recover to a certain degree so that chemo would not deplete them completely. For most people, their blood counts would recover to a safe level after a week to a week and a half, within just enough time to stay on schedule with their chemo treatments. If they did take longer to recover from chemo, it would be towards the end of their treatment. Since my first treatment had lasted five days, I only had nine days for my blood counts to drop and recover back to a safe level to start chemo again.

Unfortunately, my blood counts had been hit hard by my first treatment. While it was expected they would be depleted, compared to the expected trends from other patients, mine were significantly lower.

It wasn't the news we wanted to hear. If my blood counts were so low, it would likely take them longer to recover. It was already towards the end of the week, and I was scheduled to start chemo again at the beginning of the following week. It was unlikely my blood counts would recover to safe levels before then.

I tried not to think much of it. There was still a chance, if even a small one, that my blood counts would recover by the following week. We all hoped that I was in the upswing, where my blood counts were already starting to recover, and would recover quickly over the weekend.

February 11, 2019

Instead of heading straight to admissions, as I would usually have for chemo, we headed to the clinic. I was scheduled to start my second round of chemo that day, but with the dismal results of my blood counts the previous week, my team thought it would be best to run labs in the clinic before starting the admissions process for chemo, just in case my blood counts hadn't recovered.

Mom and I had come packed for the two-day treatment, and we were hopeful. The side effects from chemo hadn't been so bad after the first round, and I knew the sooner we got through each round, the sooner treatment would be behind me. I was even mentally prepared for the next treatment. I spent the weekend praying and strengthening my mind for what was to come.

It was almost a letdown when they told me that my lab results were just below safe levels for starting treatment.

35

It was daunting to think that one week of delaying meant one week tacked on to the end of my treatment. If I had already started to delay, was that the trend I could expect?

I shut down that line of thought quickly. When we told Megan, she reminded me that there was no sense in stressing about something that hadn't even happened yet. That aside, this delay wasn't the worst thing that could have happened.

Though I may not have needed a full week for my blood counts to recover for the next treatment, a door had opened for another opportunity. The Sunshine Kids, a foundation that raises funds to send young adults with cancer on trips to get away and meet others going through the same trials, offered me a trip to New Orleans. It was an all-expenses paid trip, usually for those under the age of eighteen, but since I was still eighteen and wouldn't be eligible for Make-A-Wish, they extended the invitation.

My team and I thought that taking the opportunity to be on a trip with other young adult cancer survivors would be worth the extra week's delay. If I tried to do another treatment before the trip started, my immune system would have been too weak for me to travel safely, and they would not have approved the trip.

I was ecstatic. I had never been to New Orleans, and this trip was planned during Mardi Gras celebrations. I let the negative thoughts about what delaying meant go and chose to focus on what exciting things the Sunshine Kids had planned for us.

February 18, 2019

When I say Sunshine Kids went all out on that trip, I mean they went *all out*. To name a few things, we shopped in the French Quarter, toured Mardi Gras World, met the cast and toured the set of NCIS New Orleans, took a pontoon boat tour, visited the National WWII Museum, and ate quite a few rounds of chargrilled oysters. We had our own game room in our hotel, where the cops who escorted us - on motorcycles, wherever we went - even got in on the fun. It was a week in paradise.

We ate at new restaurants every day and truly wanted for nothing. They even gave us money to spend whenever we shopped. Oh yeah, and we got to be in a Mardi Gras Parade, costumes, floats, throwing beads, the whole enchilada. That was an item on my bucket list that I didn't even know I had.

Mom planned on surprising me by flying out to watch me in the parade. When she got to New Orleans and started sightseeing, she saw the Sunshine Kids tour bus at a restaurant on Bourbon Street. She caught the attention of one of the cops escorting us, a seven-foot-tall guy everyone called Tiny, and asked him to tell me she said hi. Instead, he pulled her into the restaurant and pointed me out.

I had been enjoying chargrilled oysters without a single clue that Mom was in New Orleans. When I glanced up and saw her, I had to do a double take. I was still used to her long hair, and since she had cut it short for me, I didn't recognize her at first. When I finally did, I ran up to her and gave her the biggest hug.

But aside from just a week of fun, this trip was therapeutic in ways I didn't even know possible. Meeting other young cancer survivors, all in various stages of treatment, was incredible. Though I hadn't been in treatment long enough to feel this way, there would be times to come when I would start to feel alone. I knew, logically, that I wasn't the only 18-year-old cancer survivor to exist, but it was isolating. Having the friends I made on this trip was a constant reminder for me that I wasn't going through it alone and that there were others with similar young adult struggles going through cancer.

It was inspiring to see other young adults who had made it through, even another cancer survivor who had Ewing's, the same cancer I was currently fighting. Gabe had lost his right leg to Ewing's but was in remission, and it didn't take us long to become close friends. We brought each other out of our shells and even got so close we wouldn't go to our rooms for the night without sharing hugs.

I think one of the most impactful things that happened to me on this trip, though, was our trip to a local arcade to play laser tag. Up until that night, I had been wearing a hat to cover the fact that I was bald. I wasn't trying to hide it since my lack of natural eyebrows and eyelashes kind of gave me away, but I just wasn't ready to face that reality. Even being around other people who had lost their hair wasn't enough to shake me from wearing a hat, even as we sweltered in the New Orleans humidity.

Running around playing laser tag forced my hand. I couldn't stand wearing a hat after working up such a sweat. The hot flashes I had because of the birth control I was on didn't help matters at all, and I finally caved and took off my hat. One of the friends I made knew that was a hard moment for me, and we were talking about it as we went to the drink counter to get something cold to help us cool off. I was expressing that I was still wildly insecure about not having hair and how I was afraid I would be looked at with pity if people suspected it was from cancer.

We had left the drink counter and that conversation behind, but I was still wildly uncomfortable. Of course, the people I was around wouldn't judge me since most of them had lost their hair at some point, too. It was everyone else in the world I was worried about. But not long after leaving that conversation behind, the girl working the drink counter that night approached me. She told me that she overheard the conversation I had about my insecurities, and she wanted to share with me that she thought I was absolutely beautiful and brave for not wearing a hat and that I shouldn't worry. She believed the look suited me well, and before she heard our conversation, she just assumed I had made a bold fashion statement. She assured me that others would probably think the same.

I ended up crying on her shoulder, and she cried on mine. It was the encouragement I needed, and because of her, I never tried to hide my bald head again. And she was right; most people I encountered were shocked to find out I had cancer.

Her being caring enough to share those incredibly emboldening words with me would lead to one of the funniest moments of the trip, and had she not given me the courage to embrace my shiny bald head, this moment might not have happened.

As the week came to a close, Sunshine Kids threw a Mardi Gras Ball for us, and my name was drawn out of a hat to be the Queen of the Ball. Being a queen meant I got a super cool costume, complete with a tiara. But like all costume tiaras, this one had those little combs on the side that helped hold the tiara into a girl's hair. Well, seeing as I didn't have hair, the combs did me no good.

My chaperone - one of the doctors from my hospital - and I were in my room, trying to get the costume together, when we realized our best bet was to get the combs off the tiara and let it rest on my ears.

But we didn't have scissors.

So, we yanked the little teeth of the combs back and forth until the plastic weakened and broke, trying to hurry so we weren't late for the ball. It was at that moment that my chaperone looked at me with a dead-serious expression and said, "I bet you never thought you'd be in a hotel with me in New Orleans, ripping the combs off a tiara during Mardi Gras."

It was truly the most ridiculous moment, and we spent at least five minutes laughing at it.

The day the trip ended, and my group flew back to Florida, I met my new friends in the hall of our hotel and we shared a tearful goodbye. Though only a week, we had become so close and weren't ready to leave, likely knowing that we probably would not see each other again for a very long time, if ever.

I shared a particularly painful goodbye with Gabe, since he and I had become so close. We all exchanged numbers and made group chats, promising to keep in touch.

New Orleans had become somewhat of a haven for me. Sure, I still had cancer, but there were no blood tests in New Orleans, no bright red chemo bags, and no IV fluids. I knew that once we flew back, I would be whisked back to the reality of being a cancer survivor, and I wasn't ready.

Limitless

Getting off the plane in Florida, I felt like a totally different person. I hadn't covered my shiny bald head since the night in the arcade, and now that I was home, I wanted to feel the same confidence I did in New Orleans. I decided to test the waters with the person I trusted most - aside from Mom, of course. I texted Anthony to see if I could stop by his house on my way home from the airport.

When I got out of the car, he didn't even react. He just pulled me in for a hug and asked me how the trip had been. We spent some time talking, and during our conversation, I had a thought. One of those things I would start to refer to as a Rebecca-ism. With no warning, I asked Anthony what I should name the port in my chest. He didn't miss a beat before he said the first thing that came to his mind. We named my port Santana.

Chapter 5

February 25, 2019

By the time I had returned from New Orleans, emotionally recharged and encouraged, I found myself tossed unceremoniously back into reality. My doctors wasted no time getting me back in the hospital for my second treatment. It would be, blessedly, only two days. It was still nerve-wracking since I didn't know how my body would respond to a different cocktail of chemo drugs, but I already felt more confident since surviving my first treatment. I also had a better idea of the boredom to come, so I was more prepared.

The first evening I was there, I got to meet some Streeples that I hadn't yet met. I was pretty introverted at the time, so meeting new people was a little unnerving for me. And that was ignoring the fact that I was sitting in a hospital bed, bald, with no eyebrows, pale as a ghost. But as soon as they came into the room, all sense of my insecurities vanished. It was like meeting with old friends, as quickly as we all fell into an easy conversation. More to my surprise, no one asked about the elephant in the room. I was used to answering the big questions when new people came around, like how I got diagnosed, what chemo was like, and how I was handling the side effects. Instead, I found myself having a conversation about my favorite movies. I was a huge Marvel fan at the time, and I was eagerly awaiting the release of *Avengers: Endgame.* For hours, we talked about our favorite Marvel movies, theories, and hopes for the upcoming movie.

It was a much-needed reprieve from my life as a cancer survivor and a reminder that there was still a person behind the disease that currently held everyone's attention.

That night, I slept better than I had in previous hospital admissions. Having my port was now proving to be a huge blessing. Not having an IV in my arm allowed me to curl up like I preferred, and since my chest had healed, I could lay in any position I liked. I was already starting to get the hang of shutting out all the sounds. Even better, rounds for patients on chemo didn't start until sometime after 10:00 a.m., so I didn't wake up to anyone bombarding my room.

I was able to leave as soon as my chemo was done, so we only had to spend a few hours in the hospital the next day. When we finally got to leave, and I stood up to walk out, I felt a new side effect kicking in. I was *dizzy.* I was never one to get seasick, and years of marching gave me great balance. It was an entirely new feeling to stand and not quite be able to stay upright. We made it out to the car in one piece, thanks to the wheelchair, and I reclined the passenger seat back to keep the feeling at bay.

March 7, 2019

After my second treatment, the mouth sores started to appear. At first, they were just tiny sores that would pop up along the sides of my tongue or on the inside of my cheeks. They were, at that point, a minor inconvenience to my ability to eat anything salty, sour, or spicy. So, y'know, most of the foods I liked.

It also didn't take long for the neuropathy to set in. A faint numbness appeared in the tips of my fingers as if no matter how hard I pressed them, my nerves had just given up.

The real joy of my "off days" from chemo came when I got my lab results back and found out that my red blood cells and platelets were dangerously low. I got a call from the hospital with a request, or demand, really, that I come in at 8:00 a.m. the next day for a blood transfusion.

I was mortified.

I had an hour-and-a-half drive to the hospital and needed at least half an hour to be awake enough to make that drive. Never mind that I was exhausted, and these people wanted me to wake up at 6:00 a.m. on a day I would be desperately trying to catch up on the sleep that I lost from being in the hospital.

At my pushback, I was told very matter-of-factly, "You can refuse to come in for this transfusion, but if you end up in the ED because you bleed out over the weekend, don't say I didn't warn you."

Excuse me?

Apparently, being treated in a pediatric unit meant I got to be manipulated and scared into making decisions. But I didn't have the energy to fight back, or to explain to this practitioner why that was an inappropriate response, so I agreed to be there.

March 11, 2019

That was the rhythm I started to live my life by - chemo, blood tests, blood infusions, intrusive questions, and worsening side effects.

We hoped that, since my treatment was only two days, my blood counts would have more time to recover, and I wouldn't need to delay the start of my next treatment. Unfortunately, those two days of chemo packed a punch.

My blood counts were still low, and even though the blood transfusion had helped elevate my red blood cells and platelets, there was nothing that could be done about my white blood cells. Until they reached a safe level, I wouldn't be able to start my third treatment. To make things even more difficult to coordinate, since my next treatment would be a five-day stay, my team wanted to start the treatment on a Monday. Even if my white blood cells recovered within a day or two, I would have to wait a full week before starting my next treatment.

The unpredictability started to get to me. Just a few months prior, while I was at college, I had lived my life by a strict schedule. I even had a massive desk calendar with color-coordinated pens. My weeks were well planned, and I thrived off knowing what I would be doing and when.

Not knowing when I would be in the hospital for treatments started to throw me into a tailspin. I could plan to spend five days in the hospital, only to have to push the treatment back a week. If I had anything planned during that week, I would have to cancel or push those plans back in order to accommodate the treatment. If my treatments got moved, my appointments in the clinic also got moved, and all the rescheduling made it impossible to live my life by a predictable calendar.

I had to learn to let my life revolve around the ever-changing chemo schedule, and that was something I wasn't prepared for, either in practice or in how I responded to it emotionally.

Chapter 6

The third treatment stay itself was about as eventful as my others had been. I would mostly be stuck in my room but would sneak out sometimes to sit by the Fountain of Hope, or to get fro-yo from downstairs.

I started to look forward to meeting new Streeples as much as I enjoyed seeing my old friends from Streetlight. On one especially fun night, we started a massive game of Uno. I hadn't laughed as hard as I did that night since New Orleans, and laughs at the hospital were few and far between.

Being involved with Streetlight turned out to be so much more than just visits in hospital. One of the volunteers, Francisco, had become so invested in my story that when I opened up about my diagnosis and treatment, he introduced me to the director of Streetlight. Their director, Em, seemed to radiate positivity and encouragement wherever she went. Between the two of them, my room always seemed to light up when they were around. Francisco was the kind to ask questions and appreciate the human experience, and always seemed to have the wheels turning during our conversations.

Limitless

Talking to him about my diagnosis didn't feel as burdensome as it did when I had to bring up that part of my life for most others. His appreciation for the person in front of him, no matter who it was, made talking about such things a positive experience.

Having Streetlight visit was the one time in the hospital I could feel more like a human. Most of the time, it felt as if I were defined by my diagnosis. To most, I was Rebecca, the cancer patient.

That label caused friction with my team. I related more to the term cancer survivor. The term cancer patient seemed to have the undertone of a victim of cancer, in my opinion. I was no victim. If I had to be referred to in relation to the disease I had, it would be as a survivor.

At one point, I informed my team that I would prefer them to refer to me as a cancer survivor if they must refer to me in relation to my diagnosis at all. A simple request, seeing as I was the one with the life-threatening disease. I was informed that I would be called a cancer patient until I finished treatment. Cancer patients only received the title of cancer survivor after they finished treatment, not before. Their words, not mine.

I told them, in no uncertain terms, that I thought that was the dumbest thing I had ever heard. From then on, I made sure to correct them every time they called me a cancer patient. With a kind and innocent smile, of course.

By this point with my treatments, I was handling the hospital torture a little better. I figured out how to get the nurses and PCAs to coordinate meds and vitals as best they could. Instead of nurses coming in to give me my meds and then PCAs coming in to do vitals, they tried their best to get those tasks done at the same time. I still had to use the bathroom every half an hour or so, but I had accepted my fate there. Someone from Streetlight showed me how to hit a mute button on my IV pole. I still pray that God blesses them for that one.

I was finally getting the hang of dragging around Stoopid, my IV pole, and figured out how to move my bed around so that Stoopid could be on the side of the bed closest to the bathroom. That way, I

46

usually wouldn't even worry about the charging cable. I even started to learn how to sleep so that when a nurse or PCA came in, I could let them do what they needed without fully waking up.

March 25, 2019

After my treatment, I felt a little worse than the previous ones, as expected. The mouth sores now kept me from talking much, and I only ate soft foods until they subsided. If I ate at all, that is. I got up from bed only to move to the couch. If I wanted to change it up, I might have moved to the recliner instead. Exciting, I know.

The feeling of constant sickness had almost started to feel normal. If the mouth sores were held at bay and my nausea kept to a minimum, it was a good, normal day. No longer did I expect to feel like I had energy or feel like I could move without my body shaking under its own weight.

I had gone in for labs a few days after finishing chemo, as usual. I expected to hear the same results, that my blood counts had tanked past what was expected. Well, I did hear that, but not before it was revealed that I was running a fever.

You would have thought my arm was falling off from the commotion my team made. This was one of the many pieces of information that had not quite stuck with me from before my first treatment. Fevers would get me admitted to the ED to ensure I had not contracted some life-threatening infection. My team making a fuss did not help my growing anxiety as they called down to the ED and ushered me there with no clear explanation of what I should expect.

By the time I managed to get someone's attention, I was beyond asking things nicely. I more or less snarled at the first doctor who slowed down for half a second, "When can I go home?"

As if it were the most normal, nonchalant response ever, I was told that I'd be staying for a few days, at least, to make sure my blood cultures came back clear.

Days?!
I mean, it's not like I had any plans except lying in bed. But I
wanted to lay in *my* bed. In peace. Not in a hospital bed, with people
invading my space and machines beeping.

I also didn't appreciate that no one was explaining *why* it was
so big of a deal that they would be keeping me for a few days. No
matter how much I asked or in what way I asked, I got a mix of
answers that didn't line up.

"You need antibiotics."

"You may have a severe infection."

"Your blood counts are too low."

So, I was back in a hospital bed, feeling perfectly fine aside
from my growing agitation, not having a discernible clue about why
I was being kept in the place I was growing to hate. One of my
nurses noticed I didn't understand why I was being forced to stay for
what was becoming an indefinite period of time and took the time to
explain what was going on.

A fever was their warning sign that my body might be fighting
an infection. But because my blood counts were very low, and my
ANC, absolute neutrophil count, was so low, if I did have an
infection, even a minor one, my immune system would be unable to
fight it. It could turn into something as serious as sepsis if not caught
and treated with antibiotics in time. They were starting me on a type
of antibiotic that could treat most common bacterial infections while
waiting three days for my blood cultures to come back positive or
negative for a specific infection. Until those blood culture results
came back, I would be stuck.

Much to my dismay, she also explained that if the cultures
came back positive, I would likely be staying longer, either until my
blood counts and ANC increased or until I had finished a course of
antibiotics. At a maximum, I could be in the hospital for two weeks
or more.

Until the third day, I would wait. But I couldn't go outside like
I would during chemo treatments because of my low ANC. I would
be confined to my room for the foreseeable time of my stay. To make
my feeling of isolation worse, anytime someone came into my room,

they would have to wear gloves, a mask, and a gown. For my protection, they said. It felt so alien, having people in my room when I could only see their eyes through the garb.

She left me to process my new predicament. I felt perfectly fine, so being confined to a small room with a tiny window was like being held in captivity. Mom had to go back home to pack us some bags with essentials, and I asked her to bring sketchbooks, colored pencils, a book, and anything else she could find to keep me entertained.

In hindsight, all the art supplies and books would be excessive, but I was panicking. I imagined being stuck in the same room, with most options for my entertainment being taken. I couldn't go enjoy the sunshine, couldn't spontaneously hang out with friends, and couldn't take myself on a drive, so I was trying to make up for it by giving myself what options I could for entertainment.

It was a blessing that at least Streetlight was still able to visit, though they had to wear masks and gowns. I couldn't even interact with my newfound friends in a semi-normal way. But even having the Streeples there gave me the faintest sense of normalcy in such an ever-changing environment.

Because I wasn't on constant IV fluids, just IV antibiotics, I at least had hope that I could get decent rest without needing to use the restroom or being woken up by the constant beeping. I was only disturbed by having my vitals taken two or three times during the night. I started to feel comfortable and even got a little rest with so few interruptions to my sleep.

Until the residents ruined everything at 5:00 a.m. the next morning.

During chemo, I only saw my team during mid-morning rounds around 10:00 a.m. Plenty of time for me to wake up slowly and peacefully, get breakfast, and prepare for the onslaught. That was not how things worked when I was admitted for a fever.

Just after 5:00 a.m., a resident nearly busted down the door to my room - or so it seemed through the peace of my sleep - and promptly turned on every light switch he could find, including the impossibly bright LED light directly above my bed.

This man was entirely too perky. Before my eyes were even open, I was asked every question in the book. When I didn't sit up and respond as fast as he would have liked, he started moving my bed into an upright position. At this point, I'm pretty sure he was asking to get throttled, but he was moving too fast for me to get a good swing in any way.

And just like that, the lights were off, and he was out the door, leaving me to readjust my bed. Mom was turning the lights off, and we were trying to get back to sleep.

I had barely gotten back to sleep before being woken up, albeit gently this time, for morning vitals before shift change. I couldn't be mad at how much effort the nurses and PCAs put into being quick and quiet. Unlike the residents, if nurses and PCAs had to come in during the night, they cracked open the door just enough to squeeze into the room so the hall lights wouldn't wake me. They would only turn on a small light over the sink to make sure they could see, and they always spoke softly. At least there were people in the hospital who valued sleep as much as I did.

I had almost given up on sleeping, but I was so desperate. I tried one last time, and just as I drifted off...

The door was being busted down again, lights were being turned on, and voices were speaking much too loudly. I wondered, snarkily, who might be careless enough to be making that much noise.

Enter the resident, with an equally annoying attending. I thought I would be getting some new news. Maybe an update on the likelihood of going home.

Oh, how hopeful I had been at that stage.

The attending was there to ask questions. The same questions the resident asked. By this point, I was awake enough to show my snarkiness. It was like they didn't even notice, like they couldn't be bothered to read the room. By the time they left, Mom and I had given up on sleep. She got up to get a shower and much-needed coffee as I started picking at the breakfast they delivered.

When my full team came for rounds, faces full of sickeningly sweet smiles, I was informed that I could expect three separate rounds each morning.

Joy.

They told me that my blood cultures were still negative, and I hadn't had a fever since the previous day, so I could expect to go home the following day if those trends continued. That was good news, at least.

Since it was so early, I had lost hope for more sleep, so I broke out my sketchbook for the day. My hand trembled so badly I could hardly make the same confident marks on the page as I had before. My style of choice was geometric line art, and being able to draw a straight line that didn't waver was pretty central to the style, but I tried. Even as shaky as some of the lines were, by the time I came to a finished product, I was happy. I was grateful I could still do art in the first place, and the messy lines seemed to be a testament to the situation.

Despite the small reprieves from art and visits by the Streeples, I was still frustrated at the whole situation. By the time I had gotten discharged, another insanity-inducing day of early wake-up calls, boredom, and frustration later, I was ready to rampage. I'm fairly certain I ranted all the way home. God bless Mom and her patience.

I couldn't possibly fathom why I had been forced to stay in the hospital for what amounted to nothing. Precautions, sure, but it did not feel worth it to go through that kind of stress and, quite frankly, misery over precautions.

When I asked why, if I hadn't had any signs of infection, I spiked a fever, I was told that sometimes, as a patient's bone marrow starts to regenerate after treatment, it could cause a fever. I tucked that info away, promising myself that, if this did happen in the future, I would make sure it was a true fever before letting my team catch on.

The whole experience made me feel so out of control. I had never had much say in what would be happening to me, and the fact that I could just be randomly forced into a hospital stay was jarring. I had been trying so hard to balance the necessities of chemo with my quality of life and knowing that at any time I might need to drop my plans and sacrifice those moments of joy and that it could all be for a false alarm was not something I was okay with.

Chapter 7

April 8, 2019

I had barely gotten over the exasperation of the unexpected hospital captivity before I was back in for another chemo treatment. Though my stay in the hospital had caused me to delay the start of my next treatment by a few days, it still felt like no time at all before I was back for more. By this point, the treatments were starting to take a greater toll on my body. With the compounded amount of chemo in my body for even three treatments, the side effects had started to come on much quicker.

What started with my first few treatments as feeling unsteady and lightheaded now caused my blood pressure to drop so low that I had to stay lying down for most of my treatment. If I needed to get up, I had to sit up very slowly over the course of a few minutes.

During my stay, I went for an evening shower as usual. Since I was connected to fluids and my port was accessed, I had to use a shower dressing over my port. It was a large sticky piece of plastic that covered the area so that water would not get to the access point on my chest and risk an infection. A hot shower was still one of the few comforts and moments of privacy I could find to decompress, so the discomfort of the port dressing and having to drag my IV pole into the small bathroom with me was a small price to pay.

53

Cancer, it seemed, would want to steal that small luxury away from me.

I started to feel a bit lightheaded while I was in the shower, but I didn't think much of it since that was pretty normal with the chemo. Even still, I turned off the water and started to dry off. Because of the steam trapped in the tiny bathroom, I asked Mom to open the bathroom door to vent out the steam.

In an instant, I knew I was more than just lightheaded. My vision started to tunnel black around the edges, and my head seemed to fill with helium. I knew I was close to blacking out.

But over my dead body was I about to pass out with no clothes.

I willed myself to fight the blackness closing in on my vision as I threw on a t-shirt. I called out to Mom to help just as I had slipped on a pair of underwear, and at that moment, everything went in slow motion.

Mom stepped into the doorway of the bathroom just as I had started to waver and fall. She pulled the IV pole out of the way and caught me before I hit the floor. She was holding me up, yelling for a nurse, and trying to maneuver me into bed. I was absolutely no help, a dead weight in her arms. I couldn't fully pass out, but also couldn't come to consciousness because she was holding me vertically. I remember thinking that I was helping, at least trying to get my feet under me to take some of my weight off her, but apparently, I had just gone limp.

Mom got me to my bed just as the nurses started to rush in. As soon as I tipped back, I came back as if nothing had happened. I felt fine laying down but couldn't stay conscious if I tried to sit upright. As I came back to consciousness, I saw at least twenty nurses piling into my room. Just my luck, this happened during shift change, so I had both night shift and day shift nurses in my room.

I was so thankful I had gotten clothes on before I went down.

I had to explain to the nurses that, yes, I felt as if I would pass out in the shower, and, no, I didn't call for help until I had clothes on. I had lost quite enough dignity to cancer treatment, and I was holding onto what I had left for dear life.

I marveled that Mom had to have become a Supermom at that moment. She single-handedly moved my IV pole, caught me, kept my IV line from ripping out of my chest or pulling from the machine, and got me to bed within seconds.

I looked over at my Supermom, who had nearly passed out herself from the chaos of the moment. The nurses who remained were now more concerned with making sure she was okay than with me, all in good judgment. After all, I was perfectly fine as long as I didn't try to sit up.

When everything finally calmed down, I was told to not get out of bed without calling for a nurse. An instruction I promptly ignored when I had to get up to brush my teeth.

Hey, I was fully clothed and spent at least ten minutes easing the back of my bed up so I was in a sitting position. Now that I knew what it felt like to be on the verge of passing out. I didn't need a babysitter to walk three feet to the sink.

The rest of my treatment went without much excitement. I felt lightheaded and just a bit nauseous when we left the hospital, and mainly just ready to be home where I could sleep in peace.

April 15, 2019

Going in for my labs after that treatment, I was much more cautious. I checked my temperature before leaving the house and was fully prepared to take Tylenol if I had a slight fever. There was no way I would get trapped in the hospital again because of a false alarm. Luckily, my temperature was fine.

My labs, however, were not. At this point, we had started to expect this news, but it did not make it any easier to hear. My blood counts had bottomed out. Spectacularly. We didn't want to think of the implications of this yet, but we had to face reality by this point. The chemo should not have been tanking my blood counts that badly that early in treatment.

My team explained this to me but offered no solution to the problem. They had committed to giving me very high doses of chemo in the hopes that it would give me a greater chance of my cancer not spreading. Apparently, my now-imminent delays would not change their minds on that. The implication was heavy that if my blood counts were already taking such a hit, and I had experienced delays since my first treatment, I could continue to expect delays. I could also expect my eight-month treatment plan to be indefinite, as the goal was to finish 14 rounds of chemo, no matter how long it took.

I had always been a goal-oriented person, even so much as counting down the days to big events like vacations and graduation ceremonies. I didn't cope well with having such an ambiguous goal, especially when it meant staying in a perpetually sick state. Having my end goal taken away from me, with no sure time to look forward to so I could say I would be done with chemo, was devastating. Hope had become much less tangible.

To make matters and my mood worse, I felt like my body was trying to die. It felt as if my iron will was the only thing keeping my body from simply calling it quits. I was in a constant state of exhaustion that no amount of sleep could fix. My heart raced if I so much as turned over in bed. My nausea was constant, and though I hadn't thrown up, I felt as though I were seconds away at any given time. My mouth was filled with sores so painful I had a hard time talking. I even started to have worse hot flashes from the induced menopause I was experiencing, so I randomly felt like I was being flash-boiled from the inside out.

When the APRN on my team came to check on me during my appointment for labs, I finally crumbled under the pressure and allowed myself to show some vulnerability. It was something I tried not to do because I wanted to maintain a positive attitude, but I could only keep the facade up for so long. I told her how I was feeling physically and how it seemed my "better" days seemed to be less and less better after each treatment. I had hit lows I couldn't imagine, and every time I thought it couldn't get worse, it did.

It was a plea for help. I needed to know, if I had only gone through four treatments, how I was supposed to make it through ten more. I needed to be reassured that, at some point, it wouldn't get any worse. Mostly, I needed the person who was in charge of inflicting this on me to show me that she understood what it was doing, to encourage me, and to reassure me.

I was near tears, shaking both from the weakness that was now constant and from the fact that I was shattering.

She only told me, "Oh, you'll be fine. We have kids a decade younger than you going through the same treatment, and they handle it well. I can't tell you how you'll get through it, but you just will because you have to."

Until this moment, I had held out hope that my team had compassion, that the people who ordered the poison that I let in my veins at least saw the reality of what they had to do to give their patients a chance at life. Obviously, they had become desensitized.

That statement broke me. She left the room, and I lost it. Her response was so cold, impersonal, and dismissive. It completely invalidated everything I was feeling. How could I possibly be complaining when children were going through the same treatment? And I must have been a special kind of wimp if they could handle it, and I couldn't.

But at the same moment, what was left of me was shattered, and it was also forged back together. I was strengthened in that moment, and I know it must have been the work of God.

I didn't need their help or reassurance to survive. What I had inside me would pull me through whatever was to come.

Luckily, I didn't have to go completely without reassurance. Megan always checked on me after my appointments for labs and asked what had gotten me so upset. She took the time to sit with me and reassure me in much more helpful ways that I would get through. Instead of making me feel weak, she told me how strong I was for what I had endured so far. She empathized with how hard it must have been. We even joked that she could never have dealt with what her patients dealt with and that I could never deal with what my nurses dealt with. It was her encouragement that helped me put my brave face back on and walk out to keep facing what was ahead of me.

I thought I had gotten lucky in the following days. I had no hint of a fever or chills and, all things considered, felt fine. I was past the point where I had gotten a fever on my last break from treatment, so I was prepared to enjoy a few anxiety-free days, letting my blood counts recover.

Chemo had other plans for me.

This time, instead of a fever, it was shooting chest pains every time I tried to breathe.

I went straight into denial. It wasn't severe, and I was going to try everything I could before subjecting myself to a hospital stay, so I propped my pillows up, seeing if elevating my head would ease the pain.

No such luck, but I was determined. I tossed and turned, trying every position I could think of. I even ended up in the recliner. Still, no relief. Unfortunately, it was starting to rapidly get worse.

Now, I was panicking. To my surprise, my Crash Course in Chemo seemed to cover everything but shooting chest pains. I knew one of the chemo drugs I was on could affect my heart and that I would take steroids before receiving that drug to prevent that. But, if chemo had caused an issue with my heart, would chest pains be the sign?

Around 2:00 a.m., I woke Mom up to see what she thought. Of course, she wasn't thrilled that I had been having chest pains for over an hour before I woke her up, but she knew already that I would exhaust every option before going to the hospital.

My anxiety on the drive was, oddly enough, not coming from needing to go to the ED. Had it not felt like my ribs were puncturing my lungs every time I inhaled, I would have been fine. If anything, I was more agitated at the loss of sleep. I knew that since I didn't have a fever - because I checked, of course - they likely didn't have a reason to keep me for very long if they could quickly solve the chest pain issue. At least, that was the hope I was clinging to in order to keep myself sane.

Mom, however, was less calm. I glanced over at the speedometer on our drive and saw her going at least 80mph. She said if a cop tried to pull her over, she would put on her emergency flashers and keep driving to the ED. Her daughter was having what could be an emergency and she wasn't wasting any time explaining it. She had a good point.

My hope was fueled when I went into the ED, and no one panicked. It wasn't like with the fever, where everyone acted like I was going to keel over at any second. I wasn't whisked away into a room immediately. Obviously, they didn't think that it was serious, so I could let my nerves ease.

The sensory input from the hospital still unnerved me. The beeping of machines, the scent of hand sanitizer, and the trapped feeling weren't things I could just ignore, but it was just low-level anxiety. That I could handle.

Since it was still the middle of the night, I was taken back quickly. By this time, my chest pains had started to ease, driving my hope on even further. They were all but a minor annoyance by the time I was seeing a doctor after the typical barrage of vitals, blood work, and basic tests were done.

After what seemed like a million and one questions later, I was told that what I was experiencing was likely a severe flare of acid reflux, something I had never experienced in my life. Since chemo could damage the lining of the digestive tract, this was not an unexpected or serious concern.

Because it was easing up, they weren't concerned about sending me home, and I was not about to argue with that logic. Oh, and I would now have another medication to take to prevent flares.

"Wonderful, should we add that to the morning handful or evening handful of pills?" I asked.

Apparently, they had their sense of sarcasm surgically removed when they became doctors because they very seriously answered that I should take acid reflux meds in the morning before breakfast. Tough crowd, those doctors were.

Limitless

On the way home, I tried not to let my frustration get the best of me. At 4:00 a.m., after not sleeping all night, it was hard to not get caught up in the sea of thoughts.

How could I let myself panic like that? It was all over a little acid reflux, and Mom and I were both short on sleep and more than a little snarky because of it. But at least I would be sleeping in my own bed that night, with no residents breaking down my door at 5:00 a.m. That was a positive thought I could latch onto.

Chapter 8

April 18, 2019

I managed to stay away from the hospital while I recovered from chemo. No fevers - at least, none that couldn't be controlled by Tylenol. Wink, wink. No more acid reflux flares, and though my threshold for feeling "good" was lower and lower after every treatment, I was able to function well enough to see friends, go to church, and go shopping if I wanted.

My ANC, however, took its sweet time to recover. I went in for labs every few days, and it took nearly a week and a half for it to recuperate enough that I could start treatment. It was both a relief and a disappointment to finally go in for my fifth treatment.

It was a relief that I knew the quicker I got the treatments behind me, the closer I would be to finishing chemo. But that fact hardly did much to counter the dread that filled me when I started that round of chemo. In the time I had been away from the hospital, I had finally started to feel better. The constant nausea had dissipated, the shaking through my whole body eased, and I had some semblance of energy again. Knowing that all of those symptoms would be coming back, knowing I couldn't prevent them and that avoiding the chemo simply wasn't an option, was dreadful.

But I buckled down and did what I had to do. I knew that one day, though that day was an ambiguous point somewhere in my not-near-enough future, I wouldn't have to fight it anymore.

That round of treatment went by fairly uneventfully. I showered with the door open so I wouldn't get overheated and pass out. I went outside as often as I could manage, though the timing of meds, fluids needing to be changed, and even my bladder kept me from spending as much time outside as I would have liked.

But when we did get things coordinated - having a full bag of fluids, making sure I wouldn't need any meds, and having my vitals taken - I could look forward to a trip through the underground tunnel to the Fountain of Hope. On a lucky day, Mom and I could be out for 45 minutes to an hour before I would need to be back. Some days, we would even grab a snack on our way. Most days, our choices were between Starbucks and the fro-yo shop, but some days, we would get lucky and catch the Chick-fil-A truck.

The only hindrance to my time out was the mask I was "required" to wear since I was becoming too susceptible to infections. Already nauseous, breathing in my stale, humid air was the most miserable feeling. And with that, I couldn't breathe in the fresh air. I was trying to be good, but I was out of sorts enough as it was.

Mom, the clever woman she is, helped me find a way around that problem. Our first stop would always be to get some sort of snack or drink. To enjoy it, I would need to take the mask off. Then, if I lost track of what she was getting at, she would remind me when doctors or nurses would walk by to make sure I was drinking plenty. Hydration is so important on chemo, y'know.

I don't know how I would have survived without Mom looking out for me.

After about three months of treatments, I was starting to have hope that maybe, if I hadn't thrown up yet, I wouldn't. It was one of the aspects of chemo I had dreaded from day one. Even during long hours on the football field during marching band camps and rehearsals, I had never thrown up, so I hoped the trend would continue.

Well, my hope was dashed.

A few days into this treatment, the nausea was really starting to kick in. I fought it tooth and nail, getting higher doses of nausea meds, trying to move slowly, and avoiding strong scents like cafeteria food and hand sanitizer. One of my nurses even introduced me to a trick of hers - sniffing alcohol pads. I don't know what it is about the scent of alcohol, but it would take the edge off the particularly bad waves of nausea.

Usually, when food was delivered to my room, Mom would place it as far away from me as possible and wouldn't open the containers. But somehow, one slipped past her. As the food service lady very sweetly set my tray in front of me and opened the lid, the smell hit me like a brick to the face.

Mom saw my face pale, and with some of that Supermom agility, she had a trash bucket in front of me as I heaved. I'm pretty sure once I was done, she walked into the bathroom and threw up, too. What a pair we were.

She kept a strict eye on the food trays from that day on, and I no longer ate anything they brought me.

It wasn't just limited to the cafeteria food, though. Mom decided to get me a taco salad from downstairs that night since I hadn't eaten anything because of the nausea. I was ecstatic since taco salads were one of my favorite foods. The sight of a crunchy taco bowl filled with all my favorite fillings ignited my appetite, and I ate a good portion of the meal.

It was great! Right up until the moment the taco salad made a reappearance. To this day, I have avoided taco salads like the plague.

With the worsening nausea, my time outside became invaluable. Fresh air flooding my senses seemed to be one of the only things that could keep it at bay. That, and sniffing alcohol pads like it was no one's business. My nurses started leaving handfuls with me anytime they came to my room because they did work in a pinch.

April 21, 2019

As I expected, my side effects came back with a vengeance in the days following chemo. I shook like a chihuahua, though it was much less adorable in my case. As soon as I stopped receiving chemo, the threat of hurling everywhere became less, but I still felt like it all the time. This time, though, I had the worst case of mouth sores. Within days, my cheeks, tongue, and gums were covered in ulcer-like sores. I couldn't move my mouth to drink without whimpering in agony. I couldn't even swallow.

When I went in for labs, I took a notebook and pen to write down what I would need to say. Upon writing out that I couldn't move my mouth, my team of geniuses told me they needed to see how bad the sores were.

If looks could kill.

Again, I get it. They needed to see how bad it was. That didn't take away the fact that I wanted to cry each second I had to hold my mouth open, my teeth scraping against the sores covering my mouth.

It didn't need to be said at that point, but my labs came back dismally low. What a shocker.

My team was always so enthusiastic when I went in for labs the following days. They were optimistic that my blood counts would somehow recover quickly - unlike the past five treatments, where they dropped like the Titanic pretty predictably.

Which was weird because I couldn't share their sentiment. Recovered blood counts meant I would have to start chemo sooner, and that is just not something to get excited about. At least, not for the one living with the body being slowly poisoned by chemo.

I understood their intent. They wanted to get me through treatments on schedule so I could have an end date to look forward to. That's not to say that their excitement to start chemo and their subsequent disappointment when my blood counts were still in the garbage as if it weren't predictable by this point, didn't grate my nerves.

64

I knew that, despite their optimism that maybe this time I would recover quickly, I would be delayed again. I had already accepted that that was going to be my journey with chemo, even if I also had to accept that every delay meant stretching my end-of-chemo date farther and farther away.

There was only so much I could handle to stress over. I couldn't control my delays, so I made myself come to a place of acceptance. Why stress over what I couldn't control? Instead, I was determined to try to enjoy the reprieve.

April 26, 2019

That week, it would have been hard to get me down. Despite the mouth sores, low labs, and non-existent energy, it was finally a week that I had been looking forward to for months. *Avengers: Endgame* was premiering, and my friend and I had opening-day tickets.

After having my entire life dictated for months upon months, I was taking control of this one thing. I didn't even let the info slip to my team because I didn't want the germ speech about how bad a movie theater would be for my immune system.

In the days leading up to *Endgame*, my mouth sores were mostly healed, I had an appetite, and I had energy. Everything was going great.

Until it wasn't.

Oh, come on, you didn't think it was going to be that easy for me, did you?

The night before the premiere, I felt the tell-tale chills I had been on edge about for so long, and when I checked, I was running a fever. I was determined to avoid what I knew was inevitable for as long as I could, so I took a handful of Tylenol, turned my heating pad on under the layers of blankets I kept on my bed, and tried to get some sleep.

The chills would subside for a few hours, but as soon as the Tylenol wore off, they would come back. So, the cycle went on until I woke up the next morning. I was weak and exhausted. Even though it was mid-May in Florida, I dressed in a long-sleeved shirt and grabbed my jacket. If Tylenol could keep the fever at bay, it wouldn't be bad enough to call off *Endgame*.

My friend and I met at her house and planned on getting lunch and hanging out before heading to the movie. When she asked why I hardly ate, I told her it was nausea from the chemo. When she asked why I was huddled under a blanket with my jacket, I told her it was just chemo making my body weird. I kept taking Tylenol every few hours, and it kept the fever and chills at bay.

She seemed suspicious, rightfully so. She knew me well enough, but she also knew me well enough to not push the matter. I knew that, likely, I would need to be admitted to the hospital. In my head, though, that could wait a few hours.

I was quiet on the drive there. I didn't even sing along when "Holding Onto You" by Twenty One Pilots, my all-time favorite song, came on. I was just trying to survive to get through the movie.

We went all out for *Endgame.* We got the biggest bucket of popcorn they had, candy, large sodas, the whole nine yards. We even brought Marvel-themed blankets to curl up in. The theater we chose had reclining seats, so we were set. I took more Tylenol just before we arrived, and it had kicked in by the time we got settled.

I had only gotten invested in the MCU movies that year, binge-watching all the previous movies on the days I didn't feel like moving from the couch. I had a hard time remembering the details of most of the movies, but I had the main plot down. That day would be my first experience watching a Marvel movie on opening weekend, and I was not disappointed.

It felt incredible to do a normal thing for once. All the delays and postponed appointments were starting to get to me. I was worried I would end up in chemo the week of the premiere and would feel too sick to go. But as we got caught up in the movie, I almost forgot my current life situation. I was just a normal 18-year-old going to the movies. I ate absurd amounts of popcorn, cried my eyes out, and screamed during the epic Captain America scene. It was such a wonderful feeling to be the Rebecca I had been just a few months prior.

By the time we were leaving the theater, the Tylenol wasn't working. Instead of hanging out, I made my excuses and headed home, saying I was just exhausted from the excitement and emotional trauma of the movie. When I got home, Mom was home from work for the evening, and she immediately knew something was wrong. She knew what the chills meant and didn't say anything about how long she suspected I had been having them before that point. She just helped get our bags together and got us in the car.

I tried to drown out the torrent of thoughts I knew had been on the way with music. It almost worked until "Avalanche" by Bring Me the Horizon came on. That song had been on my playlist for years, thanks to Anthony. But until that moment, I hadn't realized just how relatable the song was to being a cancer survivor. I have yet to hear a song describe the feelings that I had been having so accurately.

It didn't take long for the facade I had been holding up for so long to crumble. I knew this was different than the first time I had a fever. The first time, I felt fine. This time, I felt like my body was shutting down.

On top of it all, I dreaded facing the doctors I would see and the looks I would get when I would have to tell them I was symptomatic for over 24 hours before coming in. They wouldn't understand. How could they? They weren't the ones in my head. They weren't the ones who weighed the risk - no matter how quickly - of enjoying one normal-life thing before being subjected to the hospital. I knew what I was doing could put me at risk. But there were two sides to that coin. If I didn't go do the one thing I had been looking forward to for so long, what would it have done to my already fragile mental health?

As I expected, the moment I got to the ED, I was rushed back to a room. There was an upside to knowing what to expect because I wasn't thrown off by the flurry of tests. A flu test, blood test, blood cultures, and a chest X-ray. As much as knowing what to expect drove my anxiety through the roof on our way to the ED, it was helping to keep my panic at bay.

It also helped me steel myself for the incredulous looks I got from the doctors when they found out I had waited so long to come in. I wasn't expecting to be told about how they had another patient who came in for sepsis, looking perfectly fine one minute, who coded and was gone five minutes later. It was always fear with those doctors. What they didn't realize is that, unless it was spiders or clowns, I was not so easily shaken. Even needles no longer sent my knees shaking. Quite the opposite of the intent they had, I became even more determined to survive, if only to prove them wrong.

I stopped trying to explain it after a few attempts and just let them think I was being reckless. I didn't care. They weren't the ones having their entire lives turned upside down and controlled by a disease they didn't ask for. How could I expect them to understand what that was like if they simply were not empathetic enough to try to?

I didn't have the energy to keep fighting them since my shivering was becoming worse and worse. I had gone from being able to sit up and speak to curling up under the paper-thin blanket to try to find any relief. Mom started questioning why my shivering could be kept at bay at home but worsened so much when we got to the ED. The resident she questioned told her it was likely because of the IV fluids being pushed at such a high speed through my bloodstream. If the infection was in my blood, as it likely was, it would be pushing the bacteria quickly through my bloodstream.

The resident mercifully ordered the fluids to be turned to a much slower speed, and the shivering eased up almost immediately.

I had gotten myself mostly pulled together by the time I was admitted to the floor and requested that I see my therapist as soon as she was available the next morning. I knew, even through trying to be the strong, unshakable one, that I would need support because, likely, I had sepsis.

It felt like my body went about shutting down. I hadn't eaten, and I barely drank, so I had to be hooked up to fluids. When the time came for rounds the next morning, I put the barest amount of effort into giving the resident who woke me up an attitude.

As expected, I was told that I had sepsis. I would be admitted until my ANC came up and my blood cultures were negative, and I could expect ten days in the hospital, if not longer. It took every ounce of energy I had to not fall asleep during the conversation because it was just confirming suspicions I already had. Again, I was chastised for waiting so long to come in. I was told that it wasn't worth it. I stayed unapologetic but shook my head and acted like I agreed so I could get out of the lecture.

I started to feel too awful to fully grasp what it meant to have sepsis. If anyone explained what it was beyond telling me that the bacteria I had contracted had made its way to my blood, I didn't process it. I knew from my last stay that I wouldn't be leaving in three days, though I didn't quite understand that with sepsis, I may not be leaving the hospital at all.

Because of my non-existent immune system, everyone wore the usual "for my safety" getup of masks, gowns, and gloves. I was told I wouldn't be able to leave my room. It was all for my safety. The day was a blur of people coming in and out of my room since I didn't have the mental capacity to process who they were or why they were there.

It was like my body had gone into power-saver mode. I didn't want to wake up, eat, drink, or move. I just wanted to hibernate until I could wake up and feel better.

Better, of course, being relative. Ideally, I wanted to feel like I had the energy to go on a hike, do a Zumba class, or even read. By that point, feeling like I could sit up and hold my eyes open at the same time would have constituted as "better."

By the time my therapist made it to me, I had thoroughly over-thought the idea of therapy. The previous times she had seen me, I was handling things really well. All she had to do was reinforce good coping mechanisms and offer some encouragement. Now, she would be seeing me at a low point, and I didn't know how to handle that.

Though it makes absolutely no sense, I didn't like the idea of her or anyone else seeing me not coping well. I wanted everyone to see my strong, optimistic side. I had to constantly remind myself that, when she got there, I needed to *not* fake it and that she wouldn't judge or shame me for not being at my emotional best.

After hearing the doctor's reactions to my movie theater rebellion, I expected her to lecture me about how reckless I had been. But after explaining why I was in the hospital in the first place, she was the first person aside from Mom to truly understand what was going on.

She explained to me that, despite what everyone was telling me, I hadn't been aiming to risk my life to see a movie. I had decided to gain a precious ounce of control back in my life.

Since before I had even been diagnosed, I was being told what to do, how to do it, when to do it, and where to do it.

"Be here for a biopsy tomorrow morning."

"This is the chemo you're going to take."

"This is when you'll be here for blood work."

"Come in for a blood transfusion Friday at 8:00 a.m."

"You're going to stay in the hospital indefinitely because of sepsis."

At that point, I was even being told what kind of surgery I would be having after my sixth treatment.

After four months, I finally had the opportunity to make a single decision for myself. One that would make or break my ability to continue coping with the lack of control I had in my life. She helped me realize that, whether I knew it or not, had I yielded to my symptoms and skipped the movie, I may have started to give up my fight because of the lack of quality of life.

It was that phrase again, *quality of life.*

No one ever talked about that in medical settings, at least not where I was treated. My doctors were so focused on treating my disease they seemed to forget the human being attached to it and the human need to have some control, make decisions, and simply *live*. It was so easy to get sucked into cancer survivorship, even to the point of losing memories of what life before cancer actually was, that I was in desperate need of some reminder of what kind of life I was striving to return to.

My team was willing to sacrifice my quality of life for a little while to increase my quantity of life, with very little regard for my ability to cope with that decision. That was why it was so easy for them to recommend staying at home all the time between treatments.

They may have witnessed what cancer treatment did to their patients, but they did not truly understand what it did.

By the end of our conversation, I felt validated that the strong feelings I was having were not delusional and reckless but human. We also addressed the other growing issue of the panic I would feel anytime I came near the hospital. We agreed together that a mild anti-depressant medication would be a good way to help get me through treatment.

It's sad to think about, but that may have been the first actual decision I had made since my diagnosis. She did not dictate that she thought it best for me to take another medication but actually took time to explain the risks and benefits and left the choice up to me. I readily agreed because by that point, my anxiety and depression had been slipping farther and farther into a place where I could not control my way- or, as we liked to joke, optimism my way - out of it.

I slept most of the day and avoided the hospital food at all costs. Even the smell sent a wave of nausea through my whole body. When Mom finally convinced me to eat, I had half of a serving of Cinnamon Toast Crunch and a few grapes.

It wasn't that I was giving up, far from. I just could not summon the energy to do much more than sleep. I wasn't hungry, and eating the small handful of food that I was able to get down took so long that it used up what little energy I had.

I spent the day napping on and off, hoping to have enough energy to see Streetlight, even for just a few minutes. By the time they came and left, I had to take a nap to recover. I attempted a shower before bed that night, hoping it would help me feel a little better. It was a mercy that I was able to be unhooked from my fluids long enough to shower, so at the very least, I didn't have to haul Stoopid around and be attached to a leash. I still had to use the shower dressing, but I barely noticed through the freedom of being off an IV.

That night, during shift change, a new nurse came into my room. That wasn't unusual, since I was used to seeing new nurses, but this guy stood out from the second he walked in. His name was Zack, and he stopped by to check and make sure I was all good before he was scheduled to be in for meds later. He was so energetic and upbeat; it was hard for me to keep feeling so low.

He ended up popping in not long after to tell us he was being moved to the transplant unit for the night, and I was genuinely disappointed. He seemed like someone I would get along with.

I was so exhausted that I barely registered when Stoopid started beeping in the middle of the night. When nurses came in for meds or PCAs for vitals, I woke up just enough to stick my wrist outside of the covers for them to scan my armband and take my blood pressure before huddling back under the covers and crashing.

The next morning, I had just enough venom to let the residents know that 5:00 a.m. was a sacrilegious hour to be asking questions and fell back into sleep in the middle of the conversation with them.

Later, during rounds, I was told that they had confirmed I had sepsis but were still waiting on blood cultures to determine what bacteria had caused it and where it came from. My team had told me previously that they expected that I would pick up whatever bacteria was in my blood through socializing. They always demanded I stay home when I wasn't in treatment to minimize the risk of catching something, and I always ignored them. I needed to get out and do *something* to feel alive. Naturally, they started to kindly lay into me for not heeding their warnings.

With the antibiotics so far, it seemed as though my condition was improving. My temperature, though still occasionally spiking to a slight fever, was lower and more stable. My ANC, however, was still dangerously low. Until it improved, I would not be able to go home.

At breakfast that morning, one of my nurses came in and asked me if I had filled out an advanced directive. She explained that it would outline my wishes should I become unable to speak those wishes for myself.

She left me to fill out the forms, but I couldn't even comprehend them, no matter how many times I read them. I also, quite frankly, didn't see a point. Though I couldn't put the words to it at the time, I knew that I didn't want to give in to the idea that I might need an advanced directive. I had no plans of ever not being able to make decisions for myself, much less going into end-of-life care, and I felt that if I had filled those forms out, I would have accepted it as a possibility.

It was a line I wasn't willing to cross.

My days fell into a rhythm after that. I learned how to sleep through most of the interruptions during the night. Residents woke me up way too early for rounds, and I gained more energy each day to find more creative ways to tell them how much I hated it. If I managed to eat, it was an insignificant amount of Cinnamon Toast Crunch and grapes. I napped, visited with Streetlight, and napped more.

Those kinds of days allowed for plenty of introspection. As much as I started to struggle with memory loss, I used the time to try to remember parts of my life that weren't defined by cancer.

One in particular that I tried to cling to was the talent show I got roped into my senior year. The music honor society I was involved in put on a talent show as a fundraiser every year, and I usually spent my time behind the scenes. For some reason, Anthony, myself, and one other member of the drumline got voluntold to put together an act.

At first, we only planned to run through some of our drumline cadences and be done. But our competitive sides got the best of us. We spent hours on the phone planning out our act. We combined our best cadences into a montage. Between the three of us, we planned out how to keep six drums going the entire act, to the point of us switching who played which drums to feature each of us on a solo. We even ended the act with a drum battle.

We thought we had everything planned out until our need to win got the best of us yet again. We thought it would be cool to have whoever was doing the solo play with light-up drumsticks, which eventually led to blacklights on stage, white-taped drumsticks, and white tape on our blacked-out outfits.

Somehow, we pulled all of this together in a week. I think we all ended up skipping a few classes to practice our act before the talent show and stayed after classes for a few days. By the time we made it to the stage the night of the show, we couldn't sit still. We fed off each other's energy, which generally made us a pain to be around. That night, it made us unable to stop bouncing off the walls. Our act was last, so by the time we made it on stage, we had plenty of energy to burn.

It felt like it was over in seconds, but our act ended up being over six minutes. The winner was announced just a few moments later, and when they called us for first place, we were ecstatic. When they handed us the prize money we had won, we all yelled at the same time, "We're going to Disney!"

It was hard for me to believe that the talent show had only been a year prior. Then, I could run around on stage for six minutes playing drums, and at that moment, I didn't think I had the strength in my hands to even hold a drumstick. But I chose to see my situation in a totally different light. Instead of seeing myself for what I could no longer do, I wanted to look forward to what I would be able to do again. It gave me hope to hold onto and imagine myself doing what I loved again.

One morning, I was told that they had identified the bacteria that had caused the original infection. Usually, it originated from outside environments, which is why they tell people who are receiving chemo to limit their contact with people and to stay home as much as possible.

For the record, I was horrible at that. If I did end up feeling decent enough to go outside, see friends, or go to an event I had the energy to handle, I went. I knew I wouldn't survive cancer by letting my quality of life suffer so greatly. My doctors tried to convince me to play it safe, even to the point of using scare tactics to make their point, but I refused. I had to live in what small ways I could. What was the point of fighting so hard to live if I couldn't, y'know, *live?*

The smug look I gave my team was very intentional as they explained, after days of hounding me, "This is what happens when you don't listen to us and go out while you are so immunocompromised!" that the bacteria that caused my infection was actually the kind of bacteria humans already have in their digestive tracts.

Basically, my immune system was so compromised that bacteria that was usually fine, and even helpful in my body's system, became a problem when left unchecked.

It took a few more days before my fever stopped completely, and at that point, I was told I could go home when, firstly, I had three days of negative blood cultures and, secondly, when my ANC recovered to a specified point.

Well, it was a goal, at least. Not a goal that I could put any effort into, aside from praying and begging my body to just *cooperate*, but a goal. The first few days after this news, I had so much hope. I would wait in anticipation for the results of my blood cultures and labs each morning. The first morning I had negative blood cultures, I nearly used up all the energy I mustered from my mid-morning nap in excitement.

I begged my nurses to let me celebrate by going outside for just a few minutes. The Lord was looking out for me that day because I had a charge nurse who I am now convinced was an angel. She came to my room with a wheelchair, unhooked me from my fluids, and told me that my ANC was still too low to be allowed out of my room. But, if she didn't see me leave the room, and if I wore a mask until I got outside just to be safe, she wouldn't know and wouldn't be able to stop me. *Wink wink.*

We bolted as soon as she went into another room. I could have cried at the feeling of the sun on my skin. And the fresh, unfiltered air, sweet Heavens. Air that moved and brought with it the scents of cars, perfumes, lunches, trees, concrete, and sunshine. I didn't know it was possible to smell sunshine until that moment.

And the sounds.

All I had heard for days was the air conditioner, my IV pump, beeping, and a loud kind of silence. But outside after so many days, I heard birds, voices, wind, leaves brushing across the concrete, shoes stepping along different parts of the ground, and cars driving past.

It was a chaotic symphony of real life sweeping across my senses and more than any medication they could give me, it was *healing.*

Coming back into my room felt like being sealed in a tomb of sensory deprivation. Back to the scent of hand sanitizer and over-filtered, sterile air, horrible combinations of unnatural colors, and no sunlight. I knew that if I was going to survive these stays, I would need to make it a habit to get outside at least once a day.

My outing took so much energy that I slept for the rest of the afternoon, only waking up to see the Streeples. When I woke up, I realized that I had the faintest shred of an appetite. The idea of eating the hospital food turned my stomach nearly inside out, so Mom went downstairs to the Subway in the cafe. I ate a few inches of a sub, more than I had in the previous days combined, and though my sleep that night wasn't as restful, it was much more peaceful.

My hope in the following days began to dwindle as each day's lab results showed that my ANC was not improving enough to allow me to go home. It was hardly improving *at all.* I had negative cultures each day, had no fevers, and my energy and appetite were slowly but surely returning with each day I spent going outside, but my immune system was not recovering.

With my energy, my attitude returned. When the residents asked me questions during morning rounds, I gave snarky answers.

"How are you feeling this morning?"

"I *was* feeling great until you decided to interrupt my sleep."

Or "I would be feeling a lot better if I was waking up in my own bed. In a few hours. Not answering your stupid questions."

I even had the audacity to wrap myself up in the blankets so that when they came in and tried to wake me up by pulling back my covers, they had to work for it.

Finally, after about a week, my ANC started coming back up, and within three more days, I was discharged. Since I was still on a course of IV antibiotics, to be sent home, I would have to have my antibiotics through my port. My nurses trained Mom on how to connect and disconnect the bulb of antibiotics from my port and set up a home health care nurse to come check on us.

In comparison to four more days in the hospital, we would do just about anything to go home. We weren't entirely sure why they were sending a home health care nurse since our nurses had trained Mom, and I would be getting three doses of antibiotics a day, but we didn't ask. Not when we were being handed discharge papers.

The nurse was scheduled to come the evening we got home, which was strange to us since she was not scheduled to come when I would need to be hooked up to antibiotics. But even more strange to us was that the nurse they sent was about 80 years old and seemed to need a nurse of her own. She could barely make it up the steps to our house, and it took her nearly ten minutes to get my vitals.

When she was done, I told her I was going to get a drink out of the fridge and gave Mom the "follow me" look. I told her I didn't know what the point of sending a nurse was but that I didn't trust her to be anywhere near my port. She agreed and helped make excuses for the nurse to leave.

The following day, we had a different nurse but ran into the same issue. This nurse admitted she wasn't familiar with how to use a port. Granted, that wasn't uncommon. Ports are pretty specialized devices, so unless a nurse worked in a specialty that used them, they wouldn't be trained. It was weird to us that they were sending us nurses who didn't know how to give me the care that I would need, though, so we called the hospital and told them to call off the nurses.

We finished out the four days of antibiotics with no issues, and I could finally have Mom de-access my port. I had been showering with the sticky port dressings on for two weeks straight, and the skin on my chest and shoulder had started to turn red and burn from the adhesive. My skin had already been so fragile from the effects of chemo but ripping the adhesive off every day had started to become an issue.

I had a feeling that would be an issue I could avoid for a while, though. My ANC had been recovering, but it was recovering from nothing, and progress was slow. I didn't imagine I would be going in for another round of chemo anytime soon.

Chapter 9

May 10, 2019

My threshold for feeling better had dropped significantly since having sepsis. My head seemed to be constantly in a fog. Chemo brain was really becoming noticeable. It's not just that I couldn't remember things clearly, as some would think. I couldn't grasp onto thoughts, and if I could, I would have a hard time turning those thoughts into words.

I would watch movies and see an actor I recognized, but I couldn't remember where I recognized them. Or I would, but I couldn't recall the name or details of the movie.

I was never good with names, but all of a sudden it seemed that I couldn't match names with faces and couldn't place where I knew someone from.

I struggled to find the words I needed to describe things or form sentences.

Mom noticed one morning that I had started to confuse which medications I was supposed to take and when. Up until that point, I had been handling my medications on my own, but I reached a point where I couldn't even remember what each pill was for. I tried to resist giving up that bit of independence, but I eventually relented to let Mom take over.

It was hard to slowly lose more and more ability to function. I could handle the physical effects, but not even being able to think clearly to take care of myself was a hard pill to swallow.

Worst of all, I started to lose memories I found precious from my childhood and high school. It's like my life started to disappear and be consumed by the present I was stuck in.

I tried to remember things like vacations Mom and I took, but details had started to fade. I tried to talk to Mom about the trips, but she would ask me if I remembered certain things, and I would have to tell her I didn't. I couldn't remember the places we stayed or the food we tried. Some days, I think I only remembered some things based on seeing pictures.

It was like being closed out of myself. Surviving cancer wasn't *me.* I was the girl who leaned over the railing of the tallest lighthouse in the United States to see how far we were away from the ground. I was the girl who bribed Mom to take us over the Mackinac Bridge in Michigan because I loved bridges, and she was scared of them. But suddenly, those details started to slip away, and all I knew was what was right in front of me.

If I tried to visualize what it felt like to inhabit my mind, I pictured myself suspended in slow motion, with everything and everyone around me moving too quickly for me to follow. If I tried to grab onto a thought, I seemed to move too slowly, and it would slip away if it were even within my grasp at all.

Physically, my usual side effects took longer to ease, and I couldn't seem to shake the fatigue. It felt like trying to move through syrup. My muscles were slow to respond, my body moving too slowly under the weight of illness.

I was a shell of the sharp, energetic Rebecca that I had been for 18 years, and I was powerless to do anything about it.

May 13, 2019

By the time my blood counts had recovered, my body still had not. I entered the hospital for chemo, knowing I wasn't physically ready, even if my labs said I was.

I tried so hard to willpower myself through it. I told myself I felt better until I started to believe it. I told myself that I was ready for another round of chemo. It was only two days. I could handle that.

"Handle" is a term to be used very, very loosely.

Did I survive it with my will still intact? Yes. But that was about all that was intact by the time I left the hospital. It seemed like before the first bag of chemo had made it through my veins, my head was swimming with a combination of low blood pressure and nausea. If I needed to get out of bed for any reason, I needed a five-minute head start to sit up slowly and sniff alcohol wipes until the nausea subsided.

Streetlight came, and I laid back in bed, content to let them talk. Listening to them was a much-needed distraction, so even though I didn't have the energy to join the conversation, it was nice to just listen.

When I tried to sit up in a wheelchair to get discharged, my body refused to sit vertically. I would pass out constantly until Mom got me back into bed, claiming to the nurses I was just resting until she took our bags and had valet bring the car around.

I did make it back into the wheelchair, but I immediately passed out. No amount of will could keep the black spots from tunneling in until my head nodded back against Mom. Trust me; I was trying my best to make myself stay conscious. It was one of the first times my will would fail over the demands of my body.

Knowing that if I had been caught passing out, I would be kept in the hospital longer, Mom improvised. She waited until no nurses were watching us, held my head upright, and bolted with me in the wheelchair. Between passing out, I heard her lean down and whisper encouragement to me to hang on until we got in the car. I also heard her reassure the concerned medical staff that I was just tired and nauseous from chemo, and I was resting my eyes until I got to the car.

We made it to the car, and she wrestled my ragdoll body into the front seat, leaned the seat almost all the way back, and I stopped passing out. But then, I started throwing up. Mom would stop the car, help me to not puke all over the place, and keep driving once I could handle the movement.

By the time we got home, I had become ever so slightly more stable than when we left. She managed, through sheer force of will, to get me in the house and into bed, and I slept for the rest of the day.

May 21, 2019

Having cancer was like being in a toxic relationship. It just took and took and took until there was nothing left. I had lost so much to chemo and was holding on so tightly to the things I had left. One of those things, after I lost the ability to keep track of my medications, was driving myself to my appointments for labs. It was a small bit of independence, and it helped me feel like I was still capable of doing something aside from existing.

I woke up one morning to get ready for the drive and found Mom had not gone to work yet. I was on edge immediately. I knew deep down that I wasn't up to driving myself, but I wasn't ready to give up that little joy that I had. Before I could get too agitated, Mom told me she had planned on taking me to my appointment so we could go get some comfort food together. She knew I hadn't been feeling well but had a decent appetite, so she wanted us to get a Culver's burger and concrete mixer.

I immediately diffused. I would let her come along if it meant free food. That moment was much more than just a pick-me-up idea on Mom's part, though. She knew I wasn't capable of driving. That day, a strong wind could have knocked me over, but she also knew that I was in too vulnerable of a place to have more of my independence chipped away. Instead of confronting me about my inability to drive, she turned it around into something more positive. It was enough to keep me from feeling too incapable while keeping me safe.

May 25, 2019

In the following days, my condition did not improve as it usually did. My blood counts had not recovered, either. I was playing the waiting game, going in for labs every few days to see if I had recovered enough for my next treatment.

Mom always had our overnight bags packed each time I went in for labs. We hoped that I would recover enough to start my next treatment, but we were never surprised when the answer continued to be no. We even stopped trying to keep track of how much longer my treatments would last. It was too depressing to keep up with.

Instead of focusing on the length of my treatment, I tried to focus on the things I could do with the extra time to feel slightly less zombie-like. We tried to keep our lives as normal as possible between treatments. We tried to go out to eat and go shopping. I would try to hang out with friends, and most of the time, it worked. My spirits, despite the circumstances and the pain and sickness I constantly felt, stayed high.

I would do my makeup to go out, mostly because I used it to trick myself into feeling better. And I looked really weird without eyebrows. A few people would tell me they thought my choice to shave my head was such a bold statement. I looked like a force to be reckoned with. Most were shocked to find out that it wasn't my choice at all and told me they never would have guessed that I had cancer. It was always an encouragement to know that, even if I felt like absolute garbage, it wasn't showing too obviously.

Along with those conversations also came some comical questions. I was asked countless times how I knew how to do my makeup without a hairline. How did I know where my forehead stopped, and my "hairline" started? I was even asked if I used shampoo, body wash, or facial cleanser on my bald head.

When I did my makeup, I would blend the foundation up past my hairline until it faded at the top of my head. As for what I used, I would usually just wash my head with body wash.

As I was getting ready for another appointment for labs, I took my temperature, as I usually did. My body shook with anxiety when I saw that I had a very slight fever. Not wanting to repeat the last time, I took a dose of Tylenol before leaving the house for my appointment, and by the time I got there, I had no fever.

When I finally dragged myself into bed that night, though, my fever had come back with a vengeance. I took more Tylenol. I was absolutely petrified at the idea of going back to the hospital with a fever. This time, the Tylenol did no good. I turned on the heating pad I kept in my bed, huddled under more blankets, and added a hat to my nighttime attire. Within an hour, I was shivering uncontrollably. It took another hour before I woke Mom up to admit that I had a fever and would need to go to the ED.

I think she saw the anxiety and conflict on my face because she wasn't upset that I had waited or that I tried to take Tylenol to avoid it happening. She just grabbed our overnight bags and got us ready to go.

The closer we got to the hospital, the more my body reacted. My chest would tighten, nearly strangling my words when I tried to talk. My breath shook every time I tried to inhale. When we crossed into the side of town I associated with the hospital, I would go quiet and still. It wasn't a mental fear as much as it was a physiological dread.

Once at the ED, I was almost immediately taken to a room. They wanted to start an IV, but I insisted they access my port, as I knew I would have to have it accessed once I got admitted to the floor anyway.

Big mistake.

While the nurses on the floor and in the clinic knew how to access ports, the ED nurses were less familiar with the process. They knew *how* to, but they didn't practice it often. That meant much more misery for me as they missed their target multiple times. To access my port, they would have to press around the area where the port was on my chest to find the center of the device. There was a small area right in the middle, indicated by three tiny bumps, where the needle could be placed successfully. They nearly bruised my chest with how heavy-handed they had been. During this whole process, I was still freezing cold and shivering. I huddled under the single blanket they gave me, so thin I could nearly read a book through it. The minute they started the fluids, it seemed like it only worsened the chills. I shook so hard, so uncontrollably, that my body started to cramp.

Mom lay beside me in the tiny bed, covering me with her own body to try to keep me warm and still. I had started crying to the point of whimpering at the full-body pain that came with the chills.

Though we begged for more blankets or a heated blanket, the nurses refused sharply. I had a fever, and it would make the fever worse. But seeing me in so much pain, Momma Bear came out. Suffice it to say, I had heated blankets coming my way.

By the time they dosed me with Tylenol and started antibiotics, the shivering had mercifully stopped. At that point, however, my body had taken a downhill turn. I was drained of any strength, and my thoughts were clouded. All I wanted to do was sleep. It's as if the moment I surrendered to the idea that something was wrong, my body started to shut down.

As the resident in charge was taking me up to the floor, she explained to me that if I were any worse, I would have been taken to the ICU.

As soon as I made it to my floor, I let myself shut down. I figured sleeping was better than worrying about the implications of being in the hospital again. I already had enough to worry about, like surviving sepsis, part two.

That, admittedly, was going much less smoothly than the previous time. I slept more, ate even less, and even going out once a day to get some sunshine was a struggle. If it wasn't for Mom doing the heavy lifting, I think I would have stayed in bed.

Anytime I tried to get a shower, the smell of the towels and the soap they wanted me to use had my nausea ruining my peace. On top of that, the shower covers I had to use to keep my port dry started tearing at my skin when I tried to remove them. I had a ring of torn, tender, raw flash around my port, but if I wanted a shower, I didn't have a choice.

I was trying to return to my usual attempts at optimism despite how much more difficult it had been to recover.

As if God decided to send someone to help raise my spirits, my door opened at shift changed, and I heard a voice I had been waiting to hear for a few weeks. It was Zack, whisper-yelling, "Wassuuuuuup?!"

I was ecstatic! I asked him how things had gone on the transplant floor he got transferred to the first time I met him, and he told me he was absolutely *not* doing that again. Apparently, he and another nurse were arguing over who would get to be my nurse for the night. He was pretty proud of himself for winning.

As soon as he had made his rounds, he came in to tell me that my team had ordered a blood transfusion. Because of the risk of a bad reaction, anytime I got a blood transfusion, a nurse would have to be in the room with me for at least fifteen minutes. Mom and I had been watching Big Hero 6, my favorite movie at the time, and we asked if he had seen it.

He had not, and we were appalled. We joked that he wasn't allowed back for another shift until he watched the movie. He did redeem himself, though, when I mentioned Twenty One Pilots, and he said he loved their music. We got to chat about the shows we had been to and our favorite moments, and the conversation lifted my spirits despite the sickness I continued to feel.

The next morning, with breakfast, came an advanced directives packet that I threw, very ceremoniously, into the trash. With my current state of mind, I didn't have the capacity to understand it, anyway. But even still, I was determined to stay alive. If that meant willing myself through chemo and another fight with sepsis, I would.

86

Just like it had been when I got diagnosed, I wasn't in denial of what I had. I knew sepsis was bad news. I didn't fully grasp just how bad, but I got the picture. I just refused to let it hold power over my mind if I couldn't refuse it out of my body altogether. If I started to let the idea of death creep into my mind, it might have taken hold, and that was simply unacceptable.

We knew we were in for nearly two weeks of misery, so we started getting creative about how to handle the hospital stay. To ease the nausea from the scents of the hospital, Mom started spraying everything down in Bath and Body Works sprays, and I, defiant as always, stopped using the body wash my team wanted me to use.

We had been learning which nurses were the ones who would let us out to go sit at the fountain, and whenever they were on shift, we would let them know we'd be sneaking out whenever they couldn't see us. Usually, they were the ones to tell us when there weren't any doctors around so we could escape, but it was fun to continue the joke with them.

It was nearly a week into my stay before I felt decent enough to see Streetlight, and though I still barely had the energy to sustain much of a conversation, they still helped pull me through until I could be released after ten days in the hospital.

Like the last time, I would be sent home with my port accessed to finish off my course of antibiotics. Unlike last time, we specifically requested that home health care *not* be sent to our house. We had plans to take a long weekend out of town for my birthday, much to the dismay of my team. We let them go on trying to convince us to stay in town - I could get sick again, we'd be too far away from them, I was at too much of a risk, blah blah blah - and then told them that if they expected me to survive chemo, they'd deal with me going out of town for a few days for my birthday, end of discussion.

Limitless

Chapter 10

Going on a weekend trip for my birthday was proving to be more difficult than we had anticipated. The antibiotics I was sent home with had to be refrigerated, so we had to plan on keeping a cooler with us. We had to make our plans around the antibiotic schedule, a half an hour infusion every eight hours. Then we had to deal with having my port accessed, which meant carrying around shower covers and worrying about doing anything that would open the flimsy dressing or cause my port to be de-accessed.

Our plan pre-diagnosis was to go white water rafting, a hope I had clung to until the most recent hospital stay. When I realized I had too much stacked against me, I conceded to a low commitment weekend under the promise that we would white water raft on my next birthday.

It was those thoughts that became non-negotiable to me. "If" was not a word I liked to use. I would see my next birthday. I would be well enough to white water raft. I had no earthly idea how, but I would. Well, I did have an idea, but it certainly wasn't earthly. I lived with constant reassurance that my prayers and the prayers from those who knew me were working. Every once in a while, Mom would get a message from someone in a different state that they had visited a church and had all prayed for me. Someone from that church would visit another church, and the cycle continued.

Some days I really didn't know what to pray for. Most of my prayers were fairly short sighted. I realized quickly that focusing on the end goal could be doing more harm than good. It was much easier to focus on the short-term goals. I prayed for the immediate needs, like my blood counts recovering so I could get out of the hospital, or for the nausea to not be so bad.

As for the long-term goals, like finishing chemo, I had unexplainable confidence in that. Deep down, I felt that I was going through what I was going through for a reason. It didn't anger me that I couldn't fathom the reason. It didn't even bother me that I may never know the reason. But I had this kind of trust that, for whatever reason, God had allowed the trial to be passed to me, and that one day, He would walk me out of it.

Until then, I had a birthday to celebrate. We decided to make a quick trip to Orlando to experience The Wheel - a 400-foot-tall Ferris Wheel, and the tallest observation wheel on the east coast. If I couldn't have my adrenaline from falling down a waterfall in nothing but a raft and life jacket, I would get it from heights.

In order to celebrate on my birthday weekend, we would have had to leave a few days after being discharged from the hospital. It was important to me after all the control chemo had taken, to still celebrate my birthday when we usually would, without delays. I couldn't let chemo take that from me.

On our way down to Orlando, we found a sunflower field to stop at for fun. Since sunflowers were my favorite flower at the time, it was the perfect addition to our trip. The field was a summer U-Pick event, like a farmer's market, and admission to the field came with free flowers. Despite the fact that we were traveling, I couldn't resist the opportunity to pick a few sunflowers to take with us.

Because of chemo, my heat tolerance was horrible, which was bad news living in Florida. It didn't take long before the combination of wicked heat and humidity had me pouring sweat and feeling faint. Naturally, I refused to not enjoy my full time in the sunflower field despite feeling like I was being steamed. Once I was good and ready, we came in from the field and continued to Orlando.

It was a good thing we planned on getting to our hotel and staying in that night because, by the time we arrived, I was exhausted.

Usually, during our travels, we would wake up early and have the full day to do whatever we had planned, but we knew better for this trip. With the effects of chemo and sepsis on my body, I could sleep more than twelve hours a night and still be exhausted. So, we planned to wake up mid-morning to have time to get ready and head over to Icon Park. We also tried to figure out just how late I could sleep while still having enough time to get ready and be out before check-out.

When Mom woke me up that morning, I knew immediately I wasn't feeling up to it. But I tried. I got up and was in the process of getting dressed when I accepted that, at that point, I couldn't hold the weight of my own body up. I wasn't ready to give up, though, so I told Mom I was going to lie down for a little while longer. She went downstairs to ask about a late check-out, and I fell asleep praying that cancer wouldn't ruin my birthday.

God had my back, as always. I woke up for the second time and felt so much better. I knew it could only have been a small miracle. Usually, waking up in the state I had been in the first time would have been a sign that I was going to be spending my day in bed.

The lobby of the hotel we stayed at had a small gift shop, and as Mom was checking out, I grabbed a few postcards. As I looked around, I overheard bits of the conversation Mom was having with the man at the front desk. I gathered through the hushed tones that he had asked her if I was the daughter they had spoken about earlier, and she had confirmed that I was.

When I went to pay for the postcards a few minutes later, I saw the look, not of pity, but of grief, in the man's eyes. He did not charge me for the postcards I had, and Mom later confirmed that she had spoken to him about a late check-out and told him why, and he waived the hotel's late check-out fee for us.

Pulling into Icon Park, I caught the pre-adrenaline rush thrill when I laid eyes on The Wheel. It was massive, easily the tallest structure for miles. Despite how thin the whole structure was, the closed-in compartments barely swayed as they rotated.

The heat in Orlando was stifling, and the humidity seemed to make it press down on us. Of course, the sun was blazing, not a cloud in sight. I knew it would be miserable with my new heat sensitivity, but I was even more determined after the almost-mishap of our morning.

I must have looked like a vampire walking through Icon Park to The Wheel. I dodged the sunlight as much as I could, ducking into the buildings with air conditioners on high and dashing from shadow to shadow to try to keep as cool as possible. It didn't help that I was pale as an LED light and just as bright with the sun bouncing off my bald head.

Despite my efforts, I was still drenched in sweat and more than a little shaky once we got to the building that housed the ticket booth for The Wheel. Luckily for us, it was a quiet day in Icon Park, and there hadn't been a line, either for tickets, or to get onto The Wheel.

We approached the platform to enter the enclosed compartments and realized, much to my thrill, that The Wheel did not stop for boarding. To get into the compartment, we would have to time our steps. The compartments weren't moving fast by any means, but after being stuck in hospital rooms for way too long, even this small thrill was electrifying.

I was relieved to realize that, upon making it into the compartment, it was air-conditioned, and we had it all to ourselves. It couldn't have gotten much better at that point.

Each wall was glass from floor to ceiling, and each had a display showing what could be seen from miles away. With the clarity of the day we had, we could see Disney World, Universal Studios, SeaWorld, and all of Downtown Orlando. I couldn't stop bouncing from window to window, trying to take in as much of the view as I could. For a few minutes, I totally forgot about how awful I had felt that morning. It was another one of those precious moments of normalcy, where it didn't matter that I had a needle in the port in my chest or that I would likely sleep on the way home after being worn out by excitement. At that moment, I felt like myself again.

The ride took about 15 minutes, and by the time we stepped out of the compartment - again, without the ride actually stopping - my head was swimming with the adrenaline high. It was as clear as my head had felt in months.

Getting this small reprieve from my current reality helped me get myself together to face all that I knew would be ahead of me. Specifically, planning for the surgery to remove my tumor. The only thing standing between me and the surgery was my blood counts. They would have to be even higher than the levels they needed to be to do chemo.

My team was hopeful that my blood counts would recover sooner rather than later because if they took too long, my surgeon would be out of town. In that case, I would need to do another round of chemo before the surgery.

I actually had the same hopes because I knew I would get a break from chemo if I had the surgery. I was desperate enough to have more of a break from chemo that I would have gladly undergone a highly invasive, high-risk surgery to get away from it. I would have had to do it either way, so the sooner the better.

My team pulled me along on this emotional roller coaster every few days when I would come in for labs. They would start off with such high hopes that my blood counts would be recovered enough, then would come back in disappointment when they weren't. It didn't take me very long to start ignoring their wild emotions. I didn't have the energy.

After nearly two weeks of waiting, my labs showed enough recovery to do more chemo but not surgery. My team made the decision for me that I would do another round of chemo while my surgeon was out of town.

I was questioning the logic of this approach because I had a bad feeling about doing another round of chemo. If both previous rounds of chemo had caused me to have sepsis and delay for nearly a month, it seemed more logical to me to wait two weeks and do surgery rather than risk waiting another month or more before I could have the surgery.

Though I didn't follow their logic, I didn't question them, either. I didn't know I was allowed to, but even if I did, I wouldn't have been able to express those concerns. There were days that I couldn't even form a complete sentence without pausing, trying to find the word I was looking for, and then losing my thoughts completely. So often, Mom would give me a few seconds to try to work it out in my head before finishing my sentence so I would stay on track.

I cringed every time I heard recordings of myself. The woman who had once been so confident in her use of words now used fillers - like, um, uh - every few words. I did giggle at the memory of my eighth-grade history teacher and how my use of the word "like" would have given him a conniption.

I was given the weekend to prepare for my next round of chemo. Since it would be another five-day treatment, they wanted to start on a Monday. I think my team thought it a mercy to give me time to "prepare" for another round of treatment, but I don't think they understood that it was far from merciful. The anticipation was awful, knowing what would be coming. Even worse, knowing that a week and a half stay was likely to follow chemo.

That weekend was full of torment. I tried to do everything I could to make sure it went by slowly, but it only seemed to rush by faster. I tried to enjoy the time I had when I felt relatively healthy, but I couldn't fully enjoy anything with the knowledge of what Monday would bring looming over me.

Chapter 11

The drive to the hospital for chemo should have freaked me out. Based on my reactions to my previous trips to the hospital, I should have felt something - agitation, anger, anxiety, dread, depression, *something*. I knew that I *should* be feeling something, but I couldn't. I was calm and even indifferent. It's like I was incapable of feeling anything at all. My head felt muted, like the parts of my brain that would usually be screaming at me to turn around and drive in any direction but to the hospital were locked in a soundproof room in my brain. I knew they were there and, by all means, should have been in control, but I just couldn't hear them.

Well, at least the antidepressants were kicking in.

Since I had been in a perpetual state of nausea for months now, it didn't take the first dose of chemo long to have me begging for stronger nausea meds, which they gave me without much convincing after I started puking. Once that was under control, things went about as normal as expected.

Normal, until a group of Streeples burst into my room one night with cupcakes and a huge banner that read "Happy Birthday Rebecca," singing Happy Birthday.

I could have cried. Okay, fine, I was crying.

The banner was hand painted with Marvel superheroes all over it. Even the cupcakes were decorated with different superheroes. Someone from Streetlight, knowing my favorite animal was a hedgehog, crocheted a small hedgehog as a gift.

For the next few hours, I had a group of Streeples rotating in and out of my room. Em had stopped by to hang out with us, and I got to share with her that because Mom and I chose to travel for birthdays instead of throw parties, this was my first surprise birthday party.

Honestly, I couldn't have asked for a better first surprise party. Despite running back and forth to the bathroom because of all the fluids I was on, I felt normal. The banner they made was so huge it took all the attention away from the horrible colors of the room. Even without the banner, the Streeples made me feel like any other person at a surprise party thrown by her friends.

Actually getting the party in the works, though, had been quite a task. Em told me that they had been planning the party for weeks. Every time I came in for labs to start chemo, they would get everything ready to go, only to have to delay when my blood counts were too low. Apparently, they had a custom Marvel cake made, but the cake did not survive the wait. They hoped that my blood counts would come up soon enough to enjoy the cake that they had kept frozen, but then I got admitted for sepsis.

They chose not to throw the party then because they knew I would have been too sick to enjoy it. When I finally did come in for chemo, they were as excited to throw the party as I had been to be surprised.

The party fueled me through my remaining days of chemo. Though I had stayed sick, even to the point of carrying around the very dignified bright green sick bag with me when I managed to get out to the fountain, I was holding onto the party and the love I had felt. It, like The Wheel and *Endgame,* became a reminder of what real life would be like on the other side of cancer treatment.

Going home from chemo at that point was just as anxiety-inducing as being in the hospital. Five out of six previous treatments

96

had been problematic in some way. I had been delayed for every treatment, had two false alarm emergency department visits, and two unexpected stays for sepsis. The delays were getting longer, and the false alarms had turned into true emergencies. It was hard to deny the fact that things were progressing, and not positively.

Even optimism can only go so far when reality gets involved.

I couldn't enjoy time at home when I was just waiting for the ball to drop, and to see how bad the drop would be. Every night after watching a movie, I would wait for the chills to start. It would have kept me from sleeping, had chemo not caused such an overwhelming exhaustion that made me sleep whether I wanted to or not. And every moment before I would fall asleep would be spent worrying.

I stopped making plans for fear that they would be canceled if I suddenly got a fever. Not having anything to look forward to was killing my morale, but I knew to look forward to something only to have it taken from me would be worse. Neither option was great, but it was choosing the least devastating out of the two. I had been able to see *Endgame* and go on my birthday trip, and it felt like my luck on that end had been running low.

Every day, I didn't end up in the hospital, which made the next day even worse. When I finally did feel the chills start to take over my entire body one night, I felt such opposing emotions I almost stopped feeling anything at all - relief and dread.

July 6, 2019

I didn't even try to fight it. I took Tylenol but didn't crawl back under the covers to see if it would work. I knew it wouldn't. I woke Mom up, and by the time we got in the car to make the trip to the ED, the relief and dread fused to form a new emotion I hadn't dealt with yet.

Desolation.

I had never, and still did not, fear death. And fear had no part in this new feeling I was processing. I had simply lost hope. I had gone through sepsis twice, with each time getting worse, so I knew what to expect. At least ten days in the hospital. Weeks after that, before my blood counts would recover. Weeks more added to my treatment time. I wouldn't get to have the surgery we were planning. There was no telling how long it would be before I could hit that milestone in chemo.

My treatment was only supposed to last eight to nine months, tops. I was at month seven, barely halfway through treatment. I did the quick math. When I survived this fight with sepsis - not if, mind you - I would likely have another eight months of treatment if my delays didn't keep getting longer and longer.

No tangible milestones, forward progress at a halt again, and finally, no hope. I couldn't be convinced to hope at that point. I had barely survived the previous seven months with my mental health intact, and I had no clue how I could possibly survive another eight. How my body, for that matter, could survive another eight.

Even my antidepressant meds couldn't numb the emotions that crashed over me on the way to the ED. To say I cried would have been the understatement of the decade. I wept. I wept for every moment in the past seven months that I made myself stay strong and optimistic. I wept the way I probably should have when I got diagnosed. I wept for the loss of seven months of my life and for the next eight that I was likely to lose as well.

I pulled myself together enough to speak to admissions when we got to the ED and to speak when doctors and nurses asked questions, but the tears still streamed down my cheeks.

By the time I had been taken to a room, I was shivering uncontrollably again. Just as I expected. Mom didn't bother for pleasantries this time as she demanded the nurses bring in heated blankets. She lay beside me in the single-person hospital bed, using her body to help stop the shivering.

It didn't take long for the shaking along my entire body to cause my muscles to lock up and cramp. Now, I was crying in pain. My body would give out, unable to provide the energy it took to shiver, and a few seconds later, it would start again, unable to stop shivering.

It took all of ten minutes from the time I had gone into the room to the time Mom decided she had had enough of watching me suffer. I thought it had been hours, but time crawls in situations like those.

Mom got out of bed, hunted down a nurse, and ordered the nurse to slow down the fluids they had set up for me, remembering the theory we had talked about the first time I found myself in this situation. The nurse tried to argue, but Mom wasn't having it. She threatened to stop the fluids herself if they didn't turn them down.

I would have enjoyed the show had I not been in so much agony.

The relief was almost instant. The minute the fluids weren't running at top speed through my system, the chills became manageable. And then they stopped entirely.

Eventually, I emerged from eight layers of hospital blankets, which equated to maybe three normal blankets for how thin they were. I stopped shaking, and mostly stopped crying. Not because I stopped feeling, but because I had nothing left to fuel my body. The shivering had taken every last bit of energy I had, and my body was ready to shut down.

It wasn't the kind of exhaustion that made me want to sleep. It was the kind of exhaustion that made moving my head, breathing, and even blinking nearly impossible.

I wasn't going to die, not on my watch, but I also couldn't will myself into living. I had nothing to back up my commands to my body to keep going.

But somehow, I kept living. Somehow, I ended up on my usual floor instead of in the ICU. Somehow, I woke up the next morning to residents barging in my room.

I could barely hold my eyes open, but the moment they opened to show me where I was, I started crying. Not weeping, no matter how much I wanted to. I didn't have the energy for that. Just letting tears stream down my face until the residents would let me fall back into the mercy of sleep.

And that was how I spent the first day. When I woke up, I cried silently and with jarring stillness.

The advanced directives pamphlet showed up with breakfast, as usual, and if I had the energy to rip it up, I would have.

I wasn't going to die.

It was the next day before I stopped being so weepy. Emotionally, I was no better, so I just assumed my body had run out of tears to cry or had run out of energy to keep producing tears.

Mom begged me to eat, even to the point of cutting up grapes and feeding them to me by hand. I would eat a handful at a time before needing to stop to nap again. My nurses begged me to drink, but all I could manage was a few sips at a time.

I didn't make the effort to shower. I didn't really want to anyways. I wasn't trying to give up, but I also wasn't trying to keep going. I was just stuck, with no energy to try in either direction.

My therapist had come in at some point, but I was barely able to talk. Mom filled her in on what was going on, and she told us that though it would take a few days to kick in, she could prescribe the maximum dose of my antidepressants. I agreed but couldn't muster the energy to speak.

I wanted to. Goodness, I wanted to find my way out of the limbo. I wanted to grasp onto something to help pull me into wanting to survive. I wanted to stop crying every waking moment and be strong again. I just couldn't.

It was three days into this existential suspension that I finally admitted to Mom while she was lying beside me in the hospital bed that I had barely moved from, that I thought I had lost the will to live. It was not that I wanted to stop living; I just lost the will to keep trying.

It's a confusing thing to try to describe. "I've lost the will to live" kind of sounds like "I want to die," but it wasn't for me. I wanted so badly to live. I just couldn't figure out how, and even if I could, living to see more days of sickness and hospital stays and my body fighting so hard against chemo wasn't an existence I wanted anymore. Much less for the eight or nine more months I would be stuck in that existence.

My nurses and PCAs had tried everything to spark the fire they knew I still had, but nothing worked. One PCA even flat out refused to leave my room until I smiled. She talked to me about food: chocolate cakes and lobster tails and all you can eat buffets waiting for me when I left the hospital. I still cried, but I cracked a smile.

It was the promise Mom made to me in that moment that gave me a reason to have the will to keep living. I couldn't see past my current existence as a cancer survivor to see why I should keep trying. I simply didn't have the mental energy to. All I could see was the countless days, weeks, and months I would spend in the revolving door I was already stuck in. Chemo, home, sepsis, home, repeat.

I needed the reminder that I wouldn't be stuck as a cancer survivor forever, and I needed a reminder that there was hope for real life beyond what I was seeing. Even when I was home last, I couldn't enjoy the peace of home without worrying about when the ball would drop. I chose not to make plans so I wouldn't have to cancel them, and at that time, I had lost sight of anything that wasn't directly in front of me.

The promise she had made was more like a bargain, something in exchange for my willingness to survive long enough to leave the hospital one more time. It wasn't extravagant. It was simply a reminder that there would be life past cancer because if I wanted what she promised me, I would have to get to that life.

She promised me a hedgehog.

Limitless

Chapter 12

Yep, you read that right. A hedgehog. I had wanted one for years but was never in the position as a busy high schooler or college student to have one.

And it was that promise, something so simple and, to some, maybe a little insignificant, that gave me hope. Because it wasn't just about the hedgehog. It was the idea that one day, I wouldn't be in the hospital every other week. One day, I would be healthy and, dare I say, maybe even normal again, and I could have my dream pet.

So that was the thread of hope that I grasped onto to survive. I regained some small remnant of my will, and the thrill of that promise gave me a burst of energy enough to figure out what steps I had to take to leave the hospital.

I would have to eat. Drink water. A shower would have probably helped. I needed to go outside. I needed to interact with Streetlight.

So, I started to snack on grapes and Cinnamon Toast Crunch, one handful at a time. I tried to drink water. I pep talked myself into a shower. I was going to get out of there, if only for the hedgehog.

One nurse during this stay, a floater from another floor, had noticed the night before that all I would attempt to eat was the grapes and cereal. When he came back the following night, he brought a massive bag of grapes, and two family size boxes of Cinnamon Toast Crunch, one original and one churro flavored.

Limitless

My day nurses promised me that if I could drink a certain amount of water, they would take me off the fluids for a few hours a day so I could go outside and shower without my IV attached.

When we started letting Streetlight visit again a few days later, even though I didn't have the energy to talk for long, they did everything in their power to lift my spirits. The spark was there, and everyone who saw it was doing what they could to fan it back into that flame of willpower that had gotten me this far.

To my delight, when the night shift nurses came to the floor and started making rounds, I saw someone I had been looking forward to seeing for a while. It was Zack!

I had been saving some confetti from a Twenty One Pilots concert I had been to for him, and I carried it with me every time I went to the hospital in hopes that he would be there. I lit up when he walked in and gave it to him while we took a few minutes to catch up. I filled him in on the weekend trip for my birthday and the surprise party from Streetlight, and he told me about a Twenty One Pilots show he went to.

A few hours later, right as I was about to fall asleep, I saw the light brighten up my room as my door opened, and I heard Zack half whisper a "Happy Birthday." Then I felt something hit my bed. I looked, and he had found a comic book-themed pillowcase that had been on the floor to give out to patients. He was out the door before I could thank him.

I didn't know if I would get a chance to talk to him again or when he would be on shift next, so I wrote a thank you note on a paper towel and set it on the counter.

I forgot if he spelled his name with a k or an h, though, so I had to start the note with, "Zack - or is it Zach?"

Before his shift ended the next morning, he woke me up during his rounds just enough to tell me I had it right and that he was glad I liked it.

It was moments like that, the connections I made, that would pull me through my treatment. Without my nurses taking the time to catch up with me and Streetlight making me feel more human, it would have been so easy to lose all sense of my humanity and

104

become the disease I was being treated for. Cancer treatment is consuming and constant. As I said, it is a full-time job. Those moments played such a huge part in reminding me of who I was and pushing me through those less-than-desirable times.

Though things were going better, and I had regained my will to live, I still had my moments. I was stuck in the hospital, and the days dragged on with no news that told me I could look forward to leaving. It was all the same news every morning during rounds. I had sepsis, my cultures were negative, but my blood counts weren't recovering enough to be discharged.

During one of my more emotional moments, Mom asked me what she could do to help me stop crying and have a better day. I told her, almost sarcastically, that I wanted sushi and to watch *Spiderman: Into the Spiderverse*.

The movie was the easy part, but to get the sushi I wanted, she would have to drive across town to my favorite sushi place - I was *not* taking my chances with hospital cafe sushi. I didn't expect her to want to leave me alone in the hospital long enough to pick up the sushi, but she was out the door within minutes, telling me to call in my order.

Her plan worked. I was too excited about sushi to keep crying, and it was hard to stay upset while watching the movie. It was also hard to be upset at how hilarious it was for both of us to lay in the hospital bed, trying to eat sushi and watch a movie at the same time. We made it work, though.

That evening, I wanted to go outside while I was off leash. I hadn't had a nap since hours before the movie, but my nurse let me know that if I wanted an escape, it would have to be then before my next dose of antibiotics and before dark.

We made it out to the Fountain of Hope and found a park bench to sit on. I wanted to feel somewhat normal and get out of the wheelchair for a bit. Before I knew it, I had gone from sitting up, to leaning on Mom's shoulder, to sleeping with my head in her lap. With all the noises and distractions of being in the hospital, it was the most peaceful nap I had had since being admitted.

She let me sleep until the nurses called to remind us to come back in for my antibiotics, and for years, we've joked about me falling asleep on a park bench.

Over the next few days, while waiting to be released, I got stronger emotionally and physically. I even made it into the Streetlight game room to play pool with another cancer survivor and Francisco.

Mentally, though, I was on the struggle bus. Chemo brain combined with sepsis brain and my mind was just not functioning at the capacity it should have been. I couldn't remember things, process things properly, or use any sort of critical thinking. I didn't ask questions, because I just didn't know what questions I should ask.

It was at this point that my surgeon stopped by to chat. He had stopped in briefly during other stays to see how I was doing, so I expected the same from this visit.

We all knew once my blood counts had recovered to levels safe for surgery, I would be in his hands to remove the tumor from my leg. I didn't realize, though, that his intention for stopping by this time was to talk about the surgery he was planning.

I knew that it would likely take a few weeks for my blood counts to recover, so I figured this would be a conversation for later, but I was in no mental state to voice that. I could only really go with the flow and hope I was comprehending what he was saying.

He started describing how he was planning on taking the tumor out while attempting to save my leg. He even had a 3D print of my tibia and the tools he would use to make precise cuts to remove the section of bone with cancer.

The plan was to remove the bone and soft tissue that had been affected by cancer and replace the bone and part of the patellar tendon with an allograft - a nice way of saying cadaver. He would hold the bone together with a metal plate that would be a permanent addition to my leg, and if all went to plan, I wouldn't lose my leg to cancer.

I was as fascinated as I could be. I was trying to process all he was saying, but forming thoughts was like trying to walk through Jello. By the time I had caught up to him in the conversation, he was asking me if that was cool with me. I said sure, because that must have been the best option if he had put so much planning into it.

I just thought it was cool, this radical surgery he was planning. After all, I was holding an exact replica of my tibia. It didn't get much cooler than that, right?

Limitless

Chapter 13

July 26, 2019

After being discharged, I knew I would get to enjoy a few weeks of peace. My blood counts would have to recover to higher levels than usual for it to be safe to do surgery, and despite the irksome optimism of my team that they wouldn't take as long, I knew that meant a few weeks of freedom.

Sure, most of the time I liked to lean on the optimistic way of thinking. But there is a difference between optimism that takes reality into account, and optimism that is just naive. They were on the naive side if they thought, after all I had been through, that my blood counts were just going to magically recover in a week, and I'd be ready for surgery.

Knowing that things would likely be infinitely harder to cope with after surgery, Mom and I planned a weekend trip to St. Augustine to enjoy life a little before my life changed even more drastically. We had always wanted to take one of the moonlight sailboat tours in St. Augustine, and we decided it was time.

We didn't even tell my team about our plans this time. We were tired of them arguing with us or trying to convince us not to go. Our motto became "It's better to ask forgiveness than permission."

As if we would ever ask their forgiveness for living life the way it should be lived, even if I had cancer.

St. Augustine had always been a city near to my heart. Despite the too-busy streets, impossible parking, and general chaos of a tourist town, it had a charm I could never stay away from.

One of my earliest memories was of St. Augustine. I remembered flashes of that trip, clear as day and clearer even than some of my early adulthood, thanks to chemo brain. I had this Build-A-Bear named Brownie that I took everywhere with me, and before we got to St. Augustine, we got her a new pink hoodie because I insisted she would be too cold in her usual t-shirt. I remember touring Castillo de San Marcos, the Spanish fort. It was so breezy up on the top that I felt like I, at six years old, would fly right off. And I was glad that Brownie had a new jacket to keep her warm because the wind seemed to blow right through me.

We took a carriage ride through the streets of St. Augustine, which thrilled me to no end since horses were my favorite animals. I felt like a princess, like all the ones I had watched in Disney movies with their own horse-drawn carriages.

The Cathedral Basilica also became a memory forever engraved in my mind. Whether it was because of the sheer size and wondrous beauty or because Mom told me it gave her the heebie-jeebies, I can't tell you.

We ended the day at a Merry-Go-Round that I rode over and over until I was about to fall asleep on my chosen horse.

A few years later, Mom and I would go back to St. Augustine where we would climb the 219 steps to reach the top of the St. Augustine Lighthouse. Mom glued herself to the outside wall when we reached the top, while I was taking in all the views I could get from the gallery, probably even leaning over the railing to see the ground 165 feet below me.

My daredevil tendencies started early, it seems.

That trip would spark my interest in visiting and climbing lighthouses, and by the time I was diagnosed with cancer, we would have visited 88 lighthouses together across Florida, North Carolina, and Michigan.

Then there were the trips my mom, grandma, and I would take to the St. Augustine beach. That was where I learned the fine art of wave jumping. We would go out hand in hand until we were, for my ten-year-old self, chest deep, and wait for the waves to swell before either jumping over them as they came in, or getting slammed by them.

That is also where I learned that Sprite is a great drink if you end up swallowing and inhaling salt water all at the same time.

St. Augustine even had my favorite restaurant and my favorite dish of all time. Shrimp and grits from the Conch House, right on the marina, was probably the reason I grew up to be a foodie from such a young age. To this day, I have not found shrimp and grits to rival theirs.

One thing we hadn't ever done in St. Augustine, though, was shop. We never had a reason to until I told Mom I just wanted to be a tourist. Our sailboat tour wouldn't leave until sunset that evening, so we had plenty of time.

It never really ceases to amaze me, even to this day, the amount of *stuff* in those shops. We could have walked for hours and never seen the end of it. Most of it was geared towards tourists, with all the beach-themed T-shirts and nick-knacks, but we did find one shop that yielded something unique. Though there was a host of jewelry stores, we found one that had the perfect charm bracelet for me. The charm on it was a compass, outlined with the quote, "A mother's love is true north, always guiding the way home."

We debated trying something new for dinner, but I didn't feel like a trip to St. Augustine would be complete without a visit to the Conch House. While we waited, we walked the small pier at the marina, listening to live Jimmy Buffett style music.

I had forgotten just how hard it was to take selfies at the beach. I had also forgotten that after factoring in the background and where the sun was, I had to make sure the wind wasn't blowing Mom's hair in her face. I mean, I didn't have hair blowing on my face, so it was no big deal, right?

That ended with some of my most treasured pictures, capturing the moment of realization for me and the exasperation on Mom's face as I snapped pictures of her hair going everywhere.

By the time we boarded the sailboat, I was ready to wind down and relax. From the open-air sailboat, we watched the sky go from vibrant hot pinks and oranges to soft purples as the sun set behind the downtown horizon. The downtown lights blinked on with the stars that had started peeking through the darkening night sky. The farther we got from the downtown area, the more numerous the stars became.

We had live music on the boat, but in contrast to the upbeat, tropical feel of the Conch House, this music was a soft, almost intimate combination of vocals and acoustic guitar. The wind had calmed down to a gentle breeze, and the current swayed the boat into a predictable rhythm.

I spotted the lighthouse by its lantern's flash pattern, a constant and steady beat against the ever-changing city lights. I had only ever seen lighthouses during the day, but in the dark of night, I realized why lighthouses are used as a symbol of hope. There, standing above all the chaos and confusion of the city, was an unrelenting beacon that promised stability and safety.

For me, whether I realized it in the moment or not, it symbolized Jesus. Far above the chaos of the circumstances I found myself in, He was there, guiding, reassuring, and offering the promise of hope and safety if I kept my eyes on Him.

I made a small promise to myself at that moment that, no matter what happened, I would be back to climb it again when everything was over.

The farther we got from the city lights, the brighter the night sky became. It didn't take long until I found myself leaning against Mom's shoulder, staring at the stars as if it were the first time in forever I was really *seeing* the beauty of the universe that surrounded me.

And for the first time in my entire life, I saw a shooting star. I knew it was a meteor but calling it that takes the magic out of the experience. I was beyond ecstatic, and nothing could have topped the joy I felt at that moment.

Coming back to the pier broke the magic of escaping reality for most of us on the boat, the energy going from a calm peace to a rush for solid ground. Having the lights on also brought my shiny bald head to the attention of a very sweet, *very* drunk lady to my side.

"OH my goooodness honey, you have suchaperfectheadshape! I'm a hairdresser you know and bald REALLY works for you, I mean your head is soooooo round and smooth! I have too many dents in my head to pull off a shaved head but YOURS?! Absolutelyperfect," she told me, her slurred words and comical, over the top hand gestures at odds with the serious tone she was going for.

It took every ounce of self-control I had to not giggle as I thanked her, as I'm sure she thought she was having a moment with me. Though, in a way, she was. Moments like those helped me fight against the insecurities that popped up every once in a while.

Limitless

114

Chapter 14

August 2, 2019

The trip to St. Augustine had given me a peace I didn't know I needed to continue the uphill battle I was facing against chemo. Surgery was now the next step for me as soon as my blood counts had recovered to a safe level.

Honestly, no matter how the surgery was going to turn my life upside down, I was just happy that I would be spared from chemo for a few weeks while I recovered. My team apparently did not share my excitement for the break I was being given due to my blood counts being low. For them, the quicker I got to surgery, the quicker I could start chemo again. I understood, but again, they weren't dealing with what I had to live with on a daily basis because of chemo.

We would have been fine had they not tried to force me to share their point of view. Didn't I *want* to have the surgery to get my tumors removed? Didn't I *want* to get back to chemo and finish up my treatments?

Well, yeah, but forgive me for enjoying the little break from the torture. It's not like I was actively sabotaging my blood counts. I was just making the most out of the time I was given because of that.

If they wanted me to *want* to have a "radical" surgery and take drugs that wrecked my body, they had lost touch with just how awful what their patients were going through really was. I was getting pretty fed up with how they couldn't seem to empathize with why I might be relieved to have a break from everything I had to go through. I could understand why they thought the way they did, but they seemed to be incapable of putting themselves in my shoes to understand why I thought the way I did.

The same thoughts echoed for me during my pre-op appointment with my surgeon. He seemed so excited to do this surgery, almost to the point of not understanding what he was about to put me through.

He recapped what he had already shared with me during my previous hospital stay. Taking stuff out, replacing it with cadaver parts, adding metal. It sounded like he would be making a puzzle out of my leg. But that wasn't all.

There was a definite possibility that if they got in my leg and realized the damage that the tumor had done was more extensive, they might be forced to amputate.

He made the statement as if it were just a normal Tuesday. Well, I guess for an orthopedic surgeon, it was. It certainly wasn't for me. Before I could even process that bomb drop, he was moving on. He was *sure* that he would be able to save my leg.

But, even if I got to keep my leg, I probably wouldn't be able to walk for at least a year. Even then, I would probably use crutches or a walker for the rest of my life.

Before I could even question what the point was of saving my leg, if I couldn't use it, he was happily explaining that he was so sure I would get to keep my leg, and that was what mattered! Right?

Between the brain fog and the influx of information I had just received, I barely had time to process even a fraction of that conversation before I signed the consent forms. The thoughts in my head sounded something like *I could keep my leg, maybe, probably, but I won't walk for a very long time, if at all, by myself, and doctors know best, so I should trust him, right?*

But I could trust my team, they knew what was best. So, I could sign the consent form. I could trust them.

Couldn't I?

August 5, 2019

Grasping for one last shred of independence while I could still walk on my own, I told Mom I wanted to drive myself to my pre-op MRI the day before surgery.

My blood counts were high enough, consent forms were signed, and the date was confirmed. All they needed was an updated scan, and we would be ready.

Well, they would be ready. I didn't know if I could ever be ready. It had taken a few days, but I managed to process what was ahead of me. They would take my leg apart and put it back together with parts that didn't belong to me, and I would hope that I could one day walk with a cane or walker.

Not only did I need independence for what seemed like one last time, I needed some time alone. I figured that after surgery, I would be getting very little of that for a while.

I managed to hold myself together fairly well until I arrived at the hospital for my MRI. I barely got through the doors before something in my chest broke apart. It became almost impossible to breathe.

It took a force not of my own to keep me walking towards the check-in desk, not away from it. All I wanted to do was to run. But I couldn't, so I checked in, and followed a nurse back to where I would wait to be called for my MRI.

As I got situated on the table before the 45-minute MRI would start, the tech asked me if I would like to listen to any music. I requested Twenty One Pilots. As the scan started, "Car Radio" came on, and my last bit of resolve to hold it together broke. I cried, trying my best to stay silent and still so I didn't interrupt the accuracy of the scans. Mercifully, it didn't take long for me to fall asleep.

117

Limitless

As I left, I felt a weight heavy against my shoulders and my chest. The following day, when my surgery was scheduled, my life was likely to change in a way that even my will couldn't stop.

August 6, 2019

Only two people knew about my upcoming surgery - my mom, of course, and Anthony. I was going through too much to have anyone else involved, especially knowing the responses to my diagnosis.

I had very little idea of what to expect. As far as invasive surgeries go, I had my port placed at the beginning of treatment. That was hardly a comparison to what was about to happen. Even though I had a decent grasp on the process of the surgery and the length of recovery, I was pretty clueless about what that would mean for me in a practical sense. I knew I would face a barrage of questions and opinions if I told anyone, and I didn't have the mental capacity to deal with everyone else's response to *my* surgery.

Getting diagnosed with cancer taught me enough about how people respond to major things like that. On top of being told what everyone thought about what was about to happen to me, the idea of having to comfort other people while I was falling apart was unbearable. I was the one that needed comfort, for Heaven's sake.

Telling everyone that I would be okay was one thing. That is par for the course for surgery. I don't mean providing reassurance. For so many of the people who were in my life at the time, it wasn't reassurance I would be giving. I would have been calming their emotions, and it was an act I couldn't balance when my own were hardly in check.

On top of that, I did not want anyone to come to see me. I didn't even know if I would wake up with both legs still attached, and I definitely didn't want anyone showing up, asking how I was, if they could get me anything, if I needed anything, if I was in pain, if I was okay.

118

I could only deal with so much, and I was very near my max. I couldn't deal with the pity, the assumptions, the worry, the visitors. Aside from Mom and Anthony, I didn't trust anyone to respect my boundaries and not show up or call unexpectedly.

I did tell Mom that, if she wanted someone to wait with her during the long hours I would be in surgery, she was welcome to invite someone, but she was in the same boat that I was. She didn't want to deal with any possible drama, so it was easier if she waited alone.

Plus, it's not like we had much support in those months following my diagnosis anyway. Once the diagnosis hype died down, everyone seemed to move on with their lives. So, it wasn't an unusual feeling to face this life-altering moment just the two of us.

Going into pre-op for this surgery was the single most dehumanizing experience I have ever had. From the second I was called back from the waiting area, I felt like livestock being herded around. I was not a human. I was a body with a destination.

For everyone who was working there, it was just their day-to-day routine. They had to get people from one place to the next, ready for whatever surgery they were being prepped for. They seemed to forget that for most of us, it was not normal. For those of us being prepped, we were anxious, and scared, and we were looking for reassurance that we wouldn't find.

It was lucky for me that I had done the process before, but being slightly familiar with the process did nothing to ease my nerves. I couldn't take a step without wondering if those were the last steps I would ever take by myself. Or if they were the last steps I would take with my own leg.

The first thing after being asked to confirm my date of birth was being handed a bag and told to change into what was in the bag and only what was in the bag.

And bonus, for me, since I was a woman of childbearing age, to take a pregnancy test while I was at it. Which wasn't the worst thing in the world until I was told that when I came out, wearing what could only be described as glorified newspapers, I would need to take said pregnancy test across the room and place it on a sink. In full view of every other human being in the unit.

Because modesty was not a word in the pre-op dictionary.

Well, it's not like I was in a position to argue, so I started changing. At least they upgraded the glorified newspapers to actually wrap all the way around before closing, so I wasn't trying to hold my gown closed while traipsing all over the unit.

As I reached the bottom of the bag, I started laughing. Not a genuine laugh, of course. More like a slightly unhinged, *you have got to be kidding me,* kind of laugh.

There was a hairnet.

They gave me, with my bald head, a hairnet.

Look, I know it comes in every pre-op bag, but I was not in a good place mentally. It was laugh or lose it. I chose to laugh.

When I came out, I was immediately ushered, first to the sink to drop off my pregnancy test, then to a curtained-off area to get prepped for surgery.

Well, at least I was finally out of the public eye.

Upon getting situated on the bed, a nurse came in to start placing sensors for ECG monitoring. Which was not a huge deal, until he pulled open my paper gown with no warning to start placing the sensors over my chest and sides.

Wow, at least take me to dinner first.

Again, laugh at it or break down.

Another fine example of things nurses do daily that are so normal for them, but so jarring for patients.

I finally accepted that I wasn't surviving the day with any dignity. I was holding onto a tiny shred of it until this point, and I lost hope for that the second the gown came open.

I knew that next, I would be turned into a pincushion. My fear of needles had long since disappeared since I had been getting poked multiple times a week for eight months, but this wasn't Megan, my trusted clinic nurse. These were nurses who would try to start the IV in my hand, where it was virtually impossible to find a vein.

I tried to reason with the nurse to start an IV anywhere but my hand and to place the one in my hand after I had been put out. I tried to tell her that, even in my arms, my veins were hard to find. She would save me a lot of unneeded discomfort if she would just try for my forearm instead.

I was told that anesthesiology liked the IVs started in the hand, so that is what she would do. And I really didn't have the nerve left to fight it. In fact, I was starting to dissociate. I couldn't have fought her if I tried. It was like my consciousness was leaving my body while I stayed awake. I was shutting down, losing the ability to advocate for what I needed.

She tried and failed multiple times to get an IV in my hand. After spending way too long having her pushing and pulling and twisting the needle in and out of my hand, she got it placed. She hadn't noticed that while she fought to get the IV placed, I had started panicking and started to cry. I struggled to breathe. No one was listening to me, and no one even acted like there was a person attached to the body that they were doing whatever they wanted to.

I cried and kept crying through each nurse and doctor who came by to ask an unending onslaught of questions. They didn't introduce themselves; they didn't pause for even a second to ask if I was okay. They just asked their questions and left.

In between the questions, Mom held me and let me lose it. She was the only thing keeping me grounded and the only thing making me feel like I was still a human being. So, when they told her she had to leave, I lost it. Whatever small bit of sanity I had left slipped out of my grasp. Making matters worse was the fact that with her went my glasses. Without my glasses, I couldn't see what was going on around me, and the only person in the entire building I trusted had to leave.

I was surrounded by people I didn't trust, whose names I didn't even know, and whose faces I couldn't see. I could barely breathe through the panic rising through me. No one was talking to me, no one was trying to help. They just talked over me, talking through the details of the surgery as if I weren't breaking down right in front of them.

With no warning, I felt my head swim as if I had been dragged underwater. Everything started fading. I couldn't move, couldn't communicate that something was wrong. Right before everything slipped away from me completely, I was convinced that I was dying. I had to be dying. But no one was doing anything about it. They were all still talking, not paying attention, while I slipped farther and farther away.

The only thing that clued me into the fact that I hadn't died was the fact that I shouldn't have been in such pain. I tried to call out to stop the pain, but I couldn't. I felt a stabbing pain through my hip, and my entire leg started to throb like it was about to explode. It was like the night terrors I had been haunted by since being diagnosed. I was aware enough to want to yell, but my body couldn't move to escape the pain, and I couldn't do much more than loudly hum without having control of my mouth to form any words.

Just as I started to really panic, it all slipped away.

Then it all came back.

I would come back to awareness just long enough to know that whatever was happening was definitely wrong, but before I could place where I was or what was happening, it would slip away from me again.

Each time I came back, I would pick up a little more of what was going on around me, and each time I went back out it was like I was being reset. I would come back, fully unaware of the little clues I had picked up during my last few seconds of awareness. So, each time, I thought I was dying, again and again and again.

During one burst of awareness, I caught a glimpse of one of the nurses reaching for my hand and heard her whispering to me that I was okay.

Her hand became a lifeline. Each time I came back a little and still felt her hand squeezing mine, I didn't panic quite so badly. At one point, I looked up to see her looking back down at me, telling me that I was okay and safe. As long as she didn't let go of my hand, I would believe it.

Chapter 15

I came back again and didn't feel anyone holding my hand. I wanted to panic, but I was so very heavy. I just wanted to go back to sleep. The next time I came back, I felt someone rubbing my hand, and knew it must have been Mom. She is the only one who would know how to rub my hand that way..

I couldn't find the energy needed to open my eyes, but I could take inventory of my body and my surroundings.

The constant beeping clued me in that I was in the hospital. I had survived the surgery. That was good, at least.

Something was squeezing my right leg. I thought maybe they had absolutely lost it and were taking my blood pressure from my leg. But I felt the blood pressure cuff around my arm, so whatever was on my leg wasn't for that.

Then I realized I could only feel one leg. The first movement I made was to stretch my legs, and I only felt one. I started to wonder if maybe I had lost my leg. I was too tired to try to ask why I couldn't feel my leg, much less open my eyes, so I devised another plan. I started rolling my right leg back and forth until I felt my foot hit something. It was reassuring. Something was down there, and I figured I could try to look when I got enough strength.

I tried to stretch my arms, and pain shot through the inside of them. Okay, no moving my arms either. I guess the focus would be on getting my eyes open. Somehow, that was much harder.

When I finally managed, the room had been dimmed. I couldn't see much, but I did see Mom's face come into view. She was talking to me softly, but I really couldn't make out what she was saying. If she was calm, though, I could be calm.

When I tried to talk to her, my throat protested. Big time. It was so dry and sore.

Okay, new priority. Get water.

I started rasping to Mom that I needed water, and she held a straw up to my lips. If she would have let me, I would have kept drinking until the cup was empty. The cold soothed my throat immediately, and I felt like I hadn't had anything to drink in ages.

I tried to move my arms again, but pain stabbed through them. I had felt the pain before, usually when I had spent too long holding the phone up to my ear. They had been held immobile, bent for much too long. I needed a heating pad. That would be my next priority. Sitting up to see if I still had my leg would be hard if I couldn't extend my arms.

With impeccable timing, my post-op nurse came in through the curtains, blocking off my small room. *Curtains.*

That was good. If they had any bad news for me, I might have been put into a private room like they did after my biopsy when I got diagnosed.

I noticed immediately that he was so much kinder than the pre-op nurses had been. He spoke softly and slowly and actually seemed concerned.

I mumbled that I needed heating pads. I tried to convey that my arms were sore, but I felt like I was epically failing on the coherency side of things. He understood, though, and said he would be back soon.

While I waited, I let Mom rub my arms over what I realized were multiple IVs. One in each hand and one in each forearm.

Thank God I had been out when they placed those. The one in my hand was bad enough.

Mom helped me sip water while we waited, and I slowly became more and more aware of myself. I still couldn't feel my leg, and whatever was squeezing my right leg was starting to tick me off

124

a little. Mom told me it was a wrap that would help with my circulation since I would be in bed for a few days. Understanding the "why" did not help the fact that it was adding more sensory input than I was capable of handling.

It was now a matter of eliminating extra sensory inputs so that I didn't go into a sensory overload breakdown. I wanted at least two of the four IVs out, and I needed my arms.

It didn't take long before my nurse came back in holding...not heating pads. But he had the most excited, triumphant smile.

He explained that it was taking too long to get heating pads from a different floor, and he knew I was in pain, so he improvised.

He ran water through the break room coffee machine and filled sealable plastic bags with hand towels to hold the water, wrapping the whole bag in dry towels to keep the heat from burning my arms. I could not help but to smile at the look on his face.

But I smiled more at the fact that he cared. Though my mind had already initiated erasing the memories of how awful pre-op had been, having a nurse who treated me like a human being and was so thoughtful and reassuring.

He helped place the makeshift heating pads against my arms, telling me that if he needed to run more water through the coffee machine, to just let him know. He took out one IV from my hand, and one from my other forearm, so I was a little more comfortable.

He left me with a new cup of ice water since I had devoured the first one with some crackers. He said the faster I could hold down food, the faster I could be admitted to a private room.

Little did he know I was starving. By the time he came back just fifteen minutes later, I was sitting up, and the crackers were gone. His heating pads had worked wonders to get my arms moving, and with that I felt okay to start moving to sit up. I told him the only issues I ever have with surgery and anesthesia is that I would be starving when I woke up.

He told me to wait out the crackers while he took a quick break for dinner, and we could talk about food if I held the crackers down.

It was a relief to sit up and see that I hadn't lost my leg during surgery. I also realized that I hadn't been able to feel it because of the

125

nerve blocks that were inserted into the front and back of my hip. Well, no sensation was way better than pain.

When my nurse came back, we started chatting about how his break was, and he told me he had a Cuban sandwich from the cafe upstairs. The look I gave him must have told him I was serious about being hungry after surgery.

Ten minutes later, he was back in my room with a to-go box. A Cuban sandwich and fries. He said he had gone all the way back up to the cafe to get me something to put on my stomach, and I had to promise him I would take it slow. I could eat a quarter of the sandwich, and if I didn't throw up by the time he came back, I could eat however much I liked.

I could have cried.

The kindness was overwhelming after eight months of dealing with what I had put up with from my team.

After realizing that I wasn't bluffing about being able to eat whatever I wanted after surgeries, he let me finish off the sandwich and fries.

Before surgery, I was given the option to spend the five days I would be admitted on the adult surgical floor where I had my surgery or on my usual floor where I received chemo.

Stay on a floor with strange nurses who I had never met, or stay on a floor with nurses I had spent months getting to know and who, more importantly, knew me. Was that even a choice?

Because I had my surgery in the South Tower, we had to use the underground tunnel to get me to the North Tower and my usual admissions floor. I was thrilled. I knew I wouldn't likely be leaving my room during this stay, so going through the tunnel was a fun trip to take before I would be stuck in my room for five days.

When I got settled into my room, almost every nurse on shift that night came to my room to see me and congratulate me for getting through surgery. I was glad that if I had to be stuck anywhere for five days, it was with my nurses.

Megan had even stayed late after her shift in the clinic to come see me. Seeing her brightened me up even in the haze I had been in. I had gone back to napping off and on after finishing my Cuban sandwich, but when she came into my room, I was wide awake.

Though I wasn't in pain, per se, I was far from comfortable. There was a small area on my left thigh that still had sensation between the nerve blocks, deadening the sensation on the front and back side of my leg. Naturally, that one spot of sensation had to be where the skin had been taken for a skin graft during surgery. Oh, and the immobilization brace that went from thigh to ankle sat *right* over the skin graft site. I was certain they had branded my leg with scalding metal for the way that spot had been burning.

Anytime I had to move, I had to work around my leg, which was dead weight. Between the two nerve block lines and two drains coming out of my leg, I came to the horrifying realization that I would be sleeping on my back for a while. As a side sleeper, I knew many restless nights were on the way.

When I got settled, Mom went out to grab some snacks since she finally felt okay leaving my side. I had been dozing until she came back absolutely beaming.

She told me that she saw some of my team in the hallway, and they let her know that my surgeon had gotten clean margins with the tumor removal. I didn't have cancer anymore.

I was in remission!

I was ecstatic. We knew from my diagnosis that the tumor was localized to the bone and soft tissue of my left leg, so clean margins meant that we could worry less about the cancer spreading. The only major concern at that point was cancer cells that just hadn't been detected by other tests. That was why I would finish seven more rounds of chemo after surgery to kill any remaining cancer cells.

But while we celebrated together, I felt something drop in my stomach a little. Why hadn't they come to tell me? That was amazing, morale-boosting news. I should have been celebrating with my team. But I quickly moved on from that line of thinking. I no longer had detectable cancer in my body. At the moment, I was too busy celebrating with Mom, but as I processed the events of that day in my mind, I had some questions for my team during rounds the next morning.

Limitless

By the time the next morning came, I was a mix of celebratory and grouchy. It depended on who came into my room. My nurses and PCAs all got the news that I was in remission, news that came with many happy tears. Plus, I almost never got snarky with my nurses. They cared for me with so much love and kindness.

The residents that came into my room at 5:00 am, as usual, caught the snarky side. Hey, someone had to take one for the team, and residents and I already had a history.

I had gotten next to no sleep from the fact that I was stuck on my back like a flipped turtle. No sleep meant too much thinking, and too much thinking meant I pondered all night why it wasn't a priority for my team to tell me I was in remission. I didn't ask the residents about that, though, since I had planned those questions for my lead oncologist and her nurse practitioner.

As we waited for rounds with my whole team, my day shift nurses came in to get me set up for the day. They took out my catheter - nope, not talking about that - and had a bedside toilet set up in my room.

Oh. Heck. No.

I had lost enough dignity in the past 36 hours, and I was putting my foot down.

The one I could still move, just to clarify.

Over my dead body, would I be using that thing, and I told them as much.

God bless my nurses. They asked what my plan was for using the bathroom, and I told them in no uncertain terms that either they could help me get to the actual bathroom or they could get out of my way.

They knew me a little too well and wisely chose option one.

Their plan was to wheel my bed as close to the bathroom as possible, untangle me from the mass of lines and tubes surrounding me, lift my leg out of the bed since I had no control of it, and I would use crutches to get the rest of the way into the bathroom. So, less than 24 hours after surgery, I was up and out of bed, crutching myself to the bathroom.

Would it have been easier to just use the one beside the bed? Absolutely. But easy wasn't in my vocabulary since being diagnosed with cancer.

Stubborn and determined were, though.

By the time my team made it to my room for rounds, I was feeling quite feisty. Bad news for them.

I listened patiently while they told me how the surgery went and my plan for recovery. When they asked me if I had any questions, I asked, a little naively, "So, if they got clean margins, that means I don't have cancer anymore, right?"

"Nope!"

"That means that, technically, I'm in remission now?"

"You are! Isn't that so exciting?"

Bless their hearts, they didn't see it coming. "When did you plan on telling me that I was in remission? Or did you think that wasn't information I would want to have?"

Silence.

"Well, most patients don't celebrate being in remission until their treatment is over, so we thought it would be more exciting to tell you once you finished treatment."

"Last I checked, remission isn't when you finish treatment; it's when you don't have signs of cancer anymore. And since you got clean margins, that sounds like not having cancer anymore. Did you not think that I would want to celebrate that after all I've been through?"

They deflected the question quite awkwardly and made for their exit. I was feeling pretty satisfied with myself. I hoped it was a lesson they would take to heart.

It didn't take longer after my team left before I started feeling some much more intense discomfort. Every hour, I could use the pump attached to my nerve blocks to get an extra dose of pain medication. Up until this point, it had been working.

We called my nurse in, and she let me know that pain management had not set up a schedule for oral pain meds so she could give me what they had on order. Sounded like a plan.

And the plan worked. For about three hours.

The pain started to creep back. I thought nerve blocks were supposed to, y'know, block the pain. I used the pump for an extra dose of pain meds, to no avail. According to my nurse, I would have to wait another hour until I could have oral pain meds again.

By the time that hour was up, my leg felt like it was going to implode. And explode. I could feel the swelling straining against the limits of my skin and the incision, but I also felt like everything in my leg was trying to crumble under the pressure.

When my nurse asked me where my pain was on the pain scale, I told her it was a nine.

After the oral pain meds kicked in, the pain eased to maybe a six, but it didn't take long for it to come back with a vengeance.

I started getting weepy. I had an impressive pain tolerance, but once the threshold was reached, I started to lose it.

Mom expressed concern to my nurse, who told her that she was also concerned. She had never seen me cry from pain, and she knew it must have been bad.

She reached out to pain management, and by the time a resident stopped by, the threshold had been long since passed. My leg felt like it was being crushed. I started to feel every broken section of bone, every screw drilled through the bone, every piece of soft tissue that had been scraped away.

After checking the nerve blocks, the resident told me, without a shred of empathy, "It's normal to expect some pain after surgery. You'll be fine."

Well, I guess I was wasting his precious time, as if managing pain wasn't in his title. He walked out without another word while my nurse looked on in horror.

She wasn't having it. She called every oncologist on the floor. To my surprise, it was the doctor who was my chaperone on the trip to New Orleans that made it to my room first. I couldn't even say hey to her. I could barely control my breathing.

All it took was one look at me and a shared look between Mom, my nurse, and the doctor, and there was an unspoken agreement that if I had reached the point of crying where I couldn't breathe or speak, something was majorly wrong. Calls were made to my lead oncologist and my surgeon, and within twenty minutes, my oncologist, my nurse, and the head of pain management were in my room. I got no small amount of satisfaction that the pain management resident who had been so very helpful before was cowering behind the head of pain management.

It was determined that my nerve blocks had been turned off. For the past six hours, I had nothing to stop me from feeling everything that had been done to my leg.

Within half an hour of the nerve blocks being turned back on, the pain was completely gone, and my leg was back to being a numb, dead weight. By that time, my oral pain meds had been put on a schedule. Everything was fixed.

Except for my mental health, of course.

The pain had gone, but the imprint of the pain hadn't left my mind so easily. I hadn't eaten in hours and was too nauseous to even try to eat. I didn't want to move for fear it would come back. It took hours for me to trust that the nerve blocks really were going to work again.

By the next morning, after a decent but exhaustion-induced night of sleep, I was ready to try to take on the world again. My surgeon had stopped by between rounds and offered a look at my post-op x-rays. Call me deranged, but I wanted to see what was going on in my leg. I even thought it was cool to be able to see where the allograft met my own bone and the plate that held the whole thing together.

My leg was like a high-stakes puzzle.

To make it even better, that day was the day they would need to change the dressing on my leg. I could see the scars for myself.

Nothing could really prepare me for what I would see. The incision they made started above my knee and extended all the way down to just above my ankle. To the side of my knee, where my tumor used to be, was where the skin graft from my thigh now lay above the muscle they had moved from my calf.

It looked wicked. I was going to have the coolest scar to show when I told people about how I survived cancer.

The nurses showed Mom how to change the dressing since she would have to change it when we got discharged. She is one tough lady because being handed that task was not for the faint of heart.

Over the next few days, I got pretty nimble on crutches, going back and forth from my bed to the bathroom. I mean, as nimble as I could be with my leg dangling limp and immobile behind me. Physical therapy would come in, usually during the most inconvenient times - I swear that I had a camera on me to know exactly when I would try to take a nap - and once they realized I had no problems getting up and around, I politely but firmly told them they didn't need to come back.

If I hadn't been in the hospital, those few days might have almost been what I could consider fun. Em and Francisco visited almost every day, along with the Streeples. Since I didn't have chemo dulling my senses or sepsis eating away at my brain, I could interact with them for as long as I wanted without getting tired. Their being around actually energized me, and when they had to leave, I was left with a kind of mental clarity and energy I hadn't had in a while.

It was day four before anything else eventful happened. During rounds, I was informed that it was time to start preparing for my discharge from the hospital. I thought nothing could ever make hearing that news less than amazing. But it meant that pain management would need to stop by to turn off the nerve blocks to see if I could tolerate the pain without them.

I had spent my fair share of time without nerve blocks, and I wasn't ready to do that again. But when pain management stopped by, they reassured me that by this point, I should be able to tolerate the pain with oral meds. If it was too intense at first, they could "trick" my body by turning the nerve blocks on and then back off again.

For most patients, that might not have been that big of a deal. But by this time, my trust in doctors was waning. My team was about as communicative as a group of snails, and the pain from the first day after surgery was still imprinted on my mind. What other choice

132

did I have, though? I wanted to go home. And in order to get home, I had to be able to get along without the nerve blocks.

So, turning off the nerve blocks, it was. Pain management had assured me that if I told them my pain had reached a point where I couldn't handle it, they would turn the nerve blocks back on immediately.

Waiting to see if I could tolerate being off the nerve blocks was like taking my first dose of chemo all over again. I was so wracked by anxiety that I couldn't do anything. I just waited for things to go wrong.

Unlike my first dose of chemo, this time, it didn't go so smoothly. I knew to expect pain, but I had also gotten to know a whole new level of pain, and I refused to go there again. Unfortunately, it didn't take long before I got weepy. It wasn't that the pain was that bad. Mom was watching me like a hawk, ready to call for pain management the second things got out of hand. It was the memory. I had felt that growing ache and how quickly it became unbearable just a few days before, and I started to panic at the idea of facing that kind of agony again.

Pain management was in my room before things got too bad, luckily, and turned the nerve blocks back on as promised. They reassured me that it wasn't uncommon for that to happen, and that when they tried again the following day things would go smoother.

All I could think about was having to do that again. I tried to distract myself, but my mind kept drifting back to the fear of feeling that kind of pain again and, worse, what would happen if I did. While the pain management team was in, they told me that if I couldn't tolerate being off the nerve blocks, they had to explore other options for keeping my pain at bay.

By options, of course, they meant they'd explore the backup plan they already had in place. Options were more of an illusion in my situation.

If I couldn't tolerate being without the nerve blocks, I would have to stay longer in the hospital. That didn't seem so bad, in comparison to suffering, until they told me that leaving the nerve blocks in longer than five days was an infection risk. They would need to replace the nerve blocks if I couldn't leave the hospital.

All it took was a nightmare-like image of those flashes of consciousness in pre-op when they were placing the nerve blocks to fill me with terror. There was no way I'd let them put me through that again, but I couldn't tolerate that level of ten-out-of-ten pain. It was a no-win situation.

I spent the remainder of that day worrying and praying. It would take me a few years to understand that those two things typically did not go hand-in-hand, but I was a work in progress. I didn't know that worrying didn't have to be a part of my emotions, because I could throw all of my worries to God and trust Him to take care of things.

I did notice that when I prayed, I could not worry. It was when I stopped praying that the fear would creep back up. But as the time came closer for the nerve blocks to be turned back off the next day, I couldn't form the words to pray, and the worrying took over.

I was a nervous wreck by the time pain management came in the following day to turn the nerve blocks off. I lay in bed, just waiting for the pain and pressure to come flaring back. But it never did. Of course, without being completely numb, I felt some pain. But it reached a manageable level and stayed there. Even hours later, as I was being prepared for discharge, it was kept at bay.

As we were preparing for discharge, a home health representative stopped by. Mom and I shared a knowing look. That was going to be a disaster.

They wanted to send nurses to our house to help Mom change the dressing on my leg, and they weren't taking no for an answer. No matter that the dressings needed to be changed once a day, and they would be stopping by every three or four days. They insisted we needed help.

We realized that trying to talk to most medical professionals was like talking to a brick wall. They wanted to do what they had planned, and they didn't really care what we preferred.

Mom agreed to let them come help when I had given up on resisting and then explained that she would just have to make sure we weren't at the house whenever they wanted to stop by.

Before I could run for the hills out of the hospital, I had to get rid of all the tubes and wires connected to me. Getting the IVs out of my arms wasn't so bad. To the doctors who had come to remove the drains and nerve blocks, this part was no big deal. To them, they were just pulling a few IV lines and tubes from my body.

For me, they were *pulling a few IV lines and tubes from my body.*

When they got ahold of the first drain tube and pulled, I expected to feel more than just a slight tug. But that's all there was. Same for the second drain tube. It was a little odd, feeling the tug coming from the inside of my leg, but nothing too unpleasant.

And that's where I learned to never, ever get comfortable in the hospital. Because when they started to pull the first nerve block line from my lower back, I could have jumped out of bed and run from them if I had any use of my leg. The second one, placed in the front of my hip, was worse. I felt it being pulled from deep in my thigh all the way up through my hip.

I couldn't help the glare that shot daggers at the doctor responsible for my misery as he happily announced that he was done. Easy for him to say, since he wasn't having foreign objects pulled from the depths of his recently mutilated leg.

I was so ready to be home, in peace. No beeping machines, no getting tangled in the six different lines I was attached to, my own clothes, and, oh.

A hot shower. I was going to spend hours in my shower when I got home. I don't care what they say, wiping down with disinfecting foam is not anywhere near the same. Cleansing, yes. Satisfying, no.

Breathing in the fresh air and feeling the sunshine for the first time in five days nearly brought tears to my eyes. I almost wanted to drive home with the windows down just to breathe in the fresh air.

For the first time in a while, I was feeling hopeful again. I made it through my surgery. I would be given a few weeks off from chemo so that I could heal properly, and most of that time would be spent at home. I would only have to leave to follow up with my surgeon every week, and that wasn't at the hospital. It was like a vacation!

Okay, the world's saddest vacation, but still.

My priority now was to rest and recover. That I could handle.

Chapter 16

August 12, 2019

Recovery was not nearly as gloriously relaxing as I had hoped.

I hadn't even made it to the house before reality hit me. Upon pulling into the yard, we encountered our first obstacle: the front porch.

We had a local church group who heard my story come in to build a wheelchair ramp up the two steps that it would take to get me onto the porch and into the house, but it had not been finished yet. Dragging me, in my wheelchair, up those two steps did not seem like a good option either.

After much deliberation, our friend, Doug, used his gift of ingenuity to come up with a plan. We would use a dolly.

Yep, I would need to stand on one leg on the platform of the dolly while Doug hauled me up the steps. After the fact, it was hilarious. I was not having a great time in the moment, though.

It's not that I didn't trust Mom and Doug to get me up the steps. They laid out a plank of wood to make a makeshift ramp, eliminating the bumpy ride of the steps. But the second Doug tilted the dolly back, I started questioning just how much I trusted his plan. He leaned me and the dolly almost all the way back and started to haul me up the steps. I was holding on for dear life, looking to Mom to help make sure I wouldn't tilt off either side.

The whole ordeal was over in seconds, but I was perfectly happy to get back in my wheelchair. I was trying to be Little Miss Independent again, since I had the energy, and insisted I roll myself into the house.

What I had not anticipated was the attachment on my wheelchair for my leg. I wasn't allowed to bend my leg for at least six weeks, so my wheelchair had a leg rest that stuck straight out. I had never tried to steer a wheelchair with my leg sticking straight out in front of me before, and the learning curve for that particular skill was steep.

Sure, I could let Mom steer me around everywhere, but where was the fun in that? I was clinging to whatever small bits of independence I could still have, and wheeling myself around was one thing I wasn't ready to give up just yet. Wheeling myself around even earned me the nickname Hot Wheels from Mom.

Being in the house meant I was that much closer to the thing I had been waiting for. It was time for that shower.

A long, hot shower was my therapy, so not having one for five days was absolutely miserable. One of the first things on my agenda upon getting home was to get a shower and wash off the hospital. And tape residue. And glue.

Yeah, they used glue to hold the nerve blocks in place. Years of medical research, and the best they could come up with was blobs of glue.

I was so excited to get a shower that I completely overlooked some of the obvious barriers. I had over 30 stitches and a fresh skin graft. I also couldn't move my leg and had to keep the immobilizing brace on.

Luckily, Mom was thinking. She already had a trash bag and duct tape waiting. Showering was about to get a whole lot more complicated.

Instead of being able to get undressed and hop in the shower, I had to leave on enough clothes to keep my dwindling dignity so Mom could seal the trash bag around my leg with duct tape. Then, I could undress the rest of the way and scooch on one leg and crutches from wherever I was sitting to the tub.

Then there was the shower chair. In order to keep my leg out of the water, I had to sit with one side facing the shower head. The tub was narrow, so I couldn't face completely away from the shower head. It also meant I had next to no movement to get to my other leg. We took the shower head down so I could actually wash down, which I did probably eight times to feel like I had gotten the hospital feeling off my skin, but then came the next problem.

I just wanted to sit under the water. I had to call Mom in and play the "don't look" game so she could put the shower head back up.

Until I got my stitches out, my showers would be a little more difficult than I hoped, but even a difficult shower was better than wiping down in the hospital.

Through all the chaos, I still kept my positivity. I was home, and no matter how difficult it may have been, home was better than the hospital. Really, I would rather go through more difficulties at home than for things to be easy in the hospital.

By the time I got in bed, I was exhausted just from existing. I was so ready to curl up and - wait. There would be no curling up like I usually would. Until my pain eased up, I would be a back sleeper. Well, at least it was my bed.

I fought most of the night with my instincts to curl onto my side. I would try to roll over and wake up from pain shooting through my leg. I ended up figuring out how to sleep on my side from the waist up and face-up from the waist down.

The next morning, though it wasn't the like-the-dead sleep I was used to, just being showered and sleeping in my own bed made me feel like I could conquer the world.

I would just have to conquer breakfast first. And that is where things really started to get hilarious.

I stared at the fridge for a good two minutes, contemplating how to open it in a wheelchair with my leg sticking out in front of me. Mom offered to help, and I told her I wanted to learn how to do it myself.

I had a plan. If I did an 18-point turn, I could angle myself so that I could wheel forward, grab the handle, and wheel back to open the door. Then, I would wheel forward again to grab what I needed, hopefully before the door swung shut.

What really stumped me was getting anything from the upper cabinets. Where everything I needed was kept. I heard Mom, who apparently foresaw this minor obstacle, giggling at me from across the room.

If I stood to reach for anything, blood would rush into my already very swollen leg. That was not a pain I was willing to subject myself to yet, so we ended up moving plates, bowls, and cups to a more accessible cabinet.

Half an hour later, I had my breakfast made. After eating, I nearly needed a nap because of how much energy it took. But hey! I made myself breakfast!

The following days consisted of much of the same routine. Lots of struggle and lots of determination.

The only part of it that was truly miserable was having the dressing on my leg changed. We had to prop my leg up to unwrap the ace wrap. Since they ended up taking half of my patellar tendon and replacing it, any movement at my knee was agonizing. After being unwrapped, my leg felt like it would fall apart. I mean, it was sort of falling apart already. Not only was my tibia in pieces being held together by a metal plate, but they had to break my fibula to place the plate.

Once the wrap was off, we would have to remove the gauze pads and then the medicated cloth strips that sat directly on my incision.

The gauze and cloth strips tended to get stuck on the stitches, and the cloth strips covering where the skin graft was stuck to the healing flesh there, even though the strips were moistened.

I really don't know how Mom stomached handling my leg after it had been so brutalized, but however she did, she earned the forever title of Supermom.

As we had dreaded, the home health company sent a nurse out a few days after I had been home. Since Mom was already changing the dressings on my leg, we didn't really see the need for a nurse to be sent, but we didn't have the patience to fight it.

We decided to go ahead and have the dressings changed before the nurse arrived. We had already worked out the kinks on the best way to get the ordeal over with the least amount of discomfort possible, and we didn't want to try to teach it to this nurse, who would likely be thinking she was teaching us.

As we expected, she came in thinking we were clueless. Before we could explain to her that Mom had been taught in the hospital, and that we already changed the dressings, she was going on about the need to teach us proper wound care. She even had the audacity to tell Mom to just stand back and watch.

I didn't let her touch my leg. The only person touching me would be Mom, and we both knew the plan: let her think she was in control until she saw the fresh dressings on my leg. That would send the message. So, as she watched Mom unwrap my leg, arrogantly going on and on, we let her talk. The look on her face when she realized we had already changed the dressings and that she treated us like idiots for no reason was priceless.

The look on Mom's face was even better. I even threw in a little, "Yeah, Mom really knows what she's doing when it comes to all of this," for good measure.

By the time we went in for my first post-op appointment a week later, I had gotten pretty decent at getting around with one useless leg. I hadn't yet recovered any muscle control, so it was just dead weight, but I learned to get around it.

August 27, 2019

Post-op appointments would prove to be more of a nuisance than anything. We would always end up waiting a ridiculous amount of time to be seen after getting X-rays done. We would wait even longer once we got to a room. If we got to see my surgeon within an hour and a half of my appointment time, we were lucky.

141

Limitless

We would have to unwrap my leg once the resident came in, undoing all the work Mom had done with the dressings that morning. They would check the healing and leave us to wait for the surgeon. He would check the wound, show us the X-rays, and send us home.

It wasn't until the third week post-op that things got interesting. I would be getting my stitches out at that appointment. I couldn't have been happier, since getting my stitches out meant I could shower without a garbage bag over my leg. I stayed happy, excited even, throughout the waiting, the X-rays, and even the discomfort of unwrapping my leg.

I stayed happy until the resident pulled the first stitch. Then, I would have been perfectly happy to leave the stitches in. To remove the stitches, he had to pull the stitch away from my skin and clip it so he could pull the stitch out of my leg.

Despite all the numb spots on my leg, the nerves around my incision couldn't have been bothered to stay deadened. They were alive as could be and just as angry. I almost came out of my wheelchair when he tugged on the first stitch to clip it. When he pulled it out, I was sure he was dragging a blade across the inside of my incision.

The only pain that could have topped that agony was the pain of having my nerve blocks turned off after surgery. And I had over thirty stitches that would need to be removed.

I barely got through ten stitches before I started to pass out from the pain. Before the burning had subsided from one stitch, the resident was moving on to the next. He was trying to work quickly, thinking that the faster it was over, the better, but he didn't realize that he was leaving a trail of fire up the length of my leg.

The resident and Mom tried to move me from my wheelchair to the bed, but with my leg unwrapped, it was not stabilized. As they moved me, holding my leg as steady as they could, I thought my leg was going to break apart.

I called it quits and told them we would have to wait a few minutes for the pain to subside before we pulled the rest of the stitches. To the resident's credit, he seemed to regret the pain he was causing me, but he knew it had to be done either way, so he didn't

142

bother beating around the bush with it. He would stop if I asked, but if not, he kept going as gently as he could until the stitches were out.

By the time we were done, the nerves in my leg were on fire. I was relieved we would have to wait for my surgeon to stop by because it meant a few extra minutes no one was touching my leg.

Dressing and wrapping my leg was almost as agonizing as getting the stitches out. It was like my nerves had sounded alarm bells in response to being touched by anything. The pressure of having my leg wrapped was like trapping a fire inside the bandages.

I kept trying to hold onto a positive mindset. I wanted to believe, however naively, that the worst was behind me.

My surgeon kept a habit of reminding me of my limitations during every appointment. No bending for at least six weeks. No weight bearing for at least six months. And then the looming warning that I shouldn't expect to walk for at least a year. If ever.

The one thing I had going for me in terms of good news was that he wouldn't clear me for chemo until I had healed more. We couldn't risk the possibility of infection when my ANC inevitably bottomed out. That was one restriction I could get behind.

I don't think I ever fully believed that I would never walk again without assistance. It didn't seem realistic. After all, they had done this radical surgery to save my leg. That had to mean that I could use my leg again one day. Why else would they work so hard to save it?

I rolled that around in my brain until I came to the conclusion that they likely told me that I would never walk without assistance again to not get my hopes up. Or maybe because no one else before me had walked again after having a similar surgery. But surely, I had a chance.

Now that my stitches were out, weekly post-op appointments went back to much of the same. Waiting, X-rays, unwrapping, rewrapping, and being sent home.

I started to get comfortable. I didn't let anxiety over restarting chemo bother me; I just enjoyed the time away. My hair had started coming back in a Chia Pet style fuzz on top of my head. I stopped

143

feeling so weak and sickly. I even had the strength to start getting around the house on crutches instead of in my wheelchair.

So, when my surgeon hit me with clearance for chemo on week five, I begged him to hold off one more week.

I do mean *begged,* tears and all. And I do not beg. It was pitiful, but I wasn't ready. The idea of backtracking, going back to feeling so debilitated, even losing the little fuzz of hair I had grown back, was something I wasn't mentally prepared for.

He didn't seem to get it. How could he, since he had never had to take chemo and have his leg taken apart and put back together? He tried to convince me I was ready after having over a month off, but I wasn't. He had no right to tell me if I was ready or not.

I told him as much and didn't let up. He eventually relented, telling me he would give me one more week before he cleared me. He warned me that the longer I went without chemo, the more dangerous it would be for me. I was too petrified at the thought of going through chemo again, this time with much more limited abilities, to care about the danger. He had gotten clean margins, after all. That could afford me the extra time off.

It took me the full week to process starting chemo again. It was like the weekend-before-chemo conundrum. I was trying to enjoy that last bit of freedom but was stressing out too badly to really enjoy it.

Little did I know stressing over it would do me no good. Not because it was inevitable or because I didn't get to enjoy the week as it was, but because after being cleared for chemo and physical therapy during week six, I got hit with the news that made all the stress irrelevant.

Chapter 17

September 9, 2019

Getting cleared for PT was great and all, the idea of being able to start working on getting my leg back into a useful state exciting after it had been a useless dead weight for so long.

The idea of starting chemo sucked all the excitement right out of me. But worse was the conversation we had to have before restarting chemo. My oncology team wanted me to come in for labs before starting chemo during the following week, which we thought was fairly normal.

We realized it wasn't a normal lab appointment when at least half of my team came in to talk to me. I felt cornered, knowing that something must be wrong to be visited by this many team members, but I wanted to believe that nothing was wrong.

Maybe they had come to the conclusion that the heavy doses of chemo they were giving me before were not sustainable for another seven rounds. That would be good news, at least. But I couldn't reconcile that with the mood of the room. It wasn't a casual, change-things-up-a-little kind of vibe. There was a weight that I didn't bring into the room. It came in with the team, and I knew that couldn't mean good news.

I tried to trudge through the maze of my brain to think of reasons they would need to break news to me. If it was related to surgery, I would have heard it from my surgeon a few days prior. They got clean margins, so that should have been fine. I couldn't fathom what to expect.

They started off by explaining that because my surgeon got clean margins, there was no need for radiation. I didn't have a tumor to direct radiation at, so we would just need to finish off my treatment with more chemo to kill any stray cancer cells that couldn't be detected.

Well, that seemed like good news, so I wracked my brain for what the bad news could possibly be.

I would have never guessed that the news they were bringing was that my chemo didn't work in the first place.

I was stuck there, trying to process that news, while they rambled on. Something about taking a biopsy of the tumor after it was removed and finding that there was 0% necrosis - meaning, 0% of the cancer cells were dead. They had never come across a tumor that hadn't been affected by chemo at all. It was somewhat unheard of.

I was so lost. Not in despair or anxiety. I had just talked to my nurse practitioner a few weeks prior. I thought the tumor on my leg looked smaller after a few rounds of chemo, and I wanted her to see it. She also seemed to think the tumor was smaller, but looking back on the memory, I recalled her uncertainty that I didn't catch during our initial conversation.

I had gone that whole time thinking chemo had worked. It certainly worked to take out my immune system. It made me so sick I could barely stand upright sometimes.

It worked enough to give me sepsis three times, almost killing me each time.

But apparently it didn't work. At all.

Then, it hit me just how lucky I was to have clean margins. With a completely live tumor, if they didn't get clean margins, it could have caused the tumor to spread to other organs. Then I would really be in trouble.

No, it wasn't luck. It was no less than a miracle. There was no other explanation as to why we weren't panicking about metastatic tumors popping up. I sent up a quick prayer of thanks to God for keeping me safe from that horrible reality.

I had barely caught up with the conversation when my oncologist moved on to the new plan. Instead of continuing with the remaining seven rounds of the VDC/IE protocol, I would be treated with an entirely new chemo protocol.

Immediately, the barrage of information overload started. I guess I did a great job of looking like I was keeping up with them, but I was on the struggle bus. I was barely able to process one thought before they bounced on to the next.

Like the first time I had chemo explained to me, it was all thrown at me at once. I didn't process most of it but pieced it together over the next few days, relying on Mom to help remind me.

The new chemo protocol was called VIT - vincristine, irinotecan, and temozolomide. It would be infused for five days, in three-week cycles. That sounded great at first. More time off between treatments to recover. Though, I had started to learn what things like that really meant in the hospital. Nothing was for my comfort. If I had more time off between each treatment, it probably meant it would be much more difficult to recover from each treatment.

I tried to push that thought aside and catch back up with the conversation when I got hit with the part of the plan that had my jaw hitting the floor. I was looking at twelve rounds of chemo. At three weeks per round, that was nine more months of treatment.

Granted, with all the delays I was facing with the first protocol, I was probably looking at nine more months anyway, but my hope that the new protocol would be shorter since I didn't actually have a tumor was dashed.

On the bright side, this chemo was known to be less harsh on blood counts, and it was outpatient. I wouldn't have to stay in the hospital for a week at a time. I likely wouldn't get mouth sores anymore, and my hair would continue to grow back.

I'm glad I knew not to get too excited because the next bit of info completely negated the positives. Good news rarely ever came alone when it came to cancer. I learned that the hard way when news of clean margins came with the news of chemo not working, and I wasn't going to fall for that again. The bad news for this chemo, aside from the length of treatment, was that the side effects of this chemo were much worse.

Mild nausea would likely become uncontrollable nausea, and irinotecan specifically had been known to cause severe diarrhea.

Admittedly, the idea of my blood counts not being so badly affected seemed to cover for the idea of worse side effects. At least I would be less likely to end up in the ED for sepsis, and that had to count for something.

Since this chemo was infused in the outpatient clinic and we lived an hour and a half away, my team already had the paperwork ready for us to contact the Hope Lodge, a place for those in cancer treatments and their caregivers to stay for free during outpatient treatments.

We would have to wait for that paperwork to be processed, so I would start the new chemo the following week.

September 16, 2019

This chemo protocol was already proving to be a series of massive inconveniences. Before even being able to start a chemo infusion, I had to be at the clinic for last minute labs to confirm that my blood counts were at safe levels to receive chemo. So, I was only able to start chemo after waiting for the lab to confirm results, and then for the chemo to be ordered by my team and prepped by the pharmacy.

For the first day, I would need to take the temozolomide orally at least an hour before any infusions. Vincristine would then be infused through my port, followed by irinotecan. Each day

148

following, I would take temozolomide when I woke up and have a short infusion of irinotecan.

Between waiting for lab results, waiting for the chemo to be ordered, and waiting the hour after taking temozolomide, it could have taken four or more hours before I could even start the infusions. So, I would have to get to the hospital at 8:00 a.m. when the clinic opened and could be there until 5:00 p.m. or later, waiting to finish my infusions.

After previous arguments with my team about the early hours, I was *thrilled* about being in the clinic by 8:00 a.m.. And by thrilled, I mean I was seething, of course.

The outpatient clinic I would be treated at was on the same floor as the unit I had been previously treated at, but instead of private rooms, this unit had small curtained off rooms. Which seemed fine to me, until I tried to wait out my hours in the infusion chair with a nap, only to be kept up by every imaginable noise and disturbance.

Younger children crying, nurses talking, every machine in the unit beeping, TVs blaring, you name it.

Yeah, no naps for me.

I was already feeling miserable by the time my chemo infusions started, but, unlike my last chemo protocol, I would start to feel the effects of this chemo protocol almost immediately. Halfway through my first infusion, my stomach started to churn. By the time I was being detached from the IV, I could hardly keep myself upright and had turned pale.

It wasn't ideal since I was still in a wheelchair and only had the use of one leg. Hopping was *not* an option, so my nurses would end up almost carrying me from the infusion chair to my wheelchair.

I was so ready to get in bed and sleep off the nausea.

But my night was far from over. That would be our first night in the Hope Lodge, and we would be taken on a tour before getting settled in our room.

I was far from present by the time the tour had started. I tried to smile and show how grateful I was, but even the movement of my wheelchair seemed to send waves of nausea over me. I barely made

149

it halfway through the tour when I got Mom's attention to tell her I wasn't going to make it and needed to lay down. The manager giving us the tour was incredibly understanding and got us to our room with very little delay.

Though I didn't notice it through my beeline for the bed, our room was like a hotel suite. It had a living room space, a bedroom area with two beds and a closet, and a bathroom with an accessible walk-in shower.

I wanted a shower so badly but couldn't fathom trying to move from the bed. Mom could barely coax me into moving to change into pajamas, and I knew it would be more of an ordeal than I had the capacity to handle.

I would have to have Mom help me unwrap my leg, but I would still have to worry about keeping it straight while I tried to shower. My port was still accessed, so I would have to cover it with the dreaded shower covering.

By this time, my leg had healed enough that it didn't feel like it would crumble with any movement, so as long as I kept the immobilization brace on, I had finally been able to roll all the way onto my side to sleep. As soon as I rolled over, I was out like a light.

To my continual agitation, my team had scheduled for me to be back in the clinic at 8:00 a.m., again. My first thought upon waking up was that I would be having a few choice words with my team about the early mornings. Immediately following, my second thought was that I felt like I was falling apart at the seams.

My stomach had turned on me overnight, and the nausea was so strong I knew the usual nausea meds I had wouldn't even touch it. I would talk to my team about that after we talked about the early mornings. Priorities.

Things proceeded much faster at the clinic on the second day, since all we had to wait for was for the single chemo drug I would need infused, irinotecan, to come from the pharmacy. I had already taken temozolomide, so it would be a short infusion and I would be free for the day.

To help control my nausea, my team tried an IV dose of Benadryl before my chemo infusion started. Within minutes, I was dozing in the infusion chair. I managed to make it through the rest of the infusion with no issues, and we were able to head back to the Hope Lodge.

When we got back to the Lodge, we were told that, if I felt up to it, they would be playing Bingo in the community dining room that evening. I was determined to try, if I could. I knew I would need a little fun to get through the monotony of chemo and drug induced naps.

After sleeping through most of the day, I woke up feeling able to at least try to get to the dining room for Bingo. I was shocked to realize that, as we got into the dining room, I was easily the youngest person there. Most people were much older, the youngest being past middle age.

It hit me in a way that I wasn't expecting. After being treated in a pediatric unit for so long, I was used to being the older one. And I wasn't used to the looks, not of pity, but of dejection, that came my way. For the older people fighting their own battles with cancer, to see someone so young fighting the same battle was sobering.

The thoughts weren't one way, though. I looked at the people around me, and my heart broke. I was having a hard time as a relatively healthy young adult. I couldn't imagine trying to handle cancer being older.

Playing Bingo with chemo brain was, if you have a wicked sense of humor like I do, absolutely hilarious. Trying to process the combo that was called and then trying to find it on not one, but two Bingo cards was a monumental task. Most of the time, Mom ended up playing on four sheets with how much she was looking out for the combos on my sheet.

Being a little slow to play didn't kill my competitive spirit, though. There was a small potted cactus up for grabs on the prize table, and I was determined to bring it back to my room that night. Mom ended up winning before I did, but she told me to pick whatever prize I wanted, so I got my cactus. Hey, a win is a win.

We started to anticipate how little energy I had, but it was still shocking when we got back to my room, and all I wanted to do was get a shower and go to sleep. It was a small miracle that I even had the energy to shower after the riveting excitement of playing Bingo and winning a cactus.

Showering, as usual, was an ordeal - unwrapping my leg, covering my accessed port with the shower cover, and then trying to maneuver into the shower chair with my wheelchair without jarring my leg too badly. I had always been known to take ridiculously long showers, but this time, my shower took so long because I kept checking out mentally, staring at the wall until Mom convinced me to come stare at the wall from bed instead.

Sleeping after chemo from that point on would be such a strange experience. I was always so exhausted, which I thought would mean I would fall asleep and, after about ten to twelve hours, wake up somewhat refreshed.

Luckily, with no beeping machines, nurses, or residents invading my room, I would typically sleep through the night. But it was fitful, even though I seemed to sleep all night. And that was on a good night. If I had night terrors, it was an even worse night.

Even on a good night, I was constantly waking up because I would either jar the needle that accessed my port or because my leg would start to ache when I would toss and turn. Not to mention, I was in a different bed, so tossing and turning was imminent. I would only wake up enough to adjust to the discomfort and then fall back asleep almost instantly.

But every morning when I tried to wake up, I would feel as if I hadn't slept at all. No amount of sleep seemed to touch the ever-growing exhaustion brought on by chemo and the handfuls of meds I had to take each day.

On the third day, not only did I have to have a chemo infusion, but I would need to go to PT. By the time I got to PT, my nausea was barely controlled, and I felt too weak to even do anything. But I thought from my conversations with my surgeon that PT would be invaluable to my recovery, and I wanted the best shot at walking again, so I resolved to at least try.

When I got back into the PT clinic, instead of seeing the physical therapist that I got to know on my first visit, I was handed off to a student. It wasn't the most unheard-of thing from a teaching hospital, so it didn't really bother me.

Until the girl couldn't even get my blood pressure. Listen, patience is a virtue the Holy Spirit has been working on with me for *years*, but after being dosed with chemo and dragging myself to PT on next to no restful sleep, I had exactly no patience left. I wanted to be in and out, and the more time she wasted squeezing my arm tighter and tighter, thinking that the more the cuff inflated, the closer she got to her goal and the more time it would take me to get back to my room at the Lodge and sleep. Not to mention, I was already in enough discomfort.

Instead of being apologetic, she was arrogant. She couldn't be bothered to take responsibility for her obvious shortcomings, which dropped my patience from 0 to -10 instantly. By the time we got to doing anything, I was over it.

I let her take me through the sets of exercises she planned, which went well. Except none of them had anything to do with my leg, even though I was cleared to work on getting my range of motion back. They seemed to be focused on strengthening every other part of my body. I didn't come to PT after a dose of chemo to strengthen my back, so it felt like a complete waste of the time I could have been using to sleep.

I was agitated enough by the time we left to spend the rest of the evening grumbling to Mom about how pointless it seemed, but I figured that maybe the next week would be better since I would be recovering from chemo.

By the fifth day of chemo, I had to take Benadryl before, during, and after my infusion to keep the nausea at bay. Even worse, my stomach was worse than it had ever been. I had the worst cramps I had ever experienced, and my team was not kidding when they said the stomach issues I would have were severe.

On the drive home, I kept a nausea bag in one hand and alcohol pads in the other. I tried to keep my eyes closed so that seeing the motion of the car didn't cause me to have to use the nausea bag.

153

Limitless

All I wanted once I got home was to shower and get into bed. My port had been de-accessed before leaving the infusion clinic, so all I had to worry about was keeping my leg stabilized while it was unwrapped and out of the immobilizing brace.

My leg was stable, but I took notice of the slight bend at my knee as my leg rested in the shower. It wasn't painful, and it was certainly past the point my surgeon had started me off a few weeks before.

Well, if PT was going to work on everything but my leg, then I would work on my leg myself. I tried to extend my leg from the very slight angle at which it was resting. It protested. I guess I would too, if I hadn't moved in almost two months.

I felt the ache under my kneecap from where half of my own tendon was removed, replaced with half of a cadaver tendon. It was sore, but it didn't really hurt. At least, not in the sharp, stabbing way that told me I needed to stop. It was more like the kind of ache I felt in the bends of my arms after surgery. It was an ache of disuse. To make the ache go away, I would just need to keep moving little by little until it eased up.

Every time I extended my leg, with my ankle resting on the bottom of the tub, it seemed to want to fall apart from the inside out. It wasn't pain, not as I had learned to perceive it, but it was a feeling as if nothing were holding the puzzle of my leg together. The muscles of my lower leg had atrophied, and I knew if I strengthened them, they could help stabilize everything.

I may have been out of control with so many other aspects of my life - chemo, side effects, the whims of PT - but this, I could control. I would do what was in my power to fix my leg.

So, the following night, while watching a movie in my recliner, I started to flex the muscles I would use to extend my leg while my leg was straight. I could feel the flexed muscles tugging on the healing tendon, building up the tolerance. When I got a little sore from that, I started using my hands to pull my knee into a bend. When it got to a point where it couldn't bend farther, I would hold it there, release it, and try again, bringing it to that point until it no longer hurt.

154

Chapter 18

As I expected, the two weeks of recovery I got after my first treatment of the new chemo protocol wasn't just for my comfort. It took two full weeks for me to recover from the side effects. The first week away was to ride out the side effects, and the week after that, to make sure my blood counts had recovered. This chemo, though, was making me aware of a whole new definition of misery. I felt like I had been hit by a bus.

I had no mouth sores and didn't pass out every time I sat up. But that would have been preferable to the nausea that consumed my senses. At least with my previous chemo, I could eat. With this one, though, I had no desire to eat. Not to mention how upset my stomach had become within a few days following chemo. I cramped almost constantly and stayed close to my bathroom for the more, ah, unsavory side effects that came with the GI issues this chemo caused me.

I had the hope that if I didn't eat, maybe these symptoms would ease up. Chemo followed no such logic. If I didn't eat, the side effects were bad. If I did, they were worse. But, if not eating kept the side effects at bay, then I would only eat to keep myself alive.

It was suggested that I completely change my diet to help lessen my discomfort. Calling what I was feeling "discomfort" was like calling the Atlantic Ocean "the lake," but I didn't have the energy to point that out to anyone. My new diet pretty much consisted of the plainest foods possible. Nothing spicy, nothing acidic, nothing sour, nothing sugary, nothing salty, nothing fried, and nothing cooked in oil.

So, bread and unflavored oatmeal, basically. Delicious.

Oh, and no dairy products. Those would make the cramps of GI issues much worse, and there are few things worse than puking up milk. So, none of that, either.

Chemo had taken it a step too far. It could make me exhausted, make me pass out, make me throw up, and almost kill me. Whatever. But taking away my enjoyment of a nice cold glass of milk, pizza, cheese sticks, Oreos, and anything with, oh, what is that word? *Flavor!?* We were back in the territory of torture.

One good thing to come out of this change was that my blood counts were handling this protocol much better. Even my ANC, which suffered the most, was still within safe limits after my first set of labs were done the week after chemo. It made the long list of miseries a little more bearable to know that I likely wouldn't end up in the ED with sepsis.

That news had even given me a sliver of hope that maybe PT would have it together when I went for my weekly appointment after lab work had been done. My hope was acutely misplaced. At least the PT student managed to get my blood pressure this time. She had to use a machine instead of getting it manually, but that was about as far as we made it before I lost all hope in their abilities.

From what I knew about PT, I assumed we would be building on what we had worked on the week prior. Apparently, I assumed wrong. The "plan" for this appointment was to do exercises that weren't even related to what we did the week prior. The only saving grace was that they at least started to add in some exercises for my left leg.

156

That saving grace was quickly negated by the scar tissue massage that followed. Massage sounds like a good thing, I know. But I was stuck with a student who wasn't even capable of taking my blood pressure. Trust me, this wasn't a good thing.

Immediately upon digging the heel of her hand into the barely healed scar over my kneecap, I was howling. She mumbled an insincere apology without adjusting anything about what she was doing as if she was apologizing for my inability to handle the pain she was inflicting.

It took Mom letting Momma Bear out of the cage a little to convince her to use a bit of a lighter touch. By the time I left, I was taking an extra dose of pain medication on my way to the car.

This time, PT sent me home with homework. Basically, it was the same stuff they had me doing in the clinic with them. I was excited to have something to do to get my leg back in shape.

I stayed enthusiastic until I woke up the next morning and couldn't move my leg at all to even attempt the homework I had been sent home with. I tossed the homework papers in the trash. I was well aware that PT would cause me to be sore, but "sore" and "unable to move" are two completely different situations.

I had finally been able to stop taking my nerve meds and had been easing off my pain meds, only taking half doses at a time. I hated the literal handfuls of medications I had to take throughout the day, but I couldn't control being on most of them. Most of them were to help mitigate the side effects of chemo, so I wasn't about to stop taking those. But getting off the meds for my leg was something I could control. When they combined with my other meds, they made me feel so drugged out, and I was determined not to be like that for the rest of my life.

I wasn't about to let PT ruin my efforts by causing me so much pain I had to keep myself drugged all the time. Instead of doing the homework that didn't seem to accomplish much aside from causing me pain, I started doing my own PT.

By this time, I had worked my way up to bending my knee without using my hands, then stretching it out on the recliner to full extension with only a little discomfort. My methods were actually

157

proving to produce signs of improvement, without the need for extra doses of pain meds.

When no one was looking, I started to shift my weight ever so slightly to my left side while I stood on crutches. It wasn't as much a conscious decision to defy the limits my surgeon placed on me. More of an *if I can, then I should* kind of mentality. Why wait six months to do what I could do then?

October 7, 2019

Much to my relief, I made it to the end of my second week out of chemo successfully. No chills, no fevers, and my blood counts were likely to be recovered for my next round of chemo that would start the following Monday. I had even been able to enjoy a few days of eating actual food, since my side effects had eased up.

That, of course, only made going back to the hospital for another round of chemo a little bit more miserable, knowing that I would likely suffer worse than I had during the first round.

I had never hated being right so much.

It still took just as long to even get my infusion started since they had to wait for lab results to confirm my blood counts were recovered. After hours of waiting, the chemo finally came from the pharmacy, and luckily, I saved an hour by already having the temozolomide ready to take as soon as my lab results came back.

This time, there was hardly any delay between when my chemo infusion started and when the nausea set in. It was like a switch was flipped, and my body immediately started trying to reject the chemo. Seeing how quickly and intensely I went from my usual bubbly self to curling up in my infusion chair sniffing alcohol pads, my nurses suggested I try a stronger nausea medication. I had already been using a stronger oral medication, but I was not opposed to trying a stronger IV medication as well.

They started off with a heavy dose of Phen-Ben, and it worked within minutes. It didn't stop the nausea, but it did knock me out.

When my infusion was over, considering I was swaying on my foot - I wouldn't dare put weight on my left leg in front of anyone yet - it was clear the Phen-Ben had me past the ability of moving to the wheelchair on my own. My nurse asked me to tell her how I felt on a scale of one to ten.

"Drugged," was the answer I slurred to her.

I managed to fall back asleep on the five-minute drive to the Lodge, so it was up to Mom to get me in the wheelchair to get inside. I tried to shake off the meds, though, because I saw that there was a painting class going on that night in the dining room. I loved doing art, and I was so determined to try to keep up with doing the things that I loved.

I told Mom to wake me up right before it was time for the class to start, and when she did, I tried my best to shake off the haze clouding my mind. I managed to make it to the class, and though I was so out of it, I remember painting a city skyline at sunset. My brushstrokes were shaky and uneven since I had been constantly trembling for months, but the feeling that I had accomplished what I set out to do was such a boost for my morale.

At this point, doing things I considered normal was different from the previous months. I didn't have the energy for much, so staying alert for long enough to finish a painting was something I considered an accomplishment.

The next morning, everything had worn off, which meant I could at least get up and get ready for my infusion independently. It also meant the nausea was starting already. Mom and I decided I would start my infusion with Phen-Ben and not wait for it to get worse.

Our nurse agreed when we arrived and even said they planned on giving me Phen-Ben before chemo so I could take just Benadryl after. The nurses were the real MVPs of that hospital.

I slept through the infusion and through most of the afternoon when we got back to the Lodge. Being food motivated, I was willing to wake up that evening because an organization was bringing in dinner for the Hope Lodge residents. Not much would cause me to miss lasagna and garlic bread.

Luckily, I still had an appetite, and my side effects hadn't yet gotten so bad that I was back on my heavily restricted diet. I was determined to enjoy every bite of good food I could get until then.

It was a good thing because the next morning, the ability to enjoy food or anything really came to an end. No amount of oral nausea meds could even put a dent in the constant threat of heaving. I didn't really care if I got high from having my nose glued to an alcohol pad; I was doing everything in my power to not throw up.

I was so weak I could hardly stand to brush my teeth, and I ended up letting Mom use an ice bucket to help me brush my teeth while in my wheelchair. I was still bound and determined to dress myself, though, even if it took me half an hour and made me late for my infusion. Which it did.

What were they going to do? Tell me to come back on time the next day?

When we finally did get to the clinic waiting area after checking in, I probably looked as green with nausea as I felt. I tried to lie back in my wheelchair with my eyes closed and even asked Mom to rub my arms or my head to give me a distracting sensation.

It wasn't for lack of trying, but our efforts failed. Spectacularly.

One of the nurses passing by saw it before it happened and shoved a trash can into my lap about half a second before I threw up. And continued to throw up. And when I couldn't throw up anymore, I started to dry heave.

I didn't even notice the movement of my wheelchair through the hall with how much my head was swimming, so I was more than a little shocked to lift my head and find myself in an infusion room.

Well, that was one way to get out of the waiting room faster.

I pretty much dry-heaved until the Phen-Ben kicked in, and then I only stopped because I fell asleep.

When my team heard about what happened, they stopped by to talk about options for controlling my nausea better. I was barely conscious for the discussion, but I fought to stay awake so I could at least feel a part of the decision for what new meds I would be adding to my morning and evening handfuls.

After going through a few options, they mentioned that in the worst cases, they could prescribe Ativan. Though usually for anxiety or seizures, a lot of times, it also just knocked their patients out, and, in their words, I couldn't puke if I was sleeping.

I was done playing around, so I told them to skip the trial and error and knock me out so I wouldn't be so sick. It was one of the first decisions I had been able to make for myself, and I didn't really care about the consequences. I would have done nearly anything to not puke and heave like I had that morning.

They also coordinated other anti-nausea meds to work in tandem with Ativan. The plan would be to take Ativan the night before infusions during the week of chemo, and during the weekend after. On the morning of chemo, I would take a strong oral medication along with temozolomide. I would be given Phen-Ben before chemo, IV Zofran halfway through the infusion, and Benadryl right before leaving the clinic. It was a solid plan. If nothing could stop the nausea, then they would make sure I slept until the worst of the nausea would pass.

Heavily dosed with anti-nausea meds and yet still a bit nauseous, we left the clinic. But we couldn't go back to the Lodge since I had the absolute pleasure of dealing with - I mean, working with - physical therapy. And I was in no mood. I figured, seeing as they were situated near a cancer treatment center, they would understand. Maybe they would just work on some passive stretching and range of motion that day, seeing as I could barely move from my wheelchair.

I explained to the physical therapist - not the student, thankfully - that I wasn't feeling well since I just got out of a chemo infusion. I didn't feel as though that needed much more of an explanation since most reasonable humans can conclude that chemo sucks the life out of those taking it. Apparently, I was wrong.

The physical therapist just looked at me and said, in all seriousness, "Oh, so you're just a little nauseous? Yeah, that's normal. Anyway, I planned to get you on the exercise bike today. You should be able to handle that."

My answer to that was simple. "You try to make me do that, and I will make sure that when I puke, I puke on you."

Apparently, the threat was believable because I did not end up on the exercise bike that day.

It was not long after that that my patience hit a new low. Everything she had planned for me to do involved entirely too much moving. I knew halfway through with the way she was disregarding my warnings that she was pushing me too hard, that I would be too sore to move the next day.

As we left that appointment, I told Mom not to bother making another appointment because I would not be going back. Whether she agreed with my decision or not, she knew well enough that it was not the time to try to convince me otherwise.

The remaining two days of chemo that week were progressively worse and worse. Though, with the new plan for nausea meds, I didn't have to worry about throwing up, at least. I just couldn't seem to wake up, much less function at all.

I didn't have the energy to shower and could hardly move to get myself dressed. Though I tried, Mom had to help me since I seemed to have lost any sense of basic motor skills.

I could have just gone to infusions in my pajamas, and Mom tried to encourage me to, but I used getting dressed and even doing my makeup when I could to trick myself into thinking I felt better. If I got dressed, even if it meant Mom dressing me, I felt better about myself. Not getting dressed at all meant giving up, in a way. I wasn't ready to give up on myself like that.

I slept through most of the rest of the infusions and most of the weekend after that. It was only when I stopped taking the Ativan after the weekend that I started to be able to function a little more.

By that point, I had worked on my leg enough that I could flex and extend it nearly to a full range of motion. Anytime I stood from my wheelchair, I would allow more and more weight to shift to my left leg when no one was looking. When I walked on crutches, I put enough weight on my leg to simulate the movements of walking.

Though I had made leaps and bounds of progress, I had a bad feeling that my surgeon would not handle this news well. Anytime I went to see him, I would put on the brace and agree with him as he drilled for what seemed like the thousandth time that I still wasn't ready to bear any weight or bend my leg past a few degrees.

I knew he would have to find out one day, but I was never prepared for that day to be so soon.

Limitless

Chapter 19

October 14, 2019

Though I managed to get by the first few days without my nausea going past the point of no return into throwing up, I wasn't so lucky with my GI issues. Sparing you the details of what I had to live with, let's just say that it was miserable. The meds I took to help ease my stomach hardly worked and made me miserable, and until those symptoms started to ease during the following week, I was in absolute torment.

By that point, to say I was frustrated was an understatement. I was stuck in a wheelchair most of the time because I was too weak to move around on crutches. Even when my appetite returned, I couldn't eat anything that I craved because my body seemed intent on using anything with flavor against me.

To top it all off, I could hardly justify why I was allowing myself to be put through what I was going through. I had no evidence of cancer in my body, so there was no way to quantify if this chemo protocol was actually working or if it was all for naught. I understood the reasoning behind doing more chemo, but being the one whose body was being wrecked day in and day out didn't make it feel as worth it as my team had felt it would be. I didn't even feel as if I had control over what was happening to question if it was really worth it.

I needed to feel like I could control something and make some decisions for myself. I wracked my brain for some way to do that and landed on two conclusions.

One: I needed a new piercing.

Most people get a mental breakdown haircut. I only had fuzz on top of my head, so that wasn't an option for me. Mental breakdown piercing it was, then.

Ever since college, I had my eye on a double conch piercing for my left ear. I had been working up the nerve to tell Mom that was what I wanted when I got diagnosed, and it got pushed to the back burner. It was being moved to the front burner then, because what better way to take back a little control over my circumstances than to do the thing that cancer made me put off in the first place?

Much to my surprise, Mom didn't put up a fight over me getting a second set of piercings. She barely liked it when I cut my hair up to my shoulders in high school, so I was sure the idea of more piercings would send her into a tizzy.

The only pushback I got was not against the piercings but against the timing. She tried to convince me to get them after chemo when we knew my immune system would be better able to handle them, but I had already made up my mind. My team told me my immune system should have been handling chemo better, so I was going to take my chances.

Much more to my surprise, she told me that as long as my team didn't put up a fight, she was fine with it.

As if I would listen to my team if they did put up a fight. They weren't the ones getting drugged every three weeks to tolerate the side effects of chemo.

Naturally, they put up much more of a fight than Mom did when I told them my plans the following week during my appointment for labs. They tried to tell me no, I reminded them that they had no control over what I did when I left the hospital, and we settled on the agreement that if I absolutely had to get the piercings, I could at least wait until the week before my next round of chemo so that my immune system would be at its strongest.

This suggestion came from one of the newer doctors on my team, a fellow who was usually quieter and more observant. His suggested compromise put him on my good side immediately, not just because I was getting what I wanted - because let's face it, I was getting those piercings whether my team agreed or not - but because he was the first on my team to recognize my autonomy, and to have the empathy to express to the rest of my team why it was important to me.

Now, I had something to look forward to, and a doctor on my team I actually liked. It was shaping up to be a good day. And it would continue to be a good day, because I felt well enough to go to the store with Mom after my appointment.

Usually, I didn't have the strength to handle going to the store, even if all I had to do was sit in a wheelchair while Mom did all the thinking and moving. The idea of staying awake for the length of time it would take to get to the store, shop, and come back home was usually beyond the capacity of the energy I had.

Maybe I was on a high from defying my team and planning the piercing I had wanted for so long. Whatever the reason, I never thought I would be so thrilled to see the inside of a Walmart.

Going into a store in a wheelchair, with my leg wrapped and braced out in front of me, was full of excitement, and not just because it was my first time in ages in an actual store. In my current state, I was a magnet for attention.

The first person to take notice of me was a young girl who couldn't have been older than five. She looked at my leg, eyes wide, and whisper-yelled to her mom, "Oh no!! She's got a boo-boo!"

I could not contain my giggles when she said that, and I was still giggling when an older gentleman asked me, "What in the world did you kick?"

"Cancer" was the response that earned me a high five.

The store was being set up for Halloween, and for some reason, Mom wanted to go down the Halloween aisle. I didn't really

167

question it since I would not say no to any candy she might have gotten.

I ended up with a trick, not a treat.

I had been checking out something on one side of my wheelchair, and Mom called my attention to the other side. When I turned my head, I saw the face of a clown not two inches from my own face. Mom had to grab my shoulder to keep me from launching myself out of my wheelchair and hobbling away.

Hating clowns makes life very difficult during Halloween season. Especially having a Mom with a wicked sense of humor.

Speaking of hobbling…

Conclusion Two: I was going to start walking.

I had been working so hard on my leg and had felt how much stronger it had gotten. I could shift almost all my weight to my left side and had the movement of walking while on crutches down. My most recent X-rays showed that my bones had started to fuse to the allograft, and there was a metal plate and seven screws holding it all together.

I was over having to get up and get situated on my crutches just to walk ten steps to get a snack or a bottle of water. So, one day when I was home alone, I started to walk around, slowly lifting the crutches off the ground so I was using them less and less. My leg felt so thin and frail compared to my other leg, but it held me, and it moved as it should have.

I didn't even really celebrate the accomplishment of walking just over two months after surgery when it should have taken a year at least. It wasn't a matter of accomplishment but of necessity. Plus, why should I celebrate what I had planned on doing since the day after surgery? It was going to happen eventually, and I wasn't taken by surprise that it was happening so soon.

The hardest part of teaching myself how to walk again, surprisingly, was not the act of walking. It was figuring out how to drop that little truth bomb on Mom. Telling my surgeon? Forget about it; I'd cross that bridge when I finished circling around it for a few months.

After many long days of taking rickety steps back and forth from my living room chair, when I finally felt more secure, I decided to spring it on Mom. Not with words, though. One night, while we were in the living room together, I just hopped up and walked over to get whatever I needed and tried not to laugh at the expressions on her face.

Confusion, shock, a moment of terror, then questioning. To be honest, it was hilarious.

When she tried to ask me why I wasn't using crutches and tell me I shouldn't be on my leg, I simply told her it wasn't new and that with the brace, my leg felt strong. Once she realized that, even if she wanted to stop me, I was home alone for most of the day, the resignation set in. Once again, I was going to do what I wanted, regardless of what the doctors said.

I debated more about telling my surgeon I could walk, but the debate didn't last long. On our way to my next appointment with him, I played out how that revelation might go.

He had been adamant, reminding me at every appointment not to bear weight. He didn't seem to me like the kind to see a miracle and rejoice. He seemed like the kind that didn't believe in miracles, and he would try to scold me for the progress since it didn't follow his projected timeline.

I didn't have the energy for that sort of nonsense. I figured I would just deal with that later. Commence me circling the bridge to avoid trying to cross it.

With that conclusion in mind, I put on the brace, sat in my wheelchair, and told Mom to play along. She rolled her eyes but went along with my plans. The appointment went as well as any other, considering they all seemed to be the same. Now that the scars were mostly healed, it was just checking on the X-rays.

That week, my blood counts had taken a little longer than the previous treatments to recover. It was very minor, but my team wasn't sure if they would recover enough to start chemo the following week as it was scheduled. On my last treatment, they had barely recovered enough to start chemo, being just over the level where it was safe to do so.

That Monday, I was optimistic that my blood counts would be good to go. Not optimistic about chemo, mind you, but I was still hopeful that this chemo wouldn't cause me to delay.

Much to my joy and disappointment, they had not recovered. They weren't stuck in limbo, as they had been for so long with my previous protocol, but they just hadn't reached the level they would need to be to be considered safe.

It was a relief to not have to suffer through the effects of chemo for another week, for sure, but I had to stuff down a minor sense of dread. I refused to entertain the thoughts that I could be delayed or that I could end up septic again.

One of my team's possible solutions to this problem was to take me off one of the antibiotics I took every weekend, which they thought was causing my immune system to not recover.

To do that, I would have to do breathing treatments through a nebulizer every week instead. Breathing in vapor didn't seem so bad.

Wrongo.

Breathing in vapor of any kind is like smelling and tasting something at the same time. The scent consumes the senses. And the scent that consumed my senses for fifteen minutes during this breathing treatment, I was sure, came from a skunk. It was sharp and acrid, and it lingered.

By that point, nausea had become the baseline normal for what I constantly felt. Within two minutes of the breathing treatment, I was gagging and heaving every few breaths.

I would try to inhale through my nose as often as I could to give myself a break from the assault on my senses, only to get yelled at by the tech administering the treatment.

I told her she could breathe those vapors in after getting chemo and see what she thought of it. Harsh, I know, but I was done with medical professionals pretending that what I was constantly going through was minor and that I was overreacting.

October 28, 2019

When the next Monday came around, we were in the clinic at 8:00 a.m., bright and early, getting labs to see if I would be able to start chemo. I was getting pretty fed up with the early mornings, especially since I had taken Ativan for nausea the night before. Trying to wake up and function when Ativan says "no" is nearly impossible.

I had been dozing off the entire time we waited for lab results and the order to go through for chemo. We came to the point of expecting Mondays to be insufferably long and miserable, so I would just put in headphones and sleep as much as I could.

Luckily, my blood counts were good, and we could start chemo. Along with that came the Phen-ben, the Zofran, and the Benadryl throughout the infusion. I was barely able to lift myself out of the infusion chair by the time we were able to leave for the Hope Lodge. We barely made it out of the parking lot before I threw open the car door and puked, not even able to think clearly enough to use the nausea bag I had been holding in my hand.

I knew that sleeping would be my only relief, even with all the nausea meds in my system, so I skipped trying to shower, got into pajamas, and went straight to sleep when we got to the Lodge.

Or, I should say, Mom helped me get into pajamas. She was trying so hard to give me as much dignity as she could by not looking, but it made the process much slower and way more difficult than it needed to be. I knew every second delay in getting to sleep meant more seconds that my body could decide to throw up again, so I told her to not worry about it, and get me into pajamas however she needed to.

She still tried her best to keep her eyes averted when she could, bless her, but we got me into bed much quicker that way.

By that point, I was glad to be drugged past the point of caring. I had tried so hard to at least be able to dress myself for so long, and I had finally reached the point of giving that up, too. It would have been a hard pill to swallow had I been able to understand what giving up that bit of independence meant.

By that Wednesday, I spent most of my waking time either being a ragdoll with very little ability to move on my own or throwing up. My nurses knew to have mercy on me and only wake me up if it was absolutely necessary.

My doctors seemed to be oblivious to the preventative methods we were taking because they decided to put in orders for me to do another breathing treatment. When I woke up in the middle of my infusion to see a nebulizer in the nurse's hands, I almost lost it. There was no possible way I could stomach those fumes with the nausea I already had.

My team of doctors didn't seem to think about how that would go, though, so after taking a few breaths from the nebulizer and heaving over and over, I was near the point of a mental breakdown.

I asked my nurses to send my team in if they could find them and held back the breakdown until they got in my room. It wasn't hard, I just went back to sleep. When I woke up and saw them, I unleashed ten months of built-up frustration.

See, it wasn't just about the breathing treatments. It also wasn't just about the early mornings, which I was also about to bring to their attention.

It was everything that I had to carry and everything that I had been carrying for the past ten months. I had to subject myself to chemo treatments over and over despite what they were doing to my body. What choice did I have? I either took the chemo and got sick, so sick sometimes that I ended up admitted for sepsis, or I stopped taking the chemo and risked the cancer spreading and eventually killing me.

That on its own was heavy enough but add to that worrying about labs, worrying about a healing wound, dealing with PT, and going from not being able to function at all to trying to relearn how to function in my current wheelchair and crutch-bound state.

I was at my wit's end, and being up way too early and inhaling those vapors when I was already the sickest I had ever been was the final straw. I told them either I stopped the breathing treatments and

172

started scheduling appointments for later in the day or I stopped chemo. I couldn't possibly keep going at that rate.

It was only then that I found out from my head oncologist and her nurse practitioner, that the breathing treatment was not the only option I had to replace the antibiotic. There was a way to give a similar antibiotic through IV, which would be much more tolerable. They hadn't bothered to mention it, though, because there was a chance I could be allergic to it and because it was less effective. If I was allergic, they would just give me Benadryl and move on. No big deal.

I nearly exploded at that. There was another option, a much more tolerable option, that they didn't even bother to discuss with me and give me the right to decide. I laid into them about it.

They seemed taken aback as if they couldn't understand why I would be so upset. They didn't seem capable of understanding why I was at my wit's end, even though I explained it. As if going through eight months of chemo and almost dying three times, only to find out the chemo didn't actually work wasn't enough to drive anyone mad, on top of all the small things that had been building for so long.

We ended up agreeing to do the IV treatment instead and that they would start scheduling my appointments later. It was the only way I could fathom getting through seven more months of chemo.

Worse than that, though, the trust in my team that had been slowly breaking apart had been shattered. How could I trust a team who withheld information from me? Worse, they withheld the ability to make my own decisions, causing me to be put through so much more misery and stress before breaking down over it. They didn't even seem to be able to empathize with what I was being put through and the things I had to live with to avoid the risk of losing my life.

Limitless

Chapter 20

November 4, 2019

The rest of the week of chemo had been a blur. The amount of medication I was taking that kept me asleep made it go by quickly, though not without its fair share of misery. Like Wednesday, I either slept or threw up, with very little in between.

There seemed to be a few hours every evening, usually before the Ativan took me out, where I was conscious enough to watch YouTube videos without feeling the need to throw up, so long as I laid very still. I would watch whatever mindless entertainment I could find since I had such a hard time following much else.

It took me the entire weekend of sleeping once I got home to gain enough energy to even leave my room to watch a movie in the living room. I would eat just enough to survive, but I couldn't make myself eat much more. The more I ate, the worse the issues I would have with my stomach, and I was too exhausted to deal with the issues.

By this point, I would watch movies, and a few days later, I wouldn't even be able to remember them. If I had the energy to read, I wouldn't even be able to process what was happening in the book. I would reread pages over and over, trying to absorb what was happening, until I put the book down in frustration.

One evening, as I was trying to process the frustration of how incapable my brain seemed, I looked down at my leg from where I was leaning against the closed door of my room. My resolve to hold it together seemed to shatter when I saw how small my leg had become. My thigh was nearly half the size of my good leg. It looked so frail despite the work I had been doing. I broke down in the shower that night. I already felt so frail, in both body and mind, and seeing my leg so deteriorated told me I probably didn't look much better. I could only imagine the dark circles that had surely found a semi-permanent place under my eyes. Eyes that I knew looked more hollow and void than they'd ever been.

Once I threw my pity party and pulled myself together, I promised myself I wouldn't stop my efforts to rehab my leg, and one day, I would be able to do the same for my body.

For most of my treatment, I would be able to make it to my small church with a decent amount of consistency if I wasn't stuck in the hospital. By that point in chemo, I couldn't even trust myself to drive there, much less make it through a service. A friend of mine recommended a livestream service that he enjoyed, and if I could keep my eyes open long enough, I would join in. I don't imagine I comprehended very much, but I was trying my best. Most of the time, when I closed my eyes to try to pray, I would end up falling asleep. I knew God wouldn't fault me for the little naps I got, so I just trusted Him. He already knew what I was praying about.

While I mostly used a wheelchair at the hospital and the Hope Lodge, at home I used crutches when I needed to move around but still felt too unsteady to just walk. It took more energy, but was simpler to navigate in our smaller house, especially when I was by myself.

As I felt stronger in the days following my treatment week, I could get around more and more without crutches until I would just leave them in my room when I tried to do things like making food or moving from the bed to the recliner for a change of scenery.

November 12, 2019

By the time the day we had planned to get my piercing came, I was determined to walk in and out of the shop by myself. I think my sheer excitement fueled me. I was very slow, still learning to navigate the uneven terrain of the parking lot, but I made it inside with no problems. Half the battle was won.

In order to get any piercings done at this shop, there was an entire questionnaire to fill out. It wasn't a huge deal, until I got to the question asking if I was taking any medications, and why I was taking them.

I froze. I didn't have a clue what I was on or why. Mom had been handling my prescriptions for the better part of my treatment, but I didn't want either of us to have to list out everything I was on. It was supposed to be one of those "normal" days where I pretended the hospital didn't exist.

Mom saw my panic and told the lady helping us that I was on chemo and a handful of other medications and that we didn't think either of us would be able to list them.

Thankfully, she told us it was fine to skip that question if none of my medications were blood thinners. The crisis had been avoided, and I could go back to feeling semi-normal.

I was almost vibrating with excitement as I told her what piercing I wanted and picked out the jewelry. By the time I was in one of the areas set up for piercings, I couldn't stop grinning. The piercer was comically the opposite of me, covered in tattoos and piercings, and the whole look topped off with a stern expression.

He asked me if I was absolutely sure I wanted to do both piercings in one session. It was impatience, more than strategy, that made me say yes. His warning to my decision was simple and daunting all at once. He told me that the first piercing was going to suck, but the second one was going to *really suck.*

He was downplaying that statement. The first one wasn't that bad. It wasn't really the piercing that hurt, but the fact that after that, he had to pull a taper through with the jewelry and then fasten it. By

177

the time he was done with that, every nerve in my ear was on fire. The second piercing, going through those hypersensitive nerves just millimeters from the first, made me nearly come out of the chair.

I got an amused "Told ya so," as he pulled the taper through and adjusted the jewelry. It was over in less than two minutes from the first piercing, and in that time, I had started riding the adrenaline high I didn't expect to get, which was only fueled by seeing the piercings once they were done.

They were so worth the pain. In hindsight, they were also worth the nights I woke up yelling because I had turned over onto my left side and smacked my head against the pillow.

November 18, 2019

Admittedly, I was smiling bigger than I had in months thanks to those piercings. I kept looking in the mirror, grinning from ear to bright red, swollen ear.

I also didn't bother to hide my elation about my new accessories when I saw my team for blood work a few days later. While the nurse practitioner barely even tried to hide her displeasure, the fellow who suggested the compromise was genuinely happy for me, as if he recognized how much it had boosted my morale in the face of my situation. Of course, Megan was overjoyed at the cute new earrings.

I was so ecstatic and almost emotionally reset by my piercings that it didn't bother me when the fellow told me that my ANC was even lower than it had been at this point before my last round of chemo.

I refused to let the news ruin my good mood. Luckily, the fellow wasn't about the dramatics I had come to expect with my team. He even seemed to understand why I wasn't letting the delay bother me. I knew I would have to accept defeat eventually, but I had a few more days that week to enjoy the reprieve.

When I finally did go in for labs the following Monday, I let myself feel the emotions I had been putting off. It didn't devastate me as it usually would have, but it frustrated me. Partly because I had been at the clinic at a compromise of 10:00 a.m., only to be sent home for another week, and partly because I questioned how, if chemo didn't usually affect a patient's blood counts as badly, mine were dropping so low.

My team assumed that it was because of the damage the previous chemo protocol had done to my immune system. Usually, patients did not start the current protocol already compromised, and since I had, it was likely the reason behind the delays. I questioned why my team was continuing to allow it to happen without discussing a reduced dose or something to help the delays not happen, but I didn't voice it. Even if I wanted to, I couldn't even begin to put the question that was in my mind into words.

Even on a good day, I could hardly finish a sentence without my train of thought derailing. If I couldn't hold a normal conversation, I knew I couldn't even begin to put those thoughts into a coherent sentence.

Though the delay was frustrating, it gave me an extra week of feeling like a real human being with a semi-functional brain. Though speaking was a monumental task, I was able to start driving again, so I asked Anthony if he would grab lunch with me.

When we were in high school together, I had to learn how to walk fast to keep up with him. I had short legs as it was, and he had no mercy. I warned him before lunch that he would need to slow down because walking fast enough to keep up with his long legs was no longer a skill I possessed.

As we walked down a sidewalk to get to the restaurant we chose, he slowed down a little, but not enough to not leave me behind. All I got was a smirk as he said, without breaking stride, "Get those short legs moving, slowpoke!"

It was one of those things that only Anthony could say. No one else really shared our sense of humor, and definitely would not dare to comment on my ability to walk. From him, though, it was a sweet taste of normalcy. It was a relief to have someone who did not shy away from what I had been going through.

The comment even gave me a new goal to work on. If I could keep up with Anthony one day, I knew it would be a day I could consider myself well recovered.

At that point, my leg was taking my weight well without crutches. The muscles had started to grow again, so it wasn't as rail thin and rickety. I still had a slight jolt in my gait, but I was working on smoothing that out.

I had even started working on assisted calf raises. Since they moved my more medial calf muscle around to the front of my knee where they took the soft tissue tumor, I had to retrain the muscles in my leg to compensate for the loss.

Anytime I stood at the kitchen counter, if I had the time, I would do calf raises, transferring as much of my weight to my left leg as I could. I had mostly stopped wearing my brace at that point because any amount of walking would make the brace slide down my leg, rendering it ineffective anyways.

Of course, when I saw my oncology team or my surgeon, the brace was back on, and I was back in a wheelchair. Still circling the bridge instead of crossing it.

November 25, 2019

By the time I was back in for my next round of chemo, I was feeling good enough that the idea of going back to feeling so terrible was starting to feel like a waste. It was really bothering me that there was no way to tell if the chemo was actually working, which, considering the first protocol didn't, gave me plenty of reason to doubt why I kept putting myself through it.

On top of taking all three chemo drugs on the first day of infusions, my team informed me that they wanted me to get IV antibiotics to replace the breathing treatment done after my chemo infusions. It would extend my already much too long day, but they thought it would be best to do it on a day I would be the least sick.

For once, I couldn't argue with their logic. I had already been given enough meds to knock out a horse, so I would just spend a little more time asleep in the infusion room than in my room at the Hope Lodge.

My nurses warned me to try to watch out for any signs of allergic reactions, but we all laughed at that since I was falling asleep during the conversation. I figured if it was bad enough, I wouldn't be able to sleep through it.

It was fair logic, since I only noticed that I was, in fact, allergic to it when they woke me up to check on my halfway through the infusion. I thought I was having a really realistic dream, since my face from the eyebrows down was numb and tingly. When I tried to talk to tell them that, my tongue was also numb and, though it wasn't swollen, felt too big to try to speak through.

Since the reaction wasn't severe, it became hilarious. Because with everything else I had been going through, of course I would be allergic to antibiotics that I needed. I couldn't seem to catch a break.

In the haze of my mind, I started to gear up for a fight. I was ready to tell my team that I absolutely would not go through another breathing treatment and that I would rather take the risk of whatever the antibiotics prevented. When they told me that they would just dose me with more Benadryl to counter the reaction, I relaxed.

More sleep? I couldn't be mad about that. The more I slept, the less time I spent feeling like garbage. The week of misery went by so much faster that way.

The next day, after an infusion I slept through, we saw that the Hope Lodge was painting "Hope Rocks" in the dining room that night. The painted rocks trend had been going around, and it was my chance to join the fun.

I sat by an older gentleman who had shared his story with me. Though I don't remember it now, I remember being moved by his strength and faith. I painted the first rock for him to carry through the rest of his treatment.

Naturally, we all shared our stories of diagnosis and treatment while we painted. Those conversations usually made me nervous. At least half the time, talking to people about my treatments did not yield great results. It seemed we lived in a world of comparison, and so many people liked to play My Horse Is Bigger Than Your Horse like it was some sort of competition. I started to get used to being told by perfectly healthy people how I had it good in comparison to other people they knew in cancer treatment. How I was lucky I wasn't going through something worse.

In the Hope Lodge, though, everyone's struggle was their own. It was a safe place to share our stories without fear of judgment or comparison. It was also one of the only places we could freely talk about our awful side effects without making anyone uncomfortable. There was no competition about whose treatment was worse, no judgment for what we went through and what we all did to survive, just unconditional support. Survivors and caregivers offered to add one another to their prayer journals, which is such a selfless act when they seemed to have enough to be praying about as it is. It truly was a community of hope in the face of hopelessness.

By the time I had finished my next rock, I had used up all the energy I had left for the day. I was only there for maybe half an hour, but chemo had taken it out of me. I attempted a quick shower, knowing that my energy levels would only plummet worse during the week, and I would likely be too sick the following days.

By this point, my memory had started to become incredibly unreliable. All I can remember now are flashes, almost as if trying to remember a dream. A flash of Mom helping me get dressed or a flash of nearly being carried from the car to my wheelchair because I physically could not move.

Sometimes, the memory loss seems like a mercy. Some things, it was probably best that I don't remember. Most of the time though, it is extremely frustrating. Not only did I lose memories of things that were traumatizing, but I also lost good memories, and even memories from college, high school, and as far back as my childhood.

Mom would make a reference to something I should have remembered, but I just couldn't. Vacations, marching band events, movies, nothing in my memory was safe.

During my treatment that week, we found out the hospital was giving out tickets to the Hockey Fights Cancer game in Tampa, and we had been chosen to attend the game. It was a match between the Tampa Bay Lightning and the Florida Panthers the weekend immediately following my treatment. I expected to spend that weekend sleeping, but the idea of a little adventure to try something new was too enticing. I couldn't pass it up.

We accepted and prayed that the side effects would ease just for a day so we could enjoy the game since it was soon enough after treatment that I was usually still experiencing fairly severe side effects.

But God is a God of answered prayers, and I woke up the day of the game feeling miraculously better than I had the day before.

November 30, 2019

Mom and I knew nothing, and I do mean *nothing,* about hockey, but we were not about to turn down the chance to have some fun.

We didn't even know which team we should have been cheering for. After some Googling, we figured that since we would be in the Lightning, or Bolts, arena in Tampa, the safe bet was to cheer for the home team.

In my excitement, I tried to look up some of the basic hockey rules so I wouldn't be completely clueless, and quickly gave up. All I managed to figure out was that the game would last three twenty-minute periods. Once it got to rules, I was lost.

We planned to stay at a hotel about a block from the arena so that we didn't have to bother with parking and traffic after the game. My anticipation only grew as most of everyone in the lobby was wearing Bolts gear. At least we seemed to have chosen the right team.

I had been walking reliably enough at this point that we didn't even bother to bring my wheelchair or crutches. I hadn't even had to take pain meds in weeks, so we figured we were good to go. Even climbing up the stairs to our seats was no big deal.

Mom and I had never really been sports people. We had sat through so many football games when I was in high school that sports had ceased to thrill us. We were there for the outing but didn't expect to be thrilled with the hockey experience.

Oh boy, were we wrong.

From the puck drop, we were hooked, even if we were clueless. It was hard to not get invested in the fast-paced game. The first time half of both teams slammed against the wall and started fighting, we were enamored.

Lightning fans also know how to make noise. Every few minutes the entire stadium started chanting one thing or another, and it was addicting.

The best part? The lightning machines. Every time the Bolts scored, two lightning machines started crackling with lightning bolts on either side of the arena. The Bolts fans would stomp their feet on the floor, making it sound like thunder was coming from the arena itself.

Sorry, football fans, but football became lifeless after the constant electric - pun intended - energy that filled the arena. The Bolts won that night, and I have been the oddball hockey fan in every social setting since.

Though my leg had swollen to the point of pain that night, and I ended up needing to take pain medication, it only lasted a day or two until everything was back to normal.

During one of my routine visits with Ortho the same week, my surgeon had freed me from the infernal immobilization brace. I was so excited I almost gave away my secret, that I hadn't actually worn the brace in weeks anyways, but Mom jumped in and saved me from admitting anything.

The week before I was to start my fifth round of chemo, my labs had revealed the bad news that was becoming the usual: my ANC was too low to be likely to recover in time to start chemo the next Monday. Again.

They did, however, find a new way to make my life more stressful than it should have been. It was flu season, and they were pestering everyone they saw to get flu shots.

Let me be clear here, I am not anti-flu shot. If it helps to protect people from the flu, and they make the choice to get it, awesome!

I, however, hadn't had a flu shot in nearly a decade. The last few times I got one, I got so sick I could barely get out of bed for a week. In the ten years I stopped getting flu shots, I hadn't gotten the flu once.

I explained as much to my team, politely declining their offer for that season's flu shot, but they weren't having it. They fought me tooth and nail, saying that it was imperative. Obviously, they hadn't figured me out in the twelve months they knew me because I only fought back harder.

We went back and forth until they threatened - yes, threatened - to bring in another doctor who would "scare me into getting the flu shot."

He failed, epically. After a while, it wasn't about the logic to me; it was about the principle. I said no, so it was a no. If they couldn't respect it, they could argue themselves blue. Their disrespect for my decision only made me dig my heels in harder. So even when he told me that I might die - there they were using the death scare tactic again - I wasn't budging.

I caused quite a stir in the clinic that day. I had nurses like Megan telling me that they couldn't force me into anything if I didn't want them to and doctors coming in and out of my room, pushing me harder and harder. It only served to grow the distrust that I had been feeling towards my team for so long. I was already pretty fed up after the incident with the breathing treatments, and after the events of that appointment, not much of my trust in my team was salvageable.

Before I left, my team hadn't revealed anything about their thoughts on the fact that this would be three treatments in a row that I had delayed and that I started to have side effects I shouldn't have.

They revealed nothing, that is, until Monday morning when a large part of my team crowded my tiny infusion room. I groaned internally. Every time I had to see more than two of them at a time, something was wrong. I immediately assumed they were coming to corner me about the flu shot again since they seemed to have no respect for my ability to make decisions. Instead, they were there to finally talk about what chemo was doing to me.

My ANC had not recovered, though I wasn't surprised. But they were ready to have a conversation about it. At that, I was shocked.

They explained what I had already been conflicted about. My immune system was consistently not recovering, and I would likely continue to delay. At the rate we were going, I would also likely end up back in the ED with sepsis soon since my ANC was starting to drop into the levels where that usually happened.

For the first time in this entire, nearly year-long experience, I was given the opportunity to make a decision. I needed to decide whether I wanted to continue chemo.

Chapter 21

After nearly a year of not being a part of any major decisions and even having my own decisions questioned, this was nearly impossible. Of course, I wanted to stop chemo, but it wasn't that simple.

I knew without them having to explain it that there were risks. If there were any cancer cells still alive in my body, they could spread to other organs. We had no way to tell if the chemo was even working since I was in remission, and if we stopped chemo and the cancer did spread, I would have to be treated with far less reliable drugs.

But, if I did continue with chemo, sepsis could kill me before any recurrent cancer would have the chance. If they had lowered the dosage of chemo, it would have been significantly less effective.

It seemed like a straight 50/50 decision, with no evidence to pull in either direction. Since we hadn't been in the position to help make major decisions for so long, we asked my team what they suggested and if they had any inclination toward one decision or another.

They bluntly informed us that they could not help us in making that decision. We tried asking in different ways, trying to find any bit of information to pull us in one direction or another. They would not help us decide. It was purely up to us. Since they had advised us of the risks and benefits of both decisions, that was all the help they would offer us.

Mom and I both were at the point of snapping. How did they expect us to make that kind of decision when the bottom line was that things could go terribly wrong either way? Sepsis could kill me, or my cancer could come back. That was that.

We were sent home to decide what we wanted to do. When I say "we," though I mean myself and Mom, it was really me. Mom made it clear that she would support me either way. She knew about my struggles with autonomy and wanted me to be able to make the decision I felt most comfortable with.

December 23, 2019

Even at home, the decision had not become any clearer. Granted, nothing was clear through the chemo brain that seemed to suppress my thoughts. I was frustrated that I had spent so long having decisions taken from me, and the one time I needed my team to help me make a decision, they shut me down.

For the first time since I had been diagnosed, I had to come to terms with the idea of death. I still thought the idea was ridiculous, but it seemed to loom over both options. If I stopped chemo and any cancer cells that hadn't been killed by chemo became active, it could be deadly. On the flip side, if I kept going with chemo and ended up with sepsis for a fourth time, that could be just as deadly.

I knew I couldn't make the decision alone. I *wanted* to stop chemo, but this wasn't about what I wanted. It was about choosing whatever option would keep me alive. Alone, I had no evidence to say that one option was better than the other.

That night, I remembered the livestreamed church service I had watched a few weeks prior. The pastor was talking about asking God for signs, and how it was Biblical and even important when making major decisions.

188

So, I prayed. At the time, prayer was still a struggle for me. I hadn't yet been taught that prayer was a conversation and a way to build a relationship with God. I just prayed when everyone else seemed to pray - when people told me to pray about something and at church.

I knew God already knew, but I laid it out for Him like I would for anyone else, mostly just to see if explaining it to Him would allow me to see things from a different angle.

No new angles. I decided to just go for it and hope for the best. I prayed for a sign. I wasn't specific, I just told God that if He could give me a sign to go one way or another, it would help me out. Oh, and if He could make it really, *really* clear since I might second guess myself.

The next day when I woke up, I got my first sign, even though I didn't quite catch it. Mouth sores had started to pop up all over the inside of my mouth. Not bad enough to stop me from eating, but bad enough to be noticed. That shouldn't have happened, but it was an unlikely possibility according to my doctors, so I dismissed it as a coincidence.

A few days later, I went back in for labs, just to see if my ANC had improved at all. Much to everyone's surprise, it had not improved at all, even though a few days prior it had been trending towards improvement.

Now, I was nervous. I still couldn't feel at peace with either decision. I couldn't tell if my mouth sores and ANC were really signs or if I had just been making things up in my head. I ended up in the shower that night, crying. I was so stressed, so scared to make the wrong decision and end up in a worse situation than I already was.

I ran my hands over the prickles of new hair that had grown so well over the last few months. I looked down at my hands, and they were covered in hair. Then, I really lost it. That wasn't supposed to happen at all. My team assured me that hair loss was not a side effect of this chemo protocol, so losing my hair was-

A sign. It was a sign. And once I recognized it for what it was, I realized the mouth sores and my ANC had been signs as well.

I asked for one, and God gave me three.

189

There was the peace I had needed. I immediately stopped crying and felt myself relax for the first time in days. Then, I cried for a different reason. I could stop chemo. I was done. No more nausea, no more stomach issues, no more being drugged so badly I couldn't remember things.

Though I had looked forward to it for so long, I hadn't ever let myself consider what it would feel like to truly recover. It was a cruel thing to think of when I thought I would be spending many more months battling the side effects of chemo. This time, when I started to feel better, and the side effects subsided, I would continue to feel better.

Even "better" now held a different meaning. Better wouldn't be relative to the worst I had ever felt, but I would truly feel better. I would continue to recover. I might even start to feel normal again.

I could be done. It was such a relief that all I did for so long was just thank God, not just for the signs, but because I could trust that I could stop chemo, and everything was going to be okay because that was the decision He needed me to make.

Mom hadn't come home from work yet that day, so I texted her asking if we could go on a ride when she got home. I just wanted to be outside, and I wanted to tell her before we told anyone else.

As I expected, she was fully supportive of my decision. I think it was a relief to her as well, knowing that I wouldn't have to go through such torment anymore. I could recover and try my best to move on with my life.

Of course, my decision was met with mixed opinions from the few people I felt the need to share it with. For the most part, I was met with support and joy that I wouldn't be suffering anymore. But some still felt the need to tell me that if it were them, they wouldn't take the chance.

I tried to accept their opinions with grace, but the people who held those opinions had never been through anything like a year of chemo. I don't know how they thought it was helpful to tell me they thought I was making the wrong decision when they hadn't been through what I had been through. Had I not gotten the signs I asked for, it would have made me second-guess my decision. It was hard to maintain my composure and listen to those people, but by the grace of God, I did.

When I told my team the following Monday, I instinctively expected pushback. I had no reason, based on experience, to expect them to go along with my decision. So, I came in ready for a fight. I asked to speak to the fellow first since I knew he was more reasonable. He expressed his support for my decision and said that he was happy I was making a decision that gave me peace after everything I had gone through. He wanted me to talk to the nurse practitioner and my oncologist as well just so they could hear my reasoning.

From them, I got little more than a confirmation. They told me that if my cancer did come back, they would have a plan and that I should come in the following week to ring the chemo bell to signify I was done with treatment. Curt, but at least they weren't questioning me like I expected.

January 13, 2020

The following week, I came to the infusion clinic to ring the bell. It was something I had envisioned every time I passed the golden bell hanging by the entrance to the clinic, but I had never let myself think about it too much. Not with how long I thought I would have been in chemo.

Em and Francisco were there to celebrate with me, as well as some members of Streetlight who had come in early for their shifts. They painted a sign with the designs from the Twenty One Pilots album, Blurryface.

Megan and some of the infusion nurses had come from the clinic, as well as some of my nurses from the unit I had my first few months of treatment in.

My entire team and all my nurses lined the hall of the infusion clinic leading up to the bell, singing a song they had used for their

191

patients. They had all signed a copy of "Oh, the Places You'll Go" with encouraging quotes.

It was a time of joyful tears. I couldn't imagine what it must have been like for the nurses, who had been through so much with their patients, to see one make it to ring the bell. I wondered if their tears were maybe a mix of emotions for their patients who hadn't made it to that point. It was a sobering thought, even in the midst of all the joy.

By that time, I was well past teary, but the second I touched the corded handle of the bell, I just started sobbing. That was it; ringing the bell would signify that I was done.

So, I rang it, and turned to Em, who stood beside me helping the Streeples to hold the sign in front of me, and cried on her shoulder.

There was clapping from the rooms in the infusion clinic, which filled me with emotions I could not understand. I knew there were mothers and families of children in those rooms, all waiting for the day their child would ring the bell, and yet they were clapping for me as I did. Some even popped out of their rooms to congratulate me, with tears in their own eyes. I couldn't imagine what it must have been like to hear the bell ringing when their own children were still fighting.

I had to wonder, no matter how much I tried to shove the thought aside, how many of those kids would make it to their own bellringing. While my cancer story was starting to reach the point of a good ending, I knew that wasn't the reality for many. As I glanced around again to see the looks on my nurses' faces, I saw my own thoughts mirrored in theirs.

They had lost patients, and they had cheered patients on as they left the infusion rooms behind. It was the reality of cancer. That reality hit me along with a new emotion: Survivor's Guilt.

But that emotion was swept away in the sea of every other emotion I was feeling. I was ecstatic, of course. For the first time in over a year, I could look at my future without the dread of another treatment looming over me.

192

Despite that, I did feel freedom. I could start recovering again. And when I did start feeling better, it wouldn't be ripped away by more chemo. I could recover, and I could stay that way. Deep down, as soon as I recognized the signs from God that I should stop chemo, I felt a peace that I would not have to worry about recurrence.

So, I knew that I could move forward in peace without worry. I was going to be okay. I had known it from the beginning, and now I was walking in it.

I was going to be okay.

Limitless

Part Two: Recovery

Limitless

Chapter 22

The one thing no one really prepares you for when it comes to having cancer is surviving cancer. Plenty of people have advice about surviving chemo, but once the echo of the bell ringing fades, everyone seems to go silent.

I had my entire life laid out for me at the beginning of chemo, but when it was over, no one was handing me a Survival Guide for what in the world I was supposed to do with my life.

Recover would seem to be the obvious answer here, but it's hard to focus on doing that when you barely leave the treatment center, and everyone bombards you with questions immediately after congratulating you.

"Congratulations! So, are you going back to school?"

"We're so proud of you! Have you found a job yet?"

"It must be such a relief! Are you going to finish your degree?"

"Now that that's over, what do you want to do with your life?"

It wasn't like I was suddenly free from the hospital's clutches. I had visits with my surgeon once a month and would now have PET scans every month to make sure the cancer did not come back. I would have those visits for the rest of my life. It wasn't like I was just free to move on with my life like nothing had happened.

I certainly wasn't free of what chemo did to my body. Even if I had any sense of a plan for what happened next in my life, I was still sick. I could walk, but my leg was still unreliable. Some days, I would sit on the porch and just stare at the sky for hours, a feeling of exhaustion and deep depression heavy in my chest. Withdrawals from the Ativan, I found out. My hands still shook, and my body still felt too heavy to carry. I still had to sleep for ten to twelve hours a night just to feel even remotely rested.

Much to my dismay, I still suffered from hot flashes that had been brought on by the birth control I had been put on to try to save my reproductive system.

Even in the cold winter months, I would be bundled under layers of jackets and blankets, only to suddenly start stripping off the layers as fast as I could.

If I were home alone, you could bet I would end up in front of the open freezer door, usually in as little clothing as possible, until the hot flash subsided. It never actually helped, but it was better than just sitting there waiting for my body to cool itself off.

I think the most bothersome thing chemo had left me with, or rather, taken from me, was my cognitive ability. Chemo brain did not magically disappear.

I did find one silver lining to this problem, though. Losing my memory of books and movies meant that I could eventually experience my favorite plot twists and epic twists and turns for a second time. I remember reading a book during college that had me so entranced that I actually threw the book across the room at the conclusion because of how game-changing the plot twist was. It became one of my favorite books, but I was sad to know I would never get to experience that heart-dropping moment of realization when the last line revealed a whole new implication to the story.

But a few years later, I decided to pick up the book again and quickly realized I had completely forgotten the reason I loved it in the first place. I got to experience the ending's twist all over again.

Okay, I know that doesn't make years of memory loss worth it by any means. But if I could find even one tiny positive in a negative situation, I was taking it. And yet, though I was still recovering from what seemed like one thing after another, the questions still came.

The more questions I had to answer with "I'm not sure what I'm going to do yet," "No, I haven't gone back to school yet," or any number of responses, the more I started to feel inadequate. As if I wasn't moving on and healing fast enough. Even my team, who should have known the difficulties of the time I now found myself in, would ask those questions as if expecting me to just up and move on. As if it were that simple.

I started to feel as if I was lazy, because it had been a few weeks and I hadn't gone back to school yet. I stopped paying attention to how my body felt, and how it still needed to recover, and started paying attention to everyone else's expected timeline for my life and recovery. I spiraled into this dangerous place until Mom snapped me out of it.

I had just survived a year of cancer treatments and a massive surgery. I almost died from sepsis three times. I had no obligation to follow the timelines of people who had no idea what I had gone through. My obligation was to myself, taking as much time as I needed to recover, physically as well as mentally, before I tried to be "normal" again. Whatever that looked like, if it were months or even years, it would be okay.

It became a constant battle in my mind. I would find peace that I was recovering and taking care of myself, and then someone would mention work or school. As time went on, their incredulous expressions when I said I had no plans, at that given time, to do anything aside from recover started to weigh on me.

But I was so brilliant; how could I not go back to school? I had my whole life ahead of me; why was I waiting? Didn't I *want* to go get another degree?

The questions started to translate a little differently in my head. Didn't I want to be a contributing member of society? Wasn't I unhappy just sitting at home doing nothing? Was it okay with me to let others take care of me when I was obviously perfectly capable of taking care of myself? Was I just going to waste my and everyone else's time by doing nothing?

Sure, it's not like anyone had meant any harm in those questions. Everyone had just assumed that part of my life was behind me and that the ambitious Rebecca they knew would be excited to get back to real life.

199

But they didn't realize that I *was* so ready to get back to real life. It just wasn't that simple. I had to constantly fight to feel like I was validated for taking my time. I had to stop comparing myself and basing my worth on the timelines of those who, quite simply, were not me.

The other thing no one prepared me for is which ditch I might be hitting mentally after surviving life-threatening situations. A lot of people recover in the tame middle ground. More power to them! A lot of people, though, are so affected by their experiences that they go a little overboard.

The first mental state that survivors seem to hit is the Dismay Ditch. When it comes to moving on, this group is an overly-cautious group. They see how easily their lives can be thrown into chaos, how easily their lives can be lost, and they do everything in their power to avoid adding more risk. They tend to play by the rules, and not take chances. This gives them peace of mind.

Then, there is the Daredevil Ditch. This group moves on by throwing caution to the wind. They see how easily their lives can be thrown into chaos and how easily their lives can be lost, and they want to live their lives to the absolute fullest before something else happens. The rule book goes out the window. They tend to think that, since tragedy can come out of nowhere for no good reason, they shouldn't worry about causing further risk to their lives, and they should experience everything they possibly can.

I, to no one's surprise, ended up in the Daredevil Ditch.

Suddenly, I wanted to climb mountains, hike perilous trails, swim with sharks, and wring every bit of thrill and experience out of life. I started a bucket list to keep track of everything I wanted to do. It quickly reached nearly 150 activities and destinations, including climbing the Seven High Points, visiting every continent, and hiking the Triple Crown, which is completing the Appalachian Trail, the Pacific Crest Trail, and the Continental Divide Trail.

Had I lost my mind? A little. I wasn't in denial about it. I just realized how quickly my life could be taken from me. And I don't mean death. I didn't die during chemo, but my life was taken. My life was no longer mine. I didn't have the freedom to do what I wanted to do. The things I had done, I had to fight to do them, sometimes facing consequences later. I was no longer content to let life pass me by. I wanted to experience everything on this planet and even beyond - commercial spaceflight, anyone? - has to offer.

Immediately, I started planning our first adventure. We were going white water rafting. We did some research and found a rafting company in North Georgia near Helen, a German town we had always wanted to visit.

Mom, trusting my trip planning skills a bit too much, handed me her credit card and said the two words she now thinks twice before saying to me, "Book it."

What she did not realize was that this rafting company offered two different rafting day trip options. One was a beginner trip with class I, II, and III rapids. The second was for beginners and experienced rafters alike, crossing class III, IV, and V rapids.

It was with no hesitation that I booked the second trip option.

January 14, 2020

Before I could get to my much-needed adrenaline rush vacation, planned for my birthday in June, I had to face a new type of torment the hospital would inflict on me: PET Scans.

I would be getting scans for the rest of my life, but for the first five years post-treatment, it would be much more intensive. PET scans were how my team would monitor my body to ensure that, if my cancer was going to recur, they could catch it early. With Ewing's Sarcoma, the risk for recurrence is high. Since my first chemo protocol didn't work, and I stopped my second within a few treatments, I was considered at high risk for recurrence.

For the first six months, I would go in for scans every month. For a year after that, every three months. From then until year five after treatment, every six months. After year five, I would need scans every year for the rest of my life.

201

It didn't seem so bad, nothing really compared to how often I was in the hospital for cancer treatment. My team even thought it would make my life easier to coordinate seeing my surgeon on the days I had scans so I could get it all done in one trip.

It seemed like a good plan until it actually happened.

For a PET scan, I would need to fast, which became problem number one. It wasn't like a blood test, where we could schedule it early, get it done in an hour, and then go out for brunch. It was a whole ordeal.

They scheduled my scan for 9:00 a.m., which wasn't the worst thing in the world. Except, they wanted me in the clinic first for blood work before going to another center on campus for scans. So, I had to be in the clinic by 8:00 a.m. for blood work and to have my port accessed, and then rush over to the other center for scans at 9:00 a.m.

However, a PET scan was not a quick in-and-out kind of situation. After having a radioactive tracer injected through my port, I had to wait for an hour and a half while the tracer made its way through my body.

While this tracer worked its way through my system, I would be left to sit in a tiny curtained-off room until I could go for my scans.

After waking up at 6:00 a.m. to get ready, it would be around 10:30 a.m., and I still had not eaten. The scans themselves took all of half an hour, landing us at 11:00 a.m. when I left the center where I got scans. My team expected me to head straight back to the clinic where I could get my port de-accessed and find out my results.

Absolutely not. Heads were going to roll if I did not get food in my stomach. I didn't care if they were waiting on me; I was making a detour to Culver's to get a Double Bacon Deluxe and Onion Rings.

Even after getting something to eat, I was still snarky. I was exhausted and stressed out from the unknown process of scans, and we were headed towards my least favorite place on the planet. Crossing the intersection where my brain divided the fun side of town from the hospital side of town set me into an instant anxiety spiral.

I wasn't worried about the results of the scans. I had a kind of faith I didn't even know existed that cancer was no longer something I had to worry about. But, crossing that intersection, my subconscious took over. The hospital was a place where I experienced so much pain and torment. My subconscious didn't know that treatment was done and that I was just in for scan results. It just sent me into an instant state of panic that I could not get control of.

Since I still "wasn't allowed" to walk, I had to use crutches, to my further annoyance. It didn't take long for the smells around the hospital to have me near heaving, and by the time I got to the clinic floor, I was a nauseous, anxious, agitated, exhausted mess. Luckily for everyone, Megan was there to get me calm again in a way only she seemed to be able to do.

I should have known to expect the unexpected, but I hadn't caught on to that yet. What I expected was for my team to come in and tell me my scans were clear without any unnecessary drama. I already wanted to limit my interaction with them as much as I could, so I hoped they would make it short, sweet, and simple.

What I got instead was theatrics that I did not have the patience for. When my team filed into my room, asking me if I was ready to know the results of my scans as if they were asking if I wanted to know that day's winning lottery number, my eye started twitching.

The smiley, teasing tone, as if what they saw on my scans was something worth creating more anticipation over, had me leveling them with a stare and a raised eyebrow. I was not in the mood to play. I knew what the results were because I knew God was in control of it. But for anyone who would have had the usual "Scanxiety," that tone would have created more tension and uncertainty than was necessary. Maybe it was cute to the little kids, but I couldn't imagine that being tolerable to parents who just wanted to know if their child was still healthy or not.

On top of that, I still had to go see my surgeon that day, and my capacity for ridiculousness was waning, quickly. When they told me my scans were clear, my response was something along the lines of an "I knew it." I was out the door minutes later.

Luckily, appointments with my surgeon were much less animated. Once I finally did get into a room to see him after the usual hour wait time, it was usually a glance at the X-rays taken upon my arrival, a quick look at the progress with my leg, a reminder of my limitations, and that was that.

Of course, he didn't see the full extent of the progress I had made, just what I knew he wanted to see. A little more bending, full extension at my knee, little things like that.

When the nurse practitioner on my oncology team called to coordinate my next round of scans and my next appointment with Ortho, I explained that we would need to set up the appointments at least a week apart. She insisted it would be easier for me to just get them all done in one day. I *insisted* back that she was not the one who had to handle all the appointments in one day. The fact that I would explain that concept to her for the next six months proved to me she did not have the capacity to empathize with what I was going through.

January 19, 2020

Over the next six months, I would live through the vicious cycle of scans and recovery. I could not seem to fully recover mentally. Though I seemed to get my anxiety and frustration from scans under control, it seemed like within a few days of getting some peace, I would have an appointment, either for scans or with my surgeon.

On the flip side, my physical recovery, without chemo destroying my body every few weeks, became like a game. The game started with something Doug and I had long awaited: The Medieval Festival.

We had gone, dragging Mom along, when I was in high school, and it had been a blast. But this time, Doug wanted to dress up and really get involved with all the fun.

We cautioned him that with my leg, I likely wouldn't be able to walk around all day. The swelling alone would be a problem if that pain did stay at bay. He pondered that for a day or two and came back with the game changing idea. He would just build a cart to pull me around on.

It seems simple enough, but you have to know Doug. He wasn't talking about a little wagon painted to look the part. A week later, he came home with wagon wheels. Three feet tall, wooden wagon wheels. His idea was to build a cart from the ground up, literally, starting with the wheels.

The ideas only went farther and farther. He wanted to make an apothecary to go on the back and weapons to hang around the sides. It would be covered in case it got too hot. Oh, and we couldn't forget the insulated cooler compartment under the seat for drinks.

In a few weeks, a seat had been built and upholstered above the wheels, covered by a high ceiling. It could be towed by hand, like a hand-drawn rickshaw. Once it was done, Doug would pull it up and down the driveway each night to build his endurance.

After that came the weapons. Handmade, of course, by Doug in his shop. Swords of all styles, daggers, and a mace, all hanging from the sides of the wagon. He made me a dagger, the hilt made from a deer antler he found in the woods near his house, that I could wear with my costume.

By the time we got to the festival, even the jesters at the front gate couldn't come up with something to say to insult us. They just stared, jaws dropped, at the scene.

We all had our cloaks on, daggers at our sides. I was seated on the wagon being pulled behind Doug, and Mom was trailing beside us. We had at least ten handmade weapons hanging on the sides of the wagon, also decorated with various antlers and bones. We were quite the sight to behold, and Doug was proud to tell everyone how he built this wagon from the ground up.

We got plenty of attention the entire day. I met an orc in full costume who held his sword up to my throat for a picture and plague doctors who gave me a vial of "blood." Mom, much to her dismay, met a special effects makeup artist on stilts, his long bony fingers, and smiling skull face sent her running to hide behind me.

When it came time for the parade around the festival grounds, we even got invited to join in with them. Doug was ecstatic, nearly dancing through the whole parade. That weekend was the first time I would experience what it was like to be adaptive instead of disabled. I learned that to do the things I wanted to do, it wasn't going to be about either being able to do it or not. It was about finding ways, some much more creative than others, to do what I wanted despite my new limitations.

Chapter 23

February 11, 2020

For most people, being told that they would never walk without assistance might be something they come to acceptance with. For me, it was a challenge. One that I had already overcome.

But the thrill of walking again, completely independently, after being told I wouldn't, kindled a need to keep doing *more.* If I could walk, what else could I do?

A month after finishing chemo, my dad planned a trip out to North Carolina for us to see some family we hadn't visited in a while. As a born and raised Florida girl, I had always been enamored with the mountains, so it didn't take long for my aunt and uncle to take us driving on the Blue Ridge Parkway. Every chance we got, I would ask to stop to take in the scenery, especially as we moved higher up in the mountains.

It was at one of these stops that we found ourselves on a "short" hike to reach a waterfall. I'm not sure whose idea it originally was, but I have no doubt I was the instigator who pushed us all to the trail. I didn't even think of my leg as we started down the nearly two-mile trail that led to a few waterfalls. I had been walking with so much ease over the past few weeks that it didn't register in my mind as any reason to not take on the hike.

I also forgot that "hiking" in North Carolina did not even share a line in the dictionary with "hiking" in Florida. Walking through flat even trails in Florida was nothing compared to the climbing and winding paths I now faced. Somehow, doubt was nowhere in my mind as I traversed the ascents and descents over rock bridges and boulder stairs.

The trail ended where the main waterfall flowed into a river at the bottom of a boardwalk of steps. It was a steep descent down the stairs, but the reward of staring up at the falls had me overlooking the burn in my thighs from all the stairs.

Climbing back up was a different story. When the excitement of the trail had been had, I had to get back up the stairs and back on the trail. Most of the two miles back to the truck were uphill, ending only after we had climbed a steep incline to the parking lot.

I hadn't done that much in over a year. Though spontaneous hiking wasn't out of the norm for me, it was something that had been put on hold during chemo. Yet somehow, I had hiked a trail nearly five miles in the mountains just five months after surgery. Aside from the trembling muscles in my legs and burning in my lungs, it felt so *normal*.

I didn't quite process how much of a feat it was until later that evening. I was overwhelmed with emotions at the idea that I could finally do something without being weighed down by cancer. I didn't have to worry about being sick or having side effects get in my way. I could do something on a whim without being held back.

April 9, 2020

After a few more months of the vicious scan cycle, I had come to find somewhat of a peace with it. I adjusted to the routine and prepared accordingly. To never interrupt the peace, I ended up never telling my surgeon about my ability to walk - and now, hike. I figured, needing scans for the rest of my life, he would find out eventually.

In my comfort, I had not expected the routine with my surgeon to be broken. Instead of checking out the X-rays and the movement of my leg and sending me on my way, he surprised me. At eight months post-op, he wanted me to try to walk.

I panicked. I had about five seconds to form a plan since I had hobbled in on crutches, expecting the usual. I wasn't supposed to even attempt walking for a year, so I thought I had more time to plan out how I would reveal the good news.

In those five seconds, my sense of humor found a foothold. I decided to play the game he decided to play that day. So, as he explained that he and his resident would be beside me as I tried to take my first steps without my crutches, I schooled my face into a nervous, hesitant smile. I stood up and made a big deal of pushing my weight onto my left leg, standing and adjusting as if it were a foreign feeling.

And then I walked across the room.

It was a good thing my surgeon was sitting because it looked like he had gone pale enough to pass out. I just shrugged my shoulders, bringing my hands up as I gave him an "Well?" expression.

The resident started giggling to himself as my surgeon finally pulled his jaw off the floor. His only response as I walked circles around the room was to comment that I must have been walking for months.

I expected a celebratory response. After all, not only had his surgery been successful, but I had surpassed the odds and did what they hadn't expected me to do. That should have made it extra successful.

Apparently, he did not share that sentiment. I had to sit through a lecture about how reckless I had been in trying to walk before he cleared me to walk and how careful I should be about walking, even then.

209

But wasn't the whole point of saving my leg so that I could use it again? Why in the world would they save my leg, only for me to not be able to use it?

I was confused. It made no sense to me, and even worse was the fact that I was being chastised for what I figured should have been great news.

I figured he was just being overly cautious. Maybe he was the mother hen type. That, or a pessimist. So, I zoned out his lecture and nodded whenever it seemed like he expected a nod. He was saying something about the possibility of the repairs only lasting a certain amount of time, but I couldn't fathom why they would put me through such an intense surgery and recovery to save my leg if the repairs wouldn't last. I wasn't about to let negativity cloud the joy of being able to walk, so I put it out of my head completely.

Chemo had taken so much from me for a year, and I was ready to start living again. I wasn't going to waste the opportunity after having to fight for it for so long.

May 18, 2020

It wasn't long after that eye-opening appointment that I decided I wanted to take my recovery to another level. Em and Francisco wanted to make an addition to a video they had filmed of me during chemo, and we had tossed around ideas trying to find what would be the best setting.

We decided on something that had been a staple in my life before being diagnosed, something that would show my recovery coming full circle.

I was going to climb a lighthouse, and what better one to attempt climbing than the St. Augustine Lighthouse.

After climbing nearly 30 lighthouses with Mom prior to chemo, this seemed like the perfect way to show that my recovery was coming full circle. Plus, I was way overdue for one of those little adrenaline rushes I would get after leaning over the railing of the gallery.

It had been a goal of mine since before surgery to climb lighthouses again, but it became somewhat of an unspoken goal. It felt so naive to even think I would be able to do something with that kind of impact on my leg. If I wouldn't even be able to walk, then how could I even dream of getting up a lighthouse again.

But once I had taken steps, even shaky, unsteady ones, I felt less and less naive. If I could walk against all odds, then certainly climbing a lighthouse wouldn't be unheard of. So, I let myself get excited about the possibility, and when we decided to climb a lighthouse for the video, I could hardly wait for the day we planned to make the attempt.

Standing in front of one of the tallest lighthouses in Florida nearly ten months after surgery, though, was a new set of emotions. I had absolutely no doubt I would make it to the top, but to lay eyes upon a goal, a very tall goal with a lot of steps, after being told how impossible it would be, I felt doubt try to creep its way in.

Of course, that didn't last long. Doctors did not get to decide where my limits were, and their own doubt wasn't going to stop me from pushing past every limit that had been set on me.

I was the first to start the climb since everyone wanted me to be the first to reach the top. Once I started, I never wanted to stop. Sure, my legs were on fire, and my lungs felt as if they could not get enough air, but my soul felt like it had been set free.

After surgery, I felt as if I could quantify my limits. It wasn't just about never walking again. It was never running, never climbing, never hiking, never jumping, never dancing, and never doing a thousand other things. Each of those limits had an individual hold on me, weighing me down with sorrow. But with every step I took towards the top of the tower, I shook off the grief that had been holding me.

By the time I had reached the top, grinning wildly, I was convinced I had no limits. If I did, I wanted to find them and then find ways to break through them just as I had the ones that had been attached to me. I wanted to keep feeling that rush. Adrenaline, sure.

But I wanted to keep feeling the rush of doing what seemed impossible, the thrill of life being lived to its fullest.

While Francisco got his camera set up, I leaned over the edge of the railing and stared at the scenery around me. I even found the channel where Mom and I had taken the sailboat tour, where I promised myself I would climb a lighthouse again. It hadn't even been a year since I made the promise to myself, and by the grace of God, I could call it fulfilled.

June 3, 2020

Living life to the fullest also meant making sure my surgeon knew exactly what kind of life I had been living. If I had to go deal with him every month, I wasn't going to hold back on letting him know what I had been up to.

I had been growing closer to God in the months since stopping chemo, and I had started to realize just how much of a gift God was giving me. I had survived cancer and had overcome the limits put on me. It was a gift I wasn't going to waste. It also wasn't a gift I was going to hide. I had started to see just what God had brought me through, and I wasn't going to be shy about showing it.

We settled into an agree-to-disagree kind of rhythm. I would tell him about what I had been up to, or planned to be up to, he would remind me that he thought it was all dangerous and a terrible idea, I would dismiss him, he would dismiss me, and I would be on my way.

It wasn't exactly the provider-patient relationship one would hope for when they were stuck seeing their provider for the rest of their life, but I wasn't going to hide the things I had been up to from him. I wasn't going to pretend as I had the first few months after surgery. I certainly was not going to be ashamed of surviving and not playing the victim. Even if it meant our appointments were tense, I would not cower.

It was at one of these tense appointments where it came up that, according to my X-rays, the bones had fused together so well it was hard to tell where my own bone had been cut and where the allograft had started. This was nearly unheard of in any surgery that used a bone allograft. I knew it had to be God giving me another gift, another bit of proof that what He decided for me was greater than what any doctor could dictate over me.

Limitless

Chapter 24

June 8, 2020

The time had come, six months after finishing chemo, for us to embark on my long-awaited adventure: white water rafting. I had been counting down the days, and it was finally time. I had bags packed and ready to go by the front door the night before we left.

More bags, as Mom would point out, than her. Overpacking was usual for me. But this time, it was justified. I had a clothes bag, a makeup bag, a GoPro bag, and a camera bag. Mom didn't think I needed a suitcase for a three-day trip, so it ended up being four smaller bags. Really, I think that was poor planning on her part.

I could barely sit still throughout the six-hour drive to Clayton, Georgia. It wasn't just from excitement. After six months, my energy slowly returned, and compared to sleeping all the time, I was bouncing off the walls.

We got to Clayton late that evening, and even managed to get a hotel room with a hot tub. Score! Though, I figured that luxury was best enjoyed after a long day of getting beaten up by the rapids. Since we planned to spend the day after the rafting trip in Helen, Georgia, a German town, we had a German themed birthday celebration in the hotel that night.

Usually, since we took trips for birthdays, we didn't bother with gifts. The trip itself was a gift enough. But Mom went all out that year with just about everything I had mentioned in the past year that I had wanted. Thanks to chemo, I didn't even remember saying I wanted half of it until she handed it to me.

Looking on the bright side of chemo brain, it did make for great birthday surprises!

The next morning, after eating a light breakfast in a cute diner, we found our way to the Southeastern Expeditions rafting headquarters. We were the ultimate tourists, with our matching dry-fit water shirts, water-proof phone cases, and my Go-Pro.

I never actually told Mom we wouldn't be going on the beginner's rafting trip. So when they called for the beginners rafting trip, and she started to follow that crowd to their guide, her look as I tugged her back towards me could have been summed up in the phrase, "What have you done?!"

We always had a habit of doing something new every trip we took, rarely doing the same thing twice to experience everything we could. Following that logic, I figured if we were only going to go white water rafting once, we should get the full experience. She didn't disagree, but she still thought I had lost my mind.

We boarded the bus that took the intermediate rafters down to the river and held on for dear life as the bus crept down the steep, winding mountainside road. I was expecting a good adrenaline rush from the trip but didn't expect it to start before we even got to the water. We couldn't even see the road from our window, just the drop-offs down the side of the mountain. I thought it was awesome, while Mom refused to even glance out the window.

We made it down to the starting point and followed our guide to a raft. It was just us, our guide, and a woman who had rafted the beginner's trip the day before.

The look I caught from Mom when she realized our raft was all, basically, beginners was sidesplitting. We had a very experienced guide, so we would be fine. She wasn't buying it.

Luckily, the trip started off on very easy rapids, and we picked up on the basics quickly. Our guide taught us the different commands

216

he would shout - what side would paddle, what direction to paddle, how many times - and all we had to do was do what he said and trust that he knew what he was doing. My favorite command was when we maneuvered our raft into the position to go over a rapid, and all that was left for us to do was throw ourselves to the center of the raft and hold on for dear life as we went over.

I was giggling wildly over every one of the smaller rapids and was so glad I had chosen the intermediate trip. The small rapids were fun, but the bigger rapids? I couldn't wait to get near those.

During one of the lulls on the river between rapids, the woman rafting with us asked, very sweetly, to address the elephant in the raft, the giant knee to ankle scar on my leg. We had given our guide a very brief warning so he was aware, but hadn't given many details.

I gave a quick rundown of the story, earning the typical "Are you crazy?" looks when I got to the part where I told them my leg was reconstructed with metal and cadaver bone. When I told them we had never been rafting before, the look shifted into one mixed with admiration. It's not often, it seems, that they see the daredevil type of cancer survivors.

Soon after, we approached our first higher class rapid. From our angle, it looked more like a small waterfall. Our guide gave us a choice to go around it on an easier route or to go over it. When no one seemed to want to decide, I decided for us. Over the waterfall we would go.

Once we got the raft in a good position, our guide shouted to dive to the center and hold on until we got over the falls. Part of the way down, our raft seemed to drop out from under us, and all I could feel was water rushing up around me. This, of course, only made my giggles of absolute, unfiltered joy even louder.

As the trip went on, my joy did not falter in the least. Each rapid sent thrills through me, keeping me on a steady adrenaline high. Each time I started to mellow, we found ourselves doing something to up the ante each time.

One such activity included cliff jumping. Into rapids. From a 30-foot cliff.

Somehow, I managed to convince Mom to jump with me. Maybe it was because she knew I absolutely would not do it alone and would regret it for the rest of my life, but we climbed our way to the edge of the cliff, hand in hand.

There was, however, a minor miscommunication between us. I thought we were jumping on the one, two, three, *go,* countdown. Mom thought we were jumping on the one, two, *three,* countdown.

When she went on three, she dragged me down with her. Which was great for me because it felt like being pushed. I didn't have the chance to hesitate.

Another thing about jumping into rivers that we Floridians did not account for was the current. We knew we were jumping into fast-moving rapids, but we didn't quite realize we would go under and be 50 feet downstream by the time we had resurfaced.

I still haven't found a way to rival that boost of terror fueled adrenaline yet. Trust me, I've been looking.

By the time I got back to the bank, I was beaming. Mom, not so much, as she was just laughing at how I must have lost it for thinking that was fun.

Further down, we stopped for a quick packed lunch provided by the tour. Before we settled on a rock sitting right over the river, we had the option to take a short hike to a waterfall. *Hike,* of course, meant trekking over the ledge of earth ten feet above the river, crawling under fallen trees, and scrambling up rocks and boulders. My definition of a good time, Mom's definition of "for the birds."

But walking up to the waterfall took our breath away as much as hitting the chilly water after jumping from the cliff. It was the tallest waterfall I ever remember seeing, falling from the mountainside ledges and onto uneven levels of boulders before hitting the ground in front of us.

And the *sound.* We had been surrounded by a constant rush and bubble of the river water, but this was a roar. It was consuming. Not just the sound, but the full sensory experience. Our skin was misted with the crisp water from the waterfall; the sun was just enough to help warm us after being doused in the rapids. The air itself, though warm, was crisp and clear. Refreshing, like no hospital-filtered air could ever be. It was like the first real lungful of air I had in over a year, and I was devouring it.

Sitting on the sun-warmed tabletop of the rock overlooking the river, with the waterfall rushing at our backs, rivaled any restaurant experience we ever had. Just as it had stepping out onto the gallery of the St. Augustine lighthouse, my soul felt free and overflowing with life. Not simply an existence, being moved through the minutes and hours and days and years. Real, untamed life.

And we were nowhere near done with the adventure. It wasn't long before we found ourselves being swept over another short waterfall, this time going down on the side of the raft. And when all the rafts on the tour had paused on the bank downstream from the rapid, one of the guides called for a raft to volunteer.

My raft had not learned from our previous experiences together and didn't think to stop me before I volunteered for whatever task was in front of us.

A task to paddle back upstream to the basin under the curved drop-off of the rapid. For what reason, I did not know, nor did I care. We paddled like mad against the rushing current until our guide called for us to stop paddling.

But we were not swept back downstream. Instead, our raft was now caught in the right spot under the rapid to be tossed and bucked around, spinning in circles. We stayed in the spin of the rapid, the raft eventually being pulled under us so much that I only felt it with my foot directly under us. When the raft came back up, our guide called for us to paddle ourselves out of the spin, and back to the bank.

Apparently, I had been near screaming in joy. It was the coolest, craziest, wildest experience I had ever had, and it just kept getting better.

After a few more hours of braving rapids, our raft mellowed out into a calm section of the river, and we could take a breather. If we could draw in a breath upon turning to the back of the raft to see two mountains towering over either side of the river behind us. The sun had already softened into an evening glow behind clouds,

219

throwing rays of sunshine across the sky, and the river opened into a glass-smooth expanse all around us.

There was not a sign of civilization around us. No power lines, no cars, no cell towers. Now listen, I am all for a hot shower and a strong Wi-Fi connection, but to sit in the dead center of nature, relatively untouched and wild, I felt as expansive as the scene that lay before me.

Before we could relax back onto the bus for the return trip, we had to drag our rafts back up the incline to the parking lot. After six hours of trying to stay in the raft, we were exhausted. Instead of having a team of six to carry our raft, we had three exhausted women and our guide, who ended up taking most of the weight of the raft.

Even Mom, who had been subjected to rafting down waterfalls, hiking, and jumping off a cliff, was overjoyed at the experience we had. Knowing her, she was probably more overjoyed at how I couldn't stop smiling every time I recalled any part of our trip.

Chapter 25

July 15, 2020

I lived fueled off the high of the rafting trip for weeks. I couldn't even be bothered by appointments with my oncology team or surgeon. The fellow I had come to like above the rest of my oncology team was the only one that seemed to appreciate the experience I had and how important it was to my recovery, and so he listened to the stories of the trip with his full attention.

He was the only one on any of my teams who saw past the cancer diagnosis and connected on a human level. He always asked what we had been up to and always took the time to listen to our stories of whatever adventures we had been on before sharing some of his own life with us. It made a world of difference in being able to trust him, and it made the stress of scans a little more tolerable.

During one of my appointments, I passed the hall where I had spent time in the oncology unit. I glanced at the doors to see if I could see any of my nurses through the small glass windows, and I saw Zack. I hadn't seen him in almost a year, and to my joy, he recognized me. When I ran up, he gave me a huge hug, and we got to catch up on how life had been going. I got to tell him that I had been in remission for almost a year. It was rare to get to tell someone who cared for me during chemo that I had been in remission. Once I started receiving outpatient treatments, I almost never saw my inpatient nurses. Getting to celebrate that with him was the highlight of my entire week.

Though I was still always left with weeks of trauma to work through from being forced back into the environments that caused that sort of trauma in the first place, not feeling like another patient being herded to and fro made the difference between nearly having a mental breakdown after a day of appointments, and just needing to decompress.

This appointment, though, brought some good news I had been waiting for. I was finally able to get my port removed. I had been trying to get it removed since I stopped chemo. I didn't feel it was necessary to keep. God had led me to the decision to stop chemo and had given me such peace about my future I knew beyond any doubt I would not need the infernal device again.

That wasn't the only good news, though. Since I had gone six months with no evidence of relapse, I was now only required to do scans every three months. That was a real treat since it seemed to take me a few weeks after each scan to calm down from the reminders of the traumas I endured.

But that big thing that happened in 2020 that turned all of our lives upside down - yep, I'm talking about the COVID-19 pandemic, which will be referred to as the plague from here on out - had caused all elective surgeries to be canceled until further notice.

I had stopped going to get my port accessed for scans months prior, opting for IVs to be placed instead. My fear of needles had disappeared, considering the previous year had turned me into a veritable pincushion. I hadn't even gone in for the suggested monthly port flushes to ensure it stayed accessible.

I was done and over it. So, when I was told by the fellow that elective surgeries were now back open and I could get my port removed, I was ecstatic.

I was also incredibly thankful that it has been the fellow to come with this news. Had it been any other member of my team, I know they would have discouraged removing my port so soon after treatment in case my cancer had ended up relapsing. But the fellow understood my choices, as well as my autonomy to make them, better than the rest of my team. Unlike them, he didn't fight me when I told him to book the surgery as soon as possible.

In my excitement, my curiosity got the best of me. I wondered, from what I knew about how the port was attached to a major blood vessel, how they were able to get it in there.

Pro Tip: Do not, under any circumstances, look up port placement videos.

Why? Because I did, and I regretted it.

See, it wasn't that bad, watching them cut a small line into the skin of some poor soul's chest. What was bad was watching the surgeon use their fingers to separate the skin from the muscle, creating a pocket in which they would insert the port.

That's about as far as I made it. Take it from me, don't do it.

Less than a month later, I was in pre-op with the surgeon who would be taking my port out. Having been through three surgeries already - my tumor biopsy, port placement, and tumor removal surgery - I was pretty set on what to expect. My only concern was that I had been wearing a bracelet that, once tied on, did not come off unless it was broken. It was from someone who meant a lot to me at the time, and I was not thrilled about the idea of needing to cut the bracelet off for such a minor procedure.

Oh, and I wanted to keep my port. I had spent so much time with Santana over the past year and a half, and though I was ready to have the thing removed from my chest, I wasn't quite ready to part with it. That, of course, was no big deal.

When I explained it to the surgeon, she assured me it was no big deal and that she would make sure they took measures for me to keep the bracelet on safely during my port removal. It was a blessed relief since, from my experiences with my usual teams, I had expected a fight.

Seeing different providers and having them show me the kind of respect they did really put things in perspective for me. I realized that constantly expecting a fight from any doctor I encountered wasn't normal. My oncology and surgical teams had me in a constant state of fight-or-flight mode, and I wasn't one to run from a fight.

Every other doctor I met, though, left me with a sense of calm. It was completely unnatural and a little unnerving at first, but I started to see what conversations with doctors should be like.

By the time I was being called back into the dreaded pre-op area, I had been lulled into a false sense of security. I thought I had avoided the fight, but it just came from a different person. Instead of coming from the surgeon, it was the pre-op nurses who seemed bent on making my life miserable.

Immediately upon being called back to the pre-op area, the nurse first noticed the two earrings I had left in from my recent piercing. They were still far from being fully healed, so my plan was to remove them right before surgery and put them back in immediately after.

I didn't have time to explain that, though, before she was telling me that she would get pliers and cut them out if I would not remove them.

As if I would consent to let this woman near my still-healing piercings with pliers. On top of my barely controlled anxiety about being in the hospital, even for an outpatient procedure, this nurse put me on edge.

Before I could even recover from her threat, she turned her attention to the bracelet, demanding I take it off. I told her I had already spoken to the surgeon, and she wasn't having it. Well, neither was I. We went back and forth until she gave up and passed me off to another nurse.

Rebecca: 1

Pre-Op Nurses: 0

By this time, I had been pushed to the point where my patience, already barely existent, held on by a shred of will. Will that was quickly dwindling.

The new nurse decided to fight me on the bracelet situation. I fought back. She insisted, with a smirk, that the surgeon would require me to take it off. I simply told her that we would have to wait and see.

We paused our fight there to only start a new one, this time over the IV placement. I told her what I had discovered the hard way:

224

I had small veins, best accessed in the bend of my arm with a pediatric needle. She didn't take kindly to me, "telling her how to do her job" and insisted she find a vein in my hand.

I refused to let her place an IV. There was no way I was letting that hothead near my hand with a needle. If she wanted to try the bend of my arm, she was welcome to. She insisted that anesthesiology would want it in my hand, and that was a hill she would die on.

Until the anesthesiologist came in and told her that if I didn't want an IV in my hand because I knew it wouldn't work well, she could place it in my arm, and they would place one in my hand once I had been put out.

Rebecca: 2

Pre-Op Nurses: 0

After failing to get a vein for nearly ten minutes, she had to call in a phlebotomist. I thought he and I would get along much better. Apparently, everyone on staff that day was insufferable.

My only requirement to him was that, once he found a vein, he count me down to when he would go for it. I could deal well with needles, not surprises.

When he decided to go for the vein on "2", I nearly punched him in the throat. I had been fighting tooth and nail against the ridiculous treatment I was being subjected to, and I was in no mood.

I had almost lost it completely when the nurse decided to continue the fight about the bracelet. She narrowly missed being given a piece of my mind by my surgeon coming in. The surgeon cheerily informed me that her plan was to wrap my bracelet in foam and gauze so that I could keep it on. I merely smiled sweetly over to the nurse as I thanked the surgeon, earning a very peeved look.

Rebecca: 3

Pre-Op Nurses: 0

As planned, I took out my earrings and handed them to Mom as she left the pre-op area, and doctors filled the small space. Thankfully, my dealing with the nurses was done, but my anxiety was on its way to the max, considering what I had dealt with in my previous surgery.

But instead of traumatizing me beyond all recognition, to my surprise, the entire team introduced themselves to me, telling me who they were and what they would be doing.

The anesthesiologist noticed my anxiety and offered "the good stuff" to help me calm down. He assured me that he was a heavy-handed bartender, but their communication so far had already eased my mind. More than that, I had never actually seen the inside of an operating room. Even without my glasses, I was curious about getting a glimpse of where I had spent so much time.

I declined the offer to be put out so soon and got to listen in on their pre-op preparations. After being taken into the OR, they gave me a chance to look around the best I could without my glasses. Honestly, it was pretty fascinating. It had been brighter than I expected, with equipment and machines seeming to line every inch of the walls. That was most of what I could make out through my terrible vision, but I was satisfied. They transferred me to the table in the center of the room, mercifully lined with a heated blanket so I didn't have to lay on the freezing cold metal and started the process I had never been able to witness.

I was impressed by the amount of communication I heard as they prepared. They checked and double checked everything. Most surprisingly, when they were ready, they even asked if I was ready before putting me out. I was excited to not have what felt like a parasite of a device in my chest, so I wasn't lying when I said I was ready.

Since I had always been put out to some degree in the pre-op area, I had never experienced the actual anesthetic being pushed into my IV. Before even half of the white liquid had been pushed from the syringe, I started to feel its effects. It felt like ice-cold syrup was being pushed through the vein in my arm, and I felt its path all the way through my upper arm. My brain seemed to turn liquid starting in the front of my skull, and before it had gone all the way to the back, I was out.

No sooner than I had gone under, than I was coming back up from the sea of black that I had fallen under. It didn't take me as long to start to open my eyes and move around.

Unlike my last surgery, where I felt as if I had to fight my way back to consciousness, I simply *woke up* this time. I was in no pain, and Mom was already sitting beside me.

My first sensation, naturally, was that I was hungry. So ravenously hungry. Some of the first words out of my mouth were that I wanted to go to Chuy's, a Tex-Mex restaurant I liked, as soon as we left.

My surgeon stopped by for a few seconds to hand over my port in a small jar. My nerves grated as I looked at it for the first time, remembering that video of the port placement I made the grave mistake of watching, but the feeling passed as I realized I was going to keep this little souvenir of my troubles. Maybe I'm a little warped - who wouldn't be, after all I had been through? - but I was thrilled.

Luckily for me, as soon as I had eaten a few crackers and drank some water, I was detached from my IVs and rolled to the doors towards our car.

As promised, we got to Chuy's soon after, and much to Mom's surprise, I ate an entire Chuychanga. And yes, I held it down.

My chest ached for a few days after, but it didn't last nearly as long as it had when the port was placed.

To this day, I have kept Sanatana in a small jar in my closet. It is one of the only physical reminders - aside from scars - that I have of my time in chemo. It's like a trophy.

August 5, 2020

Over the months, as my energy and mental capacity returned, I constantly debated what I wanted to do with my life. I knew that it would include school, but I felt as if going back to school at Florida Southern was an opportunity that had long since passed. I never had the opportunity to formally put a hold on my scholarships, and the idea of fighting to get them all reinstated, reapply, and move back in just seemed too much.

Plus, though I loved marine biology, my experiences had changed me. I wanted to pursue something where I could help people, particularly cancer survivors.

Many people suggested I go to medical school.

Absolutely not. I had gotten glimpses of how much time med students and doctors had to dedicate to their careers. I wanted to do something that would still let me do things like white water rafting on a regular basis. Plus, cancer had given me enough stress for a few lifetimes, I didn't need more stress from med school.

So instead of med school, many suggested nursing. That got shot down just as fast. I had witnessed all that nurses dealt with. The blood, the puke, the bodily fluids. Nope. Not for me.

My nurses had told me before that they had no idea how cancer survivors dealt with the horrors of chemo. I would simply reply that I didn't know how they dealt with the things they dealt with from us. We all agreed that I couldn't handle what they went through and that they couldn't handle what I went through.

Radiography though, that was a viable option. It was relatively hands-off, but still had direct interaction with patients. I reflected on how, through the stress and frustration of scans, the techs who walked with me through the process of scans helped encourage me.

Through getting scans every month, I got to know the techs who walked me through the process of my PET scans. They were able to see past the cancer diagnosis and treated me like any other person when they came in. We talked about books, movies, and weekend adventures and eventually ended up on a first-name basis.

Despite the fasting and early mornings, I did start to look forward to seeing the techs each month. We formed a connection, and they made the process of going through scans a little less miserable. I wanted to be able to do that for someone else.

Since I had gotten my associate's degree before graduating from high school, I was only one class away from being able to enter the Radiography program at one of the local colleges.

That was the good news. The bad? It was Anatomy and Physiology, a notoriously difficult class as it was, and I was recovering from chemo brain.

But I knew few limits, so I went for it. I applied, got accepted, and got set up for an online only section of the class to start at the end of the summer break.

I was ecstatic. I had found a purpose and a goal to work toward. Even better, I knew I would be able to help people once I had gone through the two-year Radiography program.

In a testament to my optimism, it took a few months before A&P finally broke me. In comparison to how truly messed up my head was during chemo, I felt as if my brain was working just fine.

Until I was in the middle of midterms and couldn't quite remember…well, anything. Taking an online class that was usually meant to be an in-person, hands-on class was already a challenge. Doing it when my brain was working at approximately 42% of its usual capacity was playing a new game in expert mode after skipping the tutorial.

But I was determined. I spent my time on YouTube, going through the CrashCourse A&P playlist, trying desperately to figure out what in the world was going on.

I was scraping by, managing fairly well with a high B, and I fought with beating myself up over it. In high school, I always stayed near the top of my class. I was the classic overachiever, never settling for anything less than an A, even while juggling college classes, high school classes, band, and indoor drumline. I made it work. So how was it that all I had to focus on was one single class, and I couldn't keep an A?

I had to constantly remind myself that I was doing this after a year of chemo and drugs that knocked me out for days at a time. Considering that, I thought I was doing pretty well.

I managed to pull my grade up to an A, just barely, and I was thrilled with that progress. I had a few assignments left before finals, and as long as I could manage well on those last few tasks, I would finish the class with an A. I even calculated just how high I would need to score on each to keep the A.

But on the third to last assignment before finals, something had come over me. I was lethargic, and all I wanted to do was sleep. I barely got an A.

229

Limitless

By the last assignment before finals, I had barely passed and could barely keep my eyes open. I was back at a B and questioning how I was supposed to pass finals.

Just a few days before finals, I found myself in bed, barely able to keep myself awake and barely able to breathe. After eleven months of dodging the wretched virus that had taken over the world, I had caught the plague.

November 20, 2020

I denied it for days, while the symptoms seemed more like a really bad cold. I took as much Vitamin C and Alka Seltzer as was safe and hoped for the best. It wasn't until my ability to breathe had started to dwindle that I broke down, calling my college to see if it would be possible to take my finals another time.

Unfortunately, I would not be able to take them again until finals week the following semester, but that was the least of my problems. It seemed that the minute I had admitted to having the plague, my body gave in. Within a few days, I couldn't sit up without losing my ability to breathe. If I got up, I would gasp for air, taking in shallow breaths that barely kept me conscious until I could lay back down. I had Mom make me the broth from chicken soup, and I would drink it through a straw from a water bottle. It was the only thing I could hold down.

During the worst of the virus, Mom nearly begged me to go to the hospital. But trauma or not, I had heard the stories of plague patients going into the hospital. There was no way I was going to go to the hospital and be separated from Mom for however long it took. I knew how fragile my will to live could get when it came to that place. I wasn't about to go to the hospital and give up what little fight I had left.

I stayed home, keeping to myself as much as I could, but Mom wasn't about to leave me alone. She lay beside me, sometimes just letting me sleep and sometimes begging me to stop being so

230

stubborn. At one point, I used what little breath I could manage to tell her that if this was going to be what killed me, it could kill me at home, where I was comfortable, not in the hospital, isolated, scared, and alone.

Whether she liked it or not, she seemed to follow that logic. Never mind that, in my own mind, I still thought dying was the most ridiculous idea. I had survived cancer, and I was not about to get taken out by a virus.

At times when I fought to draw a breath, I would just pray. I wasn't asking for anything. I was just telling God that I didn't plan on dying anytime soon. Over and over, I would repeat that cancer couldn't kill me, and neither would the plague. After three days of gasping for air and living off broth, my breathing started to deepen again. Day by day, my breaths became less shallow, and I could speak full sentences again. It wasn't long before I was up and moving, showering and eating and watching movies.

It took nearly a month before I could consider myself somewhat recovered. My gauge for recovery had been singing in the car. Just after recovering from the plague, I couldn't keep up with some songs that I had been able to before, ones that required longer stretches between taking breaths. But by the time Christmas came, I was singing Christmas music in my car like nothing had ever happened.

Just like cancer, I had put the plague behind me. Another thing that I had survived, through the grace and power of God alone. By the time I had gone in for my next set of scans, I had all but forgotten the fourth near-death experience of my life.

My body, though, had not. The images of my lungs on the CT results had thrown my team into a full-blown - and unnecessary - panic. One that would lead to traumatic experiences that made chemo look like child's play.

Limitless

Chapter 26

January 13, 2021

Going to appointments for my scan results had been a heavy burden on me for quite a few months. All the hassle to get results I already knew would be clear became less and less worth it. It became more and more evidence of God's healing work in my life, but all the stress and anxiety for something I already knew seemed redundant.

Going in for my appointment for results this time, I was already on edge, as I usually was. I wanted to get in and get out. I was fairly unfazed when they sent a nurse in for an extra blood test, thinking they just needed to recheck the results of my usual labs. I was so unfazed to the point where I was halfway out of my chair when my team came in, asking them in a tone that clearly meant I knew the answer if my scans were, in fact, clear again. Their initial panicked looks only confused me because I knew deep in my spirit that my cancer had not relapsed.

So, what in the world could be causing the panic? I was sure I wouldn't wait long to find out.

Apparently, having the plague a few months prior had left my lungs looking a bit…messy. I believe the description they used was "ground glass." They expressed that tumor recurrence for Ewing's did not present that way, not explaining their panic.

I immediately went into no-big-deal mode. I explained that I had dealt with a rough case of the plague about two months prior, so it would make sense for my lungs to look so bad.

To them, though, that answer wasn't good enough. Before they even came to me with the results, they had gotten the results, decided to run extra labs, and connected some dots that I had forgotten about.

Right after I had stopped chemo the previous year, I noticed some hardened tissue under the skin on the underside of my lower legs. After an ultrasound, it was determined that it had been caused by trauma from surgery and recovery.

Now, it seemed to be more than the result of trauma because my team explained that because I had this hardened tissue and my lungs looked so bad on the scans, they took the liberty of ordering a blood test that would indicate whether I might have had an autoimmune disease.

And just my luck, the blood tests indicated that there was a possibility I did have an autoimmune disease. Hence the panic.

Having that thrown at me within the span of a few minutes, I tried to process what that meant for me. But for the life of me, I couldn't imagine how a little hardened tissue in my legs and abnormal lung scans could be related. Especially when the lung issues could likely be explained.

By the time I started to question the logic there, I was informed that my team connected with the immunology team at my hospital and that I would be contacted for an evaluation.

Wait, woah, stop. Rewind and freeze.

Dealing with new doctors was going to be a no-go. I could barely deal with the ones I already had without having panic attacks; I was not about to try to deal with new ones trying to diagnose me with something based on evidence I could not make sense of.

When I tried to ask them to explain their logic, I was met with resistance. I could ask immunology when I got there.

So, I tried a different route. I told them that since they couldn't explain their logic to me, I thought it would be best to wait until my next set of scans in a few months to see if my lungs would clear up.

They told me no. Not that they didn't suggest doing that for whatever reason. Not that I could, but it was a bad idea. Simply, no. I was going to see immunology. They would call me soon.

Oh, and before I left, I would need to be tested for the plague. Also, with no explanation.

By the time the nurse came in with the test, I had cornered myself at the far end of the exam room, putting the exam table between myself and the door. My nurse noticed that something was very off. I had never tried to get myself as far from the door as possible, and I had never reached a point where I stopped being able to communicate.

What I couldn't communicate was that I had shut down. Not only was I being told that my choice didn't matter to my team when it came to this new mystery diagnosis that no one could explain to me, but I was being asked to take another test, also for reasons that couldn't be explained. I had the plague two months before and had not been symptomatic when I came in for scans. I saw no point in going through another test after multiple scans, multiple blood draws, and multiple appointments.

Without good reason, enough was enough. I had spent a year subjecting my body to the whims of whatever my team came up with to help me. In the end, my chemo only served to almost kill me when it gave me sepsis three times. How they couldn't understand why I may want at least a little say in what was done to me, I couldn't comprehend. But in my panic about all that was happening, I couldn't express those thoughts.

My nurse didn't need the explanation. My hesitation was enough for her to go tell my team that I was not consenting to the test. She seemed to be the only one with a proper concept of consent.

My nurse practitioner came back into my room to tell me that I would not be leaving without the test. I was in my corner, trying to hold back tears. One person could only have so much forced on them. When asked to explain, to give me a good reason for why I should allow them to demand I do anything they want, I was basically given the "because we said so" speech.

235

But I was broken down. I had resisted their demands as much as the remnants of my emotional strength could allow. When my nurse came back in with the test, though she did not voice it, I saw in the look she gave me that she was not happy to follow the demands of my team.

She got it. Consent because I had been worn down to tears was not consent at all.

It took me a week to recover emotionally from that appointment. I constantly questioned what happened. I questioned the logic of why I was being sent, against my will, to immunology, and I questioned how my team, who I was supposed to trust, could be so forceful and back me against the literal and metaphoric wall as they had.

By the time I had stopped being a ball of anxiety and panic about the appointment, as Mom and I were trying to enjoy lunch together, immunology called. I was sent straight back into a full-blown anxiety attack. I stopped being able to draw a full breath the minute I ended the call, and an appointment for the following week was set up. I couldn't finish my lunch. I was in tears almost immediately.

Why couldn't they just leave me alone and let me heal?

I had rolled around the idea of something in my legs and something in my lungs causing an autoimmune disease and could never make sense of it.

February 4, 2021

I spent the whole week leading up to the appointment, panicking day and night, barely able to eat, and struggling for a good night's sleep. I had moments where the anxiety got so out of hand that I found myself stuck without being able to take any of the long breaths I had used to calm myself for so many months. Instead, I just gasped, spiraling into panic at the sensation of not getting enough air into my lungs. I was drowning without any water to drown in.

236

As far as I knew, I did not have the power to stop this immunology appointment from happening. On the day of the appointment, I dressed in an outfit that covered every inch of skin I could cover. Skinny jeans that could not be rolled up and a sweater that covered my torso and arms almost completely. It wasn't a conscious choice. It was instinct to protect myself in any way I could. If I couldn't avoid the interaction entirely, then I would make it so that I controlled how much access this new specialist would have to me.

I was having an ongoing, low-level panic attack from the minute we got into the car. I was snappy and agitated. I felt like I was being led to another death sentence. The fear I had wasn't because I was afraid of being diagnosed with something new. I still couldn't make sense of the combination of "symptoms" they used to force me into this mess in the first place. I was afraid of what would come of it.

The last time I needed to see a new doctor, I was diagnosed with cancer. That led to me walking through some of the most traumatic and painful experiences I had lived through. Not just physically but emotionally. Things I had heard from my teams had cut me deep. Deep down, I was trying to protect myself from more pain and more trauma, even if I was confident nothing was wrong with me. I didn't have to have anything wrong with me for whoever this new doctor was to find a way to hurt me.

I tried my best not to snap at the nurse who was taking my vitals before taking me to an exam room. I had a soft spot for nurses and knew she was only doing her job. She had no hand in the decisions that forced me to be in that office.

I was shaking like a leaf by the time I had been left in the exam room. And the walls. When people say it feels like the walls are closing in on them, it is not a truly accurate description.

The walls did seem to close in on me, but the room never got any smaller. That didn't stop the walls from coming in tighter and tighter. Even though, logically, they had stayed right where they were when I first got there, they seemed to be closer to crushing me by the second.

237

It was like an optical illusion. The walls never moved, but they also knew no limits in how close they seemed to get to me before the immunologist and his assistant opened the door.

The air seemed to flow back into the room at the open door. And the door, the promise of escape, was like dangling a steak in front of a starving dog.

Despite the fact that I was a free woman of decision-making age that very well could have walked out of the ever-shrinking room, I couldn't. Not that I physically couldn't walk through the door. I was being held there by my mind. My team told me I had to be there so no force in the world could will my legs to move me toward the door. I was trapped by the invisible bonds of thinking, and I had no control over what happened to me.

Due to the pandemic taking over everything around us, we had to wear masks in the appointment. Which was no big deal until I couldn't breathe. Anytime I tried to pull my mask down to get a single, full breath of cold air, the doctor would harshly demand I pull my mask back up. Panic attack or not, it wouldn't be helped by this man.

We spent nearly an hour going over my medical history. Y'know, the medical history that was in the chart right in front of this man's face. It wasn't as if he would read the chart and ask to confirm if everything was correct. He insisted on making me try to remember every aspect of my medical history for the last 20 years. He had the gall to condescend to me if I happened to miss a detail of my history.

That is if he even bothered to acknowledge me. Most of the time, he spoke directly to Mom. She, being nearly as frustrated as I was, didn't respond to him or even make eye contact. She just looked at me while I responded to try to give him the hint to speak to me.

If my nerves were shot upon entering the building, they didn't even exist once the medical history part of the appointment had been concluded. Unfortunately, that was the easy part of the ordeal.

He decided it was time to start the physical exam, and with no warning or explanation, he grabbed my arm, shoved up the sleeve of my sweater, and started prodding and pinching my arm. His assistant had the decency to tell me that he needed to feel the soft tissue in my arms to rule out certain symptoms.

Before I knew it, I was being hauled off the exam table. Apparently, he also needed to feel my back, neck, shoulders, arms, and torso. This time, the poking and prodding didn't come with any explanations. I was just told to stand and move at their will.

I felt my mind start to shut down in a way it only did when I dissociated. I started to lose control of any movement, which this doctor saw as the need to push me around more since I wasn't moving exactly when and how he specified.

As my plan of wearing a sweater had failed, so did my plan of wearing skinny jeans. He handed me a pair of baggy hospital shorts and told me to change into them. When I expressed that I wasn't comfortable doing that, he demanded that he needed to see and feel the hardened tissue in my legs, so I had no choice.

I ended up standing, both the doctor and assistant kneeling at my legs, pressing and squeezing for what seemed entirely too long. Then, for some reason, back to my arms and neck. Then back to my legs. I had hands on me constantly. When I tried to move away, long since passed my capacity for being touched, he grabbed my wrist and held me in place.

At that point, I fully dissociated. I felt nothing and could respond to nothing. I just moved around at their whim, unable to even express that something was wrong.

I ended up back on the exam table, on my back, with my head and wrist being held down. They were poking around in my mouth, their focus so intent on finding something that apparently was not there that they couldn't even recognize that I had frozen. It seemed as if I were watching what was going on from outside my own body, but I couldn't think or process what was going on.

It was only when they brought in an ultrasound cart that I managed to get across to Mom that I needed a minute. They seemed perplexed that I had interrupted their much too thorough exam to waste their precious time by needing a break, but they left the room.

I was seconds from breaking down and only got the words "Get me out of here," out before reaching the point of hyperventilation. Momma Bear had been summoned, though. My mom, a woman not much bigger than me, had turned into Shaquille O'Neal. Her presence nearly filled the room as she opened the door, me close behind, to let the two doctors know we would be leaving.

Not surprisingly, at that point, the doctor actually tried to step into the room and close the door, shutting us in. Mom nearly shoved him out of the way on her way out the door, towing me along behind her. By the time we had gotten to the car, my mental breakdown had hit me in full. I started to shake, rocking myself back and forth in the front seat as I cried. It didn't take long for me to start gasping for breath I couldn't draw. I didn't even want Mom to wait to comfort me; I was begging her to get me out of the parking lot and to get me home.

When I hadn't stopped crying after getting nearly back to our house, Mom called my therapist and got me an appointment just a bit later that afternoon, declaring that it was an emergency. I had reached a point I had never yet come to in terms of sheer panic.

I had gotten myself under enough control to take a drive to a small park near our house for the telehealth appointment. I couldn't stomach driving back to the side of town, an hour away, where my therapist's office was, right in the midst of the hospitals.

She listened while I recounted what had happened, undoubtedly noting the way I couldn't keep my hands still and how I still sniffled and wiped tears from my face, even hours later. I noted how her own face seemed to go from the schooled calm I had always known from her to an expression of pain and empathy and even a little horror.

She didn't even flinch when I ended the story by telling her that I was never going to see another doctor again. Even if I was dying, I refused to see another doctor.

She only uttered one sentence when I finished. "Rebecca, I am so, so very sorry."

After she gave me some time to compose myself, she started to gently ask questions to get a better sense of what had happened. Most memorably, we talked about why, if I expressed that I wasn't comfortable going to immunology in the first place, I had gone.

I told her that my team gave me no choice. They had called immunology before ever talking to me, and when I asked if we could just monitor my scans for a few more months, I was told no.

Her face shifted at that. There was frustration and annoyance there as she explained what I had never heard before. I, as the patient, should have been given the right to be in control of the decisions made. That if I didn't want to see immunology, I had the right to say no. And that my team's inability to let me say no was a right they should not have taken from me.

We worked through a lot in that session, though she warned me we had a lot ahead of us to work through. The biggest thing we accomplished at that point was forming a new boundary. When I went in for scans, I would only see the fellow who had never breached my trust. I would not see or interact with any other member of my oncology team, and I made it clear that if they tried to see me, I would walk out with no explanation.

Speaking of my next scan, I would be facing that torment again in three months. It was something I had started to dread and started to wish that it would only happen every six months. When I expressed it to my therapist, she reminded me that I was in control of that decision. If I felt comfortable getting scans every six months instead of every three, she would help me navigate that conversation.

We crafted a plan at the end of our session. She wanted me to send a message to my team to let them know the changes I was making to my care plan. I would no longer come in for scans every three months but every six, and when I did, I would only be seeing the fellow.

She would speak to them separately about her own thoughts about my care, but she wanted me to practice advocating for myself. I shook as I typed in my message to them. I was so sure I would be met with resistance and demands to do things their way instead of what I requested.

By the time I sent the draft to my therapist and then to my team, I was a wreck. My imagination had gone wild about how they were going to make my life miserable. Luckily for me, my therapist made sure I had not been met with resistance after all I had been through. It was a relief to know I would no longer be dealing with the members of my team who had contributed to, as well as caused their own fair share of my trauma. I still was adamant that I wouldn't be able to handle seeing any doctor, but I trusted my therapist.

It was during our next session that I found out her master plan to help me heal from the things that had happened to me. We got to the root of what was bothering me, which was the fact that I had never been able to have any control over what happened to me during the time that I had cancer and even in some situations before. I felt as if I couldn't be an active contributor to my care and that I was forced to go through with whatever a doctor told me.

Step one in my therapist's, admittedly genius, plan was to write out an introduction to any doctor I might see. That was simple enough. We talked through my expectations, my rights as a patient, my fears, and my needs, until we came up with a well-crafted intro.

Hi, my name is Rebecca. Before we start, there are things you need to know about me. Because of my medical history with cancer, I have experienced a lot of trauma and am very anxious to be here. In order for us to work together, here is what I need from you: I need you to stay on your side of the room and not come toward me without warning me. Before you make any movements or make any move to touch me, you need to tell me, and I need you to explain why you are doing what you're doing. I need you to be aware of my body language and check in with me. I need you to communicate everything you do and plan to do, and we will discuss all decisions and make them together. If you make any sudden movements, I will be out the door before you blink.

The last part I threw in to have at least a little humor. I was trying.

I felt good about coming up with that. It made me feel that if I was to see another doctor anytime soon, I would be able to communicate my needs and be a little more in control of the encounter. Deep down, I still didn't plan on needing to use it, but I didn't tell my therapist that.

But I didn't need to. She knew and told me about the second step in her master plan.

I was going to practice using that spiel with a real doctor.

You know, the literal last thing I would have ever wanted to do. But again, I trusted my therapist, and she said she would be there the entire time, so I knew I was safe.

By the time I drove up to the hospital for this mock appointment a week later, I was shaking just pulling into the parking garage. I had started to expect that reaction at that point, but I couldn't stop it from happening. I just had to ride it out.

When I finished chemo, I stopped taking the anti-depressants. I hated the way they made me feel, like I couldn't access the feelings I would expect to have. I figured that since my interactions with my doctors would be few and far between, I wouldn't need them.

I was glad I wasn't on them. If I was going to face what had become my greatest fear, I wanted to face it in its fullness. I wanted to fix the problem, not hide it behind a mask of artificial comfort.

My therapist met me in the lobby and explained that throughout this session, she would randomly ask me to rate my anxiety on a scale of one to ten.

I told her it was a seven. By the time we had gotten into the exam room, it was an eight.

She reminded me of the plan while we waited. She was bringing in a resident to help me practice advocating for myself in a real environment. I could stop at any time just by telling her, and she would not leave me alone during the entire mock appointment.

My anxiety was a five. When the doctor came in, it was an eight again. She was young and seemed so sweet, but my body was reacting despite my conscious attempt to use logic to navigate the situation.

That's the thing about PTSD. Logically, I knew I was safe and that my therapist had likely picked the least intimidating resident she could find. But after all the trauma I had been through, no amount of

243

logic could convince my brain not to scream at me to run for my life.

But as we talked through what I realized to be like a real-life annual appointment, I started to calm down. When she asked about what medications I was on, she related to how much she hated one of the ones I had been having a hard time with. Much to my shock, she was allowing herself to be a real human being who could relate to me and my struggles. It helped me trust her, even though I had just met her.

My anxiety was a five.

She asked me if it would be okay for her to start a physical exam. I was, surprisingly. The fact that she had asked without even making a move toward me eased my mind.

My anxiety was seven.

She heeded my request to explain everything she was doing, so even though she was in my personal bubble, I knew that everything she was doing had a purpose. Her communication filled the awkward silence.

My anxiety was a five.

My therapist called for us to take a break and talk through what had been going on so far. The doctor, bless her, admitted that the whole time she had been freaking out just as much as I had.

Apparently, they never teach doctors things like bedside manner, much less bedside manner with a nervous wreck of a patient. I was bewildered. For doctors whose entire job was to interact with patients, I couldn't fathom that they weren't taught how to do that.

My anxiety had dropped to a four.

Immediately upon my anxiety going so low, my therapist needed us to up the ante. We would pick up where we left off, right where I would need to lay back for the doctor to start feeling around my stomach.

Back up to a six.

Her communication had become paramount to keeping me from losing it. The last time I had been laying back on a table at immunology…well, let's just say I was too close to reliving that to not be anxious. But more than just telling me what she was about to do, this doctor was asking my permission to do anything. I was almost confused when she asked if I would be okay with her lifting my shirt enough to get to my stomach. No doctor had ever asked that before.

To my surprise, my anxiety was down to a five.

She started to explain, to my curiosity's delight, which organs she was feeling for and why. It wasn't just that I loved to understand how things worked, but I could be assured that everything she was doing was purposeful and organized.

Somehow, I was now at a four.

I was absolutely baffled at that point. It took all of half an hour for me to go from wanting to sprint out of the hospital to being, dare I say, comfortable. Even if I had tried, I wouldn't have been very anxious.

Funny how, when I simply got the communication and respect that I needed, I was perfectly fine. Who would have thought?

The other situation my therapist wanted to go over, both for my sake and for the doctor, was the bad news scenario. For me, this one would be easy. I had so much faith that I would be okay after what I experienced that bad news simply couldn't touch me. But as we continued the conversation, the doctor's respect for my responses and my autonomy to decide a course of action for myself, even in a hypothetical situation, I experienced what it should have been like to go through these hard conversations.

When I got diagnosed, the conversation was more, *this is how it is, and this is what you're going to do about it.*

In this conversation, it was more, *this is what's going on. Here are your options; let's talk about them.*

More to my ever-growing happiness, the doctor actually asked me how she could improve her delivery of bad news. While my own anxiety about that part of the conversation was about a three, she said hers had been a seven. By the time we talked through everything we had been through together, I felt confident that if I needed to see a doctor, I could handle the situation. But more than that, I felt a renewed hope in doctors. The doctor who had helped me had been so

Limitless

eager to learn how to help and how to improve, and I knew surely, she wouldn't be the only one.

February 27, 2021

Though I had felt a little better knowing that I was no longer convinced I would never see a doctor again, I was still filled with fear. We had never ruled out an autoimmune disease, and I simply was not willing to continue with that process. If I did have an autoimmune disease, I was content to let it go undiagnosed. I knew that even after the diagnosis, what I would have to go through with specialists and medications was too much.

In my ever-spiraling terror, I did what I had only just recently learned to do. I called on Jesus.

During the livestream worship service I had been watching for over a year, I started praying. I let God have all of it. I told Him that I couldn't bear to try to walk through it. Another diagnosis, more doctors, I just couldn't do it. I knew I needed Him to intervene. I had heard stories, mostly from the Bible, but a few from people I knew, of miraculous, unexplainable healings.

I had heard from certain pastors over the years that that kind of stuff just didn't happen anymore. But I heard from my livestream that it was possible, and I was conflicted; I wasn't familiar enough with the Bible to justify either position. But in my desperation, I just decided to believe it. There was no hurt in trying.

That's where the pleading and crying started. I begged God, asking that if He would just heal me, I wouldn't have to be tormented any longer. If I could just know I was okay, no autoimmune diseases, none of it, I wouldn't have to go back. I heard God called the Great Physician, so I asked Him to be my Great Physician.

After my cries had turned into wordless, tearful mumbles for help, I heard words that changed my life. Words that couldn't be heard by ears but felt more within the deepest parts of my existence. "Your faith has healed you."

246

And that is where the real tears began. I had never heard the voice of the Lord before. How I knew, I couldn't even explain. I just knew. And I knew at that moment that whatever was in my lungs had cleared. Whatever lurked in my body was gone. If there was a single cancer cell left in my body, it was no longer.

I had been set free.

Four years later, during a round of blood work to determine why I had been so severely fatigued, I was told that they had run the same antibody test that originally indicated I may have had an autoimmune disease. And wouldn't you know it, it was negative.

Limitless

Chapter 27

March 2, 2021

During the next few years, I would come to discover what a normal life for a woman in her twenties should be.

I would also come to discover that the phrase "New Normal" made me irrationally and psychotically angry. In relation to chemo, the connotation of new normal was annoyingly negative. Everyone who seemed to think it was wise to tell me what they thought my new normal would look like apparently thought I'd spend the rest of my life in pain, fighting the effects of chemo on my body, and not walking. As if I'd always be haunted by cancer. As if I would never escape it, no matter how many years, or even decades, it had been.

Yeah, no thanks.

I'm not saying life after cancer was easy-peasy. Far from. But life after cancer was a dichotomy of triumphs and failures, high points and low points, good days and bad days. I just tend to choose to focus on the positives, even in the face of the negatives.

In total contrast to how everyone seemed to think my life would change after cancer, things actually seemed to be getting better. After a year, I had been feeling so much healthier than I ever had. Sure, that could be attributed to experiencing lows beyond belief, but not having cancer in my body seemed to change everything.

I started focusing on my health. I knew one of my worst habits was being dehydrated all the time, so I worked on making sure I drank enough water. Instead of eating whatever I could stomach to survive, as I had during chemo, I became more conscious of what I ate. When I realized I would get winded walking down the driveway, I started walking every day and eventually included yoga to build up some of the strength I lost.

After a year of chemo, even yoga kicked my butt. But I was bouncing back fast. When I got to the point where I could make it through an hour of yoga without wanting to collapse, I started working on exercises to really build strength.

The problem was that I hated doing workouts by myself. When I walked, I could listen to music. When I did yoga, I could relax. But pushups and crunches were hardly something I wanted to do by myself. I needed external motivation.

The idea of a weightlifting gym intimidated me. I definitely wasn't at a place where I would feel comfortable trying to do workouts that way.

Then I had an idea. An awful idea. A wonderful, awful idea.

Yes, just like the Grinch.

What if I took up kickboxing?!

I just wanted to be able to work out in a way that was fun and didn't feel like working out. Bonus points that with kickboxing, I could learn a little self-defense, too. So, without telling Mom, I booked a tour of a local kickboxing gym to see if my idea was worth pursuing.

Truthfully, I had been interested in martial arts since I was a kid. Mom made the mistake of letting me watch *The Karate Kid*, and I was hooked. The interest had been dormant for years, but it was resurfacing with my newfound need to find my limits and walk - or jog, or kick - right past them.

Admittedly, I was a little nervous. Ever since my surgery, I had generally been treated as somewhat fragile. The attitude towards my ability to do things had been more of an avoidance attitude than an

250

adaptive one, but I wasn't one to avoid things. I wanted to know if there was a way for me to do what I wanted to with adaptations for my safety.

I was pleasantly surprised that when I let the owner of the gym know my situation, she was happy to find ways to help me adapt. I got all the info I could and then prepared myself to let Mom in on my plans.

Throughout my entire life, she had taught me to make informed decisions. Anytime I wanted to do something, she asked plenty of questions until I started learning how to answer those questions before she asked. Complete with relevant research, recent studies, and evidence.

You think I'm kidding? When I wanted to join marching band in high school, I hit her with research that showed the benefits to academics, brain health, and physical health, along with the possibility of leadership training and opportunities for scholarships.

Naturally, when I told her I wanted to take kickboxing classes, she was hesitant, to say the least. But I quickly explained that the classes I had been interested in were classes that required no contact with other people, just with a heavy bag or sparring pads. The owner had already given me ideas about how to adapt techniques to have less impact on my leg, as well as the possibility of wearing shin guards to protect my leg even further.

By the time I had finished, she couldn't have formed much of an argument against my idea. She asked to visit the gym with me, which I was totally fine with. In fact, I was offered a free class to see if it was something I liked, so I figured that would be the perfect time for her to lay eyes on what I would be involved in.

The first class had my brain absolutely boggled. I already struggle with my lefts and rights, and half the time, I held up my hands to see which one made an "L" shape for the left. I couldn't do that in boxing gloves.

To Mom's amusement, we weren't using the terms left and right but rather jab and cross, and it seemed like the second I got that down, we would switch stances, and I would just get confused.

I assumed being in band may have given me an advantage in coordination, but I was wrong, because I felt, and surely looked, like a three legged deer on ice.

Learning the different kickboxing techniques was a fun challenge, though, and I wanted to keep doing it to get the hang of it. The workout portion of the class, though, was punishing. They had enough variations on pushups to last weeks, and I did more squats than I had done in the rest of my life combined, it seemed. And don't even get me started on the ab workout.

Five straight minutes of various sit-ups, planks, leg lifts, and crunches. By the time we got done, I was exhausted, but for some reason, I felt amazing.

I had completed a kickboxing class with adaptations, and even though it was a struggle and a half, I felt accomplished. I did something that most people would have doubted I could ever do, and I felt *able.*

It was the first time I would experience adaptive athletics. I hadn't even heard of the concept until then, and I latched onto the idea. I was tired of feeling breakable, like I couldn't at least try to do the things I wanted to do.

To add to my feeling of being *able,* I had been looking forward to a new event I was going to try out: The Bolt Run 5k, presented by the Tampa Bay Lightning. Mostly, I signed up because of my newfound love of hockey. But it was also a new challenge.

The last and only 5k I had attempted was for a fundraiser in high school, and I hated every minute of it. I was not a runner, and I tried everything to get out of the event. I almost succeeded had my band director not made it mandatory. So, in retaliation, I walked every inch from start to finish.

But things were different now.

Not only was I choosing to participate, but I was also given a new perspective on life. I wasn't supposed to be walking, but I was. Why not try running? Even if just to say that I could.

Was it the smartest idea to attempt my first 5k after a few weeks of kickboxing classes while I was still sore? Probably not. But

Limitless

if the white water rafting experience had shown anything, it's that I'm known for daring ideas, not smart ideas.

The 5k was virtual, so I decided to complete it down our street, which almost perfectly measured out to a mile and a half. Going down and back, with maybe a few extra steps, I could easily complete the 5k. Mom volunteered to go with me for moral support if she could ride her bike beside me. As we set out, I knew for sure I wasn't going to be doing much running, but I wanted to jog what little bit I could.

Given that I hadn't trained at all for a 5k, running or walking, the only major goal I set was to finish within an hour. During the race, though, I set little goals on the street, like pushing myself to run until I got to the next mailbox before taking a break to walk. I'd spy a tree line up ahead and tell myself that I would start running when I got there.

About thirty minutes into the race, I realized I was almost back home and changed my original goal. I wanted to see if I could complete the race within 50 minutes. My legs had been on fire from all the running and speed walking so far, but I wanted to see if I could surpass the expectations I had set for myself.

I started running again. This time, I just ran until my legs threatened to stop, and then I walked just long enough to recover. I kept checking my tracking app, and I was going to cut it close. I ran until my whole body burned with my lungs and slowed to a walk as the tracking app signaled I had finished the 5k.

In 49 minutes, 50 seconds.

If I had been able to jump in celebration, I would have, but I had to settle for a very enthusiastic skip before I crawled into my chair on the front porch.

By the time I felt like I had the energy to climb out of the chair and into the house, I started feeling the consequences of my actions. My legs were locked up, and my left knee was angry with my antics. But no amount of stiffness and muscle soreness could diminish the excitement I had. I couldn't stop smiling, couldn't stop giggling to myself. I had done something else that I was never expected to do. I realized that had God not intervened, I would have had no business even thinking of doing a 5k.

Since growing in my relationship with God, I realized that the only explanation for why I had been able to do any of what I had been doing was because of Him. I had been constantly reminded by my surgeon that no one he had seen who had a similar surgery to mine was ever able to walk by themselves again, and I was hit with the full weight of that statement. Not only had I walked, but I had been running.

I started to thank God and celebrate with Him. After all, from what I had learned about Him, He would want to celebrate with His daughter as any father would.

As I shared how I felt and how grateful I was, I heard the voice I had come to cherish so much tell me, "I'm so proud of you! When you are with me, you are limitless."

I didn't know it was possible to beam any brighter, but somehow, I did.

May 14, 2021

Over the next few weeks, I slowly got stronger and more coordinated. I had started to grasp the concept of the different kickboxing techniques. I started to think more about jabs and crosses than lefts and rights.

Kicking was a bit more difficult. Front kicks were no big deal, but roundhouse kicks and sidekicks threw me off. If I tried to kick with my left leg, everything was fine. I would kick softly so I wouldn't damage anything, and I could pivot on my right foot just fine. When I had to pivot on my left foot and kick with my right, though, things got difficult.

Twisting was not good for my knee. Not that I can blame it since it was being held together by half of a live tendon and half of a grafted dead tendon, but still. Instead of being able to pivot into a kick, I had to adapt and step into the kick instead.

I wasn't too upset about that. At least I was able to kick at all, though I kept trying every once in a while to kick with the normal technique on both sides.

My core had started to get insanely strong over those few months as well. At first, I couldn't even do a single sit-up and could barely go through the entire five-minute round of ab workouts without stopping for breaks. But within a few weeks, I had progressed to doing sit-ups and could make it through a whole round of abs without a break.

Granted, I would collapse onto the floor, gasping for air almost immediately when the timer went off, but hey, progress is progress.

I had gotten the hang of the demands of the kickboxing class within a few months and had started getting a little too comfortable with the usual routine of the classes. Until I walked in one evening for class and saw a new coach in our kickboxing area.

He introduced himself as Darren, telling me he was the new coach for evening classes. He was over a foot taller than me, middle-aged, and had obviously been working out much longer than I had. He also told me that he could be as involved or uninvolved as I wanted him to be.

For better or for worse, I told him that he could be involved and that I wanted to be pushed. Immediately, I found myself being pushed to go a little faster during the workouts, doing more reps during each round. Or, if it seemed as if something had been a little too easy for me, Darren suggested a variation that was just a little more difficult.

During the kickboxing rounds, he pushed me to hit harder and faster. He even brought a pool noodle to bop me in the head if I started to drop my hands from guarding my face.

Of course, since I had just gotten to the point of being able to keep up with the ab workout, he found ways to make it just hard enough that I had to really push myself to keep up again.

What had I gotten myself into?

After a few classes, I realized I had gotten myself into a whole new level of fun. My competitive spirit kicked in every time I came in for class. I knew I couldn't outdo Darren in any of the workouts, but that didn't stop me from trying. Even during abs, I would try to keep up with the speed he went through the workout.

During one evening class, when it had been just me, he decided to throw another curve ball at me. For the past few months of kickboxing, I had been training on a heavy bag. A stationary heavy bag.

When I went into the gym to see him picking out kickboxing pads, I knew I was in for it. The pads would be strapped to his forearms, to be held up as targets for me to punch and kick. They also meant, knowing Darren, that my target would no longer be stationary.

Within one round of kickboxing, I had never been so tired. He had me running all over the training room floor, chasing after him to punch and kick at the pads. It didn't help that his legs were way longer than mine, so one step for him was three for me.

He seemed to be enjoying tormenting me, even though, through my groans and complaints, I was enjoying the new challenge. By the end, I could barely hold my hands up. It's not like I had a choice since I got a gentle tap on the side of the head with the pads every time my arms dropped.

On the bright side, at least the ab workout for the day didn't require the use of my arms. Or so I thought. Darren informed me that the ab workouts seemed to be getting a little too easy for me and handed me a six pound medicine ball.

Six pounds had never been so heavy.

As we both spent some time stretching out after the workout, the question of my leg, particularly the giant scar across it, came up. I had only ever mentioned that I had major surgery and that I would need to go easy on that leg.

I had never explained the story to Darren, so I decided to give him the full rundown. Chemo, sepsis, major surgery, expected outcomes, all of it. His face changed from surprised to saddened to shocked to surprised again. When I finished, all he said was, "Well, if you can do kickboxing after all that, I bet you could do a Spartan race."

256

I didn't know what it was, but with a name like Spartan, there was no way. I told him as much. But see, Darren had a way of saying, "Okay," in a high-pitched tone that dripped with sarcasm. He usually reserved that tone for when he was about to challenge me.

I listened to him explain some kind of race for psychos through the mud, with obstacles, no less. Rope climbs, monkey bars, bucket carries, and wall climbs, to name a few. I thought he had lost his mind. There was just no way I was going to attempt such a crazy race.

But the idea had been planted. If I had started kickboxing and had been working on running a 5k, what's to say I couldn't take on this Spartan race nonsense just once to say that I could?

So, two days later, when I came in for my kickboxing class, I only had to take one look at Darren to know that he already knew the damage he had done. I told him it wouldn't be anytime soon but that one day, I would attempt a Spartan race. A smirk and a double dog dare was his only reply before we started our workout.

Limitless

Chapter 28

June 24, 2021

Another one of the major changes that I experienced while getting a taste of normal life was how things in my social life changed. I was already pretty familiar with what cancer could do to my social life. Just during my year of chemo, I had been broken up with, lost close friends, gained new friends, and started a new relationship. As far as my social life went, Mom, Anthony, Em, and Francisco were the only people who were close to me when I got diagnosed and were still close to me in 2021.

That year shook me up spectacularly. The shaking started when I found out that Gabe's cancer had come back. He had already fought through one relapse with Ewing's since the trip to New Orleans, but this time, it had spread to most of his organs and his brain.

Gabe wasn't one to beat around the bush. He told me, and he didn't shy away from the fact that he was choosing not to do chemo a third time. I couldn't blame him. I had gone through the first two protocols that he had likely already gone through. Chemo would have only prolonged his life a little longer, but it would have made him suffer.

We knew what his decision meant, and I fully supported him, but I was heartbroken. We had become so close, and I knew I couldn't get to Louisianna to see him in time. As time passed, I received fewer and fewer texts from him. Days would pass between our messages, and I knew things must have gotten bad. I saw through a mutual friend that he had passed less than a month after he found out he had relapsed.

There is no word I could have found to properly describe the grief I felt at losing him. He and I had spoken a short time before he passed, and he told me he knew God. It was a relief to know I would see him again, but that fact didn't do much to ease my heartbreak.

As a cancer survivor, losing a friend to cancer was harder than any other aspect of survivorship. Survivor's guilt had been a continuing struggle for me, but it was even more so after I lost Gabe.

It was another feeling that I became too familiar with since my diagnosis. Particularly during times of celebration, like remission milestones, I would become overwhelmed. The guilt that I had survived but that so many didn't weighed heavily on me.

My heart would ache for the lives lost and for the surviving families. I would think back to ringing the chemo bell and wonder how many of those families were celebrating their own milestones - and how many were grieving losses.

No matter how much I told myself it wasn't about being more or less deserving of life and that it wasn't that there was some rule that said only a certain amount of people could survive and that I was just one of the lucky ones, I felt so much sorrow and guilt for the lives lost.

It took years, but I had to come to terms with the fact that, sometimes, God has reasons for things we simply will not understand. It is not that he is haphazardly choosing who lives and who dies. Who survives and who doesn't, and the reason why, isn't up to us to try to understand. It gave me great comfort to know that God has a reason for everything and that I could take peace in that simple fact.

August 13, 2021

Not long after Gabe passed, I would experience another loss, though not one nearly as devastating. The guy I had been dating for the past two years decided to end our relationship, and on top of the grief from losing Gabe, I spiraled into a dark place.

But then there was Trevor.

I had met Trevor through my boyfriend when we were still together, even meeting in person once, and we had gotten along well. The day we all went out to lunch together, he discovered my sense of humor - being somewhat warped since surviving a chronic, life-threatening illness - and used every opportunity to make me laugh, being the goofball he was.

I never expected it, but the day after the breakup, I got a call from Trevor. That's not to say I didn't expect support from him because I knew he was the kind of person to offer support. But he was my now-ex's closest friend. I assumed that broke some sort of guy code. Much to my surprise, he opened the conversation with an explanation, telling me that he had experienced a very similar, very heartbreaking breakup a few months prior and that he knew my pain. He wanted to be there to support me, and I was in no position to turn down a friend.

Even more to my surprise, we spent hours talking. It started with what had happened in our own relationships, and after spending a decent amount of time crying to him, he started pulling out all the stops to make me laugh. It was the only thing that even got me to smile since the breakup.

By the end of the hours-long conversation, I had laughed myself silly, and he had given me peace and reassurance that, even though I would still wrestle with my emotions for weeks, I had someone to trust as I went through a process he was all too familiar with.

It only took a few days for us to realize that our relationship was more sibling-like than anything. Between our ten-year age gap

261

and the fact that he lived in Oregon, he became the protective big brother, and I the lovingly annoying little sister. Calling Trevor every night became a habit we both looked forward to. If I didn't call him by a certain time, he would end up calling me.

It only took one phone call before we started ending our conversations with, "I love you, bro," and, "I love you, sis." Trevor was one of those people that I knew from the start was a life-long friend, and our bond grew quickly from our nightly conversations to the point where we didn't even bother to differentiate that we weren't actually siblings.

August 19, 2021

Time had come for my next set of scans after the previous fiasco, and I had dreaded every minute leading up to it. I wasn't worried anymore about seeing my team. I had made it quite clear that if I saw any of my team aside from the fellow I had grown to trust, I would walk out.

As for my surgeon, I had no intention of telling him I had been running or kickboxing. I didn't need a replay from when I told him I had been walking.

No, it wasn't that I would be seeing my teams that bothered me. It was that I had enjoyed life so thoroughly, being away from the hospital for a full six months. I had even managed to put so much of the trauma and bad memories behind me. I had avoided that side of town where the hospitals and clinics were and had been, for the first time in years, truly felt at peace.

On top of it all, I had started on a meal plan provided by my gym and had been eating meals and snacks like clockwork for weeks. The idea of fasting for scans seemed like torture.

After all the usual torment of being poked, injected with a tracer dye, and left to let it "incubate," as they phrased it, I was pleasantly surprised with just how different the appointment at oncology was.

Since I didn't have to worry about seeing my oncology team, I wasn't a bundle of nerves walking into the clinic. What little anxiety I did have from being at the hospital clinic was quickly diffused when my therapist stopped in while we waited for the results of my scans. She didn't stay long, but her presence reassured me that she had been diligent in making sure her requests were handled without any trouble.

When the fellow came in with my scan results, it was a world of difference to my usual experiences. He was mellow, in comparison to the usual high-strung energy I got from the rest of my team. And while the rest of my team jumped straight into scan results, as if I were just another box to check on their day, he sat down and asked about how things had been going.

I could tell that he genuinely cared, too. He wasn't just asking out of obligation, but he was interested to know what my life had been like, especially after the disaster of the last time I had been in for scan results. Even more to his credit, when we asked how he was, he spoke about his own life.

When it came time for us to talk about my scans, he remembered how I had always said I knew the results would be clear. He didn't bother with the dramatics, but told me what we already knew. I also found out that the appearance of my lungs, though not completely cleared, showed improvement since the last set of scans.

I didn't need the scans to tell me that. I knew that if God had healed me, whatever the scans said did not matter. I was standing on His promise of healing to me.

I decided to test the waters a little with the fellow. He had given me good reason to believe that I could trust him with my new life updates, so I took a chance to tell him about my latest hobby, kickboxing.

It didn't at all surprise me when he, after processing that shocking info, congratulated me. He was genuinely happy that I was able to do something that I enjoyed, and that it was something that would help me stay active and healthy.

For once, I had left those appointments feeling at peace with how it all went.

The next week at Ortho, though, was the usual. I still didn't like that I couldn't share the kickboxing news with my surgeon, but I wasn't going to let it bother me.

Not when I would already be bothered enough by how I was forced to go in for X-rays that showed nothing new in the last six months. It seemed pointless to me. If the bone had healed, and the incision had healed, why was I still going month after month to hear the same news?

And after hearing the same speech about how careful I needed to be, I was pretty over it. I tried to look forward to when I would only have to go for scans and X-rays once a year, but even that started to seem like pointless frustration.

One good thing did come out of going to those appointments, though. I still planned on pursuing radiography after recently completing the finals for Anatomy and Physiology that I had to postpone due to having the plague, but while I was in the clinic, I saw a poster that changed my mind about what I wanted to do as a career.

The poster mentioned a department that I had never heard of before, the Patient Advocate team at my hospital. After some Googling, I found out that Patient Advocates were a team of people who specialized in helping patients do what my therapist had been teaching me to do earlier in the year. They helped them make informed decisions, accompanied them to appointments, kept track of and coordinated appointments with different specialists, and did most of the communication to take the stress off the patient.

I was amazed that I had been involved in the medical practice as a patient for two and a half years and had no idea a team like that existed. Not only did I wish I had been able to have a Patient Advocate during chemo, but it seemed to be a new field, and I wanted to do my part in helping grow a profession I felt was much needed.

After plenty of research, I decided to start a Patient Advocacy Certificate program at the University of Miami in the fall. Education for Patient Advocates was still nonspecific, so I thought it would be a good start.

With the fall came another ingenious idea. I wanted to get a job. Being a full-time student at this point did not seem like a feasible idea, and the Patient Advocate program was a five month, self-paced certificate program. I wouldn't need to dedicate my full time to the program, and I felt like it was time for me to attempt to be a real adult again.

I knew the smart idea would be to get a part time job just to make sure I could handle the job, both mentally and physically, so I applied as a cashier at a local pharmacy in town. It didn't take long for my application to go through, and I was on the schedule, working my way through the days until my Patient Advocacy program started.

All was going well for me. I had a job that I didn't absolutely hate, though it came with its fair share of frustrations. I was about to start my education for a job I knew would give me a chance to make an impact. I had even started to feel some sense of peace and relief knowing I wouldn't have to go for scans for another few months, and when I did, I could be at ease knowing it would be a much better experience.

I also had kickboxing, which had changed my life completely in the few months I had been training. I was in the best shape of my life and felt as if I hadn't even had cancer. I felt as if I could finally move on and live life as a 21-year-old was meant to live.

Limitless

Chapter 29

It was becoming clearer to me that as I continued to heal from the hurt of the breakup I had just experienced and added more things to my plate with school and work, I craved something more in my spiritual life. I hadn't had a church to attend in person in over a year since the church I had been attending during chemo had shut down. I missed the Sunday morning experience and the feeling of a family. Sure, I absolutely loved the live stream I had been watching, but seeing all the people there who would pray and worship together sparked a longing I couldn't continue to deny.

The first and most difficult problem that I encountered, though, was that I didn't know of a church I would feel comfortable going to. The churches I had been to in the past had been ones I wasn't too eager to return to, and that would leave me going to an entirely new church. Showing up to a church that I didn't have a clue about, alone, wasn't an option.

Luckily for me, God had led me to the right place. By that, of course, I mean the dojo. For a while, I observed the people around me, and the one that stood out was Darren. And not just because he was over six feet tall. I noticed that he was the kind of person that, if I went to church, I would have wanted to be surrounded by people like him. He had never explicitly said he was a churchgoer, but I figured asking him would be a good place to start.

He invited me to his church on a Wednesday night, and it didn't take long for me to start going regularly. In the process, I found myself with a new desire in my heart. I wanted to get baptized.

The livestream I had been watching had baptisms in almost every service, and watching the joy on those people's faces as they came out of the water filled me with a longing to experience the same. It also seemed to be a continuing theme in my own studies of the Bible, and now that I was in a place where I could, I wanted to fulfill that longing.

My entire body seemed to tremble during the entire service on the Sunday we chose, not in anxiety, but in pure excitement. I could relate to those kids that get so excited for their own baptism that they would dunk themselves under the water if the pastor got too long winded.

When the end of the service came, and Darren led me to the front of the sanctuary, I was near vibrating with excitement. But the moment he started sharing my story and my reason for wanting to be baptized, everything turned into a blur until the next I knew, I was standing waist-deep in water, trying not to cry. I barely remember being taken into a dressing room to change into, essentially, a thick plastic graduation gown. I don't remember getting into the pool on a raised platform behind the main stage, with a stained-glass window backdrop painting us in bright, warm colors. I do remember seeing Darren in those rubber overalls that you see in movies where the guys go standing in a river to fly fish. That I won't be able to forget. I also couldn't forget that he seemed just as on the verge of tears as I was as we waited for the song that was being played to end.

I didn't know what to expect when I went under the water. Some say baptism is a physical act with a spiritual meaning and, much like when we pray for salvation, we don't *feel* anything. But as my back hit the water, everything disappeared. It's as if I stopped existing for the few seconds it took to go under the water and back up because all I remember after feeling the water curl up and around

268

my shoulders before my head went under, was sobbing tears of joy in Darren's arms a few seconds later.

Maybe I did stop existing for a few seconds. Maybe the Rebecca that was before baptism really did stop existing as the new Rebecca rose out of the water, a new creation. And, unlike when I prayed for salvation in sixth grade, I did feel something. I felt as if I truly was new. It was as if everything that had given me a reason to feel heavy from the weight of the life I had lived had been left behind, and I felt light as a feather. My soul itself felt light. I felt as if everything ahead of me was an opportunity to rewrite who I was through a new lens. The lens of how God saw me.

I remember being passed from person to person on the way back to the dressing room to get dried off, hugging without even knowing who it was I was hugging. I remember a lot of tears of joy, and not just my own.

Then I walked back out from the backstage entrance, and I saw Mom in the first row waiting for me, her eyes misty, and I remember breaking out into joyful sobs again when she held me in her arms.

The rest of the day was a long blur of hugs and congratulations, but there is one detail I hold close to my heart. In the celebration that was going on after I pulled away from Mom, someone shared a Bible verse with me that I have let guide me through the past few years.

"Be strong and courageous. Do not be afraid, do not be discouraged, for the Lord your God will be with you wherever you go." - Jeremiah 1:9

November 17, 2021

Within a few short months, my life started to return to the flurry of business I was used to in college. I would go to work, take my kickboxing classes after work, talk to Trevor before going to bed, and wake up to do it all over again. I was thriving at the fast pace of my life, and I was grateful that I was finding a normal that suited me.

Of course, when one of my kickboxing coaches offered to let me try out a Muay Thai class after my kickboxing class, I was all in.

While the kickboxing class didn't involve contact, Muay Thai did. It was the full-contact version of what I had been practicing for so long. Though, nothing could have prepared me for my first class. Darren was in the class with me, but I was the only woman. That should have told me I might have been out of my element. Instead, I took it as a challenge.

Most of the class went by without a hitch. We did shadowboxing drills in the mirrors, and partnered up to practice drills much like Darren and I would in kickboxing.

It was when it came time to spar that I realized I truly was out of my element. I was being handed shin pads and a mouth guard, and I couldn't help but question what I was getting myself into. I knew Darren wouldn't let me go into harm's way, but I still questioned why I chose to join the class.

I sparred with Darren first to get the hang of what it was like. Naturally, he was having a blast, tapping me on the head every time I dropped my hands. For the next round of sparring, I chose one of the older guys who seemed like maybe he wouldn't beat me up too badly.

This guy was super cool, letting me get a feel for what it was like to practice drills while someone tried to punch me. I thought things were going great until he stopped me, dropped his hands, and told me to punch him in the face.

I was absolutely mortified. Apparently, I hadn't actually been hitting him, and he wanted to get me comfortable making contact with someone. The fact that he was so kind about the whole situation made it even crazier.

Eventually, after stalling for a few seconds, I threw a punch. It was more like a tap, but he never specified how hard he wanted the punch to be. He saw through my logic and told me we weren't going to keep sparring until I *really* punched him.

At first, I didn't really like the feeling of punching someone. I liked the idea of putting what I had learned to a more practical use, but I didn't like thinking I could hurt someone.

That feeling quickly disappeared when the next round started, and I took a decent hit to the face. That's about the time I decided that if they had no qualms about hitting me, I'd be okay hitting back.

When the class was over, I decided I wanted to continue doing Muay Thai after my kickboxing classes. Despite my initial reservations, everyone I sparred with was cool and seemed to be there to help me learn.

January 12, 2022

The past few months had brought a new level of freedom and ability to my life, moving me farther away from the oppression of the hospital. After starting full contact Muay Thai at the dojo, I was given a taste of what it was like to be someone who wasn't defined by their chronic illness.

I had been contemplating it for months, but just days before my appointments, I made the decision. I decided to stop going in for scans. Permanently.

Mom, as always, backed my decision completely. I am fairly certain it worried her to not have concrete proof of my continued remission, but she knew what I was going through every time I had to visit the hospital. She understood my reason for choosing to stop scans and supported me when I told her I had made up my mind.

I considered the hoops I would have to jump through to make that happen. As if anyone at the hospital could force me to keep going, but I digress. I knew the first barrier to my long-term freedom would be simple.

My doctors were going to think I had lost my mind.

I decided to get one step ahead of that fight, so I called my therapist for a consultation. If I could get her to attest to my sanity, that was one less battle I would have to endure.

Luckily, aside from a brief line of questioning when I told her I was assured of my healing because I heard God say He healed me, I had no problem convincing her that I was making a well-thought-out decision. Understandably, she had her concerns about me hearing a disembodied voice, but I trusted her enough to give me the time to explain that, no, I did not need medication or a grippy sock vacation.

When it came to my team, I decided to tell the fellow about my decision first because in the years I had spent trying to talk to any member of my team, I only trusted him to take this news well. After an introduction from my therapist about how she had already evaluated me, I told him my plan to stop getting scans.

I wasn't even nervous. I had so much trust in him to respect my decision, and he didn't disappoint. After giving me the expected rundown of the risks I was taking, he smiled, hugged me, and told me how incredibly happy he was that I was able to be comfortable moving on from my experiences. It was incredible for me to experience that kind of respect from a doctor.

I was even a little upset at the idea of not going to see him. Even though he was my doctor, he had become someone I shared my life experiences with, and who had shared his own with me. It was difficult for me to let go of any kind of connection. It was for him, too, apparently, since there were a few bittersweet tears shed.

As I expected, he wanted me to break the news to my main oncologist and her nurse practitioner. I had to steel my nerves on that one, even if I had already expected it. I hadn't interacted with them in nearly a year, and my life had been all the better for it.

I expected a fight. These were the same people who demanded I come in for blood infusions and who couldn't even validate my feelings of despair during my weakest moments. I had no reason to expect they possessed the ability to understand where I was coming from.

Luckily, they didn't act too extravagantly when they came in. They let my therapist give her intro, and I told them in no uncertain terms that I would not be back for further treatments. The fellow relayed that he had explained the risks of my decision, and I told them my decision was not up for discussion.

They stayed in the room for less than five minutes, wished me the best, and left. The fellow made sure I knew he would always be in my corner. It was a bittersweet goodbye, but one I needed to make to start moving forward with my life.

As we left the hospital, I heard that gentle voice I had come to know whisper to me, "Go in peace and be freed from your suffering."

Parting ways with my oncology team went well, though I can't say the same about parting ways with my Ortho team.

When I told my surgeon that visit would be my last, I knew I would be met with pushback. I did not expect to be told that I was making a stupid decision. That was the straw that broke the camel's back on my patience. I hadn't decided on whether I would share my secret life of kickboxing with him, but at that moment I snapped.

I smiled calmly and proceeded to tell him that in the past year, I had started kickboxing, had learned how to run, had started full contact Muay Thai, and had been training for my first Spartan race.

I will never not be satisfied by the memory of how he paled, unable to even speak.

His only response, once he got his thoughts together, was to tell me, as he was walking out of the room, to call him *when* I would need him to fix the damage I had done to *his* leg.

The audacity, right?

His leg.

If he didn't want me to use *my* leg that he put so much effort into fixing, why would he put so much effort into salvaging it in the first place? Wasn't the whole goal to help the patient recover so they could live? Why couldn't he celebrate the victories that I had fought so hard to earn?

If that was how he was going to be, I knew then and there that I would never be calling him, no matter what may happen in my life.

It was so freeing to leave the side of town where the hospitals were, knowing I was free of scans and future visits. I had so much peace that I could live my life totally free of the hospital and the PTSD that popped up every time I went there.

Limitless

For the first time in three years, I could look to my future without the looming presence of the hospital. It was like a whole new world had opened to me.

With my last hospital visit behind me, I threw myself completely into my training.

I would show up at the dojo for kickboxing classes with Darren. After an hour of drills and fast paced workouts, I would go straight to the Muay Thai class for another hour. Only this time, it was drills and sparring rounds.

If I could make an extra kickboxing or Muay Thai class, I would. Darren didn't let me forget about his double dog dare to run a Spartan Race, and I had to prepare. Not that I had any clue what to prepare for. Darren just told me that if I could survive a class with him, followed immediately by a Muay Thai class, I'd be fine. Since it was all I had to go off of, I chose to trust him.

274

Chapter 30

Within no time, I was staring my next challenge in the face, frankly unsure of how in the world I ended up shouting, "I'm a Spartan!" at the starting line of a Spartan Sprint.

I had gone to church that morning with Darren and his family, and we changed into our racing gear and left immediately after service. I was sporting a T-shirt that said "Cancer Kicker" and as I walked out to get in the car, I was handed a poster that the college group had all signed with congratulations and encouragement.

Already being a nervous wreck, I ended up sniffling my way to the car. We were cutting it close with the time it would take to drive to the venue and our start time, so we didn't have much time for the emotional send-off, but I wasn't lost on how special the moment was.

I got the race prep rundown on the drive there. I had already eaten breakfast before church, so on the way, I was handed a protein shake and a banana. That was my pre-race snack, so I would have enough fuel to race without having to worry about needing to use a bathroom on the course.

They gave me a little bit of a crash course on some of the obstacles and what I might expect - like lots of mud - but we all knew nothing would truly prepare me for racing except to actually race.

As we expected, we cut it close. We had about ten minutes to check-in and get to the starting line, and when Darren was in a hurry, his long legs were impossible to keep up with. My warm-up for the race was the little jog I had to do to keep up with him.

All the chanting and starting line energy mixed with my nervous energy, and they used that hype to send us onto the course. I was nearing a full run trying to keep up with Darren and his long legs, and eventually had to remind him that it was like a chihuahua trying to keep up with a Great Dane.

We slowed to a jog until we got to the first obstacle, the Over Walls.

I had never had to jump over a wall or fence in my entire life, so when I approached the wall that came up to my shoulders, I just looked at Darren. I had no idea how to even start. I tried to hop up and push myself over but couldn't get high enough on my jump. Finally, he showed me how to use some of the footholds on the wall to climb over.

The course took us trudging through a lake - literally - so we ended up soaked before facing another wall. This time, it was a six-foot wall. Which I managed to get over perfectly fine, thank you very much.

With the help of the little block screwed halfway up the side of the wall for those of us who are vertically challenged.

Throughout the 3-mile course, I encountered obstacles I could do, obstacles I could do with help, and obstacles I could not do.

Most of the overhead, hanging obstacles - monkey bars, twister, beater, multi-rig, and rope climb – I took one look at and happily walked to the penalty area. Oh yeah, the penalty for not doing an obstacle in a Spartan Race was 30 burpees. Fun!

Darren helped me with obstacles like the inverted wall, z-wall, helix, and slip wall. In the Open Heats, it is okay to have race partners or teams help each other complete obstacles, so he helped me avoid quite a few burpees.

My favorite obstacles were the ones I had to use my strength for. Sandbag and bucket carries through rough terrain, and a 75-pound Atlas carry helped show me just how strong I had gotten since barely being able to hold the weight of my own body up during chemo.

Things really seemed to be going well, all things considered. Of course, until we hit the mud. I imagined the extent of the mud we would encounter was the ankle-deep stuff we had been trudging through during parts of the course. When we approached a mud pit that wound through a trail in a small patch of trees and saw racers that no doubt had to be taller than me up to their waists in mud, I gave Darren the "what did you get me into?" look.

I dropped down into the mud and was up to my thighs within a few steps. It wasn't watery swamp mud but thick, goopy, stick-to-everything mud. It was like trudging through brownie batter. I watched racers fall face first or step in a hole they couldn't see and sink chest-deep into the mud.

Unfortunately, I was one of the racers who found a hole and sank chest-deep into the muck. Darren tried to pull me up, but I was stuck. It took another racer to brace her arms under mine and lift as Darren pulled to get me unstuck. When we finally got free of the mud, Darren and I were covered. It stuck to our hands and weighed down our clothes. I felt like I was ten pounds heavier.

The course designers put the z-wall right after the mud pit, so when we approached it, our hands and feet were still covered in mud. We had to traverse the zig-zagged walls using the hand and foot pegs that stuck out from the wall. It was nearly impossible, even with Darren holding me up.

It wasn't long before we heard the music blaring in the festival area, signaling the nearing end of the race. I was starting to hit my point of exhaustion. We had been on the course for the better part of an hour and a half, and it was a whole new level of exertion. Back-to-back kickboxing and Muay Thai classes prepared me well, but Spartan Races were in a category of their own.

Spartan Races were meant to get in our heads as racers. It wasn't just a long course with obstacles. It had obstacles like the rope climb right after getting out of a mud pit, so gripping the rope was more difficult. It was a barbed wire crawl right up a hill through brownie batter mud. They definitely succeeded in mentally exhausting me because I was ready to curl up on the course and take a nap when I finally heard the music and realized we were only a few hundred feet from the finish line.

I wouldn't say it gave me a second wind. That had already been used up somewhere around the second mile, but it did fuel me enough to keep going through the last obstacles to get to the finish line. The last obstacle before we could cross was the infamous fire jump. The easiest way to jump over was to get a running start. I didn't think I had much run left in me, but I gave it my best shot. I heard Mom call out to me when we were approaching the fire.

"That's my Becca!"

That had been an inside joke between us since I was a toddler. At her graduation, when her name was called, I yelled, "That's my momma!"

At both my college and high school graduations, she yelled out, "That's my Becca!"

At that moment, it was what I needed to hear to get me to keep running so I could clear the fire and cross the finish line. When I did, I ran straight up to her, covered in mud and dust, and pulled her into a hug. I don't think she was expecting the muddy hug, but I couldn't help it. I was so excited to have completed the race. It was another step in freeing myself from the limitations that still haunted me. If I could run a Spartan, I figured there were few things I couldn't do if I put my mind to it.

I joked with Darren that I fulfilled my end of the dare. I did a Spartan Race, and I never had to do one again. He hit me with a high-pitched "Okay!" that told me he knew something I didn't. I couldn't imagine that after seeing the bruises start to pop up over my arms and feeling every muscle in my body ache, I would want to do another race.

But before the bruises had even faded, I felt it. It was like an itch I couldn't scratch. I was already starting to miss the high I felt after finishing the race. During the race, it was a weird mix of fun and misery. The feeling I got from crossing the finish line and getting the finisher medal completely masked all the misery though. I was already craving another race.

I kept hearing about this thing called a Spartan Trifecta. Particularly, there was a Trifecta Weekend later in the year in Central Florida. A Spartan Trifecta is completing three races of varying lengths in one race season. A 5k Sprint with 20 obstacles, a 10k Super with 25 obstacles, and a 21k Beast with 30 obstacles. A Trifecta Weekend was to complete all three races in one weekend.

It was absolutely crazy, I know. But doing my first race sparked something in me, and I found myself enjoying challenges. Being able to face down a challenge and complete it started to get addicting. I walked, then ran, then kickboxed, then did a Spartan Race. The problem with challenges is that they need to get progressively harder. Maybe I was skipping a few steps going from a Sprint to a Trifecta Weekend, but I had months to train for the race weekend, and I knew what to expect since I had raced the Sprint.

Plus, if I could do a Spartan Race after I was told I'd never walk normally again, I didn't see why I couldn't do a Trifecta Weekend.

It didn't take me long to realize that, while I was left pretty free and clear on the physical side, mentally, I was a mess. I quickly got acquainted with what living with post-traumatic stress disorder was like. It was glaringly obvious that something was not quite right in my mind any time I even entered the waiting room of a doctor's office. Whether it was a routine dermatology appointment or a visit to my primary care for a sinus infection, I turned into an anxious disaster who barely knew her own name.

I used the introduction my therapist put together with me to make those appointments easier, but nothing could really ease the anxiety of being in the kind of environment that caused me so much trauma.

I would try to find seating in the waiting room with my back against a wall, with as much of the room in sight as possible. Even that did little to calm the sensory assault of a waiting area. It was far too pristine, far too sterile. The mood was alarmingly calm. The air reeked of hand sanitizer. The sounds of keyboards, phones ringing, and hand sanitizer dispensers combined to leave nearly every one of my senses on edge.

When I finally made it to an all-too-quiet room, I would sit as far away from the door as possible. If I could barricade myself with the exam table between myself and the door, even better. Many times, I would find myself whispering things like, "You are safe," "You are in control here," and "They can't hurt you."

I found out the hard way that, sadly, my trauma response did not just manifest in medical settings. There were days I could hardly wear a seatbelt in the car because the pressure of the seatbelt against my shoulder where my port had been felt as if I was being physically restrained. Some days, I would hold my shirt away from my shoulder for as long as I could to avoid the feeling of a port dressing sticking to my skin.

I would find myself being overly reactive and much too agitated, only to realize I had taken a punch to the chest during sparring and my port area was bruised. Subconsciously, I had been freaking out over it.

I found out the hard way that the card readers in grocery stores had the tendency to wig me out. Even years after being in the hospital, the beeping of certain card readers sounded just a bit too similar in tone and cadence to a heart monitor. Luckily, I caught the panic attack before I ran out of Publix in frantic tears without my Chicken Tender Pub Sub. That would have been a real tragedy.

The most alarming response I had, though, was my reaction to basic interactions with people. I would nearly come out of my skin if someone held my arm for even just a second in conversation. Forget when someone would put their hand on my shoulder. I felt held down. It took me straight back to immunology.

For the most part, I had a good handle on it. I could catch my responses quickly and avoid a subsequent panic attack. But there was one specific moment that let me know I could no longer go on without addressing these responses as a problem.

One day, during some one-on-one kickboxing, Darren told me he wanted to drill sweeps a little more in-depth with me. In Muay Thai, if an opponent does manage to take your feet out from under you in a sweep, they would immediately back off. It wasn't like the MMA most people are accustomed to, where it turns into an all-out floor brawl.

Darren wanted me to learn what to do past just a sweep, mainly for self-defense purposes. He told me he would sweep me to demonstrate first, so I knew what to expect, and then he would teach me. Simple enough. Goodness knows I had been swept plenty of times in drills to not be afraid of hitting the floor.

What I wasn't ready for, though, was that immediately when he swept me, instead of backing off, he put his weight on top of me to show me how to keep someone down. Which immediately sent me into a bit of a dissociative state. He must have known because he had me on my feet within seconds. With the trust I had in him, I was able to tame the growing panic quickly and ended up learning the sweep he was trying to teach me.

But it was at that moment that I knew I couldn't keep letting subconscious fears rule me. One relatively small moment every once in a while seemed fine. But in hindsight, it wasn't just one moment every once in a while.

In response, I chose to confront my fear directly. I had been doing Muay Thai for long enough to be comfortable with it, so I decided to jump straight into discomfort.

I started going to Brazilian Jiu-Jitsu classes.

April 13, 2022

What better way to overcome my fear of being held down or restrained than to join a combat sport where I would spend entire classes being held down? Plus, it was cheaper than therapy.

My expectations of BJJ were pretty on point. As a white belt, I spent so much time being beneath someone else, just fighting to get free. I also expected to spend the majority of my time rolling with guys. The first few weeks, I would end up pinned under someone within a few seconds and immediately start to panic. I would focus so hard on trying to keep breathing that I couldn't think my way out of the predicaments I was in.

The guys I trained with were insanely respectful and perceptive, and eventually, I came to trust them, both with my training and the reason behind my training. There were times I would start to panic, and my partners would adjust their weight ever so slightly, pause, and tell me to think about how to get out. I usually didn't even have to say I was panicking. They just knew. Somehow, they even seemed to know when I was past any point of keeping my panic under control and would break apart from rolling until I got myself together.

After classes, I would go into the bathroom and collapse against the sink. I would focus on breathing until my chest didn't shake every time I inhaled. I would splash water on my face, pull myself together, and try to move on with my life.

I spent a while so focused on learning to roll and keep my panic in check that, admittedly, I sucked at BJJ. I would go through the motions during drills, but once we got to applying new techniques in rolling, it was just a game of breathing and teaching myself how to think despite my trauma responses.

But at some point, the lightbulb came on. My partners had spent so much time teaching me how to escape the predicaments I landed myself in - sometimes even going so far as to roll with me after class to teach me how to best use my small size and weight to my advantage - that the panic became less and less frequent. The escapes became more and more natural. One day, I found myself instinctually rolling so intensely with my partner that my mouthguard came out midway through the round, and I didn't even notice. It was one of the first rounds that I managed to avoid being submitted, and my partner had not gone easy on me.

That day was a huge step in my progress towards emotional healing. BJJ gave me confidence in my ability to defend myself - and maybe even inflict some damage on an opponent - that has changed

282

me completely. It has been a few years since I have even had a trauma response like I had before BJJ.

Through the triumph of BJJ and Muay Thai, though, came other forms of strife that I suffered with. Being so physically active on a leg that was hardly meant to take the abuse I hurled at it came with its drawbacks.

Much to my dismay, I had to learn to live with chronic pain. I had what felt like severe arthritis in my left knee, as well as every ache and pain I could imagine having metal and dead bone would bring. Most of the time, it was just a part of my normal life. I was so thankful to have even beaten the odds to be walking again, much less becoming a fairly high-level athlete, that I tried not to let it bother me.

Tried is the keyword there. Because there were just some days I would break down. Any time the weather and pressure outside changed, I was in pain. Particularly hard nights at kickboxing left me sore and achy. I was usually fine until it started to hold me back. If I even showed the slightest sign of a limp, I would start down the path of emotional breakdown.

In hindsight, it would happen like clockwork, just about every three or four months, when my capacity for staying positive ran out. Seemingly out of nowhere, a full breakdown would commence. For the first few years, it was just constant, seemingly never-ending pain and my attempts to hide it. But as I tried new things, pushing myself harder and harder physically, and as my desire to do more grew, my thoughts toward the miraculous surgery I had received shifted.

What started as a general bout of frustration curbed by my usual optimism became cynical questioning. I was frustrated that my only option had been this particular surgery that left me with so much suffering. I had to deal with waking up in the morning and wondering if my leg would take my weight when I got out of bed. I had to carry compression sleeves and Biofreeze with me in case the pain became particularly unbearable. I grew tired of asking my sparring partners to go easy on me when all I wanted to do was go at it for a few rounds and get the pent-up energy out of my system.

Simply put, I grew tired of being held back. That thought could be held at bay with the usual gratitude spiel I gave myself. It was a miracle I was walking anyway, so I shouldn't have been complaining.

But couldn't there have been other options? Was this surgery truly the only viable option for me? And if so, why wasn't it explained so that I could have peace of mind with the outcomes of the options I had to take?

As I pondered this during one of my scheduled breakdowns, I realized that surely there were other options that weren't shared with me. I had met someone with osteosarcoma who had his entire tibia replaced with a titanium rod. There was also Gabe, who opted for amputation.

Of course, I couldn't determine if those options were actually better for me than my reconstruction. How could I, when the pros and cons of those options weren't even presented to me? With that, I became frustrated with the lack of information that was shared with me and the lack of autonomy that I had in the decision-making process.

As I looked back, I realized that there was no decision-making process. At one point, while I was admitted for the third time for sepsis, my surgeon stopped by to share his plan for my leg. At the time, with my brain in a haze from sepsis and chemo, the plan sounded great. No other options were presented, and I didn't have the presence of mind to search for other options.

Naturally, that led to more thoughts. What if I had been given the opportunity to choose? Would I have chosen differently? Would I have come out better or worse for it?

I knew I couldn't answer those questions, but I longed for the closure that would have come from making my own decision. If I had chosen the surgery I had, at least it would have been my choice. But if I had chosen another option, like amputation, I could face the consequences of that decision with dignity, knowing it had been *my* decision, not a surgeon's.

Through the cycle I went, one day grateful that I was even doing all I was doing in the first place, and another day feeling as though my right to make my own decisions was stolen from me, and I was living with something that was very much not mine.

But throughout those months, I still focused on my goal. I still planned on running the Trifecta Weekend and had been keeping up with training at the dojo. I had even switched jobs to be a fitness kickboxing coach, so I would be spending hours a day working out with my classes. Even with my frustrations, I kept in mind that it was a miracle I was able to train for such an ambitious goal.

Limitless

Chapter 31

When the time came to make the trip to Central Florida, I had full confidence that I was ready to race and would be walking away with a Trifecta Weekend medal. What I couldn't believe was that I was finally going to do it. I had been so excited and so determined, and yet checking into our hotel in Sebring and seeing all the other racers there preparing for race day was surreal.

Here I was, having only one Sprint, hopes and dreams under my belt, in a hotel lobby with racers who had undoubtedly run quite a few races and probably a few Trifecta Weekends. It didn't feel like I didn't belong by any means. I had put in the work and made the commitment. But because I hadn't gone the distance yet, I did feel uninitiated. I figured that would change in about twelve hours, though.

It probably didn't help my nerves that I had been seeing something about a "Death Swamp" from seasoned racers on Facebook. I tried to ignore the possibility of what that could mean, knowing Spartan. I remembered the brownie batter mud from my first race and couldn't imagine how much worse this course would have to be to earn such a bold nickname.

That night felt very ritualistic, even though I hardly had anything to call a pre-race ritual. I set out my equipment - a water pack, snacks, mustard packs for cramps, shoes, compression socks, blister tape, headlamp, grip gloves, and eye black. I probably checked and double checked everything twice.

I had this hilarious idea that I would get a good night of sleep before the race so I could show up on the course fresh. Yeah, that didn't happen. The anticipation was killing me. I was facing down at least ten obstacles I had never encountered, 13 miles of uncertainty, and a Death Swamp. Aside from nerves, I was *so excited.* I had been training for months, and it was all about to pay off.

I had spent months taking every weekend to walk the bike trail we had in town. I started off at six miles a day, and eventually ended up doing fifteen miles a day. Mom, in support, took the bike out with me so I wouldn't have to spend hours on the bike trail alone. I didn't focus on running, since I knew that would likely cause worse issues with my leg, but I knew I needed to be able to walk the distance for two days in a row.

I used the time on the trail to train my mind, as well. I knew Spartan was a mental game as much as a physical one, and that the course designers would test our mental endurance as much, if not more, as our physical endurance.

I pictured myself completing obstacles, crossing finish lines, and stacking medals around my neck. I even pictured the gross, muddy hug Mom would have to endure at each finish line.

I kept picturing those images right up until I fell asleep the night before the race, only to dream about them. I dreamed about climbing walls, jumping over fires, and throwing spears at hay targets. It was like I had been running the races during the night because I hardly woke up rested when my alarm went off at 6:30 a.m.

My adrenaline was pumping enough already to send me flying out of bed to get ready.

All I could think as I layered on compression gear and my shirt that said "PHIL 4:19" was, *I'm about to run a Beast.*

Oh my God, I'm about to run a Beast!

I didn't realize that my first obstacle was actually going to be getting dressed. It seems simple, I know. I had only been doing it for 22 years at that point. But the layers got me. It was the compression socks first, *then* the leggings. Never once in my life had I put on my socks before my leggings, and it threw me off.

Honestly, it was all a familiar feeling. That meticulous prep, the checking and rechecking to make sure I had everything. It reminded me of every performance I had in high school and college, with band and indoor drumline. It was the energy that churned and rushed in my veins, waiting for the release of the start of the event. It was also that quiet performers' headspace I had learned to slip into to avoid the stage fright. The methodical dressing, packing gear, and checking my checklist all kept that wild energy at bay. Or rather, it held it off until it needed to be released.

I stayed in that headspace, quietly murmuring to myself *I'm going to run a Beast today,* every few minutes as we drove to the venue. As we parked, I could see the Elite racers on a mad dash through the course, and that energy coursing through my veins surged. I longed to be on the course after nine long months of preparation. Come what may, I was desperate to be out there.

"Out there," I realized, was on a cow farm. An active cow farm. With massive cows roaming around just beyond a fence from the course.

All through check-in and finding my race partner, who I had found through Facebook, I was shaking. I could barely contain my excitement. I was so lost in the depths of my own thoughts I didn't even blink when I popped an electrolyte tab in my mouth. My race partner handed me one after popping one of her own into a water bottle, but I was too distracted to see it. Once I realized what it was, though, it snapped me right back to the present. It took ten minutes to get the chalky saltiness out of my mouth.

It was like time was moving much too quickly, and not quickly enough, because I found myself at the four-foot wall at the entrance to the starting line. Somehow, though I was so ready to be racing, I also had a moment of panic at how I had ended up there so quickly. Was I really ready?

Limitless

My race partner and I had agreed that we would be taking the race at a moderate pace. Maybe we would run, maybe we wouldn't. She was definitely in better shape than I was but was perfectly content to go at whatever pace would get us through the race. It wasn't far in, past the first few over-walls that we ended up finding some friends in a couple that was racing together, that was also content to take things at a slower pace.

Honestly, racing like that, especially over a longer distance, seemed to be much more fun than trying to cover the great distance quickly. We all got to get to know each other, and of course, I was all too eager to share my "I was told I'd never walk again" story.

As we progressed, the walls got taller, and I was amazed at the camaraderie I saw from the racers. Other racers would stand at the walls and help those of us more vertically challenged racers up the wall, waiting for another racer to come take their place. It was unspoken.

As was the Spartan Handshake rule. If you get boosted over a wall, a random stranger might just grab your butt to help push. What happens on the course stays on the course.

But the sense of being uninitiated that I felt the previous night seemed to vanish. Once on the course, we were all out there with the same goal: to finish. It didn't matter if we could get up the ten-foot wall without any help or if we needed the Spartan Handshake. We were all out for the same thing, and we would all help each other reach that goal in whatever way we could.

The first few miles, and first few obstacles, went smoothly. The four of us fell into a comfortable pace, other racers cheered us on as we shouted our own encouragement to them. It was a thing of beauty. I was almost beginning to think maybe my nerves were for nothing.

I'm pretty sure the course designer had planned for us first-timers on the Beast to be lulled into that state of false security because as our team turned a corner through the woods, I laid eyes on it.

The Death Swamp.

290

Maybe ten feet wide, it was a path seemingly cut through a field of reeds, waist-deep in murky, dark water, with no end in sight. I remembered the cows and tried desperately not to think of what was mixed in the swampy water to make mud. Upon my first few steps, I discovered that the bottom seemed to be crushed reeds that tugged at my hiking boots and thick, sticky mud.

I had some shred of hope that maybe this part of the course wasn't very long. That maybe I could get by without going for a swim in the cow water. I held on to that delusion, trudging through the thigh and waist-deep water. Some racers, probably those who had coined the term Death Swamp, dove right in and started to swim. I hadn't yet gotten that desperate.

After 30 minutes in the Death Swamp, my hope started to dwindle. More racers dropped down for the swim. Shouts could be heard for miles at the shoes lost in the muck, never to be found again. Eventually, I finally gave up on staying out of the water as much as possible when a runner came through, splashing the cow water into my face right as I opened my mouth to catch a breath. Not three steps later, I stepped right into a hole in the mud that brought me up to my chest in the cow water. I abandoned all hope of keeping out of the water, but I still hadn't gotten desperate enough to drop down for the swim.

After 45 minutes, there was still no end in sight. The sloshing and splashing started to create a melody with the disgruntled complaints of racers and the occasional curses at the lost shoes. My hip flexors had long since started to lock up from pulling my legs through the mud and reeds, but I was determined. Plus, it's not like I had much of a choice. The medics would need an airboat to get to me if I called it.

But calling it simply wasn't an option for me. The entire trudge through the Death Swamp, easily over an hour long, I just kept letting the phrase I had used as fuel repeat in my head.

"You'll never walk again."

I determined that until I physically could not walk anymore, I wouldn't stop. We finally caught sight of racers running again, and hope was rekindled. The end was somewhere near, though it seemed as if the closer we got, the longer it took. The front of my hips screamed with every step, and I did my fair share of complaining. But eventually, we made it. Covered in mud and God knows what else, we made it out of the Death Swamp.

With ten more miles to go.

It was at that moment that I threw all previous strategies out the door. Not that I had much, but what I did have, I tossed. New plan: Put one foot in front of the other until someone put a medal around my neck. Then I could stop.

I was so thankful I had a team of friends to suffer the miles with. Alone, I would have gotten entirely too engrossed in my own thoughts. But as a team, we kept each other going.

The other thing that kept me going was the Trevor Pep Talks. He and I still called each other every night, and leading up to the race weekend, the Trifecta became a main topic of conversation for us. Trevor was never one to sugar-coat and wasn't one to coddle me. I got a range of responses from him. Some were more along the lines of, "Just put your mind to it and get it done," while others were more along the lines of, "Do you *really* think you'll give yourself any option but finishing? You'll crawl to the finish line before you quit." What stuck in my head from all the times we talked about the race was when he told me, "Of course, you're going to finish. You survived cancer. This won't stop you."

As the hours passed, we found out the downside to a later start time on a Florida race. The water stations had started to refill their water, but the water we were getting from the refills was fuming with sulfur. It was like drinking a rotten egg. We tried to conserve our own supplies of water, but it was a 13-mile race. We got desperate; we dumped liquid IV in the cups of Fart Water, held out our noses, and chugged. Spartan Racers can have a pretty wicked sense of humor, so it didn't surprise me that the gross water became known as Fart Water.

It wasn't on purpose, but it seemed to add to the race's difficulty, not giving an inch in any situation.

Though this race was absolutely miserable, I can't say that I didn't have fun. It's a bit paradoxical, I know, but through the misery of miles after miles of cow fields and obstacles, I was having a blast and making memories I will never forget.

I even got to make a memory of almost dying - not to be dramatic - and finding a husband.

Only in a Spartan race do those two things happen at the same time. Let me explain.

One of the obstacles I had never encountered before was called the Bender. It was a series of bars curving up and over my head that I would have to climb over. I was determined at this point to still attempt every obstacle, and this one was no different. One of my teammates gave me a boost to get my legs hooked on the lowest bar, and I started to climb. I would grab onto the bars over my head and then put my legs through the next set of bars to climb the obstacle.

Unfortunately, I did not account for how to get over the top of the obstacle. I was tilted back, somewhat inverted, at the top, and my grip strength was giving out. Worse, I did what every movie with heights tells you not to do. I looked down.

My 5'2" self was about fifteen feet off the ground. That's when I wanted down. But there were few options for getting down, and I made the fatal mistake of doubting myself. I learned a valuable lesson in that moment. The second I truly believe that I can't do something, I won't. But just that crazy little bit of belief, even if it's hardly rooted in reality, can get me farther than I ever thought I could go.

It was a lesson learned too late. As one of my teammates climbed to the top to help me down - which I didn't know, but the only good option for "down" in my case was "over" - I lost my grip on the bars and fell backward. Luckily, I still had my legs locked around one of the lower bars, but then I panicked. I saw a random stranger reach up to get a grip on my shoulders, but even he could barely reach me. Just as I started to get my head straight again, my calf cramped and out of habit, I straightened my leg. I was left hanging on by one leg. And then I fell head first toward the ground.

I was only hoping that Mom would forgive me for whatever disaster was about to happen...

And then I landed on my feet.

293

I hadn't broken my neck. I was still alive.

And I was looking up at the stranger who was reaching for my shoulders. This poor guy, older but certainly fit, looked as pale and panicked as I felt. He asked if I was okay, and I shook my head, asking one of my teammates to grab one of my mustard shots for my leg cramp.

I wasn't shaking like a leaf. I was trembling like Jello; it felt as if I had no bones in my body to hold me up. He made sure I was okay, my teammates helped me pull myself back together, and we continued on. We kept pace with the Man Who Saved My Life, one minute passing him and the next being passed by him.

At about the halfway point of the race, in front of all the spectators in the festival area, we would face the obstacles Rolling Mud, Dunk Wall, and Slip Wall. They're pretty self-explanatory, basically going up and over hills of mud into pits of mud, dunking under an inflatable wall in the mud, and then climbing up a slanted metal wall with only a rope, not ten feet after the Dunk Wall.

The Rolling Mud and Dunk Wall were easy to get through, as long as I didn't think about how gross that water was that I would have to submerge in, but the Slip Wall was a whole different story.

My first race, the Slip Wall and I did not get along. I made it over with the help of Darren, but it was a task for both of us. This time, I didn't know if I could even begin to get up the wall on my own, but I didn't give myself a chance to think about it. Not after learning from the Bender about the consequences of doubting myself.

I walked up, grabbed the rope, and started to climb. Somehow, I made it to the top. When I got there, still holding the rope and trying to figure out how to actually get my leg over, I heard one of my teammates asking where I was. Another replied, in an excited shout, "She's at the top!"

I was, in fact, at the top, but I had no idea how to get *over* the top. But before I could remember the Bender catastrophe about getting over the top, I heard a voice shout from the bottom, "Just commit!"

So, I did. I pushed off with one leg and wildly threw the other over, and by some miracle, my ankle made it over. Then, my knee. Then the rest of me. As I pulled myself over the wall, I screamed the most primal, victorious scream I have ever made. And I looked down to see Mom watching, screaming back at me, "That's my Becca!"

I was elated. Shaking with adrenaline but elated. Mom saw me take on the Slip Wall!

I had just started to get comfortable on the course again when we encountered my next impossible task. The Box. A six-foot vertical wall with low clearance and a rope running down the face of the wall. I knew this one wasn't for me, and I still wasn't ready to risk my neck again, so I went to pass. My teammate insisted she help me over, and she wasn't taking no for an answer. She leaned with her back against the wall, with the idea of me using her thighs and shoulders to climb up the wall.

Unfortunately, I just ended up kicking her in the face. I felt horrible, though she took it like a champ. Now that I had officially injured someone else, I was ready to take the penalty loop, but then Stranger Who Saved My Life saw me, looked me dead in the eye, and signaled me to come over to him. I was afraid of repaying his kindness by kicking him in the face or worse, but he was even more insistent than my teammate, even after I warned him of the risks of my clumsiness. He told me he didn't care; I was *going* to make it over the obstacle. We started with what I thought was the same strategy, but as soon as I got both feet on his thighs, he hooked his hands under my feet and stood up, effectively shoving me over the top of the wall.

We both continued on our way until he stopped me and held out his hand for a handshake.

"Hi, I figured since we've gotten to know each other so intimately in the past few miles, you should know that my name is Joe."

And that's when it all clicked, in embarrassing detail. When I fell upside-down on the Bender, my shirt had fallen over my head, and he was standing pretty close to make sure he could catch me. On the box, as he pushed me over the top, he got a similar amount of contact.

But hey, I was alive, and he had a pretty good sense of humor. What happens on the course stays on the course, so I told him my name and thanked him. He jokingly thanked me as well and mentioned that in some cultures, we could be considered married by then.

By that point, the course had started messing with all of our heads. If it wasn't the mud, it was the Fart Water. As racers came up to the last station that still had good water, the volunteers told us it was good water, but we shied away as if it were a trick. We wouldn't put it past them to have a little fun with us.

We all stood by as one brave soul took a small cup, sniffed at it, and then finally took a sip. When they didn't spit it out, we rushed to the table.

Exhausted as I was, I still hadn't gotten a medal, though I had stopped paying attention to the miles we had left. Every time we hit another swamp, I wanted to cry. Every time, we would hear racers confidently say that we should be finished with the mud. In my feeble hope, I trusted them. My hopes were crushed.

Around mile ten, there was one last big mud trudge, and halfway through, I just started giggling. I wasn't the only one. Other racers had been driven just as mad by the Fart Water, Swamp Trudges, and likely their own obstacle chaos stories, and all we had left was to laugh maniacally or sob. I think a few racers chose to sob, but I forced myself to laugh as I fell up to my chest in thick brownie batter mud. I kept laughing until one of my teammates pulled me from the mud, got in my face, and told me to put one foot in front of the other, that I wasn't allowed to give in.

Not that I had been thinking about it, but I needed that in-my-face moment to snap me out of the hysterics. I had a race to finish, and we were in the homestretch. Though we started at ten that morning, the sun had already started to sink from the sky. We had been on the course for hours, though no one was talking about that. We started talking about that post-race FitAid and what we planned for dinner. I was eyeballing a Sonny's BBQ on the way back to our hotel, and a few others had the same idea.

As we moved, we heard that sweet sound we had been looking for since we left the halfway point. We heard the music from the festival area. Quiet as it was, it was like the beacon of a lighthouse in a storm. We had almost made it. One foot in front of the other.

It grew louder, then softer, then louder again as we wound our way through the course. Finally, I felt some energy return to my abused and exhausted body. Already, the bruises had started popping up on my arms, as I knew they were over my stomach. I felt blisters forming on my feet. But I was almost there.

If it was possible, I may have started to move faster. Maybe by 0.1 miles per hour, but it was faster.

Just as I kept saying, I kept putting one foot in front of the other, even over the vertical cargo net that I barely had the strength to get over. It was Mom yelling for me, telling me I was almost there, that pushed me over closer to the fire jump.

And then it finally happened. I felt the weight of the finisher medal around my neck. It was a weight that almost took me to the ground. Not that it was heavy, but that I was so exhausted. Somehow, I stumbled my way to Mom, collapsed in her arms, and cried.

It wasn't a cry of pain or of misery. It was a massive emotional release. I had spent nearly eight hours on the course, pushing myself to my limits, and I could finally say I finished.

It was in those moments that I finally truly came to understand a concept I tried to understand in preparation for the race. It was the idea that, in order to appreciate the greatest things in life, you must experience the worst as well. Finishing the Beast would not have left me feeling nearly as elated had I not remembered those moments when I couldn't even get out of my hospital bed.

By the time we made it to the truck after taking pictures and celebrating with my team, Mom had to, quite literally, put me in the truck. My hip flexors were frozen from trudging through the mud, so she had to lift my legs from the ground and put them in the car. She was the real MVP of that race weekend.

That night, Sonny's Redneck Nachos never tasted as good as they did, with me still covered in mud with the medal still around my neck.

Waking up the next morning, I knew it would be willpower alone that would get me through the two races I would need to complete my Trifecta. Luckily, with one race at six miles and one at three miles, I would be spending a lot less time on the course than I did the previous day.

Or so I hoped.

As soon as I stood up, I felt the consequences of the Beast. My hip flexors were almost completely locked up, making it difficult to pull my knee up to take a step. The rest of the muscles in my body were all sore and tight, and I was covered in bruises.

But none of that compared to the fact that my shoes hadn't fully dried from the previous day's race, so I had to put on cold, wet shoes. Not nearly as bad as wet socks, but the sensation of the muddy water soaking through my dry socks was cringeworthy enough.

After completing the Beast, the 6-mile Super was much less daunting. If I could handle thirteen miles on a Spartan course, six would surely fly by. Luckily, I found another racer to team up with, so I knew the camaraderie would fuel me through.

At the first sight of mud, though, I wanted to cry. The penalty loop for failing the rope climb was another soul-sucking trudge through thigh and waist-deep mud. Luckily, it was relatively short. But not short enough to keep my hip flexors from starting to cramp. Out came the mustard shots.

Having done the Beast the day before, the course felt familiar. That was a constant reminder of how short this course was in comparison and how quickly it was going. As we passed the mile marker that would have taken us through the Death Swamp the day before, we all blew a collective sigh of relief.

I had already told my race partner about the fiasco on the Bender, so when we approached it, I took a direct route to the burpee zone. I would gladly put myself through 30 burpees over trying that obstacle again, with even less strength than I had the day before.

298

I knew during this race and the one that was to come that if I failed an obstacle the day before, chances were I was going to fail it again. I was okay with that idea and just focused on being able to complete the obstacles I had been able to overcome.

Somehow, I breezed over the Slip Wall just as easily as I had the day before. Obstacles like the Z-Wall, Cargo Nets, and even the Stairway to Sparta seemed somehow easier. So much easier, in fact, that I started having a little bit of fun with the race photographers, making goofy poses whenever I saw one hanging out.

While going over the Inverted Wall, I felt the familiar feeling of a hand on my butt, the Spartan Handshake, guiding me over safely to the foothold on the other side of the wall. As I looked down to thank the kind stranger, I started to laugh. Of all the people on the course to run into, it was Joe.

Before I knew it, I was over the finish line. Unlike the previous day, I wasn't in tears. I still wasn't done, and I had to wait on my teammates for the 3-mile Sprint. I had to focus.

I got to hang out in the Spartan Plus tent with my race partner for a while, and got to eat a light lunch, but I quickly realized sitting was a terrible idea. My hip flexors were even angrier than when I started the day, and I was truly afraid if I stayed still too long, I wouldn't be able to move for the last race.

I dragged Mom out of the tent and started walking slow laps around the festival area. As agonizing as moving *more* was, I was three miles from my Trifecta. I had already been racing for nearly 20 miles between both previous races, and I wasn't letting it go that easily. Three miles would be nothing.

As my team started to arrive, they weren't met with the usually put-together Rebecca they had known. I think some of them were shocked to see me covered in mud, walking agonizingly slow laps around the festival area, looking dangerously close to collapsing. A few of them even started walking my laps with me in solidarity.

By the time we started the Sprint, my "run" was more like a shuffling walk. I won't say it was a fast walk because it wasn't by any stretch of the imagination, but I was trying. I barely made it halfway to the first wall before I slowed back to my trudging walk, motioning my team to keep going. They kept their pace but never let me get too far behind. One of my team stayed beside me, giving me questioning looks about why I found this kind of torture so fun.

I think that almost everyone was asking the same question at that point, both racers and spectators alike. For the Trifecta Chasers, we were wondering why we put ourselves through nearly a marathon distance in two days, through mud and rough terrain, and over obstacles. Not to mention how we found it fun. At that moment, I couldn't answer that question. I was miserable. Each step was a monumental effort. I had blisters on both feet, making each step increasingly painful. Each obstacle I had to get over dug into the bruises that had colored my skin all over. My hands had nearly locked into one position, making gripping nearly impossible.

Yet there was an end in sight, and I knew the misery would be worth it.

Much to my surprise, I had somehow made it up the Slip Wall a third time, marking my final race halfway completed. Though as I went under the dunk wall, I felt the blisters on my feet start to burst open. Now, each step was truly agonizing. But I had just over a mile left. There was no way I was giving up with so little of the course left in front of me.

When I came to the last stretch of obstacles, I felt a stirring in my chest, which meant I was about to sob when I got over the finish line. I questioned whether I would actually make it to the finish line without tears. Then, as I struggled to keep my grip on the vertical cargo net, the final obstacle before the fire jump, I started to tear up as I heard Mom yell, as she had at every previous race. But instead of her usual, "That's my Becca!" she just started yelling an unending line of encouragement, telling me that I was almost done. I just had to keep going a little longer. To keep climbing. One foot in front of the other.

I barely remember jumping over the fire with the team. I was in a daze and couldn't even really believe I was done. I grabbed the medal from the volunteer, stumbled over to Mom, and handed it to her. I wanted her to be the one to put it around my neck, along with my other two, and as soon as she did, I collapsed in her arms, sobbing. She just rocked me back and forth as much as she could over the barrier separating us, telling me how proud she was and how I did it.

I completed my first Spartan Trifecta.

The feeling of having finished, having completed the thing that nearly broke me so many times, made the answer to "why" so clear. At that moment, it's not like I stopped feeling pain or that my hip flexors loosened up and my bruises disappeared. I was still miserable, and now that the race was over, I truly questioned my ability to walk back to our truck.

It wasn't that anything had changed in my situation, but it was that I had overcome. There had been so much in my way - nearly 23 miles and 90 obstacles. But over the course of those two days, I had been persistent. I had overcome my own mind, found my limits, and surpassed them.

It wasn't just the course I had overcome, either. I overcame a prognosis that said I would never walk again, much less race a Trifecta Weekend. Physically, I had not changed, but emotionally, I was a whole new person. I was the kind of person that met challenges, no matter how impossible they seemed. I was the kind of person who didn't listen to the voice in my head or voices outside of my head telling me that I couldn't do something.

I texted Trevor as soon as I could get my phone. It wasn't any surprise to him, since he knew I would get my Trifecta, but along with Mom, he was the first person I wanted to share the news with.

Before I could collapse in the truck, I had one more task ahead of me. I had to get my Trifecta Weekend medal. I choked up as I showed the volunteer my three medals and handed the huge medal to Mom. When she hugged me, I was crying tears of joy.

When I finally did make it to the truck, I refused to take the medals off. As much as they weighed my neck down at an awkward angle, I wasn't ready to let the physical reminder of my accomplishment go.

Limitless

Chapter 32

I still limped from the Spartan Trifecta Weekend by the time I decided to plan my next race. I hadn't yet attempted the Spartan Super on its own, and I wanted to test my abilities on the 10k without being exhausted from doing a Beast the day before.

It wasn't far into my training, though, before my leg had started to give me trouble. Instead of the typical knee pain I had grown so accustomed to, I was having pain like a shin splint. It wasn't the kind of pain to concern me, just a sharp, constant ache.

Though I had been well accustomed to chronic pain, I was used to it going away after a few days. Usually, the weather would cause my pain to flare, so after a few days, it would be fine again. This pain was persistent. It didn't go away after a few days or even a few weeks. I held off on the gym, hoping rest would help. I used ice, I used heat, and nothing worked.

The week before the Super, I started to get weary. Though I had been planning to race with a new team, More Heart Than Scars, I started to worry about whether or not I should race at all. I bounced back and forth in the week leading up to the race. I knew I would have no trouble sucking it up and racing. It was only six miles, and I knew what a 23-mile weekend was like. It would be nothing.

But, the constant, unending pain for what had already spanned weeks was wearing on me. I didn't want to make it worse. A few days before, I called off the race. Trevor was surprised that I would have chosen to let a race pass me by. He didn't say anything, but I could tell he wasn't buying the idea of me not racing.

The night before the race, at nearly 4:00 a.m., I had the most vivid dreams. I had dreams of racing, of rolling through the mud, of earning another medal. I woke up sobbing at the idea of missing out on something I came to love so much. So, at 5:00 a.m., I woke Mom up and told her I was racing. If I left by 6:00 a.m., I could still make it in time to race with MHTS.

I sent a text to Trevor to let him know I had changed my mind, only to get the simple response, "I know."

He explained later that he had no doubts I'd be racing. He just needed me to come to that conclusion on my own. When I asked him how in the world he knew, he told me, "Well, you are my sister." Fair enough.

I was wholly unprepared. Since I had called the race off, I didn't have my gear set out as I usually would have. I hadn't gotten my usual supply of race snacks and mustard shots. I didn't even have time to fill my Camelbak. I flew out the door and on the two-and-a-half-hour drive to the venue, praying I would make it in time. My start time with the team was at 8:45 a.m., and I was going to cut it close with the time it would take to park and check-in.

I pulled into the parking lot, Mom behind me, at 8:42 a.m. As I checked in, I asked if I could still make it for the 8:45 a.m. heat, and the volunteer told me, quite literally, if I signed the waiver and sprinted to the start line. I barely had time to pull on my grip gloves and put my race bandana on. They were already starting the starting line chants when I ran up. But instead of the usual 4-foot wall, I was met with two volunteers standing in front of a bucket of mud. I was confused but told them I was racing with MHTS. They smirked, and one reached into the bucket and slathered mud over the sides of my face.

304

When they stepped aside, I saw the 4-foot wall behind a 20-foot stretch of gravel and hay, covered by low clearance barbed wire, with smoke pouring from where the hay had been lit on fire.

Another addition to the pre-race rituals, I was staring at the newly coined Spartan Armageddon.

I was already rattled from barely making it to the starting line on time, so I wasn't intimidated or even surprised at the new addition to the course. I just dove into the smoky haze and started moving.

When I say I made it to the starting line to introduce myself to the team just as the MC yelled for us to go, I am not exaggerating in the least.

As the race started, I was almost thankful for the mud smeared on my face. I hadn't had time to apply my usual eye black, and the sun was glaring.

I made introductions with the team as we started our race. We reached the over walls, and I made my usual attempt to jump over them by myself. To my surprise, I actually made it over the wall on my first try with no help. I was over the moon, and we weren't even a mile in.

Through the race, it became clear that in the few months since the Trifecta Weekend, I had gotten so much stronger. I was hopping over the walls with relative ease and hauling around the sandbags and buckets on the heavy carries like they were nothing.

I also got to find out more about MHTS between obstacles. I met some of their members, who had scars, both visible and invisible, of their own. Their mission was to help anyone, regardless of ability, overcome the obstacles on the course, even to the point of having specialized wheelchairs to pull members through the course.

If I thought the camaraderie of the Spartan Racers was incredible before, this team gave it a whole new meaning. I heard stories of many who, like me, had been told they would never, that it would be impossible, complete Spartan races of all lengths.

I knew that I had found my people. The kind of people that the word "impossible" held no weight for.

Before I knew it, I was staring at the obstacle I had been waiting to face for the past few months. I was at the Bender.

I had spent months strategizing, troubleshooting, and planning how I was going to get over this obstacle. I also spent months trying to convince myself not to be more than a little scared of getting to the top and falling. Joe wasn't there to save me this time.

But I was encouraged by the fact that I was so much stronger than I had been in my previous races, and I was much less exhausted than when I first encountered the Bender. After a boost to get my legs wrapped around the bars, I started my climb, careful to use the bend of my arms to grip the bars rather than my hands. I quickly made it to the top and used another trick I had strategized to give myself a breather before trying to go over. I stuck my head under the top bar, using the back of my neck to hold myself in place.

My first attempt to stand on the bars and push myself over was an epic failure. None of my planning factored in how short my legs were, and no matter how hard I pushed off, I couldn't get my chest to clear the top bar. I came back to my resting position with my head through the bars and thought out a new strategy. My team was nearby, and I trusted them to help me, but I knew the one way down was over.

The idea hit me to use the leverage I had at my head to squeeze through the top two bars instead of trying to go completely over the top. It wasn't the perfect solution, and it may not have been the correct way to get over the obstacle, but it was a step in the right direction. I squeezed in between the top two bars and made my way down the bars before dropping down into the arms of my new team.

I felt pretty accomplished. Sure, in a competitive heat, that absolutely would not have counted as a completion, but I had made it farther than I did the first time I attempted the Bender. And I didn't almost break my neck. I was taking the wins where I could get them.

As we approached one of my favorite obstacles, the A-Frame Cargo Net, one of my team members asked, with a tell-tale twinkle in his eye, if I was afraid of heights. When I said no, he told me he was going to teach me a new trick. The growing sparkle in his eyes told me I was going to enjoy this trick, so I got Mom's attention from the festival area and told her to start recording.

As we climbed and nearly reached the top, my teammate told me he was going to teach me how to flip over the top of the net. I had watched some of the more experienced racers try that trick before and was down for the idea immediately.

Most of the time, at the top of the cargo net, we used the same strategy to get over the top as we would a wall. Swing one leg over, then the other, landing on our stomachs on the other side. But by flipping the cargo net, I would land on my back on the other side.

He taught me where to grip the net with my hands, where to aim my head, and then simply told me to swing my legs over my head. Commit, he said. Just like the Slip Wall. So, I did, and before I knew it, I had landed on my back, my team all screaming in excitement.

Through the course, my leg had started to ache worse and worse. The mental challenge of this race wasn't the mud and the distance but the pain.

Speaking of the mud, there was no Death Swamp there, thankfully. But what they did make sure to include was a torturous muddy barbed wire crawl. Up a hill.

It was sadistic, but that's what Spartan Racers thrive on. The barbed wire crawl wasn't so bad during the flat part of the course, but as the mud thickened, it seemed to drag me down. That's when the incline started, at what had to have been a nearly 45-degree angle. The barbed wire was so low it would catch my back if I didn't crawl nearly flat, which was a nearly impossible task going up the hill. To add insult to injury, the volunteers at the top of the hill had a water hose and would spray us down, making the mud even slicker.

I was grumbling the entire way up the muddy hill. I even grumbled at Trevor. He knew without a doubt that I would be going through this, and he would be laughing at the muddy predicament I had found myself in at his encouragement.

It was like the stories grandparents tell about how they got to school every day.

When I finally made it to the top and stood up, I felt bogged down with mud. Somehow, this was what I had missed so much.

Many of us had been racing on the same course at the Trifecta Weekend, and apparently, we all had a little post-traumatic stress going on. As we approached any of the water stations, we all eyed the little cups, sitting there so invitingly, with caution. Since I didn't have my Camelbak, I knew that either way, I would have to take the water from the station, even if it was like the Fart Water. Luckily, it was not, but I still held my nose and took it like a shot anyway.

Overall, I felt like I had gotten a good workout by the time I reached the finish line and claimed my medal. Mom got her now-traditional muddy hug, and I wasn't nearly as exhausted or beat up as I had been at the Trifecta Weekend. I felt strong. I had been able to complete more of the obstacles than I had before, and I finished in good time.

But it all came at a cost. My leg was barely taking my weight by the time I had gotten home, and when it didn't get better within a few days, causing me to visibly limp, I started to get worried.

I was so worried that I immediately went into denial, assuring myself that it had to be fine. Nothing could possibly go wrong. But over the course of a few weeks, I could barely take a step without pain shooting down my shin and into my foot like a lightning bolt.

I stuck it out, firmly in denial for as long as I could be. I wasn't willing to face the idea that maybe I had pushed the allograft too far. I held on to my delusions that I was fine right up until the day I got out of bed and stood up, only to watch my leg collapse under me, the outline of bone protruding from the middle of my tibia, right where I knew the allograft had been placed.

Limitless

Part Three: Amputation

Limitless

Chapter 33

My immediate reaction to the fact that it looked like my leg had just formed a new joint was denial. I had accepted a cancer diagnosis like it was another Tuesday, but I was not capable of accepting what was in front of me. Because after all this time, it simply could not be. I refused to think through the issue logically. I refused to acknowledge that I could hardly bear my weight.

I had just started a new job, one that I really liked. I was working at a warehouse, which meant being on my feet for the entirety of a ten-hour shift. Deep down, I knew I wouldn't make it through any part of a warehouse shift with my leg, but the alternative was something I wasn't ready to accept. The new reality I had spent so long building was crumbling, and I was still trying to hold it up.

Mom knew better than to try to force me to go to the hospital. She knew it would traumatize me worse to be forced into facing that, so she let me continue my delusion that I could go to work.

That's the thing about denial. For me, I knew my leg was broken. I knew the plate was broken. I knew my life was falling apart. I just couldn't accept it. Because if I accepted that my leg was broken, it wouldn't stop there. I would have to accept that I would have to go to the hospital. I would have to accept an inevitable

313

surgery. I would have to accept the likely long and painful recovery that would follow.

Worse, I would have to accept that I wouldn't be going to the gym or running any Spartans any time soon. I couldn't simply build a dam in my mind to only let the first of those thoughts through. Once the acceptance of my leg being broken came, the rest would come with it, as would a massive mental breakdown.

So, instead, I chose to allow myself to believe the delusion that I could ignore the obvious and go about my workday, and I wouldn't have to face what I knew was coming. I packed my lunch, put on my ID badge, and got in the car. Mom drove us halfway to work before the dam in my mind couldn't hold back the torrent of thoughts. I thought about the long walk I would have to make just to make it to my dock's work area. I thought about trying to stand mostly on one leg for ten long hours. I thought about making that long walk back and forth to the breakroom.

I kept pressing my foot into the floorboard of the truck, desperately hoping that it wouldn't bend midway down my tibia, right where that cadaver allograft sat. It kept bending.

The moment I accepted the truth and told Mom to take me to the hospital, the consequences of acceptance followed. All those realities I would have to accept - the surgeries, recovery, pain, and trauma to come - manifested in one single thought.

My life is over.

I knew this wasn't going to kill me. My life wasn't over in the sense that I was going to die. But my *life,* my mountain climbing, cave exploring, Spartan racing, weightlifting life was over. My life would now be what I had tried so hard to escape. It would be doctor appointments and physical therapy and sitting on the couch until I lost every ounce of my sanity.

So, to say that, when it hit me, I started to cry would be like saying that Hurricane Katrina was a little thunderstorm. I started sobbing. My breath came in gasps to the point where I got so lightheaded I started to pass out. I would focus so hard on my breathing that I would momentarily forget the state of my leg, and

314

when I remembered, the cycle of hyperventilating would start all over again.

That cycle continued for nearly an hour as Mom stopped by work to tell our managers what was going on, then drove us back home to pack the hospital essentials we had become all too familiar with years before.

The only reason the cycle stopped was because I had slipped into a state of dissociative numbness. I shut down so thoroughly that I felt nothing. I couldn't speak. I could barely move. I just sat in the passenger seat, eyes glazed, allowing myself to fall into a cold and calculative state of mind where everything was simple fact.

Void of feeling, I ran through the facts that were in front of me. I knew that the minute I entered the hospital and became a patient again, I could expect to lose myself in a swarm of long-buried traumas and may lose the ability to advocate for myself.

I knew that the likelihood of anything actually being done for me was low. I was simply there to get imaging to confirm the extent of the damage and to be referred back to Ortho. With that in mind, I knew that I wasn't going to let them admit me. There was no point. I wasn't going to risk what fragile bit of my mental health remained by trying to stay overnight in the hospital.

In an attempt to keep the growing panic at bay, I tried to play out the events that were about to happen in my head. I would check in to the emergency department, see a doctor for an initial consult, be taken back for X-rays, be given possibly devastating news, and go home. I was relatively calm, thinking I knew what to expect.

Unfortunately, since it had been quite a few years since my last visit to the ED, things were not as I had anticipated. Soon after signing in, I was called back, not to a bed in the ED but to another, smaller room. Much to my terror, I was told only that Mom could not go back with me.

The calm that I had carefully crafted based on predictability had been shattered. For most, being asked to follow the triage nurse into a small, unknown room would be fine. For me, I didn't know what was going on in that room. I could only speculate I'd be seeing a doctor, but the unexpected change in procedure left me with too

315

many questions. How long would I be separated from Mom? Would I get the chance to go back to her, or would they move me and not tell her where I had gone? How long would I be gone?

I took in the small room and realized it was a triage room, large enough to accommodate multiple patients. I only had a moment's calm before noticing that there was, in fact, a smaller room attached to the triage room. Great, then I had to speculate what that room was. Thankfully, I didn't have to wait long before the nurse taking my vitals told me that I would be waiting for a telehealth consult.

I thought they must have been pulling some kind of prank. They really meant to tell me that I would be seeing a doctor on a screen to put in orders for X-rays? Yes, yes, they did. After a long enough wait, I was told that, instead of going into a separate room to discuss what was going on with this telehealth doctor, I would just be seated behind a curtain for my consultation. As if a curtain would provide any privacy from the other patients in the triage room. Thankfully, my reason for being there wasn't overly personal.

I tried to remain calm about the absurdity of this new consult procedure; I really did. But when the spotty Wi-Fi connection made it nearly impossible to hold a conversation with this doctor, who looked as if he were sitting in his living room in pajamas, my patience started running on a short leash. Whenever the Wi-Fi did allow us to hold a conversation, I couldn't even hear what he was saying over the bad audio quality. Apparently, he couldn't hear me either because I was eventually speaking loud enough for the rest of the triage room to hear all about my leg and medical history. HIPAA compliant, indeed.

Thoroughly frustrated, I was returned to the waiting room with the promise of orders being put in for an X-ray. An X-ray that wouldn't happen for nearly two hours. When I was finally called back, I put all the effort I had into trying to be upbeat towards the X-ray techs I would be seeing. It wasn't their fault the hospital they worked at was a hot mess, and I always had a soft spot for radiology techs. They offered me a wheelchair, which I politely declined.

Deep down, though, I knew what they were about to see on the X-ray and what it would mean for me. I knew that once the speculation became reality, the freedom of taking my own steps would be taken from me. I wasn't ready to give up the independence of walking, so despite the pain, I limped with as much dignity as I could muster to get the X-rays done.

Up until then, I had been clinging to one last shred of hope that maybe it wasn't as bad as it seemed. Maybe a miracle would happen in the few minutes I would be on the X-ray table. Maybe I would stand up, and my leg would hold fast as it had for the past three and a half years. I was nearly begging God for that miracle as they took the X-rays. But as I stepped back onto the ground and let my leg take a little of my weight, it gave. The visible bend midway down my tibia was still there.

Despite that, I still held on to some impossible shred of hope. Hope was pulled farther from my grasp as the X-ray tech subtly asked me if my surgeons had ever warned me about the possibility of the plate in my leg needing replacement.

My heart dropped to my stomach. I had been holding onto the smallest bit of hope that maybe the plate was still intact. The allograft being broken was one thing, but the plate being broken was a whole new level of bad news. Of course, not that he told me the metal was broken. But the sympathetic look he gave me as we parted ways back at the waiting room spoke volumes.

As the hours dragged on in the waiting room, I went from trying to lean on Mom's shoulder for a nap to threatening to leave the ED. My patience was gone. If all they were going to do was tell me my leg was broken beyond their ability to do anything for me, waiting seemed pointless. It didn't help that I hadn't eaten since well before coming to the ED, and I had already been there for five hours. Hangry was an understatement.

As I kept my small group updated through our group chat, one of the amazing ladies offered to pick us up some food to get us through the night. I was in the process of learning how to accept help. I had moved to a new church that was closer to home, Destiny Community Church - DCC for short - and had gotten involved in a small group. I had learned to rely on the ladies in my small group for prayer but hadn't quite learned how to accept things like the offer of food. The bag of Fritos and Pepsi from the vending machine was only lasting so long, though, so Mom and I accepted her offer.

In the perfect timing of the hospital, I was called back to a bed not five minutes before our friend arrived with the best Burger King Whopper I had ever tasted. At least I could handle what was to come on a full stomach.

I was hoping that the absurdity of the whole situation had been behind me now that I had a bed, but I was wrong. In a similar fashion to the triage room fiasco, my bed didn't even have a curtain to give me any separation from every other patient packed into the room. Even with the hangry taken care of, the ridiculousness of the whole situation left me wondering what was next.

What was next was more frustration, of course, this time in the form of a nurse practitioner with an attitude. As I began to recount the events that led up to that moment, I was interrupted and told that she had read my file and that she already knew. Why she asked me in the first place, I do not know, if she had apparently already read my file.

Starting off on that great note, she told me with about as much empathy as a dead snail that the allograft in my leg had a transverse fracture, meaning it had broken all the way through. On top of that, the plate had also been completely broken. She cheerily told me that their on-call Ortho resident was on his way to talk me through what that would mean for me and left me to process this news.

The spark of hope I had been holding onto was such a small flicker, but I wasn't giving it up. Not yet. Not until I heard it from this resident's mouth what this meant for me and my future. I couldn't spend too long pondering what my life would look like, though, since I started pondering something far more pressing in my mind.

How did a titanium plate in my leg break?

When the resident got there, that was the first question I asked. I was blindsided by the answer that, as a team, Ortho actually expected that the allograft would break eventually and that it was likely the allograft breaking that put enough pressure on the plate that it followed suit. I was so stunned at that answer that I didn't have the capacity to ask any other questions. I just stared blankly while he explained that, since there was nothing they could do, they were considering admitting me until morning.

Mom and I refused that suggestion at the same time. The resident was smart enough not to argue. He just told us that he would get a referral into Ortho and get the discharge papers ready. As he left, I stared at the wall in front of me, processing the information I had just been given. My surgical team knew my leg was going to break again one day. On top of the fact that they essentially gave me no other options for a tumor removal surgery, the option they chose had set me up for failure.

All the talk about me never being able to walk again wasn't a question of ability. It was a warning. A badly communicated warning that should have come before the surgery when I was in my right mind. Not when I was lying in a hospital bed fighting sepsis. Because if I had known that one day I would end up right back at the hospital, unable to walk, I would not have gone along with the plan they set out for me.

I ran all that through my mind, trying to find a new angle. Some way to spin it to seem less atrocious, less devastating. But every time, I came to the same conclusions. My team had severely screwed me over, and now my life was over.

Okay, maybe that second part seems a bit dramatic. Looking back on it now, I know it does. But being the girl who was terrified of just being in a hospital, staring unforgettable traumas right in the face, hearing that her life as she knew it was about to change drastically - no more running, boxing, or even walking on her own - I think she was pretty justified in how she was feeling. What was she going to do with a broken leg, anyway?

When the first tears from that set of realizations hit, they didn't stop this time. Mom leaned up from her chair beside my hospital bed and held me while I wept. She tried to hold up the nearly see-through blanket to give me some semblance of privacy to have my breakdown to, but eventually, we gave up on hiding it. Every time I got myself together, even just a bit, I would think of just one aspect of my situation and break down again. This went on for another two hours as we awaited discharge.

I thought of how I would likely be undergoing some sort of corrective surgery soon. I remembered the pain from the last surgery, and dread filled every fiber of my being at the idea of going through that again. Then, there were thoughts of another months-long recovery. I definitely wouldn't be able to work, which meant I wouldn't be getting paid. I wouldn't be able to work out the way I had come to enjoy working out. Slowly, I watched so many aspects of my life that I had come to enjoy - my physical fitness, my job, my independence - fall apart.

And it just kept falling apart. Minute after minute, I relived watching those aspects of my life crumble, knowing there was nothing I could do about it.

The scariest thoughts came just before Mom and I nearly begged the resident to get the discharge papers signed. It had been two hours since I was told I would need to revisit Ortho, totaling nearly eight hours in the hospital. I had processed this new development in my life enough that my thoughts turned into an even more terrifying place.

After all this time, even through cancer, I had not yet had the thought that now plagued my mind. But at the roots of my despair, I finally wrestled with the thought I had tried so desperately to avoid.

Is this really God's plan for me?

Why would He have given me so many amazing years and experiences after cancer, only to let them be ripped away?

My tears hadn't stopped since it was confirmed that both the allograft and plate in my leg had broken. It was at that moment that, for the first time in my life, I had lost all hope. I had spent years fighting. From fighting for my life during cancer treatment to fighting for my ability after surgery to fighting to improve my health to fighting to find a job that I loved that would sustain me. It seemed as if my fighting had finally paid off, and just as it did, everything had been turned upside down. I would have to start fighting again.

But in the last few hours that I spent lying in the hospital bed, not even having the privacy to cry in peace, I stopped fighting. I was tired, both physically and emotionally, and so I let myself cry. I didn't stop as my nurse went over discharge instructions or as the Ortho resident brought in the objects that would seal my living nightmare in place. I could barely move or even react as he adjusted the crutches I had worked so hard to rid myself of to my height and as he strapped the immobilizing brace around my leg. I felt as if, within a few moments, I had been thrown back to square one. Crutches, a brace, and being told not to walk.

Much to the resident's credit, he didn't try to act overly enthusiastic about the situation. He didn't smile ridiculously or cheerily tell me I would be fine. He saw me where I was and met me in my despair. He offered sympathetic smiles and apologies for what I would be going through.

I tried to insist that I at least be allowed the dignity to walk myself out of the ED on crutches, but of course, I ended up being wheeled out in a wheelchair.

The moment the nurse left me to the care Mom, I tore off the brace, taking great pleasure in ripping open the Velcro straps that held it in place. It was like slamming down those old landline phones after a heated call. It was cathartic. I found the idea of immobilizing my perfectly good knee absurd, anyway. Keeping my leg frozen straight wasn't going to do me any favors when I had to learn to navigate around on crutches.

My only discharge instructions were to not put weight on my left leg and to make sure I didn't do anything to cause the fracture to become a compound fracture. Because, to my surprise, there was something that would make my current situation worse.

I finally stopped crying by the time we started our drive home at around 2:00 a.m. It wasn't out of acceptance or comfort. I didn't feel any better, and the thoughts of my life being over still haunted me. I simply didn't have enough energy to keep crying.

Or so I thought.

When I got home and finally found the privacy of my own room, I lost it in a way I had never experienced. I started crying again, but this time, I exhaled in short screams muffled by a pillow, with what little air I had in my lungs from the short, hyperventilated inhales I took.

My life is over.

My life is over.

My life is over.

Over and over until my head started to feel foggy, and I knew if I didn't get it under control, I would pass out. Mom had just turned the water in the shower off anyway, and I let that be the timer on my existential breakdown. It had to end sometime, and that was the time. I would sleep, and I would figure out the rest the next day.

But getting out of the shower and imagining being alone nearly sent me into another fit of hyperventilation. I did what any 22-year-old woman would do in the depths of despair. I hobbled my way into Mom's room and curled up in bed beside her.

Waking up the next morning yielded no better results than the night before. I awoke as I usually did after my night shifts, stretching my arms over my head and slowly letting the stretch take over my entire body. Everything seemed fine. Everything even seemed normal, as if the previous night was just some horrible nightmare. Except when the glorious morning stretch reached my legs, and I lifted my leg off the bed, I felt it. As my knee and ankle raised off the bed, the two broken halves of my bone seemed to stay suspended between my two joints like a low arching swinging bridge.

I went limp, sinking back into the bed. I still couldn't quite process it. I tried lifting my leg again to see if maybe I had just been imagining it in the haziness of sleep. But surely enough, my swinging bridge, Jenga tower of a leg still fell apart. So much for that.

I tried to distract myself by getting on my phone, but the concerned texts from friends who I had kept informed the previous night overwhelmed me. Their care and love filled my heart but trying to find the words to explain what we had found out had tears falling again.

322

I didn't want the morning, or the rest of the day, to go as the previous night had, but unless I kept myself well distracted on Facebook, I found no relief from the mental torment.

My life is over.

Random cat video.

My life is over.

Ridiculous 5-Minute Crafts Life Hacks.

My life is over.

I knew I would eventually have to face my problems. Though it pained me to think about it, if Spartan taught me one thing I could take into real life, it was that you can't avoid life's obstacles forever. You face them, overcome them, or take the penalty.

Well, I couldn't exactly take the 30-burpee penalty around my useless leg, so I decided to face it. But I couldn't think. I couldn't hear any sort of logic over the broken record "My life is over" playing in my head.

Okay, so dealing with it in my head was not going to work. But saying out loud, "My life is over," wasn't going to be any more effective than thinking about it. Therapy was an option, but finding a therapist, much less one that could deal with the host of spiritual questions building in my mind was a slim chance on a Thursday afternoon.

There was one option, though, that reignited the smoldering hope I was trying to keep alive. My DCC family. I knew the pastors offered counseling, and perhaps one of them might still have had an opening on their schedule. So, I pulled myself together and gave the church office a call. Even hearing the receptionist's voice answering the phone put my soul at ease. They were my people. I tried to keep it together while explaining that I had a medical situation come up that, if possible, I needed help processing. Thank God our associate pastor, Pastor Andrew, was able to make time later that afternoon.

The hope reignited. My life might have been over, but I was going to be okay. I just had to keep myself distracted by watching Facebook videos. There was a plan. Even if it was just one step in the plan, it was more than I started my day with.

When I got to the church office, I encountered a new obstacle. Immediately, seeing that I was on crutches, everyone was asking if I was okay. I would be, I assured them. I didn't know how, but I would be.

I managed to make it into Pastor Andrew's office and thank him for making time to see me before bursting into tears. Much to his credit, he just handed me a box of tissues and told me to cry it out until I was ready.

For the first time, I laid out my story. I survived cancer. I survived sepsis three times. I explained the parts of my story that are simply beyond logic, like how I was free of aggressive cancer when chemo had not worked. How I had walked when my surgical team had not witnessed anyone walking after a radical surgery like mine. How I was free of an autoimmune disease because I heard the voice of Jesus tell me my faith had healed me.

Then I had to explain how the leg that had carried me, miraculously, through Spartan Races, had failed me. How it seemed as if the miracles had run out. How I questioned if all those experiences with miracles and healing had even been true at all, how I had been thrown back into square one.

And somehow, during this long explanation of big feelings, I stopped crying. I still felt broken, but it had been replaced with a hunger for understanding. Maybe if I could understand where God was and what He was doing, I could rekindle my hope and face this new reality. I just couldn't stop the torrent of my own thoughts long enough to get there. I needed someone to guide my thoughts back to where they should be, and Pastor Andrew was the person.

He reminded me that just because I was facing seemingly impossible circumstances did not mean I was starting over. I must have looked beyond perplexed as I glanced at the crutches sitting against the wall because he had to ask me if I was, in fact, the same person I was during my first surgery.

Well, that was a good point. The amount of growth, especially spiritual growth that I had experienced in the past few years since my first surgery was pretty clear. So, even though I seemed to be back at square one, I was far from square one in my ability to handle the situation.

If that were true, and it certainly was, then it must remain true that all those experiences, all of the miracles I experienced, had to be true. My current situation did not negate the things that took place.

The final piece of the puzzle that fell into place was when Pastor Andrew started to explain a concept that I have carried with me all this time. It's one that I had heard about a thousand times, though I had always heard it when life was good. When life was good, I could clap my hands and "amen" to the concept all I wanted, but it didn't really hit home until I was down in the depths. Then, the lightbulb really went off.

The concept was that of expectation versus reality, and how the problem lies when those two concepts do not converge. My expectation for my life was that everything would be, and stay, amazing, but reality took a different turn that would lead to disappointment, and in my current extreme case, despair.

Lightbulb.

At that moment, I found God again. It's not that He had been anywhere else but right there beside me, but it was like a veil of negativity had been lifted, and I could put my eyes back where they should have been. It was then that I found out what true hope was.

I had known hope to be this thing that was based on what I could see, metaphorically speaking. If I could see a good resolution to the problem, then I had hope. But at that moment, I learned that real, true hope isn't based on seeing a positive outcome. It's finding joy when I couldn't see any resolution at all because the hope isn't reliant on the outcome but on who determines the outcome. I remembered that the one who brought me through cancer, kept me alive during sepsis, and healed me of an autoimmune disease was the same one who had already laid out the outcome of the situation I was in. I didn't need to know the outcome. I just needed to keep my eyes on the one who knew the game plan.

I reminded myself that, if God could take away an autoimmune disease, he could heal a broken plate. I had peace knowing that even if that healing didn't look like what I had hoped it would look like, His plan was greater.

For the first time since I had woken up the previous morning, I had a new thought running through my head.

I am going to be okay.

I faced the weekend and the inevitable call from Ortho to schedule a consultation with the new and improved swarm of thoughts in my head. I was going to be okay. God would make sure I was okay.

When Ortho called to schedule me, I had no fear, not even a hint of anxiety. I knew one thing for certain, though. I wasn't going to be consulting with the surgeon who had performed my first surgery. I may not have been in fear, but that wasn't to say I wasn't angry. There was simply no way I was going to go into an appointment to determine the course of my life with a surgeon who I couldn't trust.

Of course, the nurse coordinator who called me seemed shocked that I blatantly stated that I wanted to see another surgeon. That was no surprise. But I held firm and got scheduled with a new surgeon in the same office. This time, things would be different. I would be with a new surgeon. I would make my concerns and my needs heard. I would make my own choices, not be stuck with choices that were made for me.

Chapter 34

April 24, 2023

I had an entire weekend to think through how my appointment with this new surgeon would go. I learned from my ED experience to not use my expectations of how the appointment would go to ease my anxiety. Instead, I focused on what I could control. I knew what I wanted my life to look like. I knew the idea of spending my life using a cane or walker was out of the question. I wasn't going to be able to climb Everest or run a Spartan Ultra with a useless leg. Whatever options they gave me, and Lord knows they were going to give me every option they had in their arsenal this time, was going to be for the betterment of my life and wellbeing.

Mom knew I was ready to take any extreme measure to get my life back. I had mentioned some of those extreme measures in my scheduled mental breakdowns before my leg broke. Almost down to the week, I would become so fed up with the pain and restrictions forced on me because of my previous surgery that I would spend a day ranting about how I wish they would have given an option, any other option, to get the tumor out of my leg.

I often speculated that even if the other options had been decidedly worse, simply being in control of the choice of what happened to my leg would have given me the peace that I had been robbed of. I was ready to take that back. I think it scared Mom, seeing just how impassioned I would get laying out what I wanted from the upcoming consultation.

I kept telling her that I needed her to know what I wanted in case I became unable to voice it for myself if my trauma responses became too great. I wanted my life back. I wanted to run again, even if I hated running. I wanted to race again. I made her promise not to let them take that away from me.

On the day of my appointment, I spent a lot of time praying. I wasn't praying for a specific outcome. I had become so comforted by the idea that God had it under control that I didn't really need to pray for the outcome. I needed my strength. I prayed that He would make my mind sound against the anxiety already building. I prayed that He would help me stand firm for what I knew was best for me.

By the time I stepped into the entryway for Ortho, I truly understood the concept Pastor Andrew was trying to convey to me. I was in the same entryway where my journey started. Back in 2019, that office was where I would be poked and prodded for hours before being told they needed to biopsy the tumor on my leg the day before I was diagnosed with cancer.

I took a moment to truly let myself process how different of a woman I was from the 18-year-old that went into that same office four and a half years prior. She was so young, and so inexperienced. The woman standing in the Ortho office in 2023 had walked through so much and had grown so much through the process. She knew what she wanted, how to advocate for herself, and had a confidence that could have only come from faith.

I felt the shift in my mindset to my core. After spending all weekend feeling like I had lost my dignity to the crutches I had to use, I felt my dignity return, almost with a vengeance. I was the woman who ran a Trifecta Weekend, her first season of racing. I was the woman who almost knocked out a grown man during sparring for not heeding my warnings to lighten up. I was the woman who fought to live life to the fullest, and if I had to keep fighting for that, I would.

328

Of course, the whole appointment started by throwing me far off balance. Or trying its best to. I had come in expecting the unexpected, so when I wasn't taken to the CT room as I was told I would be when I checked in, I just brushed it off. It was the usual chaos.

Sticking to the usual routines, though, I was met first by an Ortho resident before meeting my surgeon. In a definite answer to my prayers, I felt a confidence I had never felt in the presence of doctors. Usually, I would have been timid. Not this time. When the resident finished his quick exam of my leg and asked me if I had any questions, I came in prepared to throw them off balance. I just recounted that the resident in the ED had told me that, with surgery like mine, the bone breaking was something they had expected. I asked only if that was true. I smiled calmly and thanked the resident when he affirmed that, yes, they did expect the bone to break eventually.

Meeting my new surgeon was, to my surprise, a pleasant interaction. We chatted enough that I felt confident he was, in fact, seeing a human being in front of him, not a broken leg attached to a human body that he could fix. I was still shocked, nearly out of my chair, though, when he asked what *he* could do for *me.*

I was so used to being told exactly what was going to happen to me that I was thrown off balance. In a good way. Which threw me further off balance, in a good way.

I had come in prepared to listen to some bogus idea of how to fix my leg that would certainly not be what I wanted. Opening up with a conversation about what I needed was a new situation for me. So, I told him what I wanted. I told him I was a Spartan Racer. I was an adventurer. Admittedly, I was an adrenaline junkie. I told him I needed him to get me back to doing those things. He seemed to pause to consider my words, even more to my surprise.

Then came the surgery plan he had been thinking of. His plan was to, of course, replace the metal plate in my leg. That sounded decent. Then, to repair my broken tibia, he would take the blood supply from my fibula and connect it to my tibia in hopes that it would resupply the allograft with blood and allow it to heal itself. In terms of healing time, it would be months, of course. But then he used a word I didn't particularly like.

If.

If my leg could heal itself. *If* I didn't need revision surgeries to make it work.

Then came another word I didn't like hearing.

Maybe.

If everything worked as it should, then *maybe* I'd be able to keep my leg.

He seemed quite pleased with his plan. I mean, color me impressed, it was a pretty good plan. Except for those *ifs* and *maybes.*

I knew the answer, but I still had to ask when I would be back on a Spartan course. His answer to me was laced with an attitude of, "Silly goose!" as he told me that I likely wouldn't be walking again, and for real, this time.

So, for the second time in my life, I was being told I would "never walk again." Please imagine me using dramatic air quotes when I say that.

Now we were playing the game I had come in waiting to play. In my mind, it was like a very high stakes game of chess. I needed to, for lack of better words here, manipulate him into making the moves I needed him to make. Game on.

I kept my calm, by the grace of God, and simply reminded him that I needed an option that included actually being able to use my leg again. He told me that that would be, and I quote, "Impossible."

I gave him a sweet smile and leaned back into my chair.

"Nothing is impossible."

He mirrored my stance in his own chair. I was using an old trick I learned in high school. In interrogations, the first person to speak loses, and I don't like losing. So, I met his stare with one of my own and waited. It was a tense fifteen seconds or so until he broke the silence.

He explained that, under the circumstances, this surgery was my only option. It took every ounce of my self-control not to roll my eyes at him.

330

I will forever cherish the look on his face as I smiled at him and simply stated, "Find me another option, or I'll find another surgeon."

Now, he was off balance, and I was in my element. My leg was broken. He was talking about a months-to-years-long recovery period. I had plenty of time to find a surgeon who would give me the right options.

Now being somewhat on the defensive, he explained that I wouldn't like any other options. That statement was what let loose the barrage of thoughts that had been building for years, and I was past holding them in.

I told him we needed to pause because we needed to get on the same page. I needed him to understand me. Graciously, he motioned me on.

I told him that, first and foremost, I didn't ask to be where I was, not just physically in the same office where I had suffered through pain and unbelievable sickness, but in life. I didn't ask, as a 19-year-old trying to survive cancer, to have my choices taken from me when I was too vulnerable to advocate for myself. I didn't ask for surgery where the prognosis was that I would never walk again. I asked him what kind of surgeon sees a 19-year-old whose life before cancer was full of activity and chooses a surgery where she would never walk again. I certainly didn't ask to be right back in that same office three and a half years later because their choice for me failed to hold up to the life I fought to get back to.

That's when I watched the lightbulb go off. After I finished my tirade about not having a choice in what I had been forced to endure and wanting a choice that would give me my life back, I waited. Whoever speaks first loses, so despite the awkward silence that stretched on for way too long, I waited. The nurse coordinator and the resident observing from the corner of the room didn't say a word. We all just waited.

I braced myself for what I was about to hear when my surgeon took a breath to speak. I wasn't sure what I should have expected after what I just dumped on him. But what he said when he finally did speak healed quite a few years' worth of hurt and trauma.

He started to explain that he was in the operating suite during my surgery. He watched as my surgeon cut the cancerous tumor out of my leg and perfectly fitted an allograft in, all while getting clean margins. Then he followed along with my recovery when my body didn't reject the new parts that had been added to my leg. He watched as my scars healed without signs of infection. To him and to every surgeon who witnessed that surgery, it was a miracle. It was surgical technology at its finest.

With tears in my own eyes, I listened as he explained that he now understood that, though it was a miracle for them, it wasn't a miracle for me. That they had no right to make that decision for me. For that, he began to apologize on behalf of my previous surgical team.

With that understanding now between us, I asked him to give me my options, whether I would like them or not. And when he explained that he could amputate my leg below the knee, I smiled.

We were finally getting somewhere.

Chapter 35

Surprisingly, the rest of my appointment was a success. With an amputation below the knee, some of the allograft and metal plate would still be left in my leg, which was a huge concern for me. The last thing I wanted was for a replay of my previous surgery, where I would spend a few years enjoying life with a below-the-knee prosthetic, only to be forced to get a revision surgery and have to learn how to live life as an above-the-knee amputee.

After all I'd been through, I made it clear that if the chances of what was left of the allograft breaking again, based on how active I planned on being, I would rather just go for an above-the-knee amputation first. I felt as though we had reached a good understanding, so when my surgeon suggested I go for below the knee, I trusted his judgment.

Trust, of course, was something I was hesitant to give. But, in my own journey of healing, I was trying my best to give this surgeon his own chance. I didn't want to judge him by the acts of so many other doctors and surgeons in my past, and he had been so open with me so far that, despite my reluctance, I chose to give that trust.

As my surgeon explained his new and improved plan, I felt something in my soul settle into place. By the end of the appointment, I had been given three options.

Option One: The repair surgery he had planned.

Option Two: Amputation.

Option Three: Wait for my leg to heal itself. Or, as I liked to think of it, wait for God to do the impossible if He chose.

Though deep down, even before the appointment, I had amputation on my mind, I needed time to pray about that decision. That very permanent, very irreversible decision. But I left feeling at peace.

Throughout the years, I saw my fair share of lower-limb amputees. I had even seen them on the same Spartan courses I had been on. The advancements in technology over the years had ensured that amputation was no longer a last resort, disabling option in many cases.

But one thing that left me in a slight decision paralysis was that, for the first time ever, I saw my mom cry. The idea of amputation didn't scare me, not in the least. But seeing Mom cry made me pause. I hadn't seen a single tear shed from her, not when I received my diagnosis, not when I shaved my head, and not when I told her during my last fight with sepsis that I had lost my will to live. This woman held out through the impossible and was my rock when I crumbled. But as my surgeon explained how amputation would be very likely to offer me a chance at a life of activity and adventure, I can only guess that all Mom saw was her daughter losing a limb. Her daughter, who had fought through so much, going through more pain.

I think a part of my reluctance to commit to amputation was to give Mom a chance to be okay with the decision, too. But, like the trooper she has always been, she just told me that whatever I chose to do, she would support me.

Being as okay with the decision as I was, we hadn't even made it home from the appointment before I had shared the updates with my small group leader and mentor, Takela. She told me she would pray for me, and share the update with the church staff, who had been following my new journey closely since my talk with Pastor Andrew.

That night, I called Trevor to tell him what had gone on. Just as Mom was, he was my biggest source of support. He had walked with me through life, even from a distance, and I knew he would see my decision the same way I had.

I should have expected that his immediate reaction was to ask me if I planned on submitting my application to work at IHOP. If he was at all devastated by the news, he didn't show it. He just affirmed my logic that my life would be able to return to how I wanted to live through this decision.

Then he asked me if I got upset after my amputation, would I be hopping mad. That was my brother.

That same night, I had a thought as I was getting ready for bed. I wasn't quite sure if Mom was ready for my wicked sense of humor to come out, but I couldn't hold back the joy that had come out of a certain speculation of mine. I had to tell Mom that, as soon as I had my amputation, I would only really have to shave one leg. While she smiled at me with uncertainty still in her eyes, Trevor reminded me that pedicures would now be half off for me.

Positives, people. Positives.

April 26, 2023

As I shared my decision to likely have my leg amputated, I was met with so much love and support. Looking back on it, I can't even imagine what it must have been like for my church family to hear that one of their own was facing the decision to amputate her leg. I got a glimpse into what that was like on the next Wednesday night Midweek service. So many had known that I was scheduled for a consultation with Ortho, but as I explained to them that my best option was amputation, I watched faces fall and tears come to the surface.

I was, admittedly, a little thrown off. I had such peace about losing my leg. My leg was, in my eyes, useless. It made sense to me to give it up and have a new, more reliable one replace it. But I was so firm in my peace of mind that I didn't prepare myself for the fact that, to those who considered me a sister, daughter, or granddaughter,

335

this was devastating. So, faces quickly went from tears to absolute perplexion when I quickly explained that I was okay. That I was happy, even. I was given an option that would allow me to live my life again.

As I started to leave the church sanctuary, I was met by our lead pastor, Pastor Rocky - PR, for short. He was weighed down with a look of devastation, so much so that as he approached me, *I* nearly asked *him* what was wrong. I had been smiling and laughing with some friends just a few minutes prior and, again, forgot that this news was along the lines of a tragedy.

I think everyone, PR included, was a little baffled by the idea that I was so okay with the decision I had made. But that aside, I was met with so much love, and so much support, that I was very nearly overwhelmed. My small group offered to set up a meal train, my friends offered to visit me in the hospital and to come keep me company at home after. I was asked if families could pray with me after services.

It contrasted sharply with what Mom and I experienced when I went through chemo. After the initial shock of my diagnosis passed, the support dwindled. After a while, it was just me and Mom. My support came from Em and Francisco, Anthony, and Streetlight. It even got to the point where I had asked Mom not to share updates with my family to avoid the dramatics that usually ensued. So, to experience what it was like to have a family, and one that didn't cause unnecessary drama, was an entirely new thing for me.

I knew that, unlike what we had come to expect, the support this time wouldn't dwindle once the shock and excitement from my now-upcoming surgery passed. I knew my DCC family was in it for the long haul.

It took me nearly a week to call and schedule the amputation. Though I knew that was my best option, I was still holding out for one of those impossible miracles I had come to believe in from God. I needed time to pray, and I would wake up every morning expecting my leg to suddenly be able to hold itself together. When it didn't, though, I wasn't disappointed. I trusted that God was doing what was best for me and what would best show His grace in my life.

I decided to be at peace with scheduling my amputation. I knew that God didn't need me to wait around. If it was in His plan to give me a miracle, then the date of my amputation didn't matter. I was so okay with the decision that when I found out I would have to wait a month for my amputation, I was almost disappointed. I just wanted to get on with it already. Even just a week hobbling around on crutches had driven me a little mad.

May 2, 2023

Call this one of the only times I had actually chosen to follow the advice of my team, but at the suggestion of the nurse coordinator at Ortho, I was on my way to Gainesville Prosthetics to consult with them. I can't possibly leave it up to coincidence that I chose to visit that office first, but I had a feeling urging me to go there first.

The drive there was a whole new dose of reality. I was going to visit a prosthetics clinic. It's not that I was scared, or all of a sudden, I had become less okay with my decision. It's just that it was more tangible.

Though I wasn't scared, I was nervous. I had never done anything like that before. I didn't know what I was even asking for. I hadn't even really decided what I was going to say before I was in front of the receptionist. Wing it, it was.

I stumbled through my explanation that I was planning on having an amputation soon and that I was advised to check out the local prosthetics clinics. To my surprise, they almost immediately brought me back into a consultation room.

Unlike the formality and sickeningly sterile environment of any surgical office I had ever been in, this clinic seemed real, comfortable even. Everyone I came across was so incredibly sweet. It wasn't the kind of "We have to be nice to you because you might be a patient" sweet. There was genuine care. While I waited, I was

337

given an armful of guides and magazines for those new to amputation. They offered me snacks. It was fascinating.

What floored me the most, though, was meeting who would become my prosthetist. Of the many ways I could describe her, the best word I could possibly find is that she was *chill*.

Naturally, with making a career in prosthetics, the news of amputations wasn't a huge shock for her. But I had come to expect a level of shock, devastation, and worry from even the most unshakeable people who found out what I had decided to do. When she met my news, not with pity or sadness, but with the same level of excitement I had already been feeling, I suspected I wouldn't even need to visit the other clinic.

I know it's weird to say I was excited to get my leg amputated. I wasn't necessarily excited about the amputation itself, but I was excited at the prospect of having my life back again. I had hope at the possibility of running another Spartan Race, at the hope of being able to live even a semi-normal life.

My prosthetist confirmed and even raised my hopes. Her first question to me was to ask what I wanted my life to look like after amputation. She was the first provider to ever ask that and truly mean it instead of just telling me what my life would be like. When I told her all that I wanted to do, there was no doubt from her that I would be back to living my life. When she told me that she would even run a Spartan Race with me once I got my prosthesis, I knew I had found the right place for me.

From then on, it was almost torture to not have my leg amputated so I could get a prosthesis and move on with my life. Being on crutches again completely disrupted the normal flow of my life. From the moment I woke up in the morning to the moment I got back in bed, I struggled. I would go into the kitchen to make a protein shake, only to realize that everything was in a different place. I had to get the blender from one counter, the protein powder from the cabinet, and the milk from the fridge. My fridge and the counter with the blender were on opposite sides of the kitchen, so I either had to carry the protein and the milk to the opposite counter or carry the full blender to its stand.

338

Let's not even talk about making lunch, with my prepped meals in the fridge being on the opposite side of the kitchen as my microwave, and then getting it all into the dining room. Forget silverware because that was a whole new trip into the kitchen.

This started attempts by Mom to rearrange the entire kitchen for me, which I was not ready for. I know she was just trying to help, but so much of my morale came from overcoming obstacles and adapting. Not rearranging the house to be convenient for me.

Though, when I did finally let Mom move the microwave closer to the fridge, I took no small satisfaction in watching her walk halfway across the dining room to where the microwave used to be, only to realize she had moved it.

Slowly, I had to accept that adapting for me would no longer be learning to do things in a new way. Not with crutches. The kitchen was bound to be rearranged. It was a fitting metaphor for what was about to happen in my life. Lots of rearranging.

Now, being stuck at home, unable to work at my beloved warehouse job with a broken leg, I had few options for how to entertain myself. Watching TV for hours on end would have driven me up the wall. Even staying in the confines of the house only took about a week to make me want to scream. My new routine, after years of staying busy, had become the leisurely business of waking up, scrolling through the reels Trevor sent me on Instagram, and reading. I wanted to read outside to get fresh air, but trying to carry a book and a water bottle or a tumbler of fruit-infused tea was beyond my abilities.

But Mom, my rock, always had a plan. She devised a basket with a neck strap so that when I needed to carry something somewhere around the house, I could without taking my hands away from the crutches. Getting my glass of tea anywhere was still a struggle, but it was a step back towards sanity.

Okay, fine, I could have put my tea in a bottle like my water but come on. Tea in a bottle? Where is the fun in that? It killed the aesthetic, and that was a hill I was willing to die on. Or a hill I was willing to tumble off of if you want to be more accurate about it.

Being on crutches wasn't the only major upset in my life, unfortunately. Though a small thing, it quickly became the cherry on top of the cake for my dwindling sanity: I couldn't sit, lay, or otherwise exist in the same positions I usually could. In most positions, my broken tibia would fall out of alignment and push into the surrounding muscles.

I had always been one to tuck my legs under me while sitting, or to cross my ankles, or even sit with my legs crisscrossed. Being that I was now stuck sitting for hours a day, this was not ideal.

At one point, I was at Takela's just to talk things through, and after just a few minutes of being on her couch, she asked if I was uncomfortable because I hadn't been able to sit still.

Trevor, of course, did his part to help keep me from losing my mind. We spent hours each night on the phone. Those were, thankfully, hours that would fly by. Of course, many of our conversations revolved around what it might be like for me after my amputation. I had so many questions, some more comical and some a bit existential. Would I forget I had lost my leg and fall all the time? Would I somehow manage to lose my prosthesis somewhere in the house? What would this new chapter in my life mean for relationships?

When I got a bit too existential, he would crack jokes. He told me that, if I wanted to have some fun, I could explain the loss of my leg to people who asked by saying, "Never, ever mock the banana peel."

I knew that I would just have to wait and see for many of the questions I had. Of course, that didn't stop me from asking the questions, especially not with all the free time I had to speculate.

Once I got into a rhythm, the forced break from normal life became somewhat of a blessing. Having the time to read more was something I definitely didn't take for granted, and I had plenty of time to foster new relationships with friends I was making from DCC. I got to go to midweek services, which encouraged me while I waited.

I started taking more time to do things I loved that I didn't seem to have as much time for while working. I got to do more art,

340

work on learning Italian, and even started watching some of the Crash Course subjects I had been interested in for so long.

It took a while to find my rhythm, though. I have always strived on a schedule. Routines are something I can't function without for long. So, as obsessive as it may sound, I had to start scheduling out my day. It was the only way I could actually do the things I enjoyed doing without getting stuck doomscrolling Instagram in decision paralysis.

On went my days, reading, watching TV shows and movies, learning Italian, watching Crash Course, and counting down the days. To say that was the longest month of my life was no joke.

Limitless

342

Chapter 36

May 15, 2023

The night before my amputation, I sat on my front porch, a cup of tea in my hand. No, not a bottle; a cup. I hadn't rolled down that hill yet. It was one of those dreary May nights. It looked like it should have been raining, which would have really fit the aesthetic of the whole "Night Before My Life Changed Forever" vibe, except it didn't rain. It was kind of disappointing.

I had a lot to contemplate. Though I had made an amazing friend who was an amputee, who tried to prepare me the best she could, nothing could truly prepare me for what was to come, and I knew it. It was going to get worse before it got better. Naturally, I thought about being waist-deep in the mud, in tears, reminding myself to just keep taking steps. One foot in front of the other until someone put a medal around my neck.

Well, the one foot in front of another part would be a little different. One hop at a time until they attached my cool new bionic leg? I could go with that.

Though I didn't have much to go on about what the next few months would look like, I did visualize one image. I wanted it seared into my memory. I saw myself, covered in mud, crossing a Spartan Finish Line. I saw the fire jump, the medal around my neck, and the muddy hug I would give Mom after. I saw it all with a prosthetic. I imagined what it would be like to see the finish line in the distance, knowing I had done it despite all odds.

That image became my metaphor. I was at the Starting Line, staring down the obstacles I would soon face. Finishing was not optional. One hop at a time. One obstacle at a time.

Every so often, my phone would buzz, and I would see a text or call from my DCC family, sending their prayers or offering to call and pray with me. I knew they would be my team when I reached an obstacle I couldn't overcome on my own.

On top of it all, I kept glancing at the word "goodbye" that a friend of ours, Jeff, had written in Sharpie across my left foot. Thank God for friends with a sense of humor. Okay, admittedly, I wasn't glancing at it, with the cloud-masked sky in the background, reflecting on what goodbye would mean. I kept seeing something black on my foot, and I thought it was a spider, so I kept jumping. But still. It was a reason for reflection.

Oddly enough, through all the thoughts, I wasn't scared. I didn't dread what was coming. I was nervous about having to stay in the hospital for nearly a week, but that was about it.

When Trevor called, there wasn't much to say that we hadn't already talked about, so we sat together mostly in silence, making short comments here and there. I wondered if he was having the same thoughts as I was having and if he was also quiet because of what was coming the next day.

In hindsight, I wonder what everyone else was thinking. While I was sitting on my front porch, pondering what life was going to look like in just 24 hours, feeling a mix of peace and excited anticipation, what was Trevor thinking? What was Mom thinking? What was my DCC family thinking?

Was everyone worried, or heartbroken? Or were they following my lead, seeing the next day as another chapter that was being written?

I had been asked so many times in that past month if I had grieved the coming loss of my leg. For most, I can see how there would have been grieving at losing part of a limb. I couldn't relate, though. I reflected on all the times in the past few years when my leg felt foreign to me. Every time it failed me or brought me pain, every time I couldn't trust it to carry me, I stopped feeling it as *my* leg.

For me, any part of my body, including my leg, was functional. It had to serve a purpose. My leg's purpose was obvious. It was meant to carry me, whether that was through the grocery store or up a mountain. It could no longer serve its purpose, so I could not imagine grieving something that had become a burden to me. Rather than grieving my leg, I grieved the time I had lost and would continue to lose until I got my prosthesis. Even that grief was short-lived, as it was a necessary loss to regain time to live my life in the future. A small sacrifice for a lifetime of freedom.

Even my only regret was short-lived. I didn't know that coming home from work a month before would have been my last literal steps in leading a normal life. I regretted that I hadn't been able to fully appreciate that milestone. But it's not like I would never take steps again, so I didn't ponder that thought for very long.

If the timeline that was laid out for me went as planned, it would only be a few short weeks until I could get my first prosthesis. Those steps I had so looked forward to taking weren't far away.

Through the contemplating I did that night, both with Trevor and on my own, I determined that I was at peace. Sure, there was so much uncertainty ahead of me. I just chose not to put my focus there. I chose to put my focus on God, who had brought me this far. I knew if He had brought me this far, He would surely guide me through whatever uncertainty was to come.

May 16, 2023

I figured that since I didn't freak out the night before, surely, I would lose it the next morning. I had to freak out eventually, right? Nope. I woke up smiling. It was the day I had been waiting for.

I had been invited to the women's prayer meeting at DCC, and both PR and Pastor Andrew were planning to meet me at the hospital

345

before my surgery. I knew that I had countless friends praying for me that very morning. It's hard to fear being surrounded by that kind of love. Whatever was coming, Mom and I weren't alone this time.

Hearing the prayers of the women who surrounded me and Mom that morning strengthened me in ways I can't even begin to fathom. It was a constant reminder that I wasn't alone and that I wouldn't be.

On our way to the hospital, the scheduling team called me to ask if there was any way I could come in early. A minor annoyance, considering the plan of meeting my pastors before my surgery. I made it clear that I would get there as soon as I could, but I wasn't going under until I saw my pastors. It wasn't because I felt as if my sanity and peace depended on that meeting. But to go into a surgery as big as this, I wanted to go surrounded by my people. Having that support for the first time was something I had never experienced. I wasn't letting go of that so easily.

Now, here's where my emotions started getting a little weird. I was at peace. I wasn't afraid. But my subconscious? She was a whole different story. I could tell myself all day long that I was fine, but the part of my brain that still held onto the traumas and pain I had experienced wasn't so easily convinced. For years, if I even passed through the red light leading to the side of town where the hospital was, I would start to shake with anxiety, even if I wasn't going to the hospital. Now, going back into the hospital, my subconscious trauma responses were having a field day.

Even though they asked me to come in early, I never guaranteed that I could. Instead of going straight in to check in, I detoured us to the Fountain of Hope. The same fountain I had found refuge by during chemo, even to the point of falling asleep on the park bench to get much-needed rest. I needed sunlight and fresh air. And if it delayed me enough that it gave my pastors time to get there before they tried to put me out, it was another win.

I didn't get the chance to sit there long before I got a call, surprisingly, from my surgeon. He had been at valet parking when we got out of the car and saw me going to the fountain.

Busted.

346

He let me know they had everything ready to prep me for surgery except the most important element. Me. So, I broke away from the fountain and went to check-in.

Waiting to be called into pre-op was another monster I wasn't prepared for. I had no fear of amputation. But pre-op? Especially after my last experience with nerve blocks? I prayed almost constantly to overcome that dose of terror.

The previous day during my pre-op appointments, I made sure to give the anesthesiology team a proper rundown of how pre-op would go. I recounted my previous experience with being conscious, just barely, during my nerve block placement, and how no one communicated with me. That didn't ease my nerves that they were actually going to heed those warnings.

Plus, facing down the indignity of the pre-op area was just as daunting. I dreaded the stupid paper gown and the cold, inhuman nature of the nurses.

Yeah, dread was certainly setting in.

The idea of having my leg chopped off was less daunting than the idea of pre-op, but I knew if I could just get past pre-op, I would be fine.

I just had to get past the paper gown, make sure the nurses didn't try to get a vein in my hand for an IV, and make sure the anesthesiology team put me completely out for the nerve block placement. No big deal.

As if God had personally staffed the pre-op area that morning, I was comforted to find that my nurse was actually a human being. I wasn't just the next piece of meat to be cut open that she had to prep. I explained to her that I was waiting on my pastors and that I absolutely did not want to be put under until I saw them, and she reassured me that she would hold anesthesiology back until that had happened.

Calmed, I decided to test my luck. I told her that I didn't want an IV placed in my hand because I had never had anyone get a good vein there without tormenting me. She promised me that if she wasn't 100% sure she could get a vein in my hand in one try, she would find one in my arm.

I didn't know how to handle this kindness. Not in pre-op. I was
waiting for the ball to drop. Surely, they were going to find some
way to torment me as always, right?

I thought for sure it would be that I had some swaggering
know-it-all anesthesiologist. Surely. But God, of course, had my
back there too. Why I was even worrying at this point, I don't even
know.

The anesthesiologist opened the conversation by telling me
that he had been told of my bad experiences before and that he was
going to do everything he could to ensure I had a better experience
this time.

I was wholly and truly blown away that, by some miracle, the
pre-op nurse from the previous day had actually communicated my
concerns. At this point, I simply did not know how to proceed. I
didn't feel like herded cattle. Somehow, I was starting to trust that
this team was going to take care of me.

Even the nurse, true to her word, found a good vein in my arm
to place the IV in after not finding one in my hand.

And things just kept getting better and better. Em had found a
way into the pre-op area using her badge, since she was an
employee, and surprised me by coming to hang out while I was
prepped. The nurses even ignored their rule of only allowing one
person in my pre-op room at a time.

I could tell anesthesiology was getting impatient, ready to get
the nerve blocks placed, but my nurse sweetly informed them that
she was not done with her own pre-op questions, and that she would
call them when she was ready. I caught her sly wink in my direction
as she continued with the list of questions I had already answered.

My nerves had eased almost completely by the time PR and
Pastor Andrew had gotten there. Again, in hindsight, I had to wonder
what they were thinking when I told them I was okay. It's not every
day that someone says they are okay a short time before getting a
limb removed.

My nurse looked the other way as both of my pastors and
Mom gathered in my room to pray. While they prayed for me, I spent
my time praying for Mom. I knew I was okay, but she was the one

who would have to be with her thoughts in the waiting room during the few hours my surgery would take. As she usually had, she politely declined any requests to have anyone sit with her while she waited, so I prayed for her peace.

Not a moment after Mom and my pastors left the room, the team that had been impatiently waiting crowded my room. I was almost amused since it seemed like they had waited right around the corner.

I didn't let my anxiety take over, not even when so many new people crowded in the small room. I saw the same doctor who assured me he heard my concerns. I asked him to walk me through everything he was doing before I was put out. I trusted that he would.

So, this is where it all got real.

They asked me for my date of birth. They asked me what surgery I would be having. I may have even wiggled my toes one last time. The doctors kept checking in with me as they ran through their pre-op checks, confirming that I was, in fact, the person they planned on prepping for an amputation.

The doctor I had spoken to became even more deliberate about communicating with me as they helped me roll onto my side for the nerve block placement. He reassured me that while I would feel their hands on me, they were only finding landmarks.

When they asked me if I was ready to be put out, I turned to the nurse at the head of my bed. It was the same one who had been so kind to me since I had arrived. I asked if she would hold my hand, and she wrapped her hand around mine. When I said I was ready, she grabbed a syringe filled with cloudy white fluid and pushed the plunger down with one hand while rubbing her thumb in circles over my hand with her other.

No going back.

But even up to the moment I felt my head start to swim as it felt like my brain was turning to Jello while the ice-cold anesthesia meds got pushed into my arm, I had no doubts about what I was doing. I had been silently praying whenever I wasn't being asked

349

questions, and I asked God to be with me at the last second before the room went black.

I'm not going to be dramatic and say something about waking up to a new reality because waking up from this surgery was nothing like you see in the TV shows.

It wasn't a peaceful picture of me blinking awake, asking if everything went well. Far from. Waking up from surgery is pure mental chaos.

For me, I usually hear and feel the things going on around me but rarely open my eyes. I come out of surgery in the same way I wake up every morning. I just want to go back to sleep.

When I started to hear the beeping and the chaos of the post-op ward, I wanted to pretend I hadn't woken up yet. I didn't quite comprehend where I was, but wherever I was, it was too loud. I couldn't quite get myself back to sleep, not with the excruciating pain in my leg.

I felt something being pushed into my hand, but all I wanted was to go back to sleep. Maybe the pain would go away if I went back to sleep. But someone was talking to me, and they were adamant about me pushing a button. At that point, I would push whatever button they wanted if they just let me sleep. But how could I press any buttons if I couldn't find the energy to open my eyes?

It felt as if whoever was talking was yelling in my ear. They were insistent. I needed to push a button. They kept tapping my hand. Maybe If I squeezed the thing in my hand, they'd leave me alone. Almost as soon as I did, I felt a button click down under my thumb. Thankfully, the chaos of the room faded into the background.

I don't know how many times I came in and out before I finally stayed awake. I knew Mom was beside me because I felt her rubbing my hand like she always did after surgery.

Trying to talk felt like a monumental effort, so I didn't try to ask how things went. I tried to glance down at my legs, but they were both covered, so I couldn't tell if my left leg really was shorter than my right, as it should have been. But the searing pain that wrapped around the middle of my calf when I tried to move my leg told me everything I needed to know.

Good thing I never had any doubts, because now would be a horrible time to start regretting my decisions.

I did start to question why I had been able to feel what was left of my leg, though. The last time I had nerve blocks, I couldn't feel anything from mid-thigh down. It would have worried me, if I had the mental capacity to worry. That would be a problem for another time. I would just stay still, then.

I laid still and quietly for as long as I could before the dry, sandpapery feeling in my mouth forced me to wake up and interact with the world. I didn't have to do much interacting, though, because Mom had done this with me enough times that she knew what I would need first. I barely opened my mouth when I found a straw already there.

Best mom ever.

For some reason, I barely had enough water to quench my thirst when the water ran out. I looked to see what had to have been the smallest cup I had ever seen in Mom's hands. Of course, I knew they wouldn't want me to drink too much at once after surgery. Little did they know, I was already imagining how a pizza from the third-floor cafe would taste.

Again, knowing what I would need, Mom popped the straw into her own bottle of water when no nurses were looking, and let me drink until I felt less like a dried up sponge.

She started explaining to me that the nurse had been keeping me on a steady dose of Dilaudid any time I started showing signs of being in pain, so if I started to hurt, I needed to ask.

It wasn't long before my appetite kicked in. I felt okay to send Mom away long enough to get pizza, so I kicked back to rest until she got back.

The rest was short-lived. The burning in my leg started again, but this time, it didn't subside when my nurse gave me another dose of Dilaudid. It was like the inside of my leg had been filled with lava. It didn't even subside when she gave me a dose of oral pain meds. I was waiting for my nurse to get an order for something stronger, sipping on my tiny cup of water to keep myself distracted, when a way-too-perky girl, who barely looked my age, pulled back the curtain to my "room."

At this point, I was in enough pain that I didn't want to move or talk, but I became more willing to talk when she told me she was the pain management resident on the floor. Perfect. Just who I needed to see.

It felt like someone had wrapped a molten vice around where my leg used to be. Unfortunately, that was not the worst pain I had ever felt, so I was, apparently, functioning too well for her to believe me when I told her my pain had reached eight out of ten. She cheerily explained to me that I couldn't possibly be in that much pain. I had nerve blocks, and if I was talking to her and drinking water, I was not in as much pain as I thought I was.

What next, "I should expect some pain after surgery"?

Those were, not shockingly, the next words out of her mouth. I was dumbfounded. The pain management doctor wouldn't do anything about the fact that I was *in pain.* Wonderful.

She left without another word. On to be useless to the person beside me, I was sure.

Under the influence of all the medications I was on, I couldn't pull my thoughts under control. I had just had part of my leg removed, and this doctor wanted to tell me I wasn't in as much pain as I thought I was? Just because I was able to sip water and articulate my pain? She had no idea about the things I had been through before that moment and why I was able to handle the pain so well.

I was appalled, but my only response was to cry. I was overwhelmed. I was hurting. I was half high on whatever had been in my system aside from Dilaudid. Crying was the only option I could think of at that point, so that's what I did.

Mom walked back into the room in the middle of this pitiful breakdown, expecting to see me happy to have pizza. Both of us quickly forgot the pizza. My only response to her asking what had happened was to tell her about what the doctor told me. How I described the doctor must have been in more colorful language than I used, because Mom had to stifle a laugh. But on top of that, I could

352

see my tears had brought Momma Bear back. Her baby was in pain, and her baby should not have been in pain.

It didn't take long for the nurse to come back, another dose of some sort of pain medication in her hand. I didn't really care what it was. It worked fast, and that was all that mattered.

When the pain subsided, I remembered that there was a pizza left untouched. I devoured all but a piece or two of a personal sized pizza, impressing the post-op nurses, as usual.

I was in post-op waiting for a bed to become available on the surgical floor for nearly six hours. Between my nurse being on top of things and the button attached to my nerve blocks programmed to allow me an extra dose of meds each hour, we managed to keep my pain under control.

When I finally did get to a private room, I had an agenda, and I would carry out my plans with or without the nurse's help. I wasn't going to be sitting around in the flimsy post-op gown - cloth, this time, but still. It was itchy and stiff and made my skin crawl.

That had always sparked questions for me after surgeries. I was put out in the flimsy paper gown but always awoke in a cloth gown. I tried not to imagine that someone had to get me changed from one gown to another.

I wanted clothes. Real clothes. And underwear. I had planned out well before my surgery how I planned to stay sane during a four-day hospital stay, and wearing my own clothes was first on the list.

My nurse tried to dissuade me. Big mistake. I told her that one way or another, I was going to end up in my own clothes by the end of the night. She could stay and help me or get out of my way. Wisely, she chose to stay.

Trying to get underwear on over my amputated leg, which had a brace extending almost down to the floor, two nerve blocks coming up my back from my hips, and a drain, was a task. I wasn't quite strong enough to stand, so I stayed lying back and pushed my hips off the bed with one leg while trying to get my underwear pulled up. I decided not to bother with shorts. It was a hassle enough already, and I was ready to sleep for the night, anyway.

353

Comfortably in my own clothes, feeling like a real human being again, I settled in for the night. I checked my phone, which I hadn't really thought to do in post-op with how hazy I was. I started to tear up to find over twenty messages from my DCC family, including prayers and well wishes. Even more surprisingly, almost all of them included a part of the message that said I didn't have to respond if I didn't feel like it. I replied to a few that I could, but I had very little energy. I knew everyone knew I had made it out of surgery because we tasked Takela with posting updates to our Women's Facebook group.

All things considered, things had somehow gone well that day. Though I was uncomfortable, I wasn't in severe pain. I hadn't had any traumatic experiences to scar me for life. I was even able to get up and hobble back and forth to the restroom on crutches.

Maybe things were going to be better this time.

Chapter 37

Remember when I was waiting for the ball to drop in pre-op? Well, it dropped.

Things had gone fine all throughout the night. I was in little to no pain and had even slept well. I set an alarm on my phone every hour so I could push the button to get an extra dose of pain medication through the nerve blocks. I wasn't playing around this time. I was determined for this stay to go well.

It's a pity that my determination can only go so far.

Right as shift change happened for the nurses at around 7:00 a.m., I started to feel a little more pain than I had throughout the night. What was a slight ache had turned into a light burning. The previous day's experiences told me this was not a good sign. When I tried to hit the button I had come to rely on throughout the night, the machine I was hooked up to gave me an error message.

It was out of meds.

No big deal. I would just call for a nurse. The day shift nurse could bring in my scheduled pain meds and refill the nerve blocks at the same time. It should have been fine.

It wasn't fine. Isn't that just the story of my life?

By 7:30 a.m., no one had even been sent to my room, so we called again.

And again.

And again.

Mom went to the nurse's station.

We called again.

By 9:00 a.m., no one had come but the Patient Care Assistants. They promised to find a nurse. By 9:30 a.m., still no nurse came.

A friend of mine from DCC had planned to come around that time, and I knew she would be there soon. I hoped they would get things straightened out before she got there. She was bringing Halo Donuts. But by the time she got there, no nurse had come.

The slight burning in my leg had turned into a searing pain. I couldn't help it, but just before my friend got there, I started to cry. It wasn't from the pain but from fear. I knew from my first surgery what it felt like to have no nerve blocks and no pain meds. I could only imagine what it would feel like for an amputation.

I was so scared of the pain that I knew was coming that I couldn't even eat the donuts my friend had brought. In the moment, that was one of the biggest tragedies of my life. Between me and snacks is not a good place to be.

By 10:00 a.m., I was gripping Mom's hand in my right hand and my friend's in my left. My breath was forced because every minuscule movement sent waves of searing pain down my leg.

My friend stayed with me while Mom went back out to the nurse's station, but still, no one came. She started to pray with me as she held my hand.

I could tell she was near the point of following Mom to the nurse's station and giving them a piece of her mind. I did not envy whoever was on the receiving end of her fierceness. While the nurses at the nurse's station didn't have to be on the receiving end of her wrath, Mom had hit her wit's end. Momma Bear had risen. I think they may have preferred my friend's wrath because all I heard coming down the hall from the direction of the nurse's station was Mom going off on the nurses.

11:00 a.m. passed, and still no one came.

My friend decided to head out, and I was in such pain that it felt as if the sun was sitting on my leg. I started to hyperventilate, and I was crushing Mom's hand in my own.

Mom was calling the nurses station, walking into the hall to find anyone who might be able to help.

Finally, at 11:30 a.m., a nurse came into my room with the pain management team. By this point, I was nearly incoherent. I just begged for them to do something. They refilled the nerve blocks and got me my oral pain meds, but the pain was past the point of no return.

Even worse, we found that the tubes that carried the pain medication through into the nerve blocks had been leaking. I wasn't even getting full doses of the medication. They asked me if I could roll onto my side so they could change the nerve blocks, and I told them I was afraid to move. I even told them not to move me.

What did they do? They rolled me over with about zero regard for my leg. They didn't bother to move me gently so that my freshly amputated limb didn't slam into the bed as they rolled me. If my pain had already been a ten, I experienced a fifteen. I was screaming. I was begging them to get an anesthesiologist to put me under until they resolved the problem.

Of course, that wasn't possible. Their solution was to just wait until the meds kicked in since they fixed the tubes. I got a pat on the leg - I'm genuinely surprised they didn't pat the amputated one - and a half-hearted, "Hope you feel better soon."

But I did not feel better. We called the nurse after fifteen minutes to tell her there was no change. I had been in excruciating pain for hours, so waiting it out was hardly an option. She called pain management and got orders to try an IV pain medication.

That was all great, except that in the chaos of the morning, the IV that had been placed before surgery had become dislodged from my vein. I would need a new IV.

I couldn't even stay still as she tried to place a new IV. My whole body was shuddering with every breath I took, but she was good. She got the IV placed and gave me the pain meds, explaining that it was the equivalent of IV ibuprofen.

357

Wait, ibuprofen? It felt like my leg was being crushed by the sun, and the pain management team's solution was *IV ibuprofen?*

I asked for Dilaudid. I remembered how quickly it had taken away my pain post-op the previous day, and I was tired of letting these people flounder when I was suffering so greatly. I was informed, though, that they could only give Dilaudid in post-op and not in the unit I was in.

I would have to wait another twenty minutes to see if the IV ibuprofen would work. I was on the way to losing hope that my pain was actually going to be under control, seeing as whoever was in charge of ordering meds for this situation seemed to lack the help of a functioning brain. By the time twenty minutes had passed, with no relief, Mom was back in the hall. This time, she got the attention of the pain management team as well as the nurse manager on shift.

Whatever she said must have worked because it was not even five minutes before the nurse manager came in to give me a dose of Dilaudid. But, of course, before she could give it to me, she wanted to talk about why they hadn't yet ordered it. As if I weren't lying in a bed in front of her, nearly begging to be put out of my misery.

She tried to explain that they didn't want to give me Dilaudid because it works quickly but doesn't work for long. I shot back with the idea that maybe, *just maybe,* if they gave me something to knock the pain out, the rest of the meds I had been given would have a chance at keeping it at bay. She gave me a look that told me she hadn't actually thought of it that way until I said it.

Lo and behold, within ten minutes of the dose of Dilaudid, I had gone from writhing in indescribable agony to sitting up in bed, crying more from the trauma of what happened to me than from the pain.

After things had calmed down, I was visited again by one of the doctors on the pain management team. He was convinced that the nerve blocks had been displaced and that I wasn't getting the correct dose of medication to the right places.

We tried to explain that, no, I had been in pain because my nerve blocks had been empty since 7:00 a.m. It was now nearly noon. But he was adamant. Adamant enough to suggest replacing the nerve blocks. But since I had eaten that day, I would have to be conscious.

Conscious while they poked and prodded around on my hip, placing another line deep into the sciatic nerve. While I was fully aware.

Oh, heck no.

It took the Holy Spirit Himself keeping a hand over my mouth to keep me from calling this doctor an idiot.

When the nurse manager told us that the reason I hadn't received care in nearly five hours was because of shift change, I didn't even have to comment. Mom nearly lost it on her, telling her that shift change was no excuse for lack of proper care, and certainly not for nearly five hours. Come to find out, it took all of that time to even have me assigned to a nurse in the first place.

And that was the moment Takela walked in, beanie frog in hand, wondering what happened to her baby.

Then, I started crying out of relief. Relief that I was no longer in pain and relief that my friend was there. Of course, I had to name the frog Christoph.

Now that the ordeal was over, I sent Mom downstairs to decompress, and Takela stayed with me for lunch. I was devouring food now that my pain was under control. Every time the nurse or nurse manager walked in, Takela gave them such a stare I was glad looks couldn't kill. I came to find out that my friend who had been there that morning had immediately texted Takela when she had left my room, and Takela was ready to come in, guns blazing.

At some point during the ordeal, physical therapy had come in for a visit, but we sent them away. They came back in while Takela was there, and though I was tempted to send them away again, I decided to let them stay. Their plan was to help me get dressed, and make sure I could get back and forth to the restroom. I laughed when I heard that, since I had already been up on crutches since the night before and had been dressed.

With that, they suggested we take a short walk down the hall. While I was absolutely terrified to move in case the pain came back, I decided that it would be good for my spirits to get moving a little.

359

First, though, I had to get on shorts. With the events of the morning, I hadn't gotten around to that yet, so it seemed to be the perfect time.

Takela had texted Mom some pictures of me hopping down the hall on crutches, to which her response was a desperate hope that I had remembered to put on shorts. Leave it to me to hop down the hall in my underwear.

We hoped that, since we had one major upset to the stay, the rest would be smooth sailing. I managed to make it through most of the day, being relatively pain-free. Relatively being the keyword there. After experiencing pain beyond even my own comprehension, my definition of pain had become quite flexible. I could be in what would usually be considered debilitating, crippling pain, and it now seemed only a mild discomfort to me. It made trying to use the pain scale a bit confusing since what was a four for me should have been considered at least a seven.

Later in the evening, Mom got a call and as she answered, I heard Trevor's voice. I figured he was calling to check on me, knowing that if he asked me how I was doing directly, I wouldn't give him the full answer so I wouldn't worry him.

I was almost offended when she took the call outside and came back in, only to tell me that he was just checking on me. I had slowly been working through all the texts from friends, so I couldn't be salty for too long. It was taking a lot of my energy to just exist.

I was still on edge, though. I was having a great time with Takela, but I was afraid to move. Usually, I would take every opportunity to hop in a wheelchair and get some fresh air, but I was terrified of triggering that kind of agony again. I tried my best to lie still.

My relief was short-lived. By the evening, I started to feel the burning, like a hot wire being laid across the skin of the outside of my leg. Just as it had before, before I could register that this pain was much worse than it should have been, the pressure crushed down on my leg so intensely I was sure it was going to implode. I was right back to clutching Mom's hand, begging my nurse to call pain management. After a high dose of pain meds through the nerve

360

blocks, the pain subsided from maddening to highly inconvenient. Combined with my other evening meds, I was able to sleep.

The next morning, I was determined to turn things around. A year of fighting cancer taught me that if I had the strength in my body, I needed to fight with every ounce I had to take control of my situation. I had been too passive, letting my circumstances dictate my experience. Though I was still stuck in a place that seemed to be my own circle of hell, I was going to do everything in my power to feel better.

My go-to comfort would have been a long, hot shower. Unfortunately, with two nerve blocks inserted into either side of my left hip, that was out of the option. I was still determined. If I couldn't shower, I could at least towel down and wash my hair. Surely, that was the next best thing.

After scarfing down breakfast, the PCA on the floor brought in hand towels, buckets for water, soaps, shampoos, and towels. I had made sure to pack my own shampoos and conditioners, but the amount of supplies they brought felt like a spa day.

A very depressing and clinical spa day, but hey, I was taking what I could get.

I came to find out that the foaming soap they left me was a leave-on body wash. As convenient as that sounded, the idea of leaving soap on my skin was a no-go. Mom set up the bathroom so I could wash off, sending the PCA away. This was not our first rodeo, so we knew we had our system down much better without them.

As weird as it felt to not be able to sit under hot running water, just to feel as if I could wash a little of the hospital off was so restorative. It was also the most movement I had attempted since surgery, and I did not anticipate just how different everything would be.

Trying to move without half of my leg was similar to the feeling of trying to pick something up, expecting it to be heavy, when it isn't. The left side of my body felt exactly like that, and I kept flinging myself to the right, not having that extra ten pounds to weigh my left side down.

While the plan for washing down had been fairly straightforward, Mom and I had to navigate something new. During chemo, since I had no hair to wash, that was never something we had to worry about. Now, we had to try to figure out how to get my hair washed without actually being in the shower. Leaning over the sink wasn't really an option because my balance was not there yet.

Our brainstorming led us to pull down the shower chair attachment in the stall shower, and to have me sit and lay back on it so Mom could lean over me and wash my hair. We had to use one of the buckets to prop my leg up on, and Mom had to be very careful to aim the shower head properly so I didn't get a face-full of water.

Sure, I could have used the little hair net shampoo gadget the PCA offered. But, if I didn't want to leave body wash on my skin, you have no idea how much the idea of leaving shampoo in my hair grossed me out.

All in all, it was hilarious. I giggled almost the whole time, even the few times the shower head tipped just a bit forward and hit me in the face. Even Mom, after she loosened up a bit, laughed with me at the absolute ridiculousness of the situation.

This experience would be the first time I really got to feel what it was like to laugh at myself in a hospital setting. In the chaos of trying to get dressed and get back to my bed, I had dropped some of my clothes from the previous day in front of me, right where I would need to place my crutches. No big deal; I could just kick them out of my way. So, I stuck out my foot and swept my leg to the side and… the clothes didn't move.

I was so confused. Baffled. Absolutely bamboozled. It took me a solid ten seconds to realize that the clothes weren't going anywhere as long as I used my left foot to move them. I started laughing so hard I could barely explain to Mom what had just happened.

It was then that I realized that when I wasn't in pain, I could still feel my toes. I could wiggle them, even. Or I felt them wiggle when I tried. I had to start referring to it as my not-foot. Because it was my foot, and I could feel it, but it was not.

That day, things started looking up. I was able to have visitors and not be a sobbing, emotionally drained mess the entire time. I

362

even felt up to going outside to the Fountain of Hope. In an attempt to placate us after the previous day's disaster, the nurse manager had a wheelchair sent to my room that we could keep there for whenever I wanted to go out, and I was going to take full advantage of their sucking up. We even got moved to a room with a pull-out couch for Mom.

I had visitors almost constantly, between my closest friends and my DCC family. One of my friends came into my room with a vase full of sunflowers, which were my favorite, and a huge box of Zebra Cakes. We went outside to the Fountain of Hope, where I could tell her everything that went on without being overheard. At the same time, a couple from DCC called to meet us at the fountain.

Making it outside didn't come without its struggles, but we made it. Any uneven ground jarred my leg, sending shocks of pain down to my not-foot. Even a crack in the cement was enough to make me groan in pain, but it was worth it to feel the sun and smell something other than hand sanitizer and filtered air.

I knew this couple since joining their prison ministry at DCC. I met one of my closest friends through their Pen Pal program. As they approached, I saw they were carrying something, but I couldn't make it out. As they got closer, I realized it was a hanging chandelier that my Pen Pal had made me. When she heard about my surgery, she started working on it as a surprise to brighten up my hospital room.

It wasn't just the combo of meds that had me tearing up. My friend, who no doubt had bigger things to worry about in prison, had taken her time and resources to make something for me. I was overwhelmed, both with the support I was surrounded with in person and from afar.

To add to the love I felt, my friend from church told me that she had met with some of the women in the prison to pray over me. Those who knew of me from my Pen Pal each said their own prayer over me before my surgery. Again, the overflow of emotion was flowing through the tears. To feel so loved at such a difficult time was absolutely incredible.

I stayed out as long as I could before I needed to go back to the hospital for a nap. The amount of meds in my system made staying up for longer than a few hours at a time nearly impossible.

Though things were looking up, I still worried. Every time I shifted on my bed, I felt the area near where my nerve blocks were inserted and felt that my shorts were soaked. I could only assume they hadn't properly fixed the leak from the previous day, which meant I wasn't getting the full dose of nerve-blocking medication. We had told the pain management team during morning rounds, but nothing had come of the issue.

It wasn't long before I felt the telling hot wire feeling down my leg. I wasn't playing around this time. I called my nurse immediately. Of course, in a hospital, preemptive pain management isn't a thing. At least not in my hospital. I won the fight, but it took long enough that it wasn't quite in time to stop it before it had started to get bad. I couldn't complain too much since at least it wasn't at the level it had been before. By the time pain management made it to my room to give an extra dose of meds through the nerve blocks, I was back in tears.

It was not a reassuring feeling to think to myself that maybe I should have just started telling them what they needed to hear to prevent my pain. It was less reassuring when a nurse told me that if I wanted them to be able to help prevent my pain, I needed to tell them that my pain was worse than it was.

By the time I had a second pain flare-up that evening, frustration was an understatement for what I was feeling. I was worrying constantly about the pain flaring, and I was tired of not being taken seriously. They still hadn't even fixed the leak that was keeping me from getting the full dose of pain medication. I was ready to put up the fight of my life with pain management when whoever was on call got there. I was expecting to be met with a doctor who had the same lack of compassion as the rest of the team I had encountered so far.

Instead, I was met with a sweet, calm doctor. His demeanor stopped me in my tracks and my rant right along with it. He noticed the leak and immediately set to the task of fixing it. Actually fixing it this time. He left to get a whole new set of tubing, reassuring me that he would be back within ten minutes. If he wasn't, he told me I should have my nurse start calling for him.

Within fifteen minutes, the lines had been completely replaced and tested to ensure they weren't leaking. The dose of pain meds I got through the new lines sent immediate relief to my leg, and I cried in relief. I couldn't stop thanking him. He was the first doctor to help me.

Having built this little bit of trust with him, I decided to ask what he thought about the nerve blocks being out of place. He told us that it was nonsense. Since I had felt immediate relief with the dose of pain meds he had given me, it was safe to say that the nerve blocks were correctly placed. I just wasn't getting the correct dose because the lines had been leaking.

And to think I had one of the pain management doctors trying to convince me to replace perfectly good nerve blocks.

I was able to get rest that night, now having things fairly straightened out. I had hope again.

But again, the next morning, my hope was dashed. It was a never-ending rollercoaster. The pain was flaring again. And I truly had reached my wit's end that time. Instead of calling for pain meds or for the pain management doctor on call, I got my nurse to call for the head of pain management. I was done playing around. Even my nurse was done watching me suffer since she had been my nurse for the past two days. I was prepared to let myself sit in pain, if only to prove the point to them that something was wrong.

By the time the nurse practitioner who was over the pain management team made it to my room, I was already in tears again. Good, that was part of my plan. When she asked what was wrong, I told her. I told her about the pain I had been in and about her team's lack of human emotion. I told her that the only doctor to provide any help was the one who had replaced the lines to my nerve blocks the night before.

By the time I was done, the pain was enough to have me struggling to breathe. It was the icing on top of the cake because she ordered Dilaudid. Not only did she order it for that moment, but she

365

kept it on order for whenever I might need it while she consulted the pain management team. It wasn't long after that she came back into my room with most of the team I had dealt with so far. All of them walked in with their tails between their legs except the doctor who had helped me the night before.

They finally had an explanation for what had been going on. Though they did not understand why, they determined that I had been having breakthrough pains - yeah, no kidding- which is very rare with nerve blocks. If it was caused by the leak in the lines on my nerve blocks, they didn't say it. The only explanation they had was that I was young, with healthy nerves, which might have caused the pain flares.

The new plan was to have Dilaudid on order whenever I needed it, and it was made clear that I did not have to wait for the pain to be unbearable before I could ask for it. Their new plan was to truly prevent the pain, not just treat it.

The good news, naturally, did come with bad news. Since it had been three days, and I had so many extra high-concentration doses of the pain medication through my nerve blocks, I was nearing the maximum dose I would be able to have. I was also nearing the point where it was becoming too much of an infection risk to leave the nerve blocks placed. I could leave them in one more day, but on day four, they would have to turn off the nerve blocks to see if I could tolerate the pain without them and then remove them.

Terrified was an understatement. I couldn't even handle the pain *with* the nerve blocks, and I only had one day until I wouldn't have them at all. On top of that, I didn't even have the assurance that I could replace the nerve blocks. Since I was reaching the maximum cumulative dose, the nerve blocks would not be an option soon.

I truly didn't know what was worse. Trying to handle the pain without nerve blocks or staying in the hospital longer. I know it seems like a no-brainer, but it wasn't for me. I couldn't even lean off my bed without alarms going off because they had alarmed my bed, so I couldn't get up. I almost constantly felt nauseous from the all too familiar scents of the hospital from chemo. Don't even get me started on the food. It was miserable.

Though I had spent a good deal of time praying, I started praying almost constantly. I needed the pain to be under control so I could get out of the hospital.

And God is surely faithful in answering prayers. With the Dilaudid on order, I was able to keep my pain under control, stopping the flares before they got too bad. I stayed relatively pain-free all throughout that day and the next. I was even able to roll over onto my stomach to be more comfortable.

On the next day, during morning rounds, I found out that I was going to have the drain removed from my leg. It was great news since it was a step closer to going home. I was excited about it, even. The last time I had gotten drains removed after a surgery, I recalled that it wasn't the worst experience ever. Still, I had never had drains removed after an amputation, and I was expecting the unexpected.

When I asked the surgical resident what I could expect, he described what should feel like a small pinch.

But when he started to pull the drain that had been embedded under my skin for days, the "pinch" was far from what I felt. In an attempt not to use a string of expletives, I chose my words wisely. The only thing that came to mind while it felt like a metal straw was being stabbed through my leg was, "I don't like it, I don't like it, I don't LIKE IT, IDON'TLIKEITIDON'TLIKEITIDON'TLIKEIT!"

I couldn't help but giggle when the resident asked in the sweetest, most innocent of tones, "I guess it was a little more than a pinch?"

Not long after the drain had been removed, I got a visit from Em and Francisco. Seeing them, just as it had during chemo, brightened my day beyond measure. It was impossible to be upset with them around. Especially when Francisco was talking about how he could already see me back on a Spartan course. The images I tried to conjure in my mind before surgery started to pop back up and he and I talked about how I would conquer obstacles with a prosthetic leg.

Em added her own thoughts to the conversation, and it lifted me up to hear other people join in on the idea that I would one day be so far past the experiences I was in.

May 20, 2023

The next day, they had to turn off the nerve blocks. The pain from the first day after surgery was still too fresh in my mind, and I was nearly shaking at the idea that I might have to endure that again. Though they would be able to turn the nerve blocks back on, the possibility of going through that pain again, even for a short time, was one that I could hardly bear. I did the only thing that had been able to bring me comfort since the whole ordeal had started a month earlier. I just prayed. I prayed and prayed and prayed until I realized that hours had passed and I wasn't in excruciating pain.

I wasn't entirely pain-free, of course, but it was a manageable kind of pain. A pain worth managing so I could go home and at least suffer in the comfort of my own home after a hot shower.

After I had managed for a few hours without more breakthrough pain, we all decided to pull the nerve blocks. Remembering having the drain pulled had me steeling my nerves. When the pain management doctor told me it would be just a pinch, I couldn't help but laugh out loud. I didn't believe that anymore. To my surprise, the first one really was just a pinch. A long, drawn-out pinch since it seemed like about eight inches of tubing was being pulled out of my hip, but the feeling was definitely more strange than painful. The second line came out with no pain at all.

All that stood between me and my hot shower was having my meds sent to a pharmacy and getting discharge papers signed. As I had come to expect, that didn't go smoothly at all. Since my surgeon had gone out of town after my amputation, things were being handled by my previous surgeon. True to the usual chaos, he sent all my prescriptions to the pharmacy downstairs.

The *closed* pharmacy downstairs.

They tried to send them to the pharmacy across the street. That pharmacy would close 15 minutes later.

368

I started to think that maybe everyone in this hospital shared a collective singular brain cell. Apparently, no one on my team had called dibs that morning.

We finally got them to send my prescriptions to a Walgreens pharmacy that was on our way home. Before the discharge papers even went through, I was in my wheelchair, bags packed. The minute those papers came through, I was leaving. Except, the minute those papers came through, no one from transport was available to take me down to the valet to pick up our truck.

I was about two seconds from wheeling myself to the nearest elevator when my nurse decided to just take me herself. She got the message.

Propped up in the back seat of the truck, I was finally free and headed home. All we had to do was stop by Walgreens and pick up my meds, and I would be free.

And we truly thought we were free. I stayed in the truck while Mom went in to get my prescriptions, thinking it would take her five, ten minutes tops. But then, ten minutes had passed. Then fifteen. Then thirty.

It turns out that when my old surgeon sent my prescriptions to the first pharmacy - you know, the one that was closed - that pharmacy somehow billed my insurance for all my meds. Though they weren't filled, that meant Walgreens could not bill my insurance.

They also could not fill four different narcotics for me without contacting the hospital to ensure the correct meds had been sent. As if my severed limb hadn't been proof enough that the orders weren't a mistake. It took nearly an hour and a half before they agreed to fill enough of all the meds to get me through the weekend until they could contact the pharmacy at the hospital to back out the billing.

What an absolute disaster.

Despite all that I had gone through, there was a silver lining. The support from my friends, who had become family, was something that I had never experienced, and I couldn't fathom going through that without them.

The flowers, balloons, Zebra Cakes, and visits where I was lifted in prayer were what kept me moving forward.

And, unbeknownst to me, more surprises were in store once I got home.

Chapter 38

The relief I felt when we pulled into our driveway was palpable in the air, both for me and Mom. All I wanted was a long - and I do mean hours long - hot shower, and to rest in my own bed.

Mom pulled the truck up close to the door so I had a shorter walk to get into the house, and when she opened the door, I saw something that definitely wasn't there when we had left five days earlier.

"Congrats" hung in huge letters from the entryway into our dining room, surrounded by balloons and ribbons. A huge arrangement of tropical plants had been laid out on our kitchen table, along with a gift basket. It was from Mom's best friend and his wife, Billy and Amy, who I was good friends with as well. They had the spare key to our house and had used it to plan a welcome home surprise for us.

I was overwhelmed with joy, so much so that all I could say was, "They broke into our house to surprise us!"

Okay, maybe it was overwhelm, paired with the fact that I was sort of high on all the pain meds. Either way, it was hilarious.

I didn't even wait for Mom to unload the truck. I was nearly begging for her to help me get into the shower. Because the dressings still covered my leg, I couldn't just hop - ha-ha, get it? Hop! - into the shower. There was a whole routine that needed to happen.

Limitless

We tried to set up the shower chair the hospital sent home with us. Of course, it didn't fit into our shower, where I could face away from the shower head with my leg resting on the outside of the tub. No, they hadn't been able to get insurance to approve the kind of shower chair we needed. Instead, we got a big, bulky bedside toilet that they justified could double as a shower chair.

Luckily, Amazon could deliver a proper shower chair in two days.

Then came what had to be my all-time favorite - insert sarcasm - part of showering after a leg surgery. We had to wrap my leg in a trash bag, and tape it to my thigh so water couldn't soak through to the ace bandages wrapping my leg. With the current set-up of the makeshift shower chair, my trash bag-wrapped leg was on the side that faced the shower head, so I had to be a little more careful of keeping that leg relatively dry.

As it always had, despite the effort it took, the shower felt amazing.

I washed down with body wash and shampooed my hair at least three times. After five days, it felt as though I couldn't get the cling of the hospital off my skin. Sure, that was all in my head, but there was also the sticky residue that I had to scrape and peel from everywhere on my body. Anywhere I had an IV or monitor placed, I had sticky residue. I don't even want to talk about the clumps of glue they used to hold the nerve blocks in place that I had to rip off from over my hips.

After I felt like I had finally scrubbed the hospital off my skin, I just sat under the water. It was the most comfort and relaxation I had gotten since I had left my house five days prior. I was savoring every minute of it and thanking God for modern indoor plumbing.

Everything about trying to shower and get dressed was foreign. I still wasn't used to the uneven weight distribution, so I tried not to stand for too long. I realized too quickly that our shower was built for standing. Nothing was within arm's reach of my shower chair, and it wasn't much better once I got out of the shower. Trying to dry off and get dressed while sitting was just as much of a mess. I still couldn't hop much to move around and get what I needed because each movement sent jolts of pain into my leg.

We would have to rearrange the bathroom. And install some handrails. A task for another time. I hobbled my way into the living room and sank into my recliner. I didn't realize how much I missed it. My leg was so sensitive, I had to use a massive fluffy pillow from the hospital to prop my leg up on. But once I got settled, I was happy as a clam. I was home. I could start truly recovering.

Once Mom and I both got settled for the evening, Billy and Amy wanted to come over to visit, and they wanted to bring their chihuahua, Jasper.

A little backstory about Jasper. We claimed him as our dog as much as they did. For the past few years, we would get him almost every weekend and let him spend time with us at our house. As a joke, Billy would bring over food and snacks with a label that said, "Doggy Support." We even got him for most holidays since he would get overwhelmed with the festivities at his house. We joked with Billy that we had joint custody, and weekends were when we had visitation rights.

After the week we had, I couldn't turn down seeing Jasper, even if I was exhausted. And he did not disappoint. Apparently, he had been ready to see us, and when they put him down at our front door, he tore out to get to me. He was running so fast that he nearly drifted around one of our couches and bounced off the other to land in my lap. Once he realized that something was definitely not right, he wouldn't even have anything to do with Mom. He curled up in my lap and refused to move.

He also refused to let anyone touch me. When Billy and Amy tried to come give me a hug, he was barking and growling at them. When Mom tried to help me adjust my leg, he sounded like he was about to bite her hand off.

It turns out that when Amy heard what was going on and how bad that hospital stay was, she seriously considered putting him in an oversized purse and sneaking him onto my floor so I could get some Jasper love.

By the time Billy and Amy had gotten ready to head home for the night, Jasper had other plans. They had to wrangle a very angry chihuahua away from his human, and he was not having it. We actually debated having him stay the night with us. Mom mentioned that she wasn't up for taking care of two kids that night, so Jasper did not get his way.

It worked out well, though, since the meal train my friend Kim had organized was scheduled to start that night. The idea of a meal train was for people to sign up to bring us a meal every day so that, with all we had to worry about, cooking was not one of those things.

As always, it was so good to see Kim. Along with dinner, she brought a gift bag that left me with tears in my eyes. Among some self-care items, she had a little Dori figurine from *Finding Nemo*. That absolutely cracked me up since Trevor's nickname for me when I started getting forgetful was Dori. She had heard me use the phrase "Just Keep Swimming" before and knew it would be the perfect gift. She also included a necklace with a charm that was stamped with a semicolon.

She wanted me to remember that my story was far from over.

Their visits took the rest of my energy from me, and I decided I was ready for bed. I was so excited to be back in my own bed.

I forgot one little detail though. As it was with my first leg surgery, sleeping on my side was a no-go. And I am not a back sleeper. But I was so determined. I had Mom help roll my leg into place for me to sleep on my stomach, and that was all it took for me to be out like a light.

Around 10:00 p.m., Mom came back into my room to wake me up. Except, she was fully dressed. Shoes on and everything. She told me she was taking a drive, and that Billy was hanging out in the living room in case I needed anything.

In my med-induced haze, all I could process was that Mom leaving me to the care of anyone else was highly unusual. She had gone on rides before if she had a rough week at work or something like that, but never in a situation like this.

I thought she had finally lost it. Now that I was safely home, she was having a mental breakdown and needed to take a ride at ten o'clock at night. I was worried but was so exhausted. I couldn't process what was going on other than to ask how long she would be gone.

Her telling me that she might be gone for half an hour, or two hours, she didn't know, really set off alarm bells in my head, but I barely had the chance to process that info before I was being pulled back into sleep.

Sometime near midnight, she was back in my room. Since my lights were off, and my contacts out, I couldn't really see, but I noticed that someone else was standing in the doorway to my room.

I couldn't imagine that Billy would be standing in the doorway to my room, but my mind was so foggy. I couldn't think.

Mom leaned down to ask me if I remembered the surprise she mentioned that she had for me while I was in the hospital. Admittedly, I had kind of forgotten about that. But apparently, my surprise was there. And before I could try to speculate if the figure standing at my door was my surprise, I heard a squeak.

It wasn't just any squeak. This was the sound you might associate with the sound a balloon makes as the air is let out of it.

That particular squeak was one I knew came from one person and one person only.

Trevor.

According to Trevor, who was, in fact, standing in the doorway to my room, I "shot out of bed like a corpse in a horror movie." I was up so fast that Mom had to grab my shoulder to keep me from tumbling off the foot of the bed.

Now, logically speaking, one might make the connection that Trevor had flown from Oregon, where he lived, to surprise me. But in my drug-addled brain, I was convinced of a few outlandish things.

Somehow, Trevor had teleported. One second, he was in Oregon; the next, he was in my room. That just wasn't possible.

If that wasn't possible, then I must have been so high on drugs that I hallucinated my brother in my room.

After he hugged me, I kept reaching out to touch him because surely I was dreaming. There was no way he was in my house.

To make matters even more confusing, he reached out and put something in my hand. It was a Hot Wheels turtle, something he had been saving to give me because of an inside joke. So, he must have really been there if he had handed me the turtle.

I know it sounds crazy to think that this was what was going through my head, but with the mix of meds I had been sent home on, I was certainly off my rocker enough to be thinking those things.

After we talked for a while, and I convinced myself that he really was there, I realized I could barely hold my eyes open. We all decided to get some sleep for the night. Except, the minute he left my room, I really started to question if I had been dreaming. Thankfully, I kept the Hot Wheels turtle on my nightstand to help me remember that he really was there.

The next morning, I was up way earlier than him. In his defense, he was three time zones away, and had endured sixteen hours of flights and airports. But I was so impatient to see him it took every ounce of willpower to keep myself from waking him up.

When he finally did roll out of bed and into the living room, he really shocked me. Without asking, he walked up, gave me a hug, and sat in the recliner next to mine. Trevor is not one to hug without being asked, so then I was really confused. It must have been entertaining for him because I just sat beside him and stared at him until he commented that, yes, he was sitting next to me, and I wasn't losing my mind.

Come to find out, his call to Mom wasn't just because he wanted to know how I was doing. He was worried, and when his job found out, they offered him a week off to come make sure I was okay. His call was to ask Mom if she thought him flying down to Florida was a good idea. She, of course, said yes but that they shouldn't tell me, just in case things didn't work out.

His plan was not even to tell me he was there but to sit in the kitchen drinking coffee when I woke up in the morning. To really mess with me, he wanted to tell me that I had been there all week. As well as my brain was functioning, I would have believed him.

Mom vetoed the idea because she knew I probably would have been so excited I would have fallen trying to get to him to hug him.

Considering she barely kept me from leaping off the foot of my bed to get to him the previous night, her concerns were pretty accurate.

The same morning, Mom also decided to pick Jasper up so he could hang out with us. After barking at Trevor for ten minutes straight, he finally decided to curl up on my lap as my eight-pound guard dog.

Having Trevor with me that week was by far the best thing that could have happened for both of us.

And somehow, things just kept getting better and better. I got to hang out with Trevor and binge-watch The Big Bang Theory, and I got to hang out with my friends from church since they signed up to bring us meals. I felt surrounded by love. I had my mom, my brother, my closest friends, and my dog. Even if I wanted to be depressed over my leg, it would have been nearly impossible.

To make the whole experience even more fun, Trevor and I decided to both sleep in our recliners. At first, the plan was just for me to sleep in the recliner, because it was much more comfortable since I had to mostly stay on my back and not toss and turn like I usually would. Trevor refused my offer to take my bed and decided to sleep in the recliner beside me.

This, naturally, brought some pretty hilarious moments. Since I was still getting used to moving around without part of my leg, I was told to not try to get up without either Mom or Trevor there to make sure I didn't fall. Well, one night, I had to get up. I turned to Trevor and tried to wake him, but he didn't budge. So, I grabbed my phone to call Mom. When I got back from the bathroom, Trevor asked why I hadn't woken him up. I told him I tried, and he didn't wake up. Apparently, all I actually did was sit up, stare at him for a few seconds, and then grab my phone to call Mom. Drug-addled brain indeed.

At first, Trevor was the picture of the sweet big brother. Every morning when I woke up, he got up to make me the protein shake he knew I liked. When I took naps, he would take my water bottle and fill it up. He even chose one of my favorite movies, the Princess Diaries, to watch, knowing he would have to endure the sequel on my request. He would disappear into the kitchen only to reappear with homemade granola, poached pears and ice cream, and all sorts of snacks.

Like I said, at first. Because when the newness wore off, he turned into the typical big brother. He could annoy me, and I couldn't run away. Within a few days, I kept a spray bottle full of water beside my recliner to spray him with when he annoyed me. In retaliation, he would try to touch me with his foot. He knew how much I hated feet.

Up until that point, I think some part of Mom still didn't fully believe that we were as we claimed, brother and sister in spirit. But when she walked into the living room to see him with his foot on my recliner, and me pointing a spray bottle of water at him, she realized she was dealing with warring siblings. I think some of the times she left the house, it was just to get away from our shenanigans.

May 24, 2023

Later in the week, Trevor even got to go with me to my first prosthetics appointment to get shrinkers for my leg. Like compression socks, they would help keep the swelling down in my residual limb and would be much easier to deal with than the ace bandage I had been using.

During my appointment, they had a few intake questions to ask, one being if I had anyone in my life I trusted to share what I was going through with. At the same time, Mom and I turned towards Trevor, standing against the back wall. Somehow, he - who flew 3,000 miles for his sister - was shocked that he was the answer to that question.

The time came to finally unwrap the ace bandages on my leg and replace them with the shrinker. Since my surgery, I had been instructed to keep the same dressing on it until I saw my prosthetist. I thought it was strange not to even have the wound checked while I was in the hospital, but I didn't have the capacity to question it.

Being that this wasn't my first rodeo, I knew that the incision was likely to look pretty gnarly. Stitches, probably some dried blood. I wasn't exactly prepared for what was under the bandages, though.

First off, they had only layered gauze on top of the incision. So, after ten days, we could barely even get the gauze away from the incision. We peeled, and tugged, and finally, gave up. The plan would be to just put the shrinker on over the few layers of gauze, and I could try to ease the rest off with saline when I got home.

But that's where the hard part came in. Because I still had a fresh wound and stitches, we couldn't just pull the shrinker on. We had to stretch it open and slip it on as quickly as we could. That was a two-person job. My prosthetist looked between Mom and Trevor, seeing who was going to be willing to give that task a try.

I wasn't shocked when Trevor volunteered. Not at all. I was shocked, though, when he pulled the shrinker over my newly severed leg like it was the most normal thing in the world. I had already gotten used to people shying away from my leg. It wasn't that they were grossed out, but they didn't want to take any chances of accidentally hurting me. For Trevor, it was a task that had to be done. He knew it was going to hurt, but that didn't stop it from having to be done.

Later that night, as we were at home in our recliners, I was asking him about it. Not just about how calm he was but about everything. Somewhere in our conversation, he turned to me to respond to a question I asked, but he didn't address me as "sis" like he normally would.

He addressed me as "She Wolf."

When I asked what in the world he meant by that, he explained that I started to remind him of a wolf. When wolves are trapped in a snare, they have been known to chew their own legs off to escape. Morbid, I know. But his point was that I had chosen similarly. I chose to lose part of a limb over giving up my quality of life. To him, it made perfect sense.

Of course, he couldn't just have the heartfelt moment and leave it. He then told me that, when making a lucky rabbit's foot, they use the left foot. He said I should have saved my left foot in a jar or something, and maybe it would be lucky. I think I tried to throw an empty water bottle at him for that one.

But in all seriousness, that interaction would begin to shape my own self-image. Trevor wasn't one to sugarcoat things. He wouldn't say anything like that unless he truly meant it. He said it at a time when I hadn't really started to form my new self-image and where the influence was much needed. Whether he planned it that way or not, he wanted me to see myself as strong because of my decision.

In the vulnerable state I was in after amputation, it would have been easy to absorb other perspectives and shape them into the image I saw of myself. Realizing just how much help I needed to function in my day-to-day life, I could have started to see myself as helpless. Or perhaps I could have looked at myself as being crazy for choosing to give up my leg instead of fighting to save it when there was an option that allowed me to do that. Worse, I could see my future prosthetic as something to hide or be ashamed of.

Those thoughts and more had spent plenty of time fighting for dominance in my head, but the memory of hearing my brother, who had been through so much in his own life, calling me She Wolf would put those thoughts to rest every time. It became a habit. Anytime he and I would talk during the time I spent recovering, if I started to get a little down on myself, he would remind me of who he saw me as.

As time went on, I started to get more and more sensation in my not-foot. Instead of just feeling the phantom limb, I would feel my toes start to itch. I had experienced that itch you can't quite scratch kind of thing before, but this was a whole new level. Trevor, being funny, reached over one night to where my foot would have been and scratched the air. I am not joking when I say the itching stopped.

I was perplexed. He was amused. When he realized that I still hadn't taught my brain that my foot wasn't there anymore, he had a field day. He would walk by my recliner and smack his hand across where my foot should have been, just to watch me jerk my leg back.

He had even more fun showing one of my friends who shared our wicked sense of humor. They would get me talking, and distracted, so that one of them could throw a magazine at where my foot used to be to watch me jump. Honestly, it was hysterical. I was just happy to be with friends that I could joke with.

I've said it since cancer, and I will keep saying it. There are times in life when I'm either going to laugh about it or cry about it. I'd rather choose to laugh.

Limitless

Chapter 39

Sadly, my staycation with my brother had to end eventually. He had to fly back to Oregon, and normal life had to resume.

Well, I was still discovering that normal simply did not exist anymore. I've stated my feelings towards the whole New Normal thing. But with amputation, normal goes right out the window. New, old, or otherwise. A better term for what I was learning would be New Reality.

Not long after he left - and his leaving did upset me more than the loss of part of my leg, in case you were wondering - the reality of what my life was going to be like set in. I do not mean that I started having second thoughts, or I got depressed, or anything like that. But my recovery and the realities of now having an amputated leg were able to better settle in.

Apparently, my brain had finally started to process that the foot that had been there for nearly 23 years was now missing, because those itches that were the cause of so much laughter, now turned to the dreaded phantom pain.

Phantom pain is thought to occur when the brain and spinal cord miss the usual input signals from the limb that was amputated. As the nervous system rewires itself to accommodate for the lack of signals, it sends signals to the brain that something is wrong. Unfortunately, that signal is in the form of pain.

I had the sensation of having a foot within a few days after my amputation. At first, it truly was like a phantom. I felt the shape and form of what I knew my leg should feel like, but that was it. It was just a vague shape. But then those itches started. It was as if my brain was trying to find what it knew should be there.

When there was no foot to be found, it panicked.

I could still feel that vague shape of a foot. I could feel my toes curl if I thought about curling them, and I could feel the bottom and sides of my foot. But when the phantom pain started, it felt like the bottom of my foot had turned to pins and needles. But it felt magnified as if the feeling of pins and needles could have gotten more concentrated. For a little while, it wasn't too bad. But after a few hours, it was insanity-inducing.

I felt like if I could just rub the bottom of my foot, it would go away. But I couldn't. It felt as if the pain wasn't actually there. And how could it have been if the part experiencing the pain wasn't there?

Following that logic, how can something hurt when it does not exist? And if it does not exist, then how do you make it stop?

So yeah, it messed with my head just a little bit. I would try to distract myself but to no avail. My usual outlets were out of the question. Going to a state park and hiking on crutches was not a good idea for obvious reasons. Neither was running. Trying to read didn't help at all since the pain distracted me from reading.

The only thing I found to help ease the pain was to take car rides. Mom would drive us down back roads in the middle of nowhere for as long as we could stand being in the car. It was my only reprieve. The minute I was back in the living room, the pain would start again.

The pain had become so intense within a few short days that I couldn't even fall asleep unless exhaustion pulled me under. That, or I took enough pain meds to knock out an elephant. The pain meds hardly even stopped the pain; they just put me to sleep so I didn't have to deal with it.

I would have Mom rub the stump of my leg to try to teach my brain to understand what was left. It only worked for so long. When I finally did get ahold of my surgical team, their only response was to increase my doses of Gabapentin and wait until it took effect. It would take at least two weeks for the increase in dose to be noticeable.

As if someone could stay sane for two weeks with pain so intense. Since my surgical team's solution was somewhat of a waiting game, I texted my prosthetist to see if she had any solutions that might help get the pain under control. I felt horrible texting her on a weekend, but I couldn't bear the idea of waiting until the beginning of the week.

God bless her, she replied almost instantly, sending links to instructions for how to wrap my leg properly to add compression, as well as instructions on how to do mirror therapy.

Mirror therapy is a way to, essentially, trick the brain into thinking the amputated limb is still there. For me, I would have to prop a mirror up between my legs, so that my right leg was reflected where my left leg should be. I could move my right leg and foot, and mimic those movements with my left leg. In theory, that would help the pain to ease.

I could have cried with relief when, as soon as I started moving my legs, seeing my left leg moving with my right in the mirror, the pain started to ease. For once in the past few days, I felt my sanity come back from the edge.

The only problem with that was that it only worked as long as the mirror stayed between my legs. Which wasn't a huge deal until we considered that the only mirror we had was my giant, 6-foot-tall wall mirror. We had to prop it up on the recliner, as well as a kitchen chair, to keep it held up. For as long as I could stand, I would hold that mirror up, rotating my ankles and twisting my legs around. The major downside to that was when I would need to eat, sleep, or get tired of holding the mirror, the pain would come back. I knew it would help in the long term, but I needed short-term relief while my brain learned the long-term solutions.

I tried to take matters into my own hands. I'll go ahead and give you the spoiler alert. Of all the times I have chosen to take things into my own hands, this time probably had the worst results. But I also can't understate just how desperate I was for relief. Being forced to sit on the couch and feel the pain I was feeling, with no relief, for days on end had me willing to try just about anything. Especially when my surgical team thought waiting it out was a perfectly fine idea.

I decided, after some research, that trying CBD might be a helpful solution. The only major reactions I saw to taking CBD with my handfuls of medications were drowsiness, dizziness, and confusion. A small price to pay, and, hey, maybe it would help me get some sleep.

Off we went to a shop in town that we thought was reputable. I had no idea what I was looking for. I was just hoping for the best. We were met by a very sweet, very old lady who ended up trying to sell me an entire line of CBD products. She insisted it would work best if I took four different kinds of CBD throughout the day. I had to decline all the way up until the register, and even as I was paying. I just wanted to try the stuff to see if it would work.

I ended up with a jar of gummies that would, apparently, help with my pain. On the way home, I took half of a gummy. By the time we got home, I felt absolutely nothing, so I took the other half.

And then I was asleep on the couch for two hours. I don't mean a light nap. I mean, I stopped existing for two hours. I didn't move, didn't dream, anything. But when I woke up, the pain was back. I wasn't fully ready to give up on the idea, so later that night, I tried another one. Again, I zonked out for two solid hours and woke up in pain. Except this time, I woke up a zombie. My limbs were heavy, and it felt like I was lifting weights just to move. But once I woke up, I could hardly get back to sleep.

Yeah, not working as intended.

The next day, it was back to the car rides between times practicing mirror therapy. But even in the car, while my pain had subsided, I could barely turn my head to look out the window. Everything felt like I was in the kind of dream where I would try to move, and my body just wouldn't respond. Like being immersed in a movie where everything was happening around me, and I couldn't interact with my environment.

Okay, so the CBD was a bust. But could I be blamed for trying?

May 30, 2023

The time quickly came for me to have my first follow-up appointment with my surgeon. Being only two weeks out of surgery, I questioned how it was already time to take my stitches out, but I figured my team knew what they were doing. I was almost excited to see my surgical team again. Though I hated being in the Ortho office, I wanted the milestone of having my stitches out.

I was happy and talkative with my surgeon all the way up until he unwrapped my leg and frowned. Deeply. Even I fell for it, thinking that the hardest part of my recovery was now behind me and that everything was going to be fine. As if the constant state of "It's fine until it's not" over the past few years hadn't been any indication of how things would go.

Hoping so much that everything was still fine made my heart drop even harder when I saw my surgeon frown. Honestly, I was terrified to ask. The longer I spent in denial that anything was wrong, the longer I spent in a state of bliss where everything was still okay.

It lasted about ten seconds before my surgeon told me that my incision had become necrotic. The skin around my wound, which we thought was just some gnarly scabbing, was actually dead and dying flesh.

Wonderful.

That also meant that we would have to leave the stitches in for at least another week.

I questioned how that even had happened. According to my surgeon, it was a lack of blood flow to the skin that caused it to start to die. But also, according to him, it would heal on its own. It didn't make sense to me at the time since I was processing that information, but later I would come to question that.

He was able to take some of the stitches out, mostly on the areas where the skin had healed better. Since my first experience with having stitches removed was borderline torture, I had prepared myself for a world of hurt, but no hurt came. The stitches he was able to take out came out relatively painlessly. Of course, my tolerance for pain was entirely different since being in the hospital after my amputation, but I wasn't going to take the lack of agony for granted.

One good thing did come out of my appointment, though. I was now able to shower without wrapping a trash bag around my leg. With my love for a good shower, that almost made up for the bad news of the day. Almost.

Of course, I took a comfort shower that night with no trash bag.

Over the next week, I would continue to fight with phantom pain. Many nights, I would end up in Mom's bed. She would rub my arm or back, giving me a sensation to focus on that wasn't the stabbing pins and needles pain in my leg. Some nights, it was the only way I could fall asleep.

It was also that week that I decided I wanted to go back to the gym. It had only been two weeks after surgery, and I was already missing the feeling of being able to workout and get the frustrations of life out of my system.

Mom was surprisingly okay with the idea, mostly because I asked her to come with me so she could help keep track of my crutches, water bottle, and spray for the gym equipment. I was a little short on hands with the crutches. Not to mention short on feet.

The minute I entered the gym, I knew I was in for an experience. I had to relearn every aspect of my life, and this would be no different. It started before I even entered the gym. I knew I couldn't do the same type of workout that I was used to, lifting heavy weights until my muscles trembled. I had to get around on crutches, so the use of my arms was essential. Leg days were also out completely for the indefinite future. I didn't want to try to strengthen just my right leg and create worse imbalances than what I knew would be happening.

All that being said, I had to do something. Fortunately, just hopping in on crutches from the parking lot was my warm-up and cardio for the day combined. My heart was pounding by the time I got inside. I had forgotten just how much anesthesia and pain meds sapped my strength. All in all, though, my trip to the gym was a success. I hopped around, passing my crutches to Mom and having her hand me weights when needed. The owners of my small-town gym were also incredibly supportive and helpful.

I did some of my usual weightlifting, and tried my best to use lighter weights so I wouldn't get sore. Even the lighter weights had my muscles trembling, though. Half the workout was moving between one station and another, and by the time I finished a workout that would have once been a warm-up, I was exhausted.

Surprisingly, my phantom pain stopped almost completely while I was in the zone, even though it did come back with a fury once I got home. It was like my brain had to make up for the time I wasn't in misery.

June 4, 2023

That weekend, I made my return to DCC for a Sunday morning service. The love I had been shown in the time leading up to my amputation was no comparison to the love I was shown my first Sunday back. The parking team parked us up front and called the golf cart over to get us close to the front door. Inside, I was greeted with so many hugs I was almost late to find a seat before service started.

I knew I didn't have to, but I tried my best to stand while the worship team started off the service. I was so grateful to be back with my family and so grateful to God that I had even come as far as I had past surgery that sitting just didn't feel like enough. But thirty minutes standing on one leg just wasn't happening, so I had to cave and sit.

Luckily, we chose to sit in the back row because once my phantom pain started up again, I couldn't stop shifting around. I would prop my leg up on the seat beside me, try to sit with my legs crossed, go back to sitting normally, and then start the whole cycle over again. By the end of service, I was restless and exhausted. I was so glad I was able to come in person and see my people, but I was so tired. When we made it back home, I napped for hours, the phantom pain not even stopping me from sleeping.

Heading back to Ortho for my second follow-up, I didn't bring many expectations with me. I didn't really expect to get the rest of my stitches out since my leg didn't look any better than the previous week. Actually, it looked worse.

Not worse enough to warrant any treatment, though. My surgical team decided that it was time for the rest of the stitches to come out. This time, it would be the resident I saw during rounds during my hospital admission. Since I knew I could joke with him, I teased him that my surgeon had set the bar pretty high as far as painless stitch removal. The first few stitches to come out were as painless as before. I was even starting to relax a little. But when he got to the stitches that were under the necrotic parts of my incision, I came unglued from the table.

On skin that was still hypersensitive and not fully healed, I felt each tug like he was ripping open the incision. Each time he pulled a stitch loose, it felt like dragging a hot, sharp wire under the surface of my skin. It left a searing pain in its wake.

More than once, I had to ask him to stop. I couldn't bear the constant feeling of my leg being set on fire and pulled apart. At one point, as he pulled one of the stitches, I groaned through gritted teeth and asked if he considered pulling stitches a "pinch." We both got a good laugh out of remembering when he had pulled the drain from my leg in the hospital.

Mom had been right there through each stitch, letting me grip onto her hand while she rubbed my back. I wouldn't have survived the experience without her.

Though it sucked, it was almost a relief to be in pain that was actually physical. A pain that had a physical cause and could be fixed. A pain that stopped once the action that caused it had ceased.

I tried to celebrate the milestone of having my stitches out, but there was a lingering dread that, as long as my leg had necrotic tissue, I would not be making any progress in healing. Though my team kept assuring me it would heal on its own, I had my doubts. How could something that was literally dead heal itself? That sounds like a Jesus-level miracle. Not that I didn't believe it could happen, but it would have to be just that, a miracle.

My attempt at celebration was cut even shorter when we got home, and I unwrapped my leg later that evening. Without the stitches holding the wound together on the areas with necrotic tissue, those areas had pulled completely apart. What used to be a thin incision would open up to be nearly an inch wide over the following days. The necrotic tissue still held on, with no sign of "fixing itself" anytime soon.

Limitless

392

Chapter 40

June 10, 2023

Though I had a wound that was determined not to heal and had only been an amputee for a whopping three weeks, there was one thing I was determined to follow through on: vacation.

We had been planning a trip to Dry Tortugas National Park in Key West since well before my leg broke, and after the stress and trauma of the previous month and a half, I needed a vacation. Desperately. It didn't matter to me that I would be taking this vacation on crutches. I had been cooped up in the house for as long as I could stand it.

Mom, being the more sensible of the two of us, tried to convince me to put off our trip. In hindsight, it made sense. We weren't even used to living a normal life and wouldn't be for a while. Trying to vacation with the unpredictability of not having half of my leg was crazy. But when I say I was desperate, I mean I was on the brink of losing my mind.

Since I had survived cancer, I had become used to *living*. Rarely did I spend a day relaxing at home. A relaxing weekend for me looked like going to seasonal festivals and local events, going to church events, planning lunches with friends, going hiking, you name it. Sitting at home for endless days was tormenting.

It didn't help that the things I would have liked to do to pass my time were hardly feasible. I would have wanted to read, but my head was in such a fog from the high doses of nerve medications that I could barely remember what I read. I wanted to learn Italian, but I couldn't retain any of what I learned. I tried watching Crash Course videos on YouTube, but I couldn't process any of the information. It was a frustrating loop that left me binge-watching The Rings of Power.

Okay, sure, I had been wanting to watch it for a while. But I wanted to watch it by choice, not because I couldn't move from the couch and didn't have two brain cells to rub together to do anything other than stare at a screen for hours.

Upon hearing that, Trevor told me that my two brain cells seemed to be fighting for third place.

When it came time for vacation, I was in. My leg - or lack of, really - was just a minor obstacle in my eyes. With my stubbornness, Mom quickly figured out that I wasn't backing down from this trip. Knowing that, she tried to offer the use of a wheelchair to make our lives easier.

Oh. Heck. No.

I was adamantly against that idea. I had spent long enough confined to a wheelchair during chemo, and I couldn't bear the idea of being stuck like that again.

I want to make myself clear here. I am absolutely not saying that there is any shame in using a wheelchair or any assistive device to aid in mobility. For me, using a wheelchair was something I could not bear to relive. I had fought so long for my independence after cancer, and it was a hard-won victory. I was perfectly capable of getting around on my knee scooter or on crutches, and I wasn't willing to give up that capability for what I knew would come with it.

The pitying stares. Those who were close to me knew that pity was the last thing I wanted. I didn't want to be seen as someone to feel sorry for but as someone whose strength and resilience were obvious. I had already caught those looks from strangers, feeling

394

sorry for the poor young girl who had lost her leg. I was not about to add a wheelchair to the list of reasons to be pitied.

So yeah, I would rather struggle along on crutches than feel confined. To feel incapable. My mental health was already in a fragile place dealing with my surgical team. No reason to push it over the edge.

The first challenge of our trip came before we had even left our house. Packing was very nearly a nightmare. Of course, there was the usual - clothes, shoes, toiletries, makeup. But then there was all the new stuff. The knee scooter, the crutches, the mirror for mirror therapy, the wound dressings, and the medications.

And unfortunately, the challenges did not end when we got in the truck to leave. Over the course of our trip, we would encounter so many obstacles.

We realized the importance of an accessible room on our first night. It wasn't something we even thought necessary, until we were in a room I could hardly maneuver around with crutches. Or until I tried to take a shower, and my shower chair couldn't fit in the tub.

In other rooms, we realized how much of a challenge stairs could be on crutches. We had booked our hotel in Key West long before my amputation, and by the time we were ready to go on the trip, we could not change rooms to an accessible room. The path to our room was up and down stairs, and the first night I tried to get up the stairs to my room, I lost my balance and fell, landing right on my amputated leg. The pain was an assault on every one of my senses. My ears rang, and I saw white until it subsided. It made every nerve in my body scream.

More to our frustration, we realized Key West is one of the least accessible places we could have chosen to travel to. Most shops had stairs and no ramps. Even crossing the street was difficult since the ramps to get on the sidewalk from the street were not directly across from each other.

To make matters even worse, my phantom pain had started to flare so badly I couldn't even sleep. I would end up in bed with Mom, begging her to rub my arm or my back to give me some other sensation to focus on until I could sleep.

But I wasn't going to be discouraged. I had anticipated how my life would change in unfathomable ways, and for me, it was all about living through the learning curve. It was times like this, though, where I found the beauty of humanity still tucked away.

When we asked the concierge at the front desk of our Key West hotel if we could switch rooms, and he had to tell us he didn't have any available accessible rooms, he went above and beyond to make our trip manageable. He offered to help me get up the stairs into our room, a part of the day we had dreaded. I expected him to just be around, close enough to catch me in the case that I fell.

But this man, an angel I'm sure, refused to see me struggle. As I went to make my way up the stairs, he gently lifted me from the ground onto the deck where the entrance to our room was. I was so stunned I could barely speak. His eyes held no pity, no sorrow at my situation. Only a sense of "we do what we have to do."

In one of those Only God moments, we found out that he would also be working the next morning when we had planned to check out because of a call-in. Come the next morning, he was right there to lift me from the top steps to the deck below. His only response to our gratitude was to say he was just doing his job.

He wasn't the only angel that we found during our trip. As we walked around, trying and failing at finding a shop I could access on my scooter, the shopkeepers would graciously let Mom bring merchandise to the door so I could see the shirts, stickers, and magnets from my scooter on the sidewalk.

One shopkeeper at a Key Lime shop I had been so excited to visit came out to the sidewalk to describe the different items on their menu to me. Again, not an ounce of pity. Just joy at being able to be a light for someone.

Whether they realized it or not, their acts of graciousness would help me to feel what I had been so desperate to feel for weeks. I felt capable, even if my capabilities were with modifications. I *could* go on vacation, I *could* check out shops and eat chocolate covered key lime pies on sticks.

All of these happenings led up to the main event of our vacation. We would be taking a two-hour boat tour on the Yankee

Freedom III to Dry Tortugas National Park, 70 miles off the coast of Key West. I, as usual, went all out for this day. I had a cute sundress, a sun hat, even a cute sandal. No, not sandals. Just the one.

Everything was going about as well as expected. We boarded the boat and found a table right at the bow. The ramp to get from the pier to the boat was a minor obstacle for me, and soon we had our tour brunch in hand and were on our way.

This time, the difficulties didn't come from outside circumstances but from my own ambitions. I had spent some time on the inside, watching other tourists spot fish and turtles from the outside area on the bow. A few nearly lost their hats in the wind. They beamed as they saw sights I quickly decided I needed a closer view of, so I told Mom I wanted to go out on the bow.

It was a horrible idea, really. The movement of the water caused the entire boat to sway, and I would have to navigate the movement of the boat on crutches. But I was so determined. Mom asked one of the crew if they could help me get outside. And God truly put the right people on the crew that day because the guy who came to help didn't even bat an eye when he saw me, half a limb short and on crutches, ready to brave a rocking boat to get outside. He let me know that he would be standing behind me, just in case, and to take my time getting out to the bow.

We made it out with no falling, not even a trip. When I felt the sun warm my shoulders, the ocean spray misting my face, and took in a breath of the salted air, I felt as if I were exactly where I needed to be. The guy who helped us get out chatted with Mom, and I tried to keep up with the conversation, but I couldn't tear my focus from the beauty of what was in front of me. The *world* was in front of me, in hues of emerald greens and crystal-clear blues. I could see the skeleton structures of lighthouses I had visited before in the distance.

I stood as long as my good leg could hold me up and then made my way over to a step to sit down, close enough to the railing that I could still experience the boat ride. Crew members would stop by every now and then and strike up a conversation about visiting National Parks and what it was like to spend every day on the water.

I never felt like an obligation to them, like someone they had to come to check on. I just felt like any other tourist on their boat.

When we arrived at the little island that was Dry Tortugas, I was first amazed when I stepped off the boat, only to realize that there was no wind to cool us in the dead heat of June. The air was still, humid, and nearly suffocating. Good thing I had worn the breezy sundress because I was not about to be stopped. We made our way down to the entrance to the fort, taking in both the vastness and the confinement we felt at the same time. Vastness because of the never-ending stretch of water around us, and confinement for the same reason.

We ended up following a walking tour around the fort. Every time the tour guide stopped to give some history or fun facts about the fort, Mom would pull out a small camping chair from her backpack and let me sit.

The tour eventually ended up going up the lighthouse that sat at the corner of the fort, and we had started to move back to the small gift shop when we were stopped by the tour guide. Much to my surprise, she had noticed us, though we had stayed far in the back of the tour. She offered, with not an ounce of uncertainty, to do whatever she could to get me up the lighthouse with them if I wanted to continue the tour.

I was awestruck at that point, considering she had offered to get one of the crew members to carry me up the steps of the lighthouse. And I would have taken her up on the offer had I not noticed the fact that, once on top of the massive walls of the fort, there were no safety rails.

I can be a risk-taker, but this one was one I would pass on. I also wanted to stay close to the entrance of the fort, just in case the heat started to get to me.

But even just the thought and the willingness to help me be a part of the tour in whatever way possible again brought me to grateful tears.

On the way back to Key West, I spent the entire boat ride sitting on the bow, taking in the wonders of what was around me. I saw turtles and the infamous flying fish I had been hearing about for years. And sometimes, I would just close my eyes, breathe, and *feel*. Not only was I feeling the physical sensations of what was around me, but I was feeling a part of myself come back as if coming out of hiding. That part of myself that took adventures, that didn't let things get in my way. The part of myself enjoyed life and marveled at being in the middle of God's creations.

I also felt a new part of me coming to light. It was a part of me that had stopped worrying about being pitied or felt as if I was being seen as fragile. It was a part of myself that felt strong for, at the very least, trying. It was a part of myself that was capable despite my circumstances.

But at the very core of all the feelings, I finally remembered who I was, and that an amputation could not change me. I was adventurous. I was daring. I was capable, and strong, not *because* of what I had been through, but *regardless* of what I had been through. I was still me, and I was finally finding my way back.

June 14, 2023

Getting home from vacation meant getting back to reality and dealing with things we couldn't ignore. The wound on my limb was still not healing. If anything, it was looking worse and worse. Every time I went to Ortho, I was told the same thing. It would heal on its own. No, they wouldn't debride and restitch it. No, they wouldn't refer me to plastic surgery. It would heal on its own. The dead tissue would fall away on its own, and the wound would fill itself in. There was no reason to take drastic measures.

On top of that, I was still fighting constantly to get on a medication that actually helped my phantom pains. Insurance required me to increase my doses of nerve meds and wait weeks between each increase before approving another medication.

The idea of waiting weeks in the same pain that kept me up every night seemed ridiculous. We ended up getting a prescription for stronger nerve meds and paying out of pocket for it in the hope that they would work better than what I had been taking.

I was learning that I would have to take things into my own hands, as I had many times before. Luckily, I had an army, and taking things into my own hands was a lot simpler. As the weeks dragged on, and my church family kept seeing me without a prosthetic, the question of why was raised. As word spread that I was fighting with a necrotic wound that wouldn't heal and that I had been told to wait it out, my friends started reaching out. I had nurses sharing their go-to remedies I could get on Amazon, and I even had a friend who had similar wound care woes supply me with specialized dressings to make the healing process more manageable.

According to the surgeon I had consulted with at my last visit, the best way for my wound to heal would be to dress it with dry gauze. Okay, sure, I could see his thought process. But that would mean ripping gauze off my leg every night after it had dried to the wound. Not exactly something I was willing to stomach. I had already been dreading changing the wound dressings every night. The necrotic tissue had started to peel away from the healing tissue bit by bit, and the smell was, not surprisingly, like death. That was hard enough to deal with without the idea of literally ripping gauze off the mangled flesh.

None of that even started to compare to the pain of changing the wound dressings. My nerves were already shot; even movements like bumping up against the couch sent waves of pain like electricity through my limb. I didn't want to imagine - couldn't bring myself to imagine - what slowly peeling dried gauze from the wound would feel like.

With a combination of non-stick gauze, medicinal honey, and faith filled prayers, I decided to stop relying on the nonsense my doctors were putting me through. Within a short time, I started to see the wound, once stagnant in its healing, start to knit back together. It was so deep that the healing actually started from the deepest sections. The necrotic tissue quickly peeled away completely, taking with it the sickening smell.

Within a few more weeks, I had finally reached a place of peace, being able to see the difference in the healing process every few days.

I even kept up with going to the gym when I felt up to it. Though my workouts were nowhere near the level they used to be, I felt accomplished for at least trying to stay active. I even got pretty good at maneuvering around the gym without having to ask for help too much.

It was always encouraging to be at the gym, but even more so when I met people who saw me hopping around on one leg to lift weights. They would tell me how seeing me motivated them to not skip workouts or how cool they thought it was that I wasn't letting anything stop me.

July 18, 2023

It's like my surgeon's office sensed my growing peace because they promptly destroyed it. After two months of begging for them to do something, finally giving up and taking matters into my own hands, and finally seeing some progress, they decided that maybe seeing plastic surgery was a good idea. Except, instead of giving me a call and explaining that, they just emailed me. No explanation of why they had a change of heart after all this time. I just got an email stating they were willing to refer me to plastic surgery if that's what I wanted.

After all the trauma and frustration that I had experienced since my surgery nearly three months prior, my mental health was fragile, my patience thin as the hospital blankets, and I snapped. I freaked out, thinking that somehow, something was wrong. The idea of another surgery, after I had *finally* let go of that as a possibility, scared me. More hospital time, more possibility for pain, and more risk for them to screw up again when I had finally started making some progress. To add to my frustration, the only explanation I got over the phone, nearly three days later, was that my surgeon thought

401

I would be anxious to get in my prosthetic and that a plastic surgery consultation might speed things up. Not when my wound first started showing signs of necrosis or when it had split wide open. But after two and a half months of *waiting for it to heal.*

There are not enough words in any language to accurately describe how livid I was. But, to prove my point, I made the appointment with plastic surgery. I knew after seeing the progress my wound was making, having it nearly healed, that I wouldn't risk another surgery. I didn't need a medical degree to tell me that another surgery would set me back another six weeks or more and that I would likely be healed by that point anyway.

As I suspected, plastic surgery determined that to do surgery at that point would actually be more of a setback. Even they admitted that if I had been sent to them sooner, they could have done a quick surgery that would have drastically reduced the time I spent recovering, but we had passed the time for that to be helpful.

For me, it had all felt like such a waste of time. Time that I could have spent learning how to walk again and precious time that I could have spent *living.* Going through all I had gone through with cancer, and now this, I was constantly reminded of how short life really can be. Wasting any of the precious gifts of life I had been given when that waste was absolutely preventable was agonizing.

At this point, plastic surgery was saying to consult Ortho, and Ortho was saying to consult plastic surgery, and both were saying that I could start to bear weight on a prosthetic when my wound finished healing. So, I used their assumption that I was consulting with the other specialty to my advantage.

It should not come as any surprise, at this point, that when I determined that my wound was healing enough to start working on a prosthetic, I set up an appointment for a casting of my first prosthesis.

Another thing that we seemed to not be able to get through to Ortho was that the process of casting and fabricating a prosthesis, as well as actually being able to wear and weight bear on the prosthesis, was a fairly time-consuming process. Ortho insisted that I be fully healed before even starting the process of casting, which was unnecessary. It was yet another reason on my list of ways I was frustrated with Ortho. As far as cutting the limbs off, they did great. But their knowledge of the continuing care and process of actually getting around on a prosthesis was lacking. All the more reason for me to stop waiting around on them.

The process of casting to fabrication to wearing was, though lengthy, absolutely fascinating. And unlike any other practitioner I had ever worked with, my prosthetist was all about educating and including me in the entire process.

To start the process of making a completely unique prosthesis, my prosthetist would take a cast of my residual limb to fabricate the socket or part of the prosthesis my limb fits into. For the cast, I was wearing the silicon liner that I would need to wear at all times in the socket. The liner would be wrapped with shrink wrap as a protective layer, and then my prosthetist would wrap layers of plaster around my limb. As the plaster dried, it was shaped to the exact shape of my limb.

After that, they fabricate what is called a check socket, or test socket, made of a plastic material that can be molded and shaped to make the socket as comfortable as possible.

It took about a week from the time we took a cast off my limb to when I got my first prosthesis, which was quite a fast turnaround since my prosthetics office fabricated it in-house instead of relying on an outside source. I thought that week would be an agonizing wait, but after four months - three since my surgery but four since my leg broke - a week was nothing. I had come to know what waiting was, and that week flew by so fast that I found myself on my way to prosthetics in the blink of an eye.

Limitless

Chapter 41

Finally, after three long, torturous months, I was on my way to get my first prosthesis. I was nearly bursting with excitement. Though I had adjusted quite well, mostly out of necessity, to living life on crutches and a knee scooter, I was ready to finally take a step - literally - in the direction of true recovery.

I didn't know what to expect. By this point, I think I had stopped having expectations at all. Hope, sure. But if so much of my strife came from reality not meeting my expectations, then I would make sure my expectations couldn't be a factor in that. I wasn't ever one to expect the worst and hope for the best. Expecting the worst as an overthinker meant that I would spiral too quickly into unrealistic anxieties. Instead, it would be best if I simply chose to not have expectations.

Now, realistically, I knew I would still be on crutches for a while. I wasn't going to put on the leg and walk out like normal. I had to let my limb adjust to the weight bearing gradually and would have to teach myself to pick up on the sensory cues to gain confidence in being able to walk without the sensory input of having a foot. I also knew that for the first few weeks, my time on my leg would be limited to allow my skin to adjust to the liner and the pressure of wearing a prosthesis. This wasn't going to be a situation where I put on the leg, walked out the door, and went back to normal, and I knew that. There was still plenty of work ahead of me.

That's not to say that I wasn't overjoyed. I was ecstatic. I was finally at a point in my recovery where things would be in my own hands. My abilities would rely on my drive to overcome whatever obstacles came my way, and that was on me. It was a massive comfort to know the ball would be in my court now. It wasn't up to a surgeon's decision or the timing of wound healing.

Naturally, I continued to decline offers for physical therapy. I had taught myself to walk before, and I would do it again.

I almost couldn't bear waiting until my appointment time. I sat at my house, dressed and ready, just waiting for the clock to count down to when I would leave. Sure, I could have left early, but then Mom and I would have been left sitting in the car until my appointment time, and that would have been even worse.

Luckily, I managed to remember one of the most important things I had been asked to bring. I needed to bring a left shoe to put on my prosthesis so I could safely wear it outside. After three months, I pretty much forgot that left shoes still existed. I ended up shoving all the left shoes I had into the corner of my closet, so the extra time at home helped me remember to go dig out the match to the shoe I was wearing that day.

I couldn't sit still in the car. If my knee wasn't bouncing, I was drumming my hands against my legs to the music we were listening to. Luckily, once we did get to my prosthetics office, I was well entertained. One of the prosthetists had a dog named Bubbles that kept patients company while we waited. It wasn't a long wait while my prosthetist attached my left HeyDude to my prosthetic foot, but it was enough to let the excited energy build up until my knee was bouncing again.

I was amazed to see my first leg when my prosthetist brought it into the room, complete with the matching shoe to what was on my right foot. I had already put on my liner, so I was ready to try on my new leg.

Trying to get it on was one of the strangest feelings I've ever experienced. A lot of prosthetic legs use the surface area of a person's residual limb to support the weight of a person, and that was the way mine fit. It was *tight*. The second I got it on and looked down to see what resembled a leg and a foot, I immediately tried to rotate my ankle out of habit. It absolutely short-circuited my brain to feel the muscles move to move my ankle and see the prosthetic ankle stay still.

I was seated between parallel walking bars, so as soon as I got my leg on and pulled the knee sleeve up to hold it on, I could stand. For the first time in three months, I stood on two feet. I thought it would be a moment where I found myself overwhelmed by emotion, but instead, I was too busy trying to understand what it felt like. I was standing, but I couldn't feel my foot against the ground. I only felt the pressure of standing through my residual limb, which just felt like a very tight, rigid compression sock.

For the first few minutes, I just swayed back and forth. If not being able to move my ankle short-circuited my brain, feeling myself stand without being able to feel the bottom of my foot flipped the breaker. I tried to focus on shifting weight to my left side. Though I still couldn't tolerate much weight, I knew I needed to teach myself to trust that there was something there.

I could feel what was left of my leg quickly trying to learn the signals - what pressure felt like as I swayed, what that pressure told me about the surface area of the foot I was standing on, what the bend in my knee meant for the placement of my foot under me.

I knew it would take longer than a few minutes to adjust and understand how my leg worked, so I decided to not waste any more time standing. I was standing between the parallel bars, holding on for dear life, and shifted onto my right leg. I lifted my left leg and took my first step.

The first thing I noticed was that I couldn't tell where I was placing my foot, and I had to try a few times before I got my foot in a place where I felt comfortable stepping onto it. When I rolled onto my foot, I was surprised that I didn't feel pain. Pressure, and maybe a little discomfort, sure, but it fit so well.

I don't think there were words to describe the elation of having a leg again and to be learning how to walk on my own. The hope I had tucked away in my soul for so many months that I would be able to live a normal, full life again was confirmed. It was like walking outside on a spring day after a long winter. It was full of new life, vibrancy, and warmth. It was a promise of new, beautiful things to come.

Before I left, my prosthetist adjusted my foot to make walking feel as natural as possible. I was amazed to see just how many ways she could adjust the foot.

Of course, I couldn't just go home after getting my leg. I needed to do something exciting. I needed to make use of my newfound freedom. Though, since I had about thirty minutes of wear time on my leg for that day, it would have to be a quick bit of excitement. Our first stop was lunch at a new place. Our second was Publix. It was like a whole new world, being able to walk around on two legs. I could actually look up and peruse the store without worrying about hitting someone with my knee scooter.

What amazed me the most was my emotional response to the whole situation. Putting aside expectations, I knew that there was a possibility I might have been insecure with my new prosthesis at first. I would still be on crutches, and I knew my gait would make it obvious that I was still new to using my prosthesis. I wondered if having a limp or an uneven gate would make me feel insecure. But instead of feeling insecure, I felt confident. So what if I limped? I was walking.

Our last stop was to stop by to show Billy, Amy, and the guys at Billy's shop my new custom-made accessory. There was no shortage of misty eyes when I stepped out of the truck on my leg and walked around the shop.

It was as I was explaining what it was like to wear my prosthesis that one of those Only Rebecca thoughts happened to run through my mind.

I needed to name my prosthesis.

I thought about what it had felt like that day, not just to get around but how it felt to wear a prosthesis. It was a little awkward, but endearingly so. It was a cute, dorky kind of feeling. The first name to come to mind with that kind of description was Herbert. So, Herbert it was.

Naturally, everyone got a good laugh out of the fact that I had named my leg. The coolest part, though, was when a friend looked up the meaning of the name Herbert. Originating from Old Germanic, the name Herbert actually means Illustrious Warrior. We all deemed it a fitting name.

As I had finally settled into a routine at home, after three long months, I would find myself changing up my routine yet again. This time, it took much more brain power.

August 16, 2023

As I was adjusting, gradually wearing my new leg more and more, I still spent most of the time on my knee scooter. When I did wear my leg, I still needed to use crutches. Now, I had to keep up with making sure my crutches and leg were in the same place and preferably where I could quickly trade off for my knee scooter. That doesn't seem entirely difficult, but I couldn't seem to keep track. I would take off my leg and use my crutches to get to the nearest couch. Sometimes, I would have Mom wheel my scooter over to the couch since I didn't feel like using my crutches, which meant my crutches were on one side of the house, my leg on the other side, and my scooter with me.

When I wanted to put my leg back on, I had to find the crutches and make sure they were near my leg so I could switch them out.

Despite the constant hide-and-seek with my equipment, I kept Mom busy. Even on days when I only had an hour or two to wear my leg, I was dragging her on walks. Across the street to Billy's shop was usually our route of choice, mostly so we could see Jasper. It only took a few days before I got brave enough to start taking a single step without crutches. I hardly felt any pain putting my full weight onto my leg without the assistance of the crutches, but the difficult part was balancing. Stepping down onto my leg, I felt like there was only one spot where I could find my balance. That spot seemed to be the size of a dime. If my step was off even just a little, I didn't have the muscle control to compensate, and my leg would topple to the side.

But each time I took a step unassisted, I was cataloging the information those steps gave me. I felt the balance of stepping on that dime-sized spot where everything was in balance. I felt how I would need to compensate each time I stepped just off target. I would stand in my living room when Mom was at work, and I would take single steps. I would start with both crutches, and I would lock into memory exactly what it felt like to take a good, well-balanced step. I would lift one of my crutches off the ground so I could only use one and then repeat the process. I would go through the whole process, taking multiple steps.

It didn't take long before I could reliably get around with just one crutch, and oh boy, was that fun. By that time, I was able to wear my leg as long as I needed to, so I could adapt my routine around the ability to use my leg. Even with just the use of one hand, I was thriving. I could make myself my protein shakes, no problem. I could heat up my food and get it to the table without nearly spilling it everywhere. And if I thought it was fun to have one hand back in use, I was soon to find out the kind of freedom that came from having both hands.

Freedom only came after actually remembering I could use both hands. After nearly five months of always using one hand to steer my scooter or use a crutch, I truly forgot how to use both hands. If I picked up items in both hands, I would freeze, unable to move until I put conscious thought into *how* to move. It wasn't that I wanted one hand open for balance or to catch myself if I stumbled. I simply could not remember how to move with both hands in use.

The best part about finally giving up crutches and walking independently was the response I got from my DCC family. In my usual flare for dramatics, I didn't actually tell anyone that I started walking. I just showed up one Sunday morning, both hands free, and walked into the building. I knew I had been spotted when I heard screams - yes, literal screams - coming from across the foyer. I had been spotted, and if half the church didn't know I was there, they certainly did at that moment.

The walk in to get to my seat was like a celebration. Everyone I passed was ecstatic that I had reached this milestone. And for the first time, I could hug my family with both arms. After service, PR saw me standing around talking and did a double-take. After watching me walk around, free of crutches, his eyes started to fill with happy tears. I'll never forget the joy in his voice as he looked at the person beside him and said, "It's been five months since I've seen this girl walk on her own," because with every step I took, I reminded myself of that same fact.

Being able to get around on my own, make my own food, and start to live a normal, functional, independent life did bring me to those same joyful tears every once in a while. Five months before, I was told that I wouldn't be able to do those things again. Had I gone with my surgeon's plan, I would be stuck on the couch with only the memory of what it was like to be normal.

Though I never doubted my decision to amputate, that feeling reaffirmed why I made that choice. Five months after my leg broke, I was back on my feet, walking and learning how to live life to the fullest again.

It seemed like once I started to get around on my own, I was progressing unbelievably quickly. Week by week, people commented on how I seemed to walk faster, with more of a steady gate. In the gym, I was able to get around much faster, and without needing crutches, I could get better workouts without worrying about being too sore.

Progress didn't come without its share of challenges, though. The first of which is what I started to refer to as the Sock Game. For amputees, it's pretty normal to expect volume changes in our residual limbs. In order to make sure my prosthesis fit properly, I would add socks over my liner, inside the socket, to add volume that I might lose throughout the day. I would carry socks of different thicknesses

- or ply - in a backpack everywhere I went. One minute, I would be perfectly comfortable, and the next, I would feel my residual limb hit the bottom of my socket. I would have to roll my knee sleeve down, take off my prosthesis, and figure out how many socks to add.

Usually, it wasn't that bad. But one day, I decided that I was going to do something I hadn't done in the months since my leg broke. I wanted to go to Hobby Lobby. I didn't have a plan, or anything I needed to get. I just wanted to wander around.

September 7, 2023

Admittedly, I was pushing it. I had only been wearing my leg for a few weeks, and I was still adjusting. Many days, I would hit a limit where I simply could not handle wearing my leg anymore. But I missed my Hobby Lobby trips so bad, so I decided to chance it. I carried my backpack with my socks and started wandering. Everything seemed to be going just fine. I made it around the parts of the store I wanted to see and started to head out when I felt the pain that told me I would need to add a sock.

I can only imagine what it must have looked like to everyone around when I stopped in the middle of the aisle, popped my leg off, and started adding socks. Or when I did that every few aisles because I couldn't figure out how many socks to add.

I managed to make it out to my car and ended up driving home with my leg in the passenger seat. Of course, Herbert was safely seat belted in.

September 30, 2023

If you know me at all by now, you can imagine that I was hardly content to just be able to walk. Much to the contrary, I was now even more driven to reach my major goal of being back on the

412

Spartan course. Though I had only had my leg a few weeks, and it was still wildly unpredictable, I took a giant leap of faith and decided to sign up for my first 5K. The Cancer Chomp 5K that I had made an annual goal of mine had come back around, and I was determined to not miss a year. Not over something as trivial as an amputation, of course.

Now, I had no intention of trying to run this race. I hardly had any intention of walking it. I brought my crutches, fully aware that I would likely be needing them to get through the race. But I had a leg and a whole lot of determination. Come what may, I just wanted to finish.

Em, being hugely involved with this 5K, planned to walk the race with me, and Mr. George, a friend from church, volunteered to walk along with us.

I'm not going to be that person who claims they weren't nervous before their first 5K after losing part of their leg. Oh no, I was a nervous wreck. This was a whole three miles, and I probably hadn't walked three miles in the six months it had been since my leg broke. It didn't help my nerves that, when I woke up that morning, my leg did not want to fit properly. I still wasn't willing to give up on the race, though.

I tried everything I could think of, including changing up the layers of socks I was in. But the Cancer Chomp 5K meant something to me. I had raced it the first year they held the race to benefit brain tumor patients. That race had been my fastest 5K yet, my finishing time being just under 40 minutes. To miss something so close to my heart would have been devastating for me.

That morning, for the first time since I started doing 5Ks, I had to wrestle with a thought I never had before. What if I couldn't finish? What if the circumstances of the day made it impossible to finish? What if this was the day my grit and tenacity couldn't carry me to the end?

They were hard thoughts. Not a year before, I had completed nearly marathon distances in one weekend, with obstacles, and now I was worried about my ability to finish just three miles.

I knew I had to come to peace with that possibility before the race started. My circumstances no longer allowed me to simply will my way through the challenges I set for myself. Really, my circumstances could have ended up preventing me from doing that. So, I let myself be okay with the possibility that I may not finish this race, this time. But I took solace in the fact that I would try. I would not admit defeat before the race had even begun.

If I was going to fail, I was going to fail while daring greatly.

As I expected, I made it a short distance past the starting line when I took my crutches back. We had already fallen to the very back of the racers, and I had to wrestle with the idea that I wasn't even able to keep up with those who were speed-walking at the back of the pack.

Mentally, it was just as tough as it was physically. Though I had Em and Mr. George with me, and they kept me encouraged, I was fighting my own mind. Before long, I had to take most of my weight off my leg and shift it to my arms on the crutches, and that slowed us down even more. I kept stopping anytime there was a bench to give my arms a rest and take my leg off.

It was a constant battle to overcome my thoughts. Part of me just wanted to give up. One of the race volunteers circled the course on a golf cart and asked a few times if we were okay. We even got stopped by a police officer asking if we needed a ride back. I wondered if it would even be worth it or if I was just being too stubborn.

But each time we were asked if I wanted a ride back to the starting line, I declined. I couldn't bring myself to give up, even if it was all I wanted to do. Every time the thought of giving up crossed my mind, I glanced down at the Spartan tank top I was wearing. Of all the lessons Spartan racing had taught me, it was to not give up. If I could make it through the Death Swamp, I could make it through a 5K on crutches.

It took an hour and a half, and I finally saw the home stretch of the race. It couldn't have been longer than a quarter of a mile, but it felt like I was looking at a ten-mile stretch. It didn't help that progress was slow, but Em and Mr. George kept encouraging me.

414

They held an easy conversation that kept my mind mostly off how tired I was.

When we finally turned the corner to the finish line, what I saw made every step worth it. They kept the finish line up, and the volunteers and members of Streetlight that were at the race had lined both sides of the last few steps to the finish line. As soon as they saw me turn the corner, they started cheering.

I was crying before I had even reached the volunteers. If seeing them didn't start the waterworks, Mr. George told me that he was going to stay behind me so I wouldn't be the last finisher. It took us an hour and forty-five minutes, but we finally crossed the finish line. The way the volunteers and Streetlight members surrounded us completely changed the way I had been feeling about myself.

All during the race, I had to fight the feeling of wondering why in the world I was even attempting the 5K in the first place, and why I was putting myself through so much to say I finished it. But being able to finish, and sharing that moment with Em, Mr. George, and the volunteers made me feel strong. I hadn't given up, but I was able to overcome, just as I always had.

October 28, 2023

After the 5K, I knew I had a lot of work to do in order to be ready to run a 5K for real. I still had my eyes on returning to Central Florida for the Spartan Trifecta Weekend, but I was seriously starting to doubt if I'd be able to race the entire weekend. After the setbacks that pushed back my ability to work on using a prosthesis for so long, things weren't looking good. I just wasn't ready to admit that yet.

I was looking at the Bolt Run 5K that I had been running every year since Mom and I fell in love with hockey. I figured that race would be a good indicator for how much I might be able to attempt at the Trifecta Weekend.

Luckily, I was scheduled to get a hardware upgrade. Since I had been gradually losing volume in my residual limb as the swelling from surgery went down, I was on track to get a new leg. This one would be more permanent than the hard plastic one I had been wearing and would be one I could add designs to if I chose.

I wracked my brain for days on the different designs I might want, but when the time came, I couldn't decide. I decided to stick with carbon fiber black, since it would be more likely to match any outfit I chose. The best thing about this new leg, though, was that it would have a really cool foot.

My prosthetist had researched feet that she thought would work best for me and my lifestyle and found one that met all my needs. It had an insane amount of shock absorption, the ability to rotate at the ankle, and would allow me to run if I chose. It was even good for terrain since it would bend like a real ankle if my foot hit any uneven areas while hiking or Spartan racing.

Walking on that foot was a dream. The more I got used to it, the more I forgot I was missing a leg. At first, I would have to tell people not to talk to me while I was walking so I could keep my focus on holding a steady gait. With the new prosthesis, named Herbert 2.0, and the upgraded foot, walking was as easy as it ever was, and I could hold a conversation and walk at the same time.

We even solved the problem of the Sock Game with this upgrade. My prosthetist asked if I would test out a new gadget, and I was happy to give it a try. Instead of wearing socks, I would wear an overlay inside my socket that could be inflated and deflated without ever taking my socket off. That was a game-changer since I could make adjustments anywhere without having to completely de-leg.

By this time, most people were shocked when they saw the carbon fiber below my knee. Most couldn't tell anything was missing based on seeing me walk, which was one of my biggest goals.

With the new Herbert came more endurance, and I was able to get around with very few issues. Only, when I did have issues, they were pretty significant. The extra weight of my new sporty foot caused some pulling on my residual limb, and if there was too much pulling, it would cause cramping in the muscles of my residual limb.

416

If they started to cramp, wearing my leg was pretty much a no-go for the rest of the day.

It was hard to predict when the cramping was going to happen, and usually, I would get no warning. I would be walking, and suddenly, I would need to stop wherever I was to get my leg off.

Because of this issue, when the time came for the Bolt Run, Mom and I had a contingency plan. We would be walking the bike trail near our house for the 5K, and even planned to take Jasper with us, and just in case, we decided to take my knee scooter. After trying to crutch through nearly three miles at the Cancer Chomp 5K, we decided the knee scooter was a much better idea.

I was hopeful that the cramping wouldn't happen, and for most of the first mile, I was good to go. I still couldn't quite match my pre-amputation walking pace, but I was still moving along at a decent pace. When the cramp finally did hit, I wasn't surprised, but I was super disappointed.

I missed being able to do full 5Ks, and I *really* missed when they were the warmup for longer races. I think what disappointed me the most, though, was the realization that there was less than a month until the Trifecta Weekend, and I would be missing out on it completely if I couldn't even make it the distance of a 5K. Even with my disappointment, I was determined to at least finish the 5K.

Around the time my leg cramped and I started using my scooter, Jasper decided that he wasn't really into the whole idea of walking. He ended up in the backpack Mom brought with us to put my leg in in case I couldn't wear it.

It just got worse from there. It wasn't long before I couldn't stand pressing my knee against the seat of the knee scooter. Instead of resting my knee there and propelling myself with my good leg, I ended up sitting on the seat of the knee scooter. The seat was way too low for that, making it nearly impossible to push with my legs.

Honestly, it was hilarious. Mom became more determined than me to finish the 5K. I was ready to call it quits and call Billy to get us back to the truck, but Mom decided we were finishing the 5K. She wrapped Jasper's leash around the handle of the scooter, held Herbert in one hand, and pulled me along with the other when I couldn't rest

417

my knee on the scooter to push myself. Jasper seemed to be having a great time hanging out in her backpack.

When we finally got back to the truck, we decided that 5K was worse than the hours we had spent on the bike trail when I was training for my Trifecta.

I was still pretty bummed to be calling off the Trifecta Weekend. After years of being able to push myself regardless of what my body was saying, having to heed those kinds of warnings was hard for me. But the consequences of pushing too hard with a prosthesis were far greater than they had been when I had both legs, so I set my sights on the next race weekend where I could attempt a 5K Spartan Sprint.

Chapter 42

The day had finally come. Eight months after amputation and exactly a year after my last race, I found myself standing at the starting line of a Spartan Sprint.

Looking back, there were some days I wasn't even sure I would ever take the step to racing again. I thought, usually on days when I was throwing myself a pity party, that maybe my days of racing were over. Recovery was slow. Adjusting to my prosthesis was a whole process. When I had to call off the Trifecta Weekend just a few months prior, I started to really doubt whether I would ever race again.

When I finally pulled the trigger and committed to the race, I was left with a nerve-wracking line of thought. What if I couldn't finish? Though I had gotten well-adjusted to my leg, even as much as going back to work in a warehouse, I hadn't attempted anything as insane as a Spartan Race before. I couldn't help but imagine what would happen if my leg cramped as it had before or if the terrain and mud would prove to be too much too soon.

I had to remind myself of my favorite quote, The Man In The Arena, by Theodore Roosevelt.

It is not the critic who counts; not the man who points out how the strong man stumbles, or where the doer of deeds could have done them better. The credit belongs to the man who is actually in the arena, whose face is marred by dust and sweat and blood; who strives valiantly; who errs, who comes short again and again, because there is no effort without error and shortcoming; but who does actually strive to do the deeds; who knows the great enthusiasms, the great devotions; who spends himself in a worthy cause; who at the best knows in the end the triumph of high achievement, and who at the worst, if he fails, at least fails while daring greatly, so that his place shall never be with those cold and timid souls who neither know victory nor defeat.

I refused to let those thoughts keep me from doing what I fought so hard to be able to do again. If I was going to fail, at least I tried. At least I couldn't say I gave up.

It further eased my mind to know that I had planned to race with More Heart Than Scars again, and I knew that, even if they had to carry me, they would not leave a teammate behind.

The cherry on top of the cake, though, was the video I watched before every race. It is the video Em and Francisco made of me during the stages of my treatment and recovery. It has always been the perfect race prep, but hearing myself at 18, bald and fighting cancer, saying, "If I can get through this, there's a lot that I can do that I don't think I can do," hit me right where I needed it to.

I knew, even as I contemplated success and failure on the drive to the race venue, that I was going to attempt the race. Stepping out of the car, I was flooded with uncertainty. I looked around at the racers around me and wondered how in the world I still fit in at an event like this. And yet, the reality in front of me was far from those thoughts. Other racers looked at me with encouragement, solidarity with the obstacles we would soon overcome, and with respect. I was even whisked into a Spartan Group Hug with a group of strangers I had never met. It was enough to tell me what I had been fighting to accept since I left the car. I was still one of them.

The welcome I got from More Heart Than Scars as I approached their tent was enough to completely dispel any lingering thoughts of unworthiness. I looked around at teammates who I knew would sooner carry me across the finish line than leave me behind to not finish the race. I saw teammates who I knew would be the first to offer help at any obstacle I encountered. As I took in the team around me, I became sure that once I stepped over the starting line, I would just as surely be crossing the finish line.

My chest stayed tight throughout the wait for our start time, but instead of feeling tight as if I were weighed down, I felt as if there was something in my chest straining for freedom. This part of me that I had locked away so securely over the past eight months was ready to be released.

Since at my last race with MHTS, I showed up at the starting line and had never spent any time with them before a race, I didn't know that, since we were racing a heat with Team Oscar Mike, that we were going to do a mini parade around the festival area as a team in order to get to the starting line. Cue the tears I thought I'd be holding back until the end of the race.

Music accompanied us through to the starting line, and we were surrounded by other racers cheering us on. I was accompanied by my team, hugging me and encouraging me all the way to the start. And before I knew it, we were on the course.

The terrain, while it was dry, was no issue for me, since my prosthetics team had equipped me with a foot that absorbed the movement of stepping on uneven ground. That, at least, helped give me one less thing to think of.

Approaching the walls, I started to try to strategize how I was going to get over them. My usual strategies might not have worked since I hadn't ever had a 6 or 8-foot wall to actually try them out on. Just as I started to get into my head about it, one of my teammates from MHTS grabbed my arm to get my attention, told me she had me, and got down on her hands and knees, giving me a step to get closer to the top.

I was amazed. Her willingness to help me in that way was instant and without hesitation. The other members of my team helped me get the rest of the way over, of course, with the Spartan Handshake.

Other teammates that had already made it over the wall were on the other side to catch me as I jumped down, and as I hit the ground, I started to feel what it was like to really trust my prosthesis. I was still babying my leg, of course, but hitting the ground on both legs felt so normal as if nothing had really changed since my last race.

It didn't take long before we hit the mud. Luckily, it was not Death Swamp Cow Mud, but ankle-deep, goopy mud. I mean, we were on a cow farm again, so it was probably Cow Mud, too, but I didn't think about that in the moment. As if in unspoken agreement, two of my teammates immediately came to my sides, offering their arms to help keep me steady since mud was a new terrain for me.

I tried to be Little Miss Independent for a whole 30 seconds before accepting their offered arms. I realized too quickly that I couldn't actually see into the mud to see where my foot would fall and when my foot would land. Even as sandbags and buckets were added to our mud trek, my team stayed with me, even taking the heavy objects into their own arms in a team carry to help me keep going during the tougher parts of the mud.

We took on obstacles, both my favorites and my least favorites, as a team, and not once did I have to attempt an obstacle alone. At the Atlas Carry, my team surrounded me to help me lift the 100-pound cement ball into my arms. As soon as I had a grip on it, they didn't stop cheering and encouraging me until I dropped it back at the starting point of that obstacle. We took on our plate drags together; they pushed me over walls, and they continued to hold me steady in the muddiest parts of the course. For every obstacle I could do on my own, they cheered me on, and for each obstacle I needed help with, they were at my side.

When we reached the A-Frame Cargo Net, I felt the stir of mischief and the need for a little chaos. I told my team I was going to do a front flip at the top, just as one of the team members had taught me a year before. As I had come to expect, I was met with the same look I knew I had. Our faces all said, "Challenge accepted."

Climbing the cargo net when I couldn't feel my foot was a whole new level of challenge, though. Instead of being able to look up the whole time, I had to constantly look down, through the holes of the cargo net, to make sure I placed my foot securely on the net. It definitely added to the thrill of being up in the air, getting ready to front flip over to the other side.

As I got to the top, I could feel the team's excitement mirroring my own. It was nearly palpable in the air around us. I got my hands around the net, aimed my head for the center opening between my hands, and flipped. I heard the team cheering in excitement as my feet cleared my head and landed on the other side. But just as I opened my mouth to make a shout of my own, the mud that had been lodged in the opening to my prosthetic foot flew over my head from the flip and hit me directly in the face.

To a bunch of Spartans, this was the best possible thing that could have happened, like a congratulations present from the course itself. I felt so at home at that moment. I was back where I had longed to be, and I was so happy to be back on the course, spitting mud out of my mouth with my MHTS family.

As we came through the midpoint of the course, right through the festival area, I started to look for Mom. I wanted to share with her that I had made it halfway, but in a sea of black shirts, I couldn't find her. I vowed to make her wear a neon green shirt at the next race. I knew that she was there, though, so I dove into the Rolling Mud with little hesitation, even if deep down I wanted to see her

423

there. But I shouldn't have worried because I heard the familiar call of, "That's my Becca!" right as I started to slide into the mud pit.

When I had gone under the dunk wall, my teammates were nearly losing their minds with excitement. It's not that the dunk wall was a particularly hard obstacle, but it was a staple. Getting fully submerged in the mud was a part of the whole experience, and they knew that, for me, it was a part of being back.

Just as I had come out of the mud on the other side of the inflatable wall, still stumbling around trying to get the mud out of my eyes, I felt someone grab me in a tight hug. It was Mom telling me I only had a little over a mile to go and that I would make it. She was so proud of me.

I had to keep it together. If I started crying then, it was going to be a long last mile, but to have her telling me she was proud of me was what I needed.

I couldn't have ignored the fact that, at that point in the course, I was feeling it. My leg had started to ache, and I was fatigued. I was having the time of my life, but I was *tired,* both mentally and physically. But being surrounded by my team and pushed on by Mom, I knew I could finish.

We hit the next obstacle, not twenty feet from the Dunk Wall I had just gone under. It was the Slip Wall. One of my favorites and one of the ones I could never be quite sure if I was going to be able to do. I had tackled this obstacle quite well at the Trifecta Weekend but hadn't been able to reach the top in the Super the previous year. Admittedly, the memory of just barely making it to the top that previous year, only to slide down the metal wall back to where I started, still haunted me, and I let it get farther into my head than I should have. I had gotten to the wall, taken the rope in my hands, and even took a few steps up before the doubt overtook me, and I told my team I didn't think I could do it.

That is the wrong thing to say to More Heart Than Scars.

Before I knew it, I had one person on each side, and one behind me. Two people were at the top of the wall, waiting. And everyone was cheering. I started to climb again.

It was hard to trust my leg going up this wet, slippery wall. I knew it would be there, that it would support me. But I couldn't let myself fully trust that it wasn't going to slip out from under me since I couldn't really feel how much pressure I was putting on it. I trusted my team, though, and knew that even if I slipped, they had my back.

I made it over halfway up the wall before it really started to get hard. I had less play on the rope and had to crouch lower and lower, throwing my balance off when I tried to step. My team was a step ahead. The ladies on either side of me used their own feet to anchor mine, stepping under my heels. The guy behind me kept his knee under my butt so I could lean back and get my balance before each step. And the whole time, my teammates at the top of the wall cheered, telling me to keep going, take a few more steps, and keep my eyes on them.

When I got to the top, I was exhausted. I hadn't used my muscles like that in forever, and I could feel it. But as I got within reach, my teammates grabbed my arms and started to pull me over.

That would become a moment I would hold onto, because it was a physical representation of what family does - both my DCC family and my MHTS family. They surrounded me, pushed me, encouraged me, and when I reached my own limits, carried me to help me reach my goal. It was something I wasn't used to experiencing, both in racing and in normal life, but it was something I was learning to cherish.

The last mile was even more brutal than I expected. Though there weren't many obstacles, they made up for the intensity with the mud. I leaned heavily on my teammates to keep me balanced during those long trudges, now becoming sore enough that it was becoming a bit miserable. I was past the laughing and joking phase of the race, and I just wanted to be finished. I started to tell myself what I told myself during my Trifecta attempt. One foot in front of the other until someone put a medal around my neck, then I could stop.

Luckily for me, if you want to call it luck, the last stretch of the race was not exactly something I could walk through. My wish to get off my leg was being granted. By the barbed wire crawl. Certainly not the most brutal I'd ever experienced, but for sure, the longest with the lowest clearance. As soon as I saw it coming off the Vertical Cargo Net, I knew it was going to be a blessing and a curse because I would either have to army crawl or roll through to the finish line.

But hey, at least I didn't have to walk!

I tried to do a little bit of crawling, but without being able to extend my left foot, I was dragging my toe through the mud, making more work for myself. I turned on my side and started to roll. I'd roll a few feet and stop to get my bearings. Then roll again. At some point, we all started to laugh. It was comical, me rolling through the mud, trying not to kick anyone else in the face with the leg I couldn't feel. But eventually, I made it to the end. I saw the fire jump and then the finish line, and I just froze.

I made it.

It's not like I didn't expect to. I knew I would make it to the finish line if I had to crawl through the race with my leg strapped to my back. But after all the mud, all the relearning of how to attempt obstacles, and after the discomfort in my leg turned to full-on pain, I was only a few steps away from my goal. But I didn't have time to ponder it too much, to get too emotional, because my team started to link arms. Everyone who had shared this race with me connected for the fire jump.

After all we had been through together and all the sacrifices these amazing human beings made to help me finish, I wish I could say we epically ran up to the fire, jumped over it, and crossed the finish line. But it certainly wasn't that epic because I couldn't get the running start. So, as we approached, my team stepped over, one leg on either side of the fire as I made my way across, still arm in arm.

The finish line was so close. I stumbled from the heat of the fire and had crossed before I even knew what happened, and I crossed right into the arms of my team, passing me down from hug to hug until I reached Mom.

I started to process that I had finished the race as she held me, and I went from a few disbelieving sniffles to sobs that shook my whole body. Of course, it didn't help that my team was surrounding me, telling Mom how much of a beast her daughter was.

Someone grabbed one of the medals and pulled me away from Mom long enough to slip it over my head, and I started crying more. For the first time in over a year, I felt like myself again. I was covered in mud, the weight of a medal around my neck, and I had felt the payoff of pushing through the misery to accomplish what I set out to do.

Back in the festival area, I sat and took in the day. Like the Trifecta, I kept my medal around my neck as I sat. Mom had taken my leg to the area at the finish line where racers could hose down, a scene we laughed at for days. I can only imagine what it must have looked like to see her walking a prosthetic leg through the festival area to hose the mud out of it.

I was told as I sat about the impact my race had on those watching. I was told about spectators who cried watching me finish, and about how proud my team was. How much I had been missed on the course while I recovered. It was surreal. I didn't even want to try to leave the festival area, because I didn't want to go back to reality just yet.

I just wanted to sit there with my medal, surrounded by my team. But I also wanted a long, *long,* hot shower. The want for a shower won, and we started on our way back home. I limped into the house, now definitely paying the price of being the beast my team claimed I was, but it was so worth it. To feel like myself again, to know I could do the hard things I set out to accomplish.

It was hard for me to fathom that, less than a year before, I had been in the depths of despair when my leg broke. It was the worst fear that I didn't know I had, having my mobility and independence taken away and being faced with less-than-ideal options for repair surgeries. Looking back on that, I couldn't even fathom what God had done for me in those few short months. I went from truly believing my life was over to living life to the fullest, even more so than I ever had.

Limitless

Epilogue

"If you could go back, would you change anything?"

That is my favorite question because I love the various looks I get - shock, confusion, awe - when I say that I couldn't imagine changing a thing. I'm not going to deny that it sucked at times. I won't rewrite my experiences of pain and trauma to be less than they were. They were hellish, brutal experiences at times.

But I also cannot deny what became of me and my life because of them.

So, let's just imagine for a moment, what if I didn't get cancer?

I'd probably be neck deep in student loan debt because I would have undoubtedly stayed at Florida Southern to finish my degree. Not only that, but I would have kept going. I'd probably be working on my PhD right now.

Likely, I would have moved away from my little town at some point as well, either to pursue higher education, an internship, or a job. There is truly no telling if I would have found time - made time - to find a church, and even if I had, there's no telling if it would have been one that pushed me to seek a deeper relationship with God. As much as it scares me to admit it, I don't imagine I would have.

Being so caught up in the need to climb the corporate ladder, getting more education and going farther and farther in my field, I probably wouldn't have kept up with my physical health, certainly not dedicating hours to kickboxing. Even if I had, I doubt I would have met a coach that dared me to run a Spartan Race.

So, I look now at all the aspects of my life that I love and that are important to me, and I try to imagine my life without them. Without Mom by my side as my best friend. Without the nightly calls to Trevor and the group chat shenanigans and hangouts with my best friends. Without the Spartan medals, resilience, and the confidence of what I can do when I put my mind to doing hard things. Without my More Heart Than Scars family. Without the skills and hard lessons from learning martial arts. Without the love, support, and encouragement from Em and Francisco. Without the refreshment I get from Sunday worship services at DCC. Without the wisdom shared with me by my mentor, Takela. Without the constant prayers surrounding me from my community. Without the small groups. Without the church potlucks.

Sure, my life could have been free of cancer. Right now, I wouldn't have to attach a limb every time I want to go somewhere. I wouldn't have days where I couldn't even stand the feeling of my shirt settling against that area on my chest where my port was. The beeping of credit card machines wouldn't send my heart racing. My heart wouldn't break every time I hear the name Gabe.

But I would go through every bit of pain, experience every moment of trauma, survive every near-death experience, and relive every dreadful moment woven into the tapestry of good and bad moments of my story over the past five years to step into this life of peace and joy and love I live now.

Five years ago, I had a disease that I am certain was meant to ruin my life, destroy my relationship with God, and kill me. But what was meant for evil in my life, God took and turned for the good. For every bit of misery I went through, He gave me joy. For every moment of trauma, He gave me healing. For every need, He provided. For every brush with death, He gave me life and life to the fullest.

It's unimaginable to most people to think that someone could be grateful for things like cancer and limb loss. But those things are a part of my story, and a part of the incredible story of how God has

430

worked in my life. So as crazy as it sounds, I am grateful for every part of the last five years of my life. I am who I am today because God took a story that should have been a tragedy, and He rewrote it with a victorious ending.

With the addition of my sparkling prosthetic, now named Helen after Helen of Troy, I have been able to do everything I had been able to do before, and with more security and less pain than I had been in before. I don't have to worry about my leg not being able to support me through my crazy lifestyle, and though it is not a fully pain-free solution, I am able to function much better through what comparatively little pain I do experience.

With this part of my story behind me, I can focus on what comes next. Thanks to a few miracles, I have my entire life ahead of me, and it is full of possibilities. I intend to live a life that will do those miracles justice, and though I don't know exactly what that looks like, I'm excited to find out.

Limitless

Acknowledgements

To Mom: You raised me to be the woman I am today, to chase my dreams, and to do whatever I put my mind to. You have always been there for me, and I know you always will be. Without you, I wouldn't have made it this far, both in life and in living my dream of being an author. Don't underestimate the role you played in getting this book out to the world. You were the first person to believe in me, and because of that, I was confident enough to take on a project like this. Thank you for your never-ending love and support.

To Trevor Turner: I know you're going to cringe at how sappy this sounds, but from the day you adopted me as your sister, my life has never been the same. You've taught me the meaning of loyalty and brotherly love, and you never doubted me. For you to believe in me became both an encouragement and a standard that I hold myself to. Thank you for being there to remind me of who I am.

To Heather Walden, Ashlynn Barber, and April Watson: I seriously don't know what I'd do without you ladies. From praying for me to enduring my voice message rants about the struggles of being a Do-It-Yourself Author, the support you have shown me is nothing short of astounding. You have all played a part in helping me achieve this goal, and I will be forever grateful for your friendship. Thank you for being a part of the adventure.

Limitless

To Em and Francisco Marchi: You two have been there through it all. It is such a blessing to have such amazing people in my corner. You both have been nothing but supportive during this project, and have celebrated with me through every milestone. The friendship you've shown me is the kind that lasts a lifetime, and I thank you for being a light in my life.

To Streetlight Volunteers: Thank you for the difference you have made in my life and the lives of countless others. The friendship you extended and the normalcy you brought during such a traumatic time is something I will never forget. You helped me remember who I was in the face of cancer, and that is something I will be forever grateful for.

To Pastor Rocky McKinley: Your support from the moment you heard I was writing a book was absolutely incredible. You used your own experience and wisdom to push and encourage me, and in moments of self-doubt, I thought back to the conversations where you lifted me up as a first-time author. Thank you for celebrating this book and supporting me in getting it into the hands of those who can use it.

To my DCC Family: Each and every one of you has shown me what it means to be a part of a family. You accepted me without hesitation, carried me when I couldn't carry myself, and were there for me through everything with no hesitation. I have never met a group of people so unwavering in their love. God knew what I needed when He brought me to Destiny Community Church. Thank you all for doing life with me.

To my More Heart Than Scars Family: The love you all have shown me is unparalleled. You welcomed me into your family and supported me on and off the Spartan course, and I am honored to share the role you all played in my story. Thank you all for walking with me through life and Spartan courses alike.

434

To Deanna Smith: You made shooting the cover of this book so fun! You captured exactly what I was looking for to release this book to the world. Thank you for working with me and giving me the confidence you gave me.

To Paul Flagg: You were the answer to my prayers as an editor. You helped me develop this story into something I am proud to release while encouraging me throughout the process. Thank you for the confidence you gave me to continue pursuing this dream of mine.

To Skyler Davis: My lifesaver when it came to the graphic design element of publishing. I was so scared to use the things I had designed, and you helped ease my mind with everything you critiqued for me. Thank you for letting me run so many designs by you.

To Jasper: Though you can't read this, thank you for being my snuggle buddy during long days of writing and for all the encouragement kisses.

To everyone who was a part of my journey: Whether you prayed, visited, called, or were simply in the right place at the right time to encourage and lift me up, know that I will hold those moments in my heart forever. This story was built on the interactions and influences of countless people. I wouldn't be the person I am today without those moments, so thank you for being a part of the journey.

Limitless

See Rebecca's Story at

www.rebeccadenae.com/mystory

Made in United States
Orlando, FL
21 November 2024

54263103R00251